PHOTOCHEMISTRY
OF
Air Pollution

This is Volume 9 in
PHYSICAL CHEMISTRY
A series of monographs
Edited by ERNEST M. LOEBL, *Polytechnic Institue of Brooklyn*

PHOTOCHEMISTRY
OF
Air Pollution

PHILIP A. LEIGHTON

Department of Chemistry
Stanford University
Stanford, California

1961

ACADEMIC PRESS · *New York and London*

ACADEMIC PRESS, INC.
111 Fifth Avenue, New York, New York 10003

United Kingdom Edition published by
ACADEMIC PRESS, INC. (LONDON) LTD.
Berkeley Square House, London W1X 6BA

LIBRARY OF CONGRESS CATALOG CARD NUMBER: 61-12276

Second Printing, 1971

PRINTED IN THE UNITED STATES OF AMERICA

Preface

One of the most striking developments of the past decade, both in the field of air pollution and in that of atmospheric chemistry, has been the recognition that photochemical reactions, produced by sunlight, may convert relatively innocuous pollutants into substances which constitute a nuisance, create a possible health hazard, and cause economic loss to man.

To the photochemist, the phenomenon of photochemical air pollution presents a many sided problem. For its proper solution he must first examine the intensity and spectral distribution of solar radiation in the lower atmosphere. Then he must identify the substances in polluted air which absorb this radiation and determine the rates and natures of the photochemical primary processes which result from this absorption. Next, the secondary reactions which follow must be specified, and their relative importance estimated. Finally, from this information he must attempt to describe the over-all process, from initial pollutants to final products, in terms which will be useful not only to those whose interest lies in the scientific nature of the problem, but also to those concerned with its human and economic aspects and with its control.

This book attempts to formulate the background, through a review, correlation, and analysis of existing information, upon which the solution of this problem must ultimately be based. New treatments have been applied and new concepts developed where necessary to the overall objectives; the concept of actinic irradiance in Chapter II, the discussion of stationary states in Chapter IV, the nitric oxide-ozone-nitrogen dioxide product ratio in Chapter VI, and the mechanism for sulfur dioxide photooxidation in Chapter IX may be cited as examples.

Throughout the book, estimated rates have been used as a yardstick for judging the relative importance of different reactions. This has served not only to eliminate a number of reactions on the basis that they are too slow to be important, but also to point out the many gaps in knowledge which must be bridged before a satisfactory understanding of the photochemistry of polluted air has been attained.

The book is an outgrowth of two reports prepared for the Air Pollution Foundation by Dr. William A. Perkins and the author. It draws freely from these and other reports of the Air Pollution Foundation, as well as from published papers and reports of the Stanford Research Institute, the Franklin Institute, the Scott Research Laboratory, and

v

the Los Angeles County Air Pollution Control District. To these agencies as well as to the individuals involved, the author expresses his sincere appreciation.

PHILIP A. LEIGHTON

May, 1961

Contents

Chapter I

Introduction

1. Photochemical Smog

Man, being gregarious, has chosen since time immemorial to congregate in groups, and since time immemorial his activities within the areas in which he chooses to congregate have resulted in air pollution. Though the origins of air pollution are lost in antiquity, only with the industrial revolution did it become a major problem over entire urban areas, and even now, in relatively few instances have adequate measures been taken for its areawide control.

The problems of air pollution control are rarely simple and never static. In different areas, differences in man's activities, in terrain, and in meteorological conditions produce wide differences in the characteristics of air pollution. In any given area, as man's activities change with time, so do the pollutants emitted and the resultant problems change with time. As population and industrialization increase, so do the problems become more critical and the steps required for control more severe.

One of the first, and not always the easiest, tasks of those charged with air pollution control in any given area is to recognize, define, and understand the nature of the problems particular to that area and to keep abreast of their changes. In some present day urban areas, a few specific sources of pollutants, usually industrial, are of major importance, and the problems of air pollution control are correspondingly specific. In other areas the effects result from a general merging of pollutants from many sources, and the problems are correspondingly general to the entire community.

While all cases of community air pollution share certain features in common, they also show, in different areas, wide differences in characteristics. Both London and Los Angeles smog are the results of community air pollution, and in both cases effluents from fuel combustion are the major source of pollution. The major fuels are coal and hydrocarbons in London, hydrocarbons in Los Angeles. Yet the word "smog" has quite a different meaning to a resident of London than it does to a resident of Los Angeles. London smog generally reaches its peaks in the early mornings, at temperatures of 30–40°F, while Los Angeles smog reaches its peaks at midday, with temperatures of 75–90°F. London smog generally occurs at high relative humidities accompanied by fog; Los Angeles smog occurs at low relative humidities under a clear sky. London smog is

1

accompanied by radiation or surface inversions, Los Angeles smog by subsidence or overhead inversions. To chemical agents, London smog is reducing; Los Angeles smog is oxidizing. The immediate effect of London smog on humans is bronchial irritation; in Los Angeles it is eye irritation. In both cases visibility is reduced, but this is generally more severe in London.

Even before World War II it was recognized on the basis of differences such as these that the problem of general air pollution in the Los Angeles basin is quite different from that over such cities as London, Pittsburgh, or St. Louis, and shortly after the war intensive investigations were begun on the sources and nature of the Los Angeles problem. As a result of these investigations, it is now well established that the undesirable effects of air pollution in the Los Angeles basin are chiefly due to photochemical reactions which occur in the polluted air and are initiated by solar radiation.[352]

While this type of air pollution, which has been called "photochemical smog," [364] is most advanced and has been most studied in the Los Angeles basin, it is by no means unique to that area. It has been recognized in several other areas, and with increasing population on the one hand and increasing air monitoring on the other, unless a cure is found the list of localities in which it is known to play some part will no doubt continue to expand. It is interesting to note that at least one of the areas in which photochemical smog is recognizable, the Central Valley of California, is not primarily urban.

The undesirable effects of photochemical smog include oxidant formation, eye irritation, plant damage, and reduced visibility. Among the major sources of evidence that photochemical reactions produced by sunlight are responsible for these effects are the diurnal variation in oxidant concentration and its correlation with incident solar radiation,[351,397] the correlation between the 24-hr integrated oxidant concentration and integrated solar radiation,[351] the correlation between oxidant concentration and eye irritation, plant damage, and visibility reduction,[287,351,397] and the formation of oxidant, eye irritant, and crop damage by laboratory irradiation of outside air.[132,265,397]

It is also well established that the pollutants which support these photochemical reactions in the Los Angeles basin are organic compounds and oxides of nitrogen resulting from the use of hydrocarbon fuels, and that the chief source of these pollutants is automobile exhaust. The early work of Haagen-Smit and his collaborators[172,174] first demonstrated that oxidants, including ozone, are produced by the laboratory irradiation of low concentrations of nitrogen dioxide and a variety of organic compounds, including hydrocarbons, in air. Haagen-Smit and Fox[175] also demonstrated that ozone is produced by the irradiation of automobile exhaust in air, at concentrations similar to those in the open. The irradiation of dilute automobile exhaust or of nitrogen dioxide–hydrocarbon mixtures in air, was shown by Schuck and collaborators[376,377,379] and by Morriss and Bolze[295] to lead to eye irritation, by Stephens, Darley, and Taylor[400,401] to lead to plant damage, and by Doyle and Renzetti[107] to lead to aerosol formation.

These results have been repeatedly confirmed and extended by more specific investigations to which we shall have occasion to refer in greater detail. In addition, the literature of photochemistry contains a large amount of information bearing on the reactions responsible for these effects. Our objective is to review, coordinate, and apply that information. This task has several general aspects which are defined by a consideration of the nature of photochemical reactions.

2. THE ELEMENTARY NATURE OF PHOTOCHEMICAL REACTIONS

A photochemical reaction begins with the act of absorption of radiation. By the Stark-Einstein law of photochemical equivalence this is a quantum process involving one photon per absorbing molecule. The number of molecules absorbing is therefore equal to the number of photons absorbed.

The immediate product of absorption of a photon is an excited state of the absorbing molecule, with energy in excess of the normal state equal to the energy of the photon which it absorbed. Experience has shown that light which produces only vibrational or rotational changes in the absorbing molecule is photochemically inactive, and it is only when the light absorbed results in an electronic transition that sufficiently large changes are produced to lead to chemical reaction. As most vibrational and rotational spectra lie in the infrared, and most electronic spectra in the visible and ultraviolet, it is the latter regions which are of photochemical importance.

The electronically excited molecule produced by absorption may undergo any of several fates. It may dissociate, it may react with other molecules on collision, it may internally rearrange or polymerize, or it may lose its excitation energy by fluorescence or collisional deactivation and thereby be returned to its original state. Any of these possibilities except fluorescence or collisional deactivation may serve as the initial chemical step, or primary process, in a photochemical reaction. The excited molecules may react entirely by a single primary process, or they may be divided between two or more competing processes, including fluorescence or deactivation. The sum of the rates of all the competing processes is equal to the rate of absorption.

A photochemical primary process may yield stable molecules directly, or it may yield unstable products which undergo further, or secondary, reactions. In the great majority of photochemical reactions which have been studied in detail, it has been found that the primary process consists of a dissociation of the absorbing molecule into free radicals or atoms. The free radicals or atoms then take part in secondary reactions. These reactions may lead to stable molecules which, in turn, take part in still other reactions.

In most cases the direct effects of light absorption cease with the photochemical primary process. The secondary reactions are thermal and are independent of the means by which the reactants concerned are produced. An exception to this is found in a few instances in which the primary products contain internal excitation energy, which cannot be acquired thermally at the existing temperature, and which influences their subsequent fate. In either event, if an over-all photochemical process is taken to include all steps from the initial act of absorption to the final end products, the secondary reactions are a part of that process.

3. DEFINITION OF THE PROBLEM

Following the order of the steps in an over-all photochemical process, the information required for an understanding of the photochemical reactions which occur in polluted air, and the part they play in producing the observed effects, may be listed under four general headings: radiation, absorption, primary processes, and secondary reactions.

Ideally, under the first heading it is necessary to know the intensity and spectral distribution of solar radiation in the polluted layer, particularly in the visible and ultraviolet regions, and its changes with time and other conditions. Second, it is necessary to know the specific substances in the polluted air which absorb in this region. For each absorber it is necessary to know the concentration as a function of time and the absorption coefficients throughout the region of wavelengths which lead to photochemical reaction; from these and the spectral distribution of solar radiation each absorption rate may be calculated. Third, it is necessary to know the primary processes which follow absorption, with the products which are formed and the relative rates of these processes. Fourth, one must know the secondary reactions which result from these primary processes, with the products formed and the rate constants and concentrations involved in each reaction.

Practically, for some of these specifications existing information falls far short of meeting the requirements, and, in order to even approach a satisfactory over-all picture, the gaps must be bridged by assumptions. As an example, the rates of very few of the primary processes with which we shall be concerned have been measured in air, and until they are measured assumptions based on such evidence as is available must apply. In some instances, where there is no evidence at all, estimates of upper or lower limits must be employed. Conversely, for other specifications the use of all of the information available would obscure the major problem in a mass of detail. Examples here are given by the short term variations in solar radiation and pollutant concentrations. While these variations must be considered and where necessary taken into account, for the most part the use of representative or averaged values will be more profitable.

Many of the conclusions which will be reached are based on assumptions and simplifications such as these. As more information comes in, and the assumptions and simplifications are replaced by positive knowledge, some of the conclusions will no doubt prove to be in error. To this extent the treatment here presented is of transient value; if it serves as a guide to further work its purpose will have been fulfilled.

Chapter II

Solar Radiation and Its Absorption

1. FACTORS TO BE CONSIDERED

The lower atmosphere receives visible and ultraviolet radiation during the day not only directly from the sun, but also from the sky and, by reflection, from the surface of the earth. The quantity of radiation received is dependent on the solar spectral irradiance outside the atmosphere, the solar zenith angle, the nature and amount of scattering, diffusion, and absorption of radiation by the atmosphere, and the albedo of the surface under the region of interest. Several general discussions of these effects are available.[141,143,243,250,288]

The amount of radiation absorbed by a specific substance within the polluted layer depends not only on the amount received, but on its effective path length within the layer, on the absorption coefficients and concentrations of the substance in question as well as competing substances, and on the amount and nature of scattering and diffusion of radiation within the layer.

In arriving at a practical method for estimating the rate of absorption of solar radiation in the polluted layer, each of these factors must be considered.

2. SOLAR RADIATION OUTSIDE THE ATMOSPHERE

The spectrum of the sun in the visible and near ultraviolet is essentially that of a black body radiator at about 6000°K, crossed by several thousand dark absorption lines; the Fraunhofer lines. The solar spectral irradiance, or energy per unit bandwidth, outside the atmosphere has been investigated for many years, chiefly by the classical method of Langley.[1–5,80,326,327] Spectral irradiance curves are obtained at different solar altitudes, hence different atmospheric path lengths or air masses traversed by the radiation, and the results extrapolated to zero air mass. The method is inadequate in the infrared and ultraviolet where atmospheric absorption reduces the irradiance to immeasurably small values, but has been supplemented in the ultraviolet by direct measurements from high altitude rockets.[208,225] All available data have been critically reviewed by Johnson[221] and combined into a mean solar spectral irradiance curve over the wavelength region from 0.22 to 7.0 μ (2200–70,000 A), averaged over 100-A intervals to eliminate the detailed Fraunhofer struc-

TABLE 1

MEAN SOLAR SPECTRAL IRRADIANCE OUTSIDE THE ATMOSPHERE FOR SPECTRAL
BANDWIDTHS OF 100 A CENTERED AT THE WAVELENGTHS SHOWN

	$I_{0\lambda}$			$I_{0\lambda}$	
λ (A)	Microwatts (cm^{-2} 100 A^{-1})	Photons (cm^{-2} sec^{-1} 100 A^{-1})	λ (A)	Microwatts (cm^{-2} 100 A^{-1})	Photons (cm^{-2} sec^{-1} 100 A^{-1})
2200	0.30×10^2	3.3×10^{13}	3850	11.5×10^2	2.23×10^{15}
2300	0.52×10^2	6.0×10^{13}	3900	11.2×10^2	2.20×10^{15}
2400	0.58×10^2	7.0×10^{13}	3950	12.0×10^2	2.39×10^{15}
2500	0.64×10^2	8.1×10^{13}	4000	15.4×10^2	3.10×10^{15}
2600	1.3×10^2	1.7×10^{14}	4100	19.4×10^2	4.01×10^{15}
2700	2.5×10^2	3.4×10^{14}	4200	19.2×10^2	4.06×10^{15}
2800	2.4×10^2	3.4×10^{14}	4300	17.8×10^2	3.86×10^{15}
2900	5.2×10^2	7.6×10^{14}	4400	20.3×10^2	4.50×10^{15}
2950	6.3×10^2	9.4×10^{14}	4500	22.0×10^2	5.00×10^{15}
3000	6.1×10^2	9.2×10^{14}	4600	21.6×10^2	5.00×10^{15}
3050	6.7×10^2	1.03×10^{15}	4700	21.7×10^2	5.14×10^{15}
3100	7.6×10^2	1.19×10^{15}	4800	21.6×10^2	5.22×10^{15}
3150	8.2×10^2	1.30×10^{15}	4900	19.9×10^2	4.91×10^{15}
3200	8.5×10^2	1.37×10^{15}	5000	19.8×10^2	4.98×10^{15}
3250	10.2×10^2	1.67×10^{15}	5250	19.7×10^2	5.21×10^{15}
3300	11.5×10^2	1.91×10^{15}	5500	19.5×10^2	5.40×10^{15}
3350	11.1×10^2	1.87×10^{15}	5750	18.9×10^2	5.46×10^{15}
3400	11.1×10^2	1.90×10^{15}	6000	18.1×10^2	5.47×10^{15}
3450	11.7×10^2	2.03×10^{15}	6250	17.1×10^2	5.38×10^{15}
3500	11.8×10^2	2.07×10^{15}	6500	16.2×10^2	5.30×10^{15}
3550	11.6×10^2	2.08×10^{15}	6750	15.2×10^2	5.20×10^{15}
3600	11.6×10^2	2.10×10^{15}	7000	14.4×10^2	5.08×10^{15}
3650	12.9×10^2	2.37×10^{15}	7500	12.7×10^2	4.80×10^{15}
3700	13.3×10^2	2.48×10^{15}	8000	11.3×10^2	4.55×10^{15}
3750	13.2×10^2	2.51×10^{15}	9000	8.95×10^2	4.06×10^{15}
3800	12.3×10^2	2.36×10^{15}	10000	7.25×10^2	3.65×10^{15}

ture. The values in Table 1 are taken from Johnson's data. They will vary by $\pm1.5\%$ with changes in solar intensity outside the atmosphere, and by $\pm3.5\%$ with changes in solar distance. The mean value of the solar constant, derived from these data, is 2.00 ± 0.04 cal cm^{-2} min^{-1}.

It is rather interesting to note from Table 1 that, while in terms of energy units per unit wavelength interval the maximum of solar irradiance outside the atmosphere occurs at about 4500 A, in terms of number of photons the maximum is at about 6000 A and is relatively flat. It should also be noted that even when averaged over 100-A intervals the curve of solar spectral irradiance shows several maxima and minima in

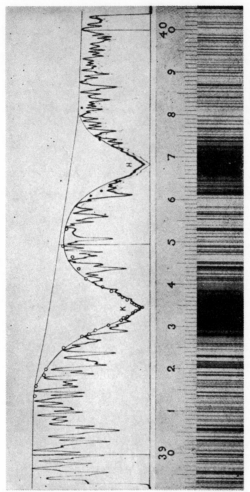

Fig. 1. Solar spectrum in the region 3900–4000 A. From E. Pettit (Ref. 327).

the region 3000–6000 A. If averages are taken over shorter intervals, these variations become sharper, and if the Fraunhofer lines are taken into account, they become sharper still.

The Fraunhofer lines show varying amounts of Doppler broadening, and some of them are quite intense. For example, Fig. 1 shows the lines in the region 3900–4000 A, together with a photoelectric tracing of the same region, obtained by Pettit.[327] The strong bands centered at 3968 and 3934 A are the Fraunhofer H and K lines, resulting from absorption by singly ionized calcium atoms in the solar atmosphere. As the tracing shows, these lines have half-widths of about 10 A, and in their center portions the spectral irradiance is less than 10% of that to either side. Several other lines shown in Fig. 1 reduce the irradiance by 50% or more. Conversely, the peaks of irradiance between the lines run from 1.3 to 1.6 times that of the average over the 100-A interval, and this is true throughout the solar ultraviolet region.

3. Air Mass and Solar Zenith Angle

The air mass, m, is the ratio of the length of path of the direct solar radiation through the atmosphere relative to the vertical path. It is a function of the solar zenith angle, or angle from a point on the earth's surface between the sun and the zenith. For solar zenith angles less than 60°, it suffices to take $m = $ secant z, where z is the zenith angle. At larger zenith angles, corrections are necessary for the curvature of the atmosphere and for refraction.[138] Some representative values are given in Table 2.

The solar zenith angle for any specific location and time may be meas-

TABLE 2

VALUES OF THE AIR MASS, m,
AT VARIOUS ZENITH ANGLES

Solar zenith angle (z)	Air mass (m)	
	Secant (z)	Corrected
15°	1.03	1.03
20°	1.06	1.06
30°	1.15	1.15
40°	1.30	1.30
45°	1.41	1.41
60°	2.00	2.00
70°	2.92	2.90
80°	5.76	5.60
85°	11.47	10.39

ured directly or may be calculated from the latitude of the location, the local hour angle, and the declination angle. The relation is

$$\cos z = \cos \text{lat.} \times \cos \text{dec.} \times \cos \text{lha} + \sin \text{lat.} \times \sin \text{dec.} \qquad \text{(II-1)}$$

Declination and local hour angles (lha) may be obtained from a solar ephemeris or nautical almanac. The solar altitude, or angle which the sun makes with the horizon, if measured in degrees is 90-Z.

The variation in solar altitude and zenith angle with time of day and season of the year is illustrated by Fig. 2, and the effect of latitude on

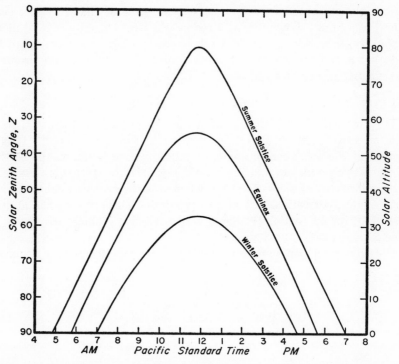

Fig. 2. Relation between solar zenith angle and time of day at Los Angeles.

these variations is shown in Fig. 3. The latitudes illustrated are very approximately those of Mexico City, Los Angeles, and London.

4. ATMOSPHERIC TRANSMISSION

Equations for estimating the amount of solar radiation which is directly transmitted by the atmosphere are based on the Bouguer-Lambert law,

$$I_{t\lambda} = I_{0\lambda}e^{-\sigma_\lambda m} \qquad \text{(II-2)}$$

$I_{0\lambda}$ and $I_{t\lambda}$ are the incident and transmitted intensities at wavelength λ, σ_λ is the attenuation coefficient at that wavelength, and m is the mass of air through which the transmitted light passes.

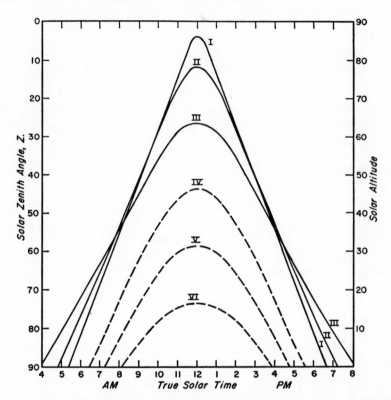

FIG. 3. Effect of latitude on solar zenith angle. On the scale of true solar time, also called apparent solar time and apparent local solar time, the sun crosses the meridian at noon. The latitudes and seasons represented are: I, 20° N lat, summer solstice; II, 35° N lat, summer solstice; III, 50° N lat, summer solstice; IV, 20° N lat, winter solstice; V, 35° N lat, winter solstice; and VI, 50° N lat, winter solstice.

Where several factors, such as molecular scattering, particulate diffusion, and absorption contribute to the attenuation, the coefficient for the total effect is the sum of the individual coefficients,

$$\sigma_\lambda = \sigma_{m\lambda} + \sigma_{p\lambda} + \sigma_{a\lambda} + \ldots \tag{II-3}$$

Setting $I_{t\lambda}/I_{0\lambda} = \mathrm{T}_\lambda$, the fraction transmitted or transmissivity, and converting to decadic logarithms,

$$\log_{10} \mathrm{T}_\lambda = -(\sigma_{m\lambda} + \sigma_{p\lambda} + \sigma_{a\lambda} + \ldots)m \log e$$
$$= -(s_{m\lambda} + s_{p\lambda} + s_{a\lambda} + \ldots)m \tag{II-4}$$

Here s_m, s_p, and s_a are the decimal or decadic attenuation coefficients for molecular scattering, particulate diffusion, and absorption.

If desired, the transmissivity with respect to each of these effects may be written separately,

$$\log_{10} T_{m\lambda} = -s_{m\lambda}m; \quad \log_{10} T_{p\lambda} = -s_{p\lambda}m; \quad \log_{10} T_{a\lambda} = -s_{a\lambda}m \quad \text{(II-5)}$$

In this case the transmissivity resulting from any combination of individual factors is simply the product of the individual fractions,

$$T_{s\lambda} = T_{m\lambda}T_{p\lambda}; \quad T_\lambda = T_{s\lambda}T_{a\lambda}; \quad \text{etc.} \quad \text{(II-6)}$$

The term $T_{s\lambda}$ is the transmissivity relative to the combined effects of scattering and diffusion. The fraction of I_0 which will be scattered and diffused will be $(1 - T_{s\lambda})T_{a\lambda}$.

5. MOLECULAR SCATTERING

The theoretical attenuation coefficient for molecular scattering is given by the equation of Rayleigh.[347] In the form in which it is usually applied to the atmosphere this equation is an approximation, involving the assumption of a homogeneous atmosphere which is of definite height and of uniform temperature and pressure throughout. For such an atmosphere, the equation may be written

$$(s_{m\lambda})_0 = \frac{32\pi^3 H_0 f \log e}{3N_0} \cdot (\eta_{0\lambda} - 1)^2\lambda^{-4} \quad \text{(II-7)}$$

Here H_0 is the height of the homogeneous atmosphere, N_0 is the number of molecules per unit volume, f is a small depolarization term which expresses the influence of the optically anisotropic molecules on the scattering,[325,429] and $\eta_{0\lambda}$ is the index of refraction of air at wavelength λ and the pressure and temperature chosen.

For a standard atmosphere at 0°C and 1 atm pressure, Penndorf [429] has selected the values $H_0 = 7.996 \times 10^5$ cm, $N_0 = 2.687 \times 10^{19}$ cm^{-3}, and $f = 1.061$. Inserting these values, if λ is expressed in microns, equation (II-7) becomes

$$(s_{m\lambda})_0 = 4.535 \times 10^4(\eta_{0\lambda} - 1)^2\lambda^{-4} \quad \text{(II-8)}$$

Values of $(\eta_{0\lambda} - 1)$ from Penndorf and of $(s_{m\lambda})_0$ from equation (II-8) are given in Table 3.

Since the index of refraction increases with decreasing wavelength, the scattering coefficient $(s_{m\lambda})_0$ increases somewhat more rapidly than does the inverse fourth power of the wavelength. This departure from an exact fourth power relationship becomes more marked at shorter wavelengths. Thus at 4000 A, the effective power of λ with which $(s_{m\lambda})_0$ varies is −4.15, while at 3000 A it is −4.3.

TABLE 3

INDICES OF REFRACTION AND MOLECULAR SCATTERING COEFFICIENTS
FOR A HOMOGENEOUS STANDARD ATMOSPHERE

Wavelength (A)	$(\eta_{0\lambda} - 1) \times 10^8$	$(s_{m\lambda})_0$	Wavelength (A)	$(\eta_{0\lambda} - 1) \times 10^8$	$(s_{m\lambda})_0$
2900	30915	0.613	4500	29592	0.0969
3000	30756	0.530	4600	29555	0.0885
3100	30616	0.461	4700	29520	0.0810
3200	30490	0.402	4800	29487	0.0743
3300	30377	0.353	4900	29457	0.0687
3400	30275	0.311	5000	29428	0.0628
3500	30182	0.275	5250	29364	0.0515
3600	30098	0.245	5500	29308	0.0426
3700	30022	0.218	5750	29260	0.0356
3800	29951	0.195	6000	29218	0.0299
3900	29887	0.175	6250	29181	0.0253
4000	29828	0.158	6500	29148	0.0216
4100	29773	0.142	6750	29118	0.0185
4200	29723	0.129	7000	29093	0.0160
4300	29676	0.117	7500	29049	0.0121
4400	29633	0.106	8000	29013	0.0093

In the actual atmosphere, the values of $s_{m\lambda}$ will depend on the vertical temperature and density profiles above the point of observation, and departures from the values in Table 3 may be substantial.[429] For a normal variety of atmospheric temperatures, approximate values of $s_{m\lambda}$ may be obtained by multiplying $(s_{m\lambda})_0$ from Table 3 by the pressure, in atmospheres, at the point of observation. The transmissivity relative to molecular scattering will then be given by

$$\log T_{m\lambda} = -(s_{m\lambda})_0 \frac{P}{P_0} \cdot m \qquad \text{(II-9)}$$

6. PARTICULATE DIFFUSION

Particulate matter in the atmosphere attenuates direct solar radiation by scattering, reflection, refraction, and diffraction, and the term "particulate diffusion" refers to the combination of these effects. If the amount, nature, and size distribution of the particulate matter were known in detail, the resulting attenuation coefficient and its variation with wavelength could be calculated by the Mie theory. But these factors are widely variable, difficult to measure, and seldom if ever definitely known, and for practical use it is necessary to introduce a simplification based on empirical results. Such simplifications are generally of the form

$$s_{p\lambda} = b\lambda^{-n} \qquad \text{(II-10)}$$

where b is a function of the number of particles and n is a function of their size. Scattering by particles of diameter less than about 0.1λ or 0.05μ will approach the Rayleigh law. With increasing particle size, the value of n will decrease from 4 toward 0. The transition from dependence on to independence of wavelength was found by Pfund [328] to set in when the ratio of particle diameter to wavelength is around unity, while Foizik [130] found the transition stage occurs for visible light when the particle diameter is between 0.5 and 2μ. Moreover, there is evidence that in this region the attenuation by particles of a given size no longer varies monotonically with wavelength, but shows a series of maxima and minima. [206,407] With a range of particle sizes, this effect will be smoothed out.

Ranz and Johnstone [346] have estimated that coagulation by collision will set a low size limit of about 0.05μ for particles which can remain in the atmosphere for long periods of time, and consider the range of diameters present to be about $0.05-10\mu$. Tunitzki [425] has calculated, on the basis of turbulent and thermal coagulation, that the particle diameter with the least tendency to collide and coagulate, hence the most likely size in the atmosphere, is 0.5μ. Ives and co-workers [216] found the same value as the most frequent particle size in a study of atmospheric pollution over American cities during the years 1931 to 1933. Particles in the photochemical smog of the Los Angeles basin range from below 0.1 to over 1μ, with a mean diameter of about 0.3μ. [276,397]

In general the larger particles in the atmosphere are found near the ground, while the smaller particles persist at higher elevations. Moreover, the number and size of the particles are not independent, but the average size is larger on hazy days than on clear days. Thus, Middleton [288] correlated the exponent n in equation (II-10) with visual range in the atmosphere, finding it to decrease from 2.1 at a visual range of 125 km to 0.8 at a range of 10 km. From the Smithsonian data for the visible region, Angström [12] found values of b usually between 0 and 0.2 (with λ in microns) and of n between 0.5 and 2. The value of n varied with atmospheric conditions and elevation above the surface; near the ground it was generally about 0.9 but with elevation it approached 2. The most generally acceptable value found by Angström was $n = 1.3$. Similar variation in n, both with altitude of the observing station and from place to place, has been reported by Linke and Borne. [263]

The variability in n with elevation and with the amount of particulate matter in the atmosphere suggests that the wavelength dependence of the particulate attenuation coefficient might better be described by using more than one term of the form of (II-10), with more than one value of n. Indeed, from an analysis of data from eight widely spaced locations, Fowle[139] concluded more than forty years ago that "the transparency of air at any place depends on three factors: the transparency of dry air itself, which depends on molecular scattering, the scatterings due to what may be termed wet haziness, and the scatterings due to dry haziness—the former associated with water vapor, the latter with dust." In accord with this conclusion, Moon[293] proposed the equation, for λ in microns,

$$\log_{10} T_{p\lambda} = -(3.75 \times 10^{-3}\lambda^{-2}w + 3.5 \times 10^{-2}\lambda^{-0.75}d)m \qquad \text{(II-11)}$$

The first term in this expression, containing λ^{-2}, was derived from Fowle's analysis, chiefly of data obtained at a 5700-ft elevation on Mt. Wilson. The coefficient w is taken as equal to the amount of precipitable water vapor in the atmosphere, measured vertically above the point of observation, and expressed in cm of liquid water. When not otherwise known, the value of w may be approximated from the formula

$$w = 2.3e_h10^{-(h/22000)} \qquad \text{(II-12)}$$

where e_h is the partial pressure of atmospheric water vapor in cm Hg at the place of observation, and h is its elevation in meters above sea level. This may on the average give values which are nearly correct, but values for individual days may be several times too large or too small.[139] Moon found that a good fit with observed transmission coefficients was obtained by using $w = 0$ for the Smithsonian Mt. Whitney data, $w = 1$ for the Mt. Wilson and Tucson data, and $w = 2$ for the Washington, D.C. data.

The second term in equation (II-11) was derived by Moon from the Smithsonian data obtained at Washington, D.C., with $d = 1$. The value of d is presumably a function of the dust content of the atmosphere; the air near the surface at the time the measurements were made was reported to have a dust count of 800 particles/cc. It will decrease with altitude; above about 3000 ft it is usually sufficient to set $d = 0$, while near the surface in an urban area it may be considerably greater than 1.

There appears to be no a priori reason, other than the empirical fit with observed data, for the first term in the Moon equation to be always proportional to, and the second term to be always independent of, the amount of precipitable water vapor in the atmosphere, and the independence of these two terms has been questioned by Angström.[12] At any rate, the Moon equation may be regarded as empirically grouping the diffusion effects of the whole range of particulate sizes in cloudless air into two terms, for small and large particles, with the wavelength coefficient $n = 2$ and 0.75, respectively. The size range contributing to the λ^{-2} term may be considered, very approximately, to be from 0.05μ to around the wavelength of light, while the diameter of particles contributing to the $\lambda^{-0.75}$ term will be around the wavelength and larger.

The values of $T_{m\lambda}$ and $T_{p\lambda}$ yielded by equations (II-9) and (II-11) are compared for a set of representative conditions in Fig. 4. For the

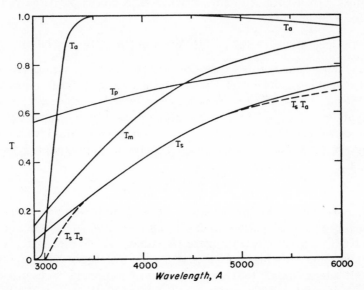

FIG. 4. Atmospheric transmission factors. T_m is the fraction transmitted relative to molecular scattering calculated from equation (II-9) with $P = 1000$ mb. T_p is the transmissivity relative to particulate diffusion, from equation (II-11) with $w = 2$ and $d = 1$. T_a is from equation (II-13) with $(O_3) = 2.2$ mm. The resultant transmissivity with respect to scattering and diffusion is $T_s = T_m T_p$, and the over-all fraction transmitted is $T_s T_a$. All values are for $m = 1.41$, corresponding to a solar zenith angle of 45°.

parameters chosen ($P = 1000$ mb, $w = 2$, $d = 1$), the attenuation by particulate diffusion exceeds that by molecular scattering above about 4500 A, while in the ultraviolet molecular scattering is dominant. More useful for estimating solar irradiance in the lower atmosphere is the combined transmittance $T_{s\lambda} = T_{m\lambda} T_{p\lambda}$. Values of this product are also shown in Fig. 4, and are given for several solar zenith angles in Table 4. At large zenith angles (low solar altitudes), the small transmittance in the ultraviolet is noteworthy.

7. ABSORPTION BY ATMOSPHERIC OZONE

In the ultraviolet and visible, through the range 2900–6800 A, the only naturally occurring absorber which need be taken into account in

TABLE 4

ATMOSPHERIC TRANSMISSIVITY RELATIVE TO SCATTERING AND DIFFUSION[a]

Wavelength (A)	$T_{s\lambda}$ at $z =$				
	0°	20°	40°	60°	80°
2900	0.165	0.147	0.098	0.027	0.00004
3000	0.203	0.183	0.125	0.041	0.00013
3100	0.241	0.220	0.157	0.058	0.00035
3200	0.280	0.258	0.190	0.078	0.00080
3300	0.318	0.295	0.224	0.101	0.00162
3400	0.354	0.331	0.258	0.125	0.00298
3500	0.389	0.364	0.292	0.151	0.00506
3600	0.422	0.399	0.324	0.178	0.00794
3700	0.453	0.430	0.356	0.205	0.0118
3800	0.482	0.460	0.385	0.232	0.0168
3900	0.508	0.486	0.413	0.258	0.0225
4000	0.534	0.514	0.442	0.286	0.0300
4100	0.558	0.538	0.468	0.312	0.0383
4200	0.580	0.560	0.491	0.336	0.0471
4300	0.601	0.581	0.513	0.360	0.0572
4400	0.620	0.601	0.535	0.384	0.0684
4500	0.637	0.618	0.555	0.406	0.0798
4600	0.652	0.635	0.573	0.426	0.0914
4700	0.668	0.650	0.590	0.445	0.104
4800	0.682	0.665	0.606	0.464	0.116
4900	0.694	0.677	0.620	0.482	0.129
5000	0.706	0.691	0.634	0.499	0.142
5250	0.733	0.719	0.667	0.538	0.176
5500	0.756	0.742	0.694	0.571	0.208
5750	0.775	0.763	0.717	0.601	0.240
6000	0.792	0.780	0.737	0.626	0.270
6250	0.805	0.794	0.754	0.649	0.297
6500	0.818	0.807	0.769	0.668	0.324
6750	0.829	0.818	0.782	0.686	0.348
7000	0.838	0.828	0.794	0.702	0.372
7500	0.854	0.844	0.814	0.727	0.411
8000	0.866	0.858	0.828	0.751	0.448

[a] Values given are $T_{s\lambda} = T_{m\lambda}T_{p\lambda}$, calculated from equations (II-9) and (II-11) with $P = 1000$ mb, $w = 2$, and $d = 1$.

estimating atmospheric transmission is the ozone in the upper atmosphere. Ozone shows two series of diffuse absorption bands in this region; the strong Huggins bands which begin about 3500 A and extend with rapidly increasing intensity to a maximum at about 2550 A, and the weak Chappuis bands, which extend from about 4500 A to above 7000 A with a maximum about 6000 A.

It is customary to express the quantity of ozone in the atmosphere in terms of the thickness of the equivalent layer of pure ozone, in millimeters or centimeters, at standard temperature and pressure. If this be denoted by (O_3), and if α_λ is the decadic absorption coefficient in corresponding units, the ozone attenuation coefficient will be $s_\lambda = \alpha_\lambda(O_3)$, and the transmissivity with respect to ozone absorption will be given by

$$\log_{10} T_{a\lambda} = -\alpha_\lambda(O_3)m \qquad \text{(II-13)}$$

The absorption coefficients for the Huggins bands have been measured by Fabry and Buisson,[122] Läuchli,[252] Ny and Choong,[316] and Inn and Tanaka.[215] The earlier investigators used ozonized oxygen and photo-

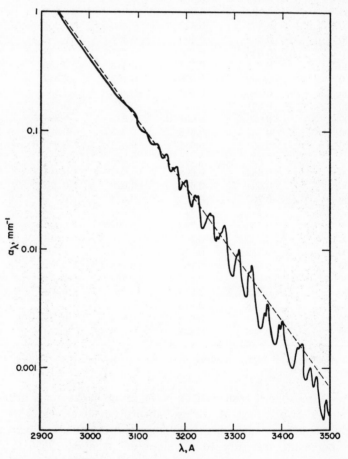

FIG. 5. Absorption coefficients of ozone, 2900–3500 A. Solid curve is from Inn and Tanaka, dashed line from Fabry and Buisson.

graphic methods, while Inn and Tanaka used pure ozone and a photo-electric detector. The latter results, which are probably somewhat more accurate, are shown in Fig. 5.

The errors introduced by taking average values of the absorption coefficient over an interval of the spectrum will be examined in Chapter III. In this case, since the bands are diffuse and the amount of absorption is slight at the wavelengths where the differences are pronounced, the error will not be large. For ozone in the region 2900–3500 A, such averages, when plotted as in Fig. 5 on a logarithmic scale against wavelength, lie very nearly on a straight line. Indeed, Fabry and Buisson expressed the results of their measurements in this region in the form of the equation

$$\log \alpha_\lambda = 16.58 - 0.00564\lambda \qquad \text{(II-14)}$$

where λ is in angstroms. The dashed line in Fig. 5 is from this equation. Below 3300 A it lies very close to the averaged values of Inn and Tanaka; above 3300 A it is somewhat higher, but here the atmospheric absorption is so slight that the difference is negligible. Numerical values of the absorption coefficient, taken from these averages, are given in Table 5.

TABLE 5

ABSORPTION COEFFICIENTS OF OZONE
IN THE ULTRAVIOLET REGION

Wavelength (A)	α_λ (mm^{-1})	Wavelength (A)	α_λ (mm^{-1})
2900	1.66	3150	0.061
2950	0.84	3200	0.032
3000	0.44	3300	0.0085
3050	0.23	3400	0.0020
3100	0.12	3500	0.0005

The absorption coefficients of Inn and Tanaka for the Chappuis bands are shown in Fig. 6, and averaged numerical values are given in Table 6.

The amount of ozone in a vertical profile of the atmosphere[104,120,121,208,329] increases with latitude from the equivalent of about a 2-mm NTP layer at the equator to between 3 and 4 mm at latitude 68°N. The amount varies with the season, with the maximum in spring and the minimum in the fall (Fig. 7). The evidence for a diurnal variation in the amount of ozone in the upper atmosphere is inconclusive; if any, it is probably small.

In applying equation (II-13), it will be convenient to select a representative value for the ozone content of the atmosphere. For most lati-

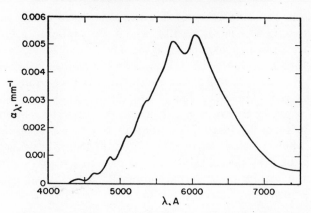

Fig. 6. Absorption coefficients of ozone, 4500–7500 A.

tudes in the United States, Fig. 7 would suggest a value of about
2.5 mm, but for Los Angeles during the months of most air pollution
(August–November), 2.2 mm would be more appropriate. Middleton[289]
selected 2.2 mm as representative on the average for middle latitudes,
while Dunkelman and Scolnik[109] estimated 2.0 mm from measurements
at 8000-ft elevation near Tucson, Arizona. On the whole, $(O_3) = 2.2$ mm
appears to be suitable, and values of $T_{a\lambda}$ estimated for this amount of
ozone are shown on Fig. 4. These values bring out rather dramatically
the cutoff of solar radiation below 3000 A by atmospheric ozone. At
2900 A the fraction transmitted by a 2.2-mm layer of ozone at $z = 45°$
is 7×10^{-6}, and at 2850 A it is 10^{-10}.

In estimating atmospheric transmission in the red and infrared beyond
about 6800 A, account must be taken of absorption by molecular oxygen,
water vapor, and carbon dioxide. Of possible interest here are the weak
absorption bands of oxygen at 7660–7590 A and 6920–6860 A, which

TABLE 6

ABSORPTION COEFFICIENTS OF OZONE
IN THE VISIBLE REGION

Wavelength (A)	$\alpha_\lambda \times 10^3$ (mm^{-1})	Wavelength (A)	$\alpha_\lambda \times 10^3$ (mm^{-1})
4750	0.5	6250	4.1
5000	1.3	6500	2.8
5250	2.3	6750	1.7
5500	3.6	7000	0.9
5750	5.2	7250	0.6
6000	5.4	7500	0.4

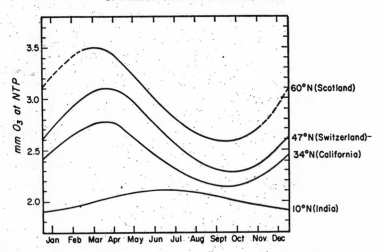

FIG. 7. Annual variation in atmospheric ozone content at different latitudes. From G. M. B. Dobson (Ref. 104).

produce the Fraunhofer dark lines A and B. The atmospheric transmission coefficients, averaged over these two bands, for $\log T_{a\lambda(O_2)} = -k_\lambda Pm$, where P is the atmospheric pressure in millibars (mb) at the level of observation, are approximately $k_\lambda = 1.5 \times 10^{-4}$ mb^{-1} for the A band and $k_\lambda = 6 \times 10^{-5}$ mb^{-1} for the B band.[140]

8. DIRECT AND SKY RADIATION

If $I_{0\lambda}$ is the solar irradiance over an interval $\Delta\lambda$ centered at wavelength λ per unit normal cross section outside the atmosphere (Table 1), on a cloudless day the direct irradiance $I_{d\lambda}$ over the same interval, per unit horizontal cross section in the lower atmosphere, will be

$$I_{d\lambda} = T_{s\lambda}T_{a\lambda}I_{0\lambda}\cos z. \qquad (II-15)$$

The light from the sky may be expressed in terms of a fraction of that which is scattered,

$$I_{s\lambda} = g(1 - T_{s\lambda})T_{a\lambda}I_{0\lambda}\cos z \qquad (II-16)$$

where $I_{s\lambda}$ is the scattered irradiance over interval $\Delta\lambda$ at wavelength λ received by each unit horizontal cross section of the lower layer and g is a fraction.

The value of g will be determined by the directional distribution of the scattered radiation and by the amount of multiple scattering. Molecular scattering is symmetrical and equal in the forward and back directions. This in itself would lead to $g = 0.5$. With particulate diffusion, however, as particle size increases the fraction of the diffuse radiation which is in the forward direction also increases, until as the diameter approaches the wavelength the diffuse radiation is almost all forward of 90° to the direction of the incident radiation.[207] This would tend to increase g. On the other hand, multiple scattering and diffusion would tend to decrease g; the fact that clouds are brighter on the top than on the bottom is an illustration of this. Any absorption by the particulate matter in the atmosphere would also decrease g.

It may be shown from the measurements of Coblentz and Stair[80] of ultraviolet sun and sky radiation on a very clear day, as well as from the calculations of sky vs. direct radiation by Deirmendjian and Sekera,[100] that under conditions of little or no particulate diffusion the value of $g = 0.5$ is closely approached. Klein[249] has reported that equations based on $g = 0.5$ yield values of the total radiation (sun + sky at all wavelengths) which are within 3 to 5% of the measured values. All in all the best procedure appears to be to adopt this value of g as a useful approximation for all conditions.[141,243,244]

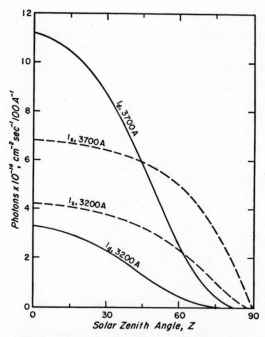

FIG. 8. Direct and sky radiation in the lower atmosphere. The ordinate gives the number of photons incident on a horizontal surface, for 10 bands of the solar spectrum centered on 3700 and 3200 A, estimated from equations (II-15) and (II-16) with $g = 0.5$ and from preceding equations for T_s and T_a with $\pi = 1000$ mb, $w = 2$, $d = 1$, and $(O_3) = 2.2$ mm.

The resulting relations between direct and sky radiation are shown, for two wavelengths in the ultraviolet, on Fig. 8. Both direct and sky radiation are, of course, at a maximum at the maximum solar altitude reached during the day, and as the solar altitude decreases, the direct radiation drops off more rapidly than does that from the sky. This is a matter of common observation with visible light. Not so commonly observed in the visible, except at the moments of sunrise and sunset, is the fact that even on a clear day the sky radiation may exceed that received directly from the sun. The conditions for which this is true may be seen by combining equations (II-15) and (II-16). The result is

$$\frac{I_{s\lambda}}{I_{d\lambda}} = \frac{g(1 - T_{s\lambda})}{T_{s\lambda}} \tag{II-17}$$

It follows from this that when $I_{s\lambda} = I_{d\lambda}$,

$$T_{s\lambda} = \frac{g}{1 + g} \tag{II-18}$$

Thus if $g = 0.5$, the direct and sky irradiance received on a horizontal surface will be equal when $T_{s\lambda} = 1/3$, and if $T_{s\lambda}$ is less than $1/3$, the sky radiation will exceed the direct. A glance at Table 4 shows that for $P = 1000$ mb, $w = 2$ and $d = 1$; this condition applies at all solar zenith angles for wavelengths of 3300 A and smaller. The amount by which the sky radiation may exceed the direct at these wavelengths is illustrated by the curves for 3200 A in Fig. 8. At longer wavelengths there is

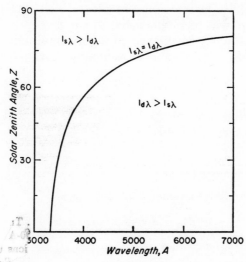

FIG. 9. Sky vs. direct radiation as a function of wavelength and solar zenith angle.

a crossover, and the zenith angle at which the crossover occurs increases with wavelength; the relation for the conditions of Table 4 and $g = 0.5$ is shown in Fig. 9. Another interesting point is that while the absolute amounts of direct and sky radiation depend on atmospheric absorption, their ratio does not; $T_{a\lambda}$ cancels out in equation (II-17).

9. Path Lengths of Solar Radiation in the Lower Atmosphere

Before applying Lamberts law to the polluted layer, it is necessary to know the path lengths L of the direct and sky radiation which traverse that layer. When the sun is at zenith angle z, the path length for direct solar radiation traversing a surface layer of the atmosphere of height h will be

$$L_d = h \text{ secant } z \tag{II-19}$$

For sky radiation the situation is much more complex. The path length of the scattered radiation which originates above the surface layer will vary from a minimum of h for that which enters the layer vertically to a maximum of $2\sqrt{hD}$ for that which enters tangentially, where D is the diameter of the earth. The average path length will depend, therefore, on the distribution of sky radiation from zenith to horizon.

A first approximation to the average path length of sky radiation in the surface layer may be obtained by considering the sky as a luminous hemisphere of uniform brightness. Viewed from the center the amount of radiation from any portion of the hemisphere will be proportional to the area of that portion, and for equal areas at different zenith angles the irradiance incident on a horizontal unit surface at the center of the hemisphere will be proportional to cos z.

If I_s is the total sky irradiance on a horizontal unit surface and θ is the fraction of sky area, the above assumptions give

$$dI_{s(z)} = kI_s \cos z\, d\theta_z \tag{II-20}$$

where k is a constant.

Now, the surface area of the hemisphere is $2\pi r^2$, and the area of the spherical segment xx' (Fig. 10) is $2\pi r^2(1 - \cos z)$. Hence

$$\frac{\text{segment area}}{\text{hemisphere area}} = 1 - \cos z = \text{versine } z \tag{II-21}$$

Therefore for annular increments of sky area

$$d\theta_z = d \text{ vers } z = \sin z\, dz \tag{II-22}$$

and equation (II-20) becomes

$$dI_{s(z)} = kI_s \cos z \sin z\, dz \tag{II-23}$$

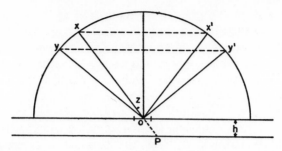

FIG. 10. Geometry of sky radiation.

Integration of this gives the irradiance from the spherical segment xx' received by a horizontal unit surface at point O (Fig. 10),

$$I_{s(z)} = \int_{z=0}^{z=z} kI_s \cos z \sin z \, dz = \frac{k}{2} I_s \sin^2 z \qquad \text{(II-24)}$$

When $z = 90°$, $\sin^2 z = 1$, and since for the whole sky $I_{s(z)} = I_s$, it follows that $k = 2$.

The irradiance from an annular segment $xx' - yy'$ bounded by angles z_1 and z_2 will then be

$$I_{s(z_1 z_2)} = I_s(\sin^2 z_2 - \sin^2 z_1) \qquad \text{(II-25)}$$

For sky radiation, the path length of that which enters a surface layer of height h at angle z will be, as for direct radiation,

$$L_{s(z)} = h \sec z \qquad \text{(II-26)}$$

The fraction of the total radiation with this path length is $d(\sin^2 z)$. Therefore, over an annular segment $z_1 z_2$ furnishing the fraction $\sin^2 z_2 - \sin^2 z_1$ of the radiation, the average path length will be

$$\overline{L}_{s(z_1 z_2)} = \frac{\int_{z_1}^{z_2} h \sec z \, d(\sin^2 z)}{\sin^2 z_2 - \sin^2 z_1} = \frac{2(\cos z_1 - \cos z_2)h}{\sin^2 z_2 - \sin^2 z_1} \qquad \text{(II-27)}$$

For the entire hemisphere this gives for the average path length of sky radiation

$$\overline{L}_s = 2h \qquad \text{(II-28)}$$

The validity of this derivation is dependent on the assumption that the sky may be regarded as a hemisphere of uniform brightness. This is an obvious approximation; the change in color of the sky between zenith and horizon shows that it cannot be true at all wavelengths, and the greater brightness of the sky near the sun shows that it will depend to some extent on the solar altitude. The change in color from zenith to horizon is due to the greater concentration of particulate matter in the lower part of the atmosphere and would suggest that at short wavelengths, with the exception of the region near the sun, the sky should be brightest at the zenith, while at long wavelengths, where particulate diffusion is dominant, it may be brightest near the horizon.

Photochemically we shall be concerned chiefly with the solar ultraviolet, and as a test of validity in this region the fractions $I_{s(z_1 z_2)}/I_s = \sin^2 z_2 - \sin^2 z_1$, from equation (II-25) may be compared with the experimental values of Luckiesh[270] for the distribution of erythymal ultraviolet ($\lambda < 3200$ A) from the sky.

TABLE 7

FRACTIONS OF I_s RECEIVED ON A HORIZONTAL SURFACE
FROM SUCCESSIVE 10 DEGREE ZONES OF THE SKY

Zone (degrees)	Calculated	Observed at $\lambda < 3200$ A	Ratio, obs/calc
0–10	0.030	0.039	1.30
10–20	0.087	0.101	1.16
20–30	0.133	0.147	1.10
30–40	0.163	0.173	1.06
40–50	0.174	0.180	1.03
50–60	0.163	0.158	0.97
60–70	0.133	0.112	0.84
70–80	0.087	0.060	0.69
80–90	0.030	0.030	1.00

This comparison (Table 7) shows, as expected, that the observed fractions exceed the calculated values near the zenith. The average path length for the distribution observed by Luckiesh may be estimated by multiplying the observed fraction of the radiation in each zone by the average path length for that zone, and summing these products. The result gives $L_{s(obs)} = 1.9h$. Since the Luckiesh values were obtained for the erythemal or lower end of the solar ultraviolet, this may be regarded as an extreme case, and at larger wavelengths a closer approach to $L_s = 2h$ or even a value longer than $2h$ may be expected. The greater sky brightness near the sun will tend to increase L_s at low solar altitudes and to decrease it at high altitudes; at $z = 60°$ (sec $z = 2$) it should have little effect. In any event, we may write $L_s = ih$, with $i = 2$ as a useful approximation.

10. ABSORPTION RATES AND ACTINIC IRRADIANCE

The starting point for estimating absorption rates in the lower layer of the atmosphere is, of course, the Lambert-Beer law. If a surface layer of height h contains an absorbing substance at concentration c, with decadic absorption coefficient α_λ, and diffusion within the layer be neglected, the average rate of absorption per unit volume, for direct and sky radiation over interval $\Delta\lambda$ centered at wavelength λ, will be[*]

$$I_{a\lambda} = \frac{I_{d\lambda}(1 - 10^{-\alpha_\lambda ch \text{ secant } z}) + I_{s\lambda}(1 - 10^{-\alpha_\lambda cih})}{h} \qquad \text{(II-29)}$$

$I_{d\lambda}$ and $I_{s\lambda}$ are the direct and sky irradiance as given by equations (II-15) and (II-16).

At the low concentrations of absorbing substances which have been reported in polluted air at times of photochemical smog formation, the absorption will generally be rather weak; that is, the attenuation of solar radiation by absorption as it passes through the polluted layer will be rather small. For weak absorption, equation (II-29) approaches the simpler form

$$I_{a\lambda} = 2.303\alpha_\lambda c(I_{d\lambda} \text{ secant } z + I_{s\lambda} \cdot i) \qquad \text{(II-30)}$$

Each wavelength interval or $\Delta\lambda$ used in the calculation will have its value of $I_{a\lambda}$, and the total rate of absorption by the substance in question will be the summation of these values over the effective range of wavelengths, or

$$I_a = \Sigma I_{a\lambda} \qquad \text{(II-31)}$$

If I_d and I_s are given in photons $cm^{-2}sec^{-1}$ and h is expressed in cm, the units of I_a will be photons $cm^{-3}sec^{-1}$. If, then, the concentration c be expressed in molecules cc^{-1}, the average fraction of the absorbing molecules which will receive photons per unit of time will be $k_a = I_a/c$. This has the dimension of time^{-1} and is equivalent to a first-order rate constant.

In ordinary practice concentrations are expressed in a variety of units, and one must take care that the units of α_λ and c are compatible. Whatever the units of c, it may be converted to molecules cc^{-1} by a conversion factor j, in which case the expression for the specific absorption rate, or average fraction receiving photons per unit time, becomes

$$k_a = \frac{I_a}{jc} \qquad \text{(II-32)}$$

For the concentration units most frequently encountered, the values of the conversion factor j are given in the tabulation.

---

[*] A more detailed and laborious equation for $I_{a\lambda}$, involving the expansion of the term for sky radiation into a series of increments over successive annular segments of sky, has been shown to be unnecessary (Ref. 255, p. 128).

Units of c	j
molecules cc^{-1}	1
moles cc^{-1}	6.02×10^{23}
moles l^{-1}	6.02×10^{20}
mm Hg at 25°C	3.24×10^{16}
equivalent layer in mm at NTP	2.69×10^{18}
atm at 25°C	2.46×10^{19}
ppm at 1 atm, 25°C	2.46×10^{13}
pphm at 1 atm, 25°C	2.46×10^{11}

Combining equations (II-30), (II-31), and (II-32) yields the expression for the specific absorption rate

$$k_a = \Sigma\ 2.303\alpha_\lambda j^{-1}(I_{d\lambda} \sec z + I_{s\lambda} \cdot i) \qquad (II\text{-}33)$$

Here the value of j will be based on the units of α_λ. The use of the weak absorption form [equation (II-30)] thus offers the advantage that it is not necessary to know the values of either c or h in order to calculate k_a; in other words, by the weak absorption equation k_a is independent of c and h.

In view of these advantages it is appropriate to inquire into the amount of error which may be introduced by using the weak absorption form. This form is equivalent to the use of only the first term in the exponential series

$$1 - 10^{-s} = s \log_e 10 - \frac{(s \log_e 10)^2}{2!} + \frac{(s \log_e 10)^3}{3!} - \ldots \qquad (II\text{-}34)$$

where $s = \alpha_\lambda ch \sec z$ for direct and $\alpha_\lambda cih$ for sky radiation. The result will be too large, and for different values of s the error is

s	% error
0.01	1.17
0.03	3.52
0.05	5.87
0.1	12.0
0.2	24.5

Of the different absorbing species known to exist in urban air the largest values of s, hence the largest errors, are given by NO_2. With NO_2 at 10 pphm in a layer 500 m deep, the median value of s for $z = 60°$ is about 0.06, hence the absorption rate calculated by equation (II-33) will be about 7% too high. At other concentrations or depths of layer the error will be approximately in proportion to each.

TABLE 8

ESTIMATED ACTINIC IRRADIANCE IN THE LOWER ATMOSPHERE[a]

λ (A)	$J_\lambda \times 10^{-15}$, photons (cm^{-2} sec^{-1} 100 A^{-1}) at $z =$				
	0°	20°	40°	60°	80°
2900	0.0014	0.0009	0.0002	—	—
3000	0.12	0.10	0.05	0.01	—
3100	0.65	0.60	0.43	0.13	0.01
3200	1.17	1.10	0.91	0.53	0.10
3300	1.83	1.75	1.48	0.96	0.26
3400	1.88	1.82	1.55	1.05	0.32
3500	2.06	1.98	1.72	1.18	0.36
3600	2.10	2.02	1.77	1.24	0.38
3700	2.48	2.40	2.11	1.50	0.46
3800	2.36	2.28	2.02	1.45	0.44
3900	2.20	2.13	1.90	1.38	0.42
4000	3.10	3.01	2.70	2.00	0.62
4100	4.01	3.90	3.51	2.63	0.82
4200	4.06	3.95	3.57	2.71	0.86
4300	3.86	3.76	3.42	2.62	0.85
4400	4.50	4.39	4.02	3.11	1.03
4500	5.00	4.88	4.48	3.51	1.19
4600	5.00	4.89	4.50	3.56	1.22
4700	5.13	5.02	4.64	3.68	1.30
4800	5.20	5.11	4.72	3.79	1.38
4900	4.88	4.78	4.44	3.59	1.33
5000	4.95	4.85	4.51	3.68	1.40
5250	5.14	5.05	4.73	3.91	1.56
5500	5.30	5.21	4.90	4.09	1.69
5750	5.32	5.23	4.92	4.14	1.75
6000	5.32	5.24	4.95	4.21	1.86
6250	5.27	5.19	4.94	4.25	2.01
6500	5.22	5.16	4.92	4.30	2.16
6750	5.16	5.10	4.89	4.32	2.29
7000	5.05	5.00	4.82	4.29	2.38
7500	4.80	4.75	4.59	4.10	2.47
8000	4.55	4.51	4.37	3.98	2.47

[a] Values given are from equation (II-37), with $I_{0\lambda}$ from Table 1, $T_{s\lambda}$ from Table 4, and $T_{a\lambda}$ from equation (II-13). Parameters employed are $P = 1000$ mb, $w = 2$, $d = 1$; $(O_3) = 2.2$ mm, $g = 0.5$, and $i = 2$.

The weak absorption equations, (II-30) and (II-33), may be reduced to a still more useful and informative form by introducing the expressions in (II-15) and (II-16) for $I_{d\lambda}$ and $I_{s\lambda}$. The results are

$$I_{a\lambda} = 2.303\alpha_\lambda c J_\lambda \tag{II-35}$$

and

$$k_a = \Sigma\, 2.303\alpha_\lambda j^{-1} J_\lambda \tag{II-36}$$

where

$$J_\lambda = I_{0\lambda} T_{a\lambda}[T_{s\lambda} + gi(1 - T_{s\lambda})\cos z] \tag{II-37}$$

The function J_λ is the heart of the discussion of solar irradiance and its absorption in the lower atmosphere and deserves examination in some detail. The significance of J_λ lies in the fact that within the limits of the assumptions and approximations involved in its derivation, it is the irradiance which would be measured by a weakly absorbing chemical actinometer with a flat horizontal surface exposed to sun and sky. Within these limits, therefore, it is the actinic irradiance to which the polluted air layer is exposed.

Since this is the case, obviously a good way to measure J_λ would be

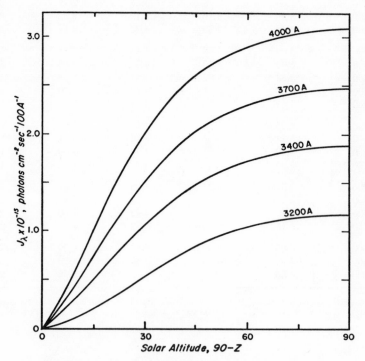

Fig. 11. Variation in actinic irradiance with solar altitude.

by use of such a chemical actinometer. Or still better, in some cases k_a might be measured directly by using the absorbing species in question as the actinometer gas. But until such measurements have been made, estimates of J_λ obtained via equation (II-37) will be useful. Using the values of $T_{s\lambda}$ and $T_{a\lambda}$ which have been judged to be representative, and taking $g = 0.5$ and $i = 2$, the resulting estimates are listed in Table 8.

The rates of the photochemical primary processes in the polluted layer of the atmosphere will be proportional to the corresponding absorption rate constants k_a, and these in turn are proportional to the summation of $\alpha_\lambda J_\lambda$ over the wavelength region which is effective. Referring to equations (II-35) to (II-37), it is seen that J_λ contains all of the parameters which vary with the solar zenith angle. The diurnal variations in J_λ, therefore, will describe the diurnal variations in the rate constants of photochemical primary processes in polluted air.

The variations in J_λ with solar altitude, and the diurnal variations for the summer and winter solstices at several latitudes are illustrated

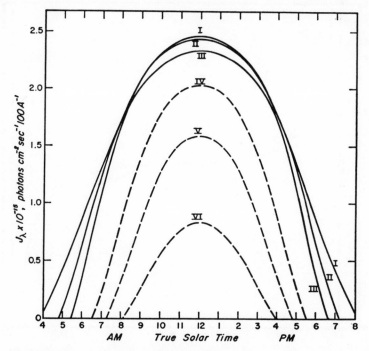

FIG. 12. Diurnal variations in actinic irradiance. Values illustrated are for the 100-A interval of the solar spectrum centered at 3700 A. The designations of the individual curves are: I, 20° N lat, summer solstice; II, 35° N lat, summer solstice; III, 50° N lat, summer solstice; IV, 20° N lat, winter solstice; V, 35° N lat, winter solstice; and VI, 50° N lat, winter solstice.

in Figs. 11 and 12. These figures bring out some interesting points. First, from Fig. 11, as the sun approaches the zenith the change in J_λ becomes slight. As a result, during the summer, when the sun reaches high altitudes at midday, the diurnal J_λ curves are broader than the solar altitude curves, and, up to about 50°N, the latitude has little effect on the maximum values attained. Comparison of curves I, II, and III in Fig. 12 with the corresponding curves in Fig. 3 shows this quite clearly. On the other hand, in winter the J_λ and solar altitude curves have much the same shape, and the maxima attained are sharply dependent on latitude.

Referring again to equation (II-37), it is seen that upon taking $g = 0.5$ and $i = 2$, these two factors cancel, whereupon at $z = 0$ this equation reduces to $J_\lambda = I_{0\lambda} T_{a\lambda}$, and even at $z = 20°$, J_λ is within a few per cent of $I_{0\lambda} T_{a\lambda}$. Since most of the ozone responsible for $T_{a\lambda}$ is in the upper atmosphere, this means, if these values of g and i are correct,

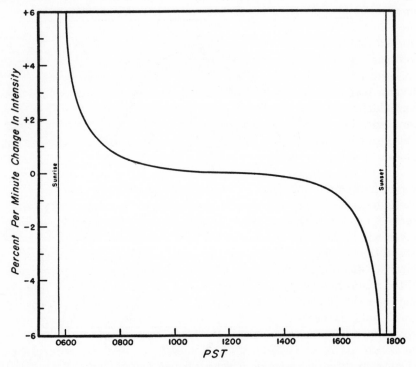

FIG. 13. Rate of change in actinic irradiance in the lower atmosphere. The rate of change plotted is for J_λ at 3700 A on the days of spring and autumn equinox at 35° N lat.

that at small solar zenith angles the actinic irradiance in the lower atmosphere is nearly independent of the elevation.

Not only the absolute values of J_λ but also their rate of change during the day are of interest, since the latter will produce corresponding changes in the rates of photochemical primary processes in the polluted layer. As illustrated in Fig. 13, over a period of several hours during the middle of the day this rate of change is rather small, but near sunrise and sunset it becomes very large. In this connection, the formulas and curves for J_λ make no allowance for refraction at sunrise and sunset, or for dawn and twilight. These would produce small toes on the curves in Figs. 11 and 12.

11. Remarks on Absorption Coefficients

In reviewing the photochemical literature, a number of instances are found in which the absorption spectrum and photochemistry of a specific substance have received a good deal of attention, but its absorption coefficients have not been reported. The reasons for this in most such instances are that absorption coefficients were not required for the purpose in hand, or that the techniques being employed did not lead to their ready determination. The result, insofar as our purposes are concerned, is that there are no data on the absorption coefficients for several possibly important absorbers in urban air. An example of this is formaldehyde. This substance may be quite important in urban air, its absorption spectrum and photochemistry have been studied in detail, but data on its absorption coefficients are not to be found. Other instances of this sort will be noted in the next chapter.

In all cases in which the absorption coefficient varies sharply with wavelength, and particularly in those cases which show discrete line structure, several points must be kept in mind in estimating absorption rates for solar radiation. The percentage transmitted by an absorbing layer will follow the Lambert-Beer law, $\log I_t/I_0 = -\alpha cL$, only if the absorption coefficient may be considered constant over the wavelength interval used in its measurement. If this is not the case, for instance if the absorption shows line structure and the bandwidth used in measuring the coefficients is greater than the individual line width, the apparent coefficients, measured over the whole bandwidth, will vary with the concentration–path length product cL.[314] If the application of such data to urban air involves a large extrapolation in the cL product, the resulting error may become appreciable. If the extrapolation is in the direction of a smaller cL product, which will generally be the case, the calculated absorption rate will be too small.

The values of J_λ in Table 8 have been computed for 100-A intervals of the solar spectrum, and in applying these values in equations (II-35) or (II-36) it will be convenient to use absorption coefficients averaged over the same intervals. This will introduce an error, the magnitude of which will increase with the strength of absorption and the amount of variation in the true absorption coefficient over the interval. Still another error may be introduced in cases of banded or discrete line absorption by the positions of the absorption maxima relative to the Fraunhofer lines. If the absorption lines and the Fraunhofer lines coincide, the calculated absorption rates over 100-A spectral intervals will be too large. Fortunately, these effects are small when the absorption is weak, and as a general rule this is the case in polluted air.

12. DIFFUSION WITHIN THE POLLUTED LAYER

The equations of the preceding sections take no account of scattering and diffusion within the polluted layer itself, yet the common observation of reduced visibility over cities suggests that these effects are of a magnitude which cannot be ignored. Pyrheliometer records obtained by Renzetti[351] show that over the period August–November 1954 the average total daily radiation (sun + sky at all wavelengths) in downtown Los Angeles was some 10% below what it would have been in the absence of pollution. Spectroradiometer measurements conducted in Pasadena by Stair[395] during part of the same period showed that the transmittance of direct solar radiation through polluted air is highly variable and at times of intense pollution may be reduced, in the ultraviolet, by more than 80%.

A striking instance of this was encountered on October 18, 1954. During the early morning of this day the air over Pasadena was exceptionally clear, but about 10:30 A.M. photochemical smog began to form and increased rapidly to a peak at about 12:30 P.M. The intensity of direct radiation at 3235 A as measured by Stair on this day is compared in Fig. 14 with calculated values for normal air.

Measurements such as illustrated in Fig. 14 immediately raise the question as to how much of the attenuation is due to particulate diffusion and how much to absorption. The range of particle sizes present is sufficient that attenuation by diffusion will generally vary monotonically with respect to wavelength, while attenuation by selective absorption will show maxima and minima corresponding to the locations of the absorption bands. Therefore by a suitable plot of transmittance against wavelength some answer to this question may be found.

If the particulate diffusion within the polluted layer obeys an equation of the form of (II-10), i.e., if $s_{p\lambda(\text{poll})} = b\lambda^{-n}$, a log-log plot of

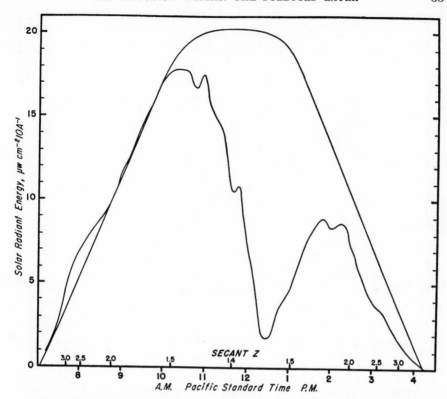

Fig. 14. Attenuation of direct solar energy by photochemical smog. Both lines represent the direct solar energy over a 10-A bandwidth centered at 3235 A, incident on a normal surface at 800-ft elevation. The smooth line is $I_{0\lambda}T_{s\lambda}T_{a\lambda}$, calculated from Table 1 and equations (II-9), (II-11), and (II-13) with $P = 985$ mb, $w = 2$, $d = 0.5$, and $(O_3) = 2$. The irregular line is the observed energy, from Stair's data for October 18, 1954 at Pasadena.

the observed attenuation coefficient of the pollutants against wavelength will give a straight line when selective absorption is unimportant, with slope equal to $-n$. Figure 15 is a plot on this basis of Stair's data for 12:30 P.M., the time of maximum attenuation, on October 18, 1954 (Fig. 14). The straight line is for $s_{p\lambda(\text{poll})} = 0.133\lambda^{-1.5}$. This wavelength coefficient, -1.5, lies in the same range as the values found by other observers for atmospheric haze (Section 6).

The increase in the observed attenuation below about 3150 A indicates absorption, and the tendency of the observed values to lie above the line in the region 3300–4200 A may be due to absorption, but the amount indicated is slight. This is to be expected on the basis of analytical determinations of the concentrations in photochemical smog of substances

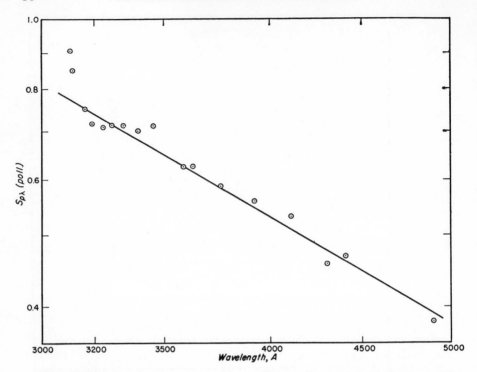

Fɪɢ. 15. Variation in the attenuation coefficient of photochemical smog with wavelength. The points are observed data from Stair (Ref. 395), the line is for $s_{p\lambda(poll)} = 0.133\lambda^{-1.5}$.

which absorb in this region. With NO_2, for example, at a concentration of 10 pphm in a layer 500 deep, at 3200 A the value of $s_{a\lambda} = 0.03$, as compared to the observed value of $s_{p\lambda(poll)} = 0.62$ at this wavelength. In any event, when plotted as in Fig. 15 the approach of the observed values to a straight line suggests that, above about 3200 A, by far the major portion of the attenuation in this instance is due to particulate diffusion.

    The effects of this amount of diffusion on the actinic irradiance and hence on absorption rates within the polluted layer will depend on its directional distribution, and of this little is known. On the one hand, if the average particle size is ~0.3μ or larger, the diffusion with respect to an individual act will be mostly in the forward direction.[207] On the other hand, multiple diffusion will tend to equalize the directional distribution, and with increasing density the situation would approach that in a cloud, with only a fraction of the diffuse radiation reaching the bottom. The diffuse radiation which originates within the layer differs in one important respect from that which originates above; as long as it remains

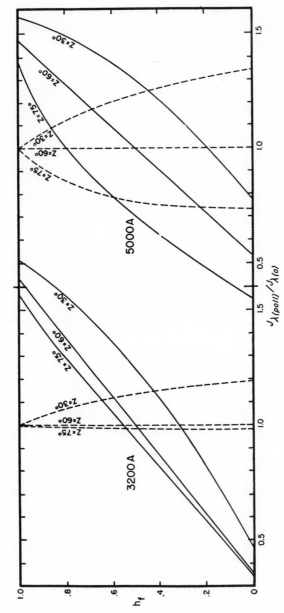

Fig. 16. Variations in actinic irradiance within the polluted layer. Solid lines are for postulate (1), dashed lines for postulate (2), h_f is the fractional height within the layer.

within the layer it is effective, no matter in which direction it is traveling.

In order to gain a feeling for the possible range of effects of diffusion on actinic irradiance within the layer, estimates of such effects for amounts of diffusion which might be expected during severe attacks of photochemical smog are presented in Figs. 16 and 17. Estimates are given in terms of the actinic irradiance relative to that in the absence of pollution, or $J_{\lambda(\text{poll})}/J_{\lambda(0)}$. They were made by dividing a polluted layer of height h into five increments of $0.2h$, and postulating two extreme situations for these increments: (1) half the radiation diffused in

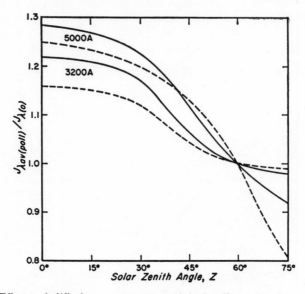

Fig. 17. Effects of diffusion on average actinic irradiance in the polluted layer. Solid lines are for postulate (1), dashed lines for postulate (2).

each increment is directed upward, and (2) none is directed upward. It was assumed that within each increment the diffuse radiation from above could be treated as an addition to sky radiation, and that from below as sky radiation in reverse. Uniform vertical distribution of pollutants within the layer was also assumed. This led to a series of simultaneous equations, quite complicated for postulate (1); these equations were solved for several solar zenith angles at two wavelengths, 3200 A with $s_{p\lambda(\text{poll})} = 0.8$, and 5000 A with $s_{p\lambda(\text{poll})} = 0.4$.

While Figs. 16 and 17 should not be regarded as more than indicative of the effects to be expected, they do bring out some interesting points. From Fig. 16 it is seen that under postulate (1) the irradiance at the top part of the layer is much higher than that at the bottom, and also is higher than it would be in the absence of pollution. At 3200 A and $z = 30°$, for instance, the estimated value of $J_{\lambda(\text{poll})}/J_{\lambda(0)}$ is over 1.5 at the top and only 0.35 at the bottom, a ratio of more than four to one. On the other hand, under postulate (2) at $z = 60°$ there is no change from top to bottom; $J_{\lambda(\text{poll})}/J_{\lambda} = 1$ at all levels. The variations from top to bottom at other zenith angles for postulate (2) are due to the change in effective path length as the result of diffusion.

Perhaps the most significant feature of these estimates is the behavior of the average actinic irradiance throughout the layer with changing solar zenith angle. In all instances the value of $J_{\lambda\text{av}(\text{poll})}/J_{\lambda(0)}$ is unity at $z = 60°$, in other words at this zenith angle diffusion has no effect on the average actinic irradiance within the layer. Also, in all instances the average actinic irradiance, relative to that in the absence of pollution, increases with solar altitude and is greater than unity when $z < 60°$.

In judging the importance of these effects, it should be remembered that the values of $s_{p\lambda(\text{poll})}$ used in arriving at Figs. 16 and 17 are rather extreme. They are even larger than the values in Fig. 15, which in turn were obtained during the few minutes of maximum attenuation shown on Fig. 14. During periods of actual formation of photochemical smog, the amount of particulate diffusion will ordinarily be smaller than this, and its effects on the actinic irradiance within the polluted layer will be less pronounced than those indicated here.

13. SURFACE REFLECTION

Surface reflection will increase the irradiance and hence increase absorption rates within the polluted layer. The amount of radiation reflected back into the atmosphere by each unit area of the earth's surface will be

TABLE 9

REPORTED ALBEDOS FOR SELECTED SURFACES

Surface	Albedo (a)	
	Visible range	Ultraviolet below 3600 A
Snow	0.46 to 0.85	0.46 to 0.85
Ocean	0.03 to 0.46	—
Forests	0.05 to 0.18	—
Fields and meadows	0.15 to 0.30	—
Bare ground	0.1 to 0.2	—
Stone (gravel, granite)	—	0.22 to 0.25
Dune sand	0.17	0.1 to 0.25
Garden soil	—	0.06

$I_{r\lambda} = aI_{t\lambda}$, where I_t is the total irradiance, direct and diffuse, transmitted by the atmosphere and incident on that area. Some values reported in the literature[141,143,151,264] for a, the fraction reflected or albedo of the surface, are given in Table 9.

Figures for the albedos of cities have apparently not been obtained, but it would appear likely from the data of Table 9 that they are of the order of 0.1 to 0.2.

14. CLOUDS

The absence of color in clouds shows that, through the visible region at least, their diffusion effects are independent of wavelength. In consequence it may be expected that the spectral distribution of the radiation which penetrates an overcast will not be substantially different from that which enters it.

The intensity, on the other hand, will be reduced to a fraction β of its clear sky value. Common observation shows that only a moderate thickness of cloud between the observer and the sun will reduce the direct radiation to zero; the radiation which penetrates is entirely diffuse.

The magnitude of β as a function of cloud type, thickness, and density has been determined by a number of observers. Table 10, from Haurwitz,[188] gives representative values.

TABLE 10

AVERAGE FRACTIONS OF INCIDENT RADIATION TRANSMITTED
BY VARIOUS CLOUD TYPES

	β						
m	Cirrus	Cirrostratus	Altocumulus	Altostratus	Stratocumulus	Stratus	Fog
1.1	0.85	0.84	0.52	0.41	0.35	0.25	0.17
2.0	0.89	0.78	0.50	0.41	0.34	0.25	0.17
3.0	0.82	0.71	0.47	0.41	0.32	0.24	0.18
4.0	0.80	0.65	0.45	0.41	0.31	0.24	0.18

These are average values and the actual values will vary widely with cloud thickness and liquid water content. Thus Neiburger[298] found the value of β through stratus over Los Angeles to vary from 0.9 with a 100-ft layer to 0.2 with a 1700-ft layer.

For partial overcasts, if γ is the fraction of cloud coverage over an area, to a rough approximation the direct irradiance reaching the lower layer, averaged over that area, will be $I_{d\lambda}(1 - \gamma)$, and the diffuse irradiance (sky + clouds) will be $I_{s\lambda}(1 - \gamma) + \beta(I_{d\lambda} + I_{s\lambda})\gamma$. Combining these two terms yields, for the total irradiance,

$$Q_\lambda = (I_{d\lambda} + I_{s\lambda})[1 - (1 - \beta)\gamma] \tag{II-38}$$

15. DISCUSSION

Of all of the factors which collectively determine the amount and spectral distribution of the radiation entering a surface layer of the atmosphere, the best established would appear to be the spectral irradiance outside the atmosphere and the attenuation by molecular scattering. The absorption coefficients of ozone are well established but no easy method exists for determining the amount of ozone in a vertical profile of the atmosphere at a given time. The measurement of the particulate content of the atmosphere and its correlation with atmospheric transmission is a field in which much remains to be accomplished. Surprisingly little data exist on the spectral distribution of sky radiation and its variation with solar elevation and atmospheric conditions. The effect of clouds is of secondary importance as intense photochemical smog generally occurs under a clear sky.

Within the layer, uncertainties exist as to what absorbing species are present, what amount of each is present, what the effective absorption coefficients are, how the concentration varies with height, and how the rate of absorption is affected by particulate diffusion.

Some of these factors are so variable and so difficult to determine that one may expect at best only approximate estimates of absorption rates. For this purpose it is proposed that equation (II-36) be employed, with the values of J_λ given in Table 8. This equation uses the weak absorption approximation, it neglects surface reflection, and it takes no account of the effects of diffusion within the absorbing layer. The weak absorption approximation will make the calculated rates too high and neglecting surface reflection will make them too low; as a result these two errors will partially cancel. Any accounting of the effects of internal diffusion on absorption rates will depend on the directional distribution of the diffused radiation and on whether the rate near the surface or the average rate throughout the layer is the more important. Until more is known of these factors, the effects of diffusion within the layer must be regarded as indeterminate.

Chapter III

Absorption Rates and Primary Photochemical Processes

1. GENERAL CONSIDERATIONS

For any photochemical reaction, the primary chemical process may be defined as the first chemical step following the act of absorption of radiation. To illustrate, let the act of absorption by substance A be expressed by the equation

$$A + h\nu \rightarrow A'$$

Among the possible reactions which the excited molecules A' may undergo are:

fluorescence	$A' \rightarrow A + h\nu$
collisional deactivation	$A' + M \rightarrow A + M$
dissociation	$A' \rightarrow D_1 + D_2 + \ldots$
direct reaction	$A' + B \rightarrow D_1 + \ldots$

Of these four, the first two reactions return the absorbing molecule to its original state, while the second two lead to chemical change. Either of the second two, therefore, may serve as the primary process in a photochemical reaction.

The primary quantum yield ϕ for any specific primary process is the ratio of the number of molecules of A' reacting by that process to the number of photons absorbed. Since the number of A' formed is equal to the number of photons absorbed, the primary quantum yield for a given process is simply the fraction of the excited molecules A' which react by that process. It is seen at once that the maximum possible value of ϕ is unity. If molecules of A' react by two or more competing processes, the sum of the yields for all the competing processes, including fluorescence and deactivation, will be unity, but the yield for a specific process may be much less than unity.

If $(A) = c$ is the concentration of the absorber, the rate of formation of A' is equal to the absorption rate, or

$$\frac{+d(A')}{dt} = I_a = k_a(A) = k_a c \qquad \text{(III-1)}$$

For weak absorption k_a, the specific absorption rate, or fraction of the molecules which absorb per unit of time, may be considered to be independent of the concentration of the absorber.

Similarly, for a primary chemical process yielding a product D_1, with primary yield ϕ, the rate of formation of D_1 will be

$$\frac{+d(D_1)}{dt} = k_a c \phi \qquad \text{(III-2)}$$

The sum of the rates of all the processes consuming A′ will be equal to the absorption rate.

In the following discussion of primary processes which may occur in urban air, specific absorption rates are calculated by equation (II-36), with values of J_λ from Table 8. Resulting values of k_a are given in sec^{-1}, and hr^{-1}. When substances have been identified only by class in polluted air, as for instance the aldehydes, the selection of specific examples for discussion is based partly on the likelihood of their presence and partly on the availability of data.

2. ABSORBING SPECIES IN POLLUTED AIR

The logical first step in any discussion of photochemical primary processes is to identify the absorbers. In the lower atmosphere, these will be the species which absorb in the photochemically active region, e.g., visible and ultraviolet, of the solar spectrum. A number of substances known or surmised to be present in the air during periods of photochemical smog formation may at once be classified as absorbers or nonabsorbers on this basis, and are so classified in Table 11. The absorbers must each be examined in turn; the nonabsorbers may be excluded from further consideration.

TABLE 11

ABSORBERS AND NONABSORBERS IN THE REGION 3000–7000 A

Absorbers	Nonabsorbers
Oxygen	Nitrogen
Ozone	Water
Nitrogen dioxide	Carbon monoxide
Sulfur dioxide	Carbon dioxide
Nitric acid and alkyl nitrates	Nitric oxide
Nitrous acid, alkyl nitrites, and nitro compounds	Sulfur trioxide and sulfuric acid
Aldehydes	Hydrocarbons
Ketones	Alcohols
Peroxides	Organic acids
Acyl nitrites, pernitrites, and nitrates	
Particulate matter	

3. Oxygen

Ordinary oxygen, O_2, absorbs very faintly in the red end of the visible spectrum. Observed in sunlight, the absorption consists of a series of bands with sharp rotational structure, sometimes referred to as the atmospheric absorption bands. The first two members of the series lie chiefly within the limits 7590–7660 A (the A band) and 6870–6920 A (the B band) and are responsible for the Fraunhofer dark lines A and B. Succeeding members, at shorter wavelengths, are so weak that they become prominent in the solar spectrum only when the sun is near the horizon. The bands are of historical interest in that the analysis by Giauque and Johnston[153] of their fine structure, observed by Dieke and Babcock[102] in the atmospheric absorption of sunlight, gave the first indication of the oxygen isotopes O^{17} and O^{18}.

The absorption coefficients of the A and B bands may be obtained, very approximately, from Fowle's tracings of the solar spectrum.[140] Averaged over the two bands, at 25°C, they are $\alpha_\lambda = 2 \times 10^{-5}$ liter mole^{-1} cm^{-1} for the A band and 7×10^{-6} liter mole^{-1} cm^{-1} for the B band. The resultant values of k_a and the rate of absorption $k_a c$, calculated for the radiation conditions of Table 8 are given in Table 12. Absorption by other members of the series will add but little to these rates.

TABLE 12

RATE OF ABSORPTION OF SOLAR RADIATION BY OXYGEN

Zenith angle (z)	k_a		$k_a c$ (pphm hr^{-1}) for $c = 2 \times 10^7$ pphm
	sec^{-1}	hr^{-1}	
0°	2.5×10^{-10}	9.0×10^{-7}	18
20°	2.4×10^{-10}	8.6×10^{-7}	17
40°	2.1×10^{-10}	7.5×10^{-7}	15
60°	1.6×10^{-10}	5.8×10^{-7}	12
80°	0.4×10^{-10}	1.4×10^{-7}	3

The extreme weakness of the absorption (in the A band the entire atmosphere at $m = 1$ will absorb only about 30% of the incident radiation) indicates a transition of very low probability. The absolute transition probability has been calculated by Childs and Mecke[41] to be about 0.14 sec^{-1}, as compared to 10^7–10^8 sec^{-1} for ordinary (electric dipole) transitions.

The transition concerned is probably

$$O_2(^3\Sigma_g^-) + h\nu \rightleftharpoons O_2'(^1\Sigma_g^+) \tag{III-3}$$

If this is the case, the low transition probability is due to the fact that it involves both a singlet-triplet (multiplicity change) and a $g \leftrightarrows g$ (magnetic dipole) intercombination.

Where selection rule violations are involved the transition probability is usually increased, and the life of the excited state is correspondingly reduced by collisions with other molecules. The probability of a magnetic dipole or $g \leftrightarrows g$ intercombination in particular may be expected to be increased by collisions. If the effect of this selection rule were entirely wiped out, an increase of some 10^5 in transition probability would result.[196] This means that while the calculated life of a free and uninfluenced O_2 ($^1\Sigma_g{}^+$) molecule is some 7 sec, in air at atmospheric pressure its life with respect to a return to the normal state may not be greater than 10^{-5} to 10^{-4} sec.

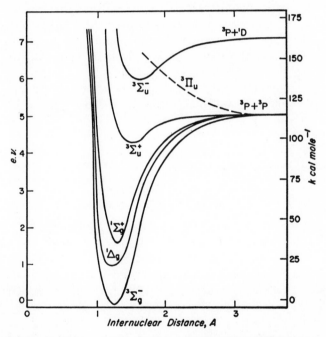

FIG. 18. Electronic states of the oxygen molecule. Potential energy as a function of internuclear distance for states of the O_2 molecule below 8 ev.

The excitation energy gained by absorption is about 37.6 kcal mole^{-1} for the A band and 41.5 kcal mole^{-1} for the B band. This is far short of the 117.3 kcal required for dissociation and is, in fact, barely enough to reach the $^1\Sigma_g{}^+$ state (Fig. 18). It follows that the excitation is almost all electronic, the excited molecule cannot spontaneously dissociate, and the only photochemical primary processes which might occur will involve direct reactiin of the electronically excited O_2 ($^1\Sigma_g{}^+$) with other molecules.

Any reaction which $^1\Sigma_g{}^+$ oxygen molecules might undergo in polluted air must compete with the deactivation of these molecules by fluorescence or collision. This competition establishes an upper limit to the possible value of ϕ for such a reaction. If t_d is the average life of the excited state with respect to deactivation and t_c the average time between its collisions with another species B, the probability that a given O_2' will undergo collision with B is

$$p = 1 - \exp\left[-(t_d/t_c)\right] \tag{III-4}$$

The value of ϕ cannot exceed p, even if the reaction should occur at every collision.

In air at 1 atm, $t_c \cong 10^{-2}/(B)$, where (B) is the concentration of reactant B in pphm, and as we have seen, for O_2' ($^1\Sigma_g{}^+$), t_d may not be larger than 10^{-5} to 10^{-4} sec. If B = 10 pphm, this gives $p \cong 10^{-2}$ to 10^{-1}. From this and the values of $k_a c$ given in Table 12, if the average life of the excited O_2 molecules produced by absorption is 10^{-5} to 10^{-4} sec, the maximum rate which may be expected for any reaction between such molecules and a pollutant at a concentration of 10 pphm is $k_a c\, p \cong 10^{-1}$ to 1 pphm hr^{-1}.

The possibility of two such reactions, one with ozone and one with hydrocarbons, has been suggested by observations in the literature.

With ozone, the energy chain

$$O + O_3 \rightarrow 2\,O_2' \;(+93 \text{ kcal}) \tag{III-5}$$
$$O_2' + O_3 \rightarrow 2\,O_2 + O \;(-24.6 \text{ kcal}) \tag{III-6}$$

was proposed by Schumacher[381] to explain the high quantum yield in the photolysis and by Ritchie[359] to explain the increase with pressure of the rate of thermal decomposition of ozone. Subsequent work on both the photolysis[190] and the thermal decomposition[411] appeared to substantiate this proposal. If the oxygen atom and ozone molecule in reaction (III-5) are both in their ground states, the reaction is exothermic by 46.5 kcal per mole of O_2. This may appear as translational, vibrational, or electronic excitation and is sufficient to produce either vibrationally excited $^3\Sigma_g{}^-$ or electronically (and vibrationally) excited $^1\Delta_g$ *or* $^1\Sigma_g{}^+$ oxygen molecules. The Wigner-Witmer correlation rules[450] permit the formation of two triplet or one triplet and one singlet, but not two singlet molecules by reaction (III-5), and permit either triplet or singlet molecules to undergo reaction (III-6). Insofar as the energetic requirements and the selection rules are required, therefore, either vibrationally excited oxygen molecules in the ground ($^3\Sigma_g{}^-$) state or electronically excited molecules in the $^1\Delta_g$ or $^1\Sigma_g{}^+$ states might serve as the chain carriers. The earlier investigators mostly assumed the excited state to be the electronic $^1\Sigma_g{}^+$, which leads to the suggestion that the excited oxygen molecules produced by absorption of red light might undergo reaction (III-6). Recently, however, Benson and Axworthy[30] have obtained evidence disputing the importance of this reaction during the thermal decomposition of ozone, while McGrath and Norrish[275] have reported that only vibrationally excited oxygen molecules in the ground ($^3\Sigma_g{}^-$) electronic state appear to be produced by reaction (III-5) during the ozone photolysis, and that the energy chain occurs only when the oxygen atoms are in the electronically excited ^1D state. We must conclude, therefore, that there is presently no evidence from this source as to whether $^1\Sigma_g{}^+$ oxygen molecules will or will not react with ozone.

With hydrocarbons, the possibility of a reaction of excited oxygen molecules is suggested by the thermal oxidation in the range 300–400°C, where the initial step appears to be[86]

$$RH + O_2 \rightarrow R + HO_2 \ (-\sim30 \text{ to } 40 \text{ kcal}) \tag{III-7}$$

There is no conclusive evidence as to whether $^1\Sigma_g{}^+$ oxygen molecules will or will not undergo this reaction at ordinary temperatures. No photochemical reaction has ever been observed on exposure of hydrocarbon–oxygen mixtures to visible light, and the possibility that such a reaction occurs at a significant rate in urban air appears rather remote.

4. Ozone

Gaseous ozone absorbs strongly in the region 2000–3500 A, with maximum at about 2550 A, and weakly in the region 4500–7000 A, with maximum around 6000 A. The relative strength of the two bands may be seen by comparing the absorption coefficients at the maxima. At the 2550 A maximum, the absorption coefficient[215] is 3250 liter mole^{-1} cm^{-1} while at the maximum around 6000 A it is about 1.25 liter mole^{-1} cm^{-1}, a ratio of 2600 to 1. Absorption coefficients at other wavelengths in the visible band, and in the ultraviolet band to the limit of solar radiation in the lower atmosphere, have been given in Chapter II. The fraction $k_{a\lambda}$ of ozone molecules in the polluted layer which will absorb photons per second in each 100-A bandwidth of the spectrum is shown in Figs. 19 and 20, and the resultant fraction absorbing or specific absorption rate, k_a, in each region is given in Table 13.

Evidence regarding the nature of the primary chemical process in each absorption region is conflicting. Both regions show diffuse bands with an apparently continuous background increasing at shorter wavelengths, which, if anything, indicates dissociation. The energy absorbed

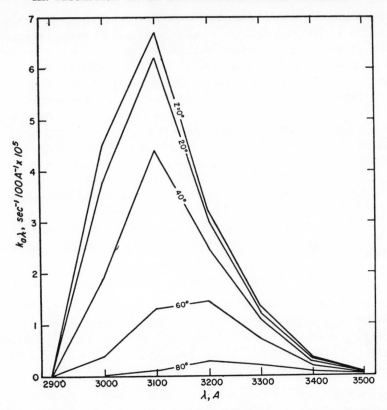

Fig. 19. Absorption of ultraviolet solar radiation by ozone in the lower atmosphere. Ordinates are the fractions of ozone molecules absorbing photons per second over 100-A bandwidths at different solar zenith angles under the actinic irradiance of Table 8.

at the long-wave limit in the visible, about 37 kcal mole^{-1}, is some 12 kcal larger than the bond dissociation energy of ozone into a normal oxygen molecule and atom. The energy absorbed at the long-wave limit in the ultraviolet is about 82 kcal mole^{-1}. The difference between the two limits, 45 kcal mole^{-1}, is greater than the 37.7 kcal mole^{-1} electronic excitation energy of a $^1\Sigma_g{}^+$ oxygen molecule, and very close to the 45.2 kcal mole^{-1} excitation of the first excited state, ^1D, of the oxygen atom. In pure ozone, absorption in both regions leads to photodecomposition with formation of oxygen. The rate laws are substantially the same in the visible and ultraviolet, but the quantum yields are not.[32,190,381] In pure dry ozone, the maximum quantum yields obtained are about 2 in the visible and 6.7 in the ultraviolet. Addition of water vapor does not affect the yield in the visible but increases that in the ultraviolet to

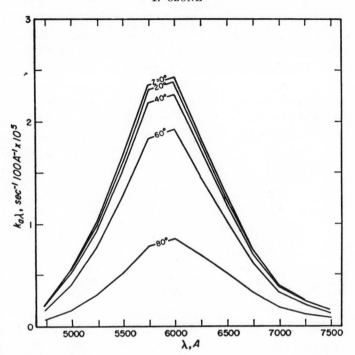

FIG. 20. Absorption of visible solar radiation by ozone in the lower atmosphere.

values as high as 130. Chain reactions, longer in the presence of water vapor, are thus indicated in the ultraviolet, but not in the visible.

To explain these observations, a primary photodissociation of ozone by both visible and ultraviolet radiation has been proposed, with that in the ultraviolet leading to more energetic products which are able to initiate chains.[32,190,381,403] Energetically, the only possible photodissociation products following absorption in the visible are an electronically

TABLE 13

RATES OF ABSORPTION OF SOLAR RADIATION BY OZONE

Solar zenith angle (z)	k_a (2900–3500 A)		k_a (4500–7500 A)	
	sec^{-1}	hr^{-1}	sec^{-1}	hr^{-1}
0°	1.61×10^{-4}	0.58	3.22×10^{-4}	1.16
20°	1.46×10^{-4}	0.52	3.16×10^{-4}	1.14
40°	1.02×10^{-4}	0.37	2.98×10^{-4}	1.07
60°	0.41×10^{-4}	0.15	2.52×10^{-4}	0.91
80°	0.06×10^{-4}	0.02	1.15×10^{-4}	0.41

normal oxygen molecule, which may however be vibrationally excited, and a normal oxygen atom. In the ultraviolet, either an electronically excited molecule or atom, or both, may be produced. Regarding deactivation processes which may compete with the dissociation, no fluorescence of ozone has been observed, but collisional deactivation is a possibility.

The possible processes and the energy required to produce each set of dissociation products from a normal ozone molecule, all in the ground vibrational state, are:

Visible

$$O_3 + h\nu \rightarrow O_3' \tag{III-8}$$
$$O_3' + M \rightarrow O_3 + M \tag{III-9}$$
$$O_3' \rightarrow O_2(^3\Sigma_g^-) + O(^3P) \ (-24.6 \text{ kcal}) \tag{III-10}$$

Ultraviolet

$$O_3 + h\nu \rightarrow O_3'' \tag{III-11}$$
$$O_3'' + M \rightarrow O_3 + M \tag{III-12}$$
$$O_3'' \rightarrow O_2(^1\Sigma_g^+) + O(^3P) \ (-62.3 \text{ kcal}) \tag{III-13}$$
$$O_3'' \rightarrow O_2(^3\Sigma_g^-) + O(^1D) \ (-69.8 \text{ kcal}) \tag{III-14}$$
$$O_3'' \rightarrow O_2(^1\Delta_g) + O(^1D) \ (-91 \text{ kcal}) \tag{III-15}$$
$$O_3'' \rightarrow O_2(^1\Sigma_g^+) + O(^1D) \ (-107.5 \text{ kcal}) \tag{III-16}$$

It is interesting to consider these reactions with respect to the rules of spin conservation. The normal ozone molecule is probably a singlet,[296] and the strong absorption in the ultraviolet indicates the initially excited state O_3'' is probably also a singlet. By the Wigner-Witmer correlation rules,[450] dissociation of a singlet into two singlet products [reactions (III-15) and (III-16)] is permitted, but dissociation into singlet and triplet [reactions (III-13) and III-14)] is not. The weak absorption in the visible indicates a forbidden transition, suggesting that the excited state O_3' might be a triplet. Whether O_3' is a singlet or a triplet, reaction (III-10) is permitted by the correlation rules.

The best evidence that the photodissociation in the ultraviolet does indeed produce ^1D oxygen atoms has been obtained by McGrath and Norrish[275,306] through observations of the absorption spectra of the products of the flash photolysis of dry and moist ozone. On photolysis of dry ozone, absorption bands due to vibrationally excited O_2 ($^3\Sigma_g^-$) molecules, with v'' up to 17, were observed, but in the presence of water vapor these bands were completely suppressed and their place was taken by strong absorption due to hydroxyl radicals. Since no reaction of the vibrationally excited $O_2(^3\Sigma_g^-)$ with water appears possible, and the reaction $O(^3P) + H_2O \rightarrow 2$ OH is endothermic by 18 kcal mole^{-1}, the only reasonable possibility of a mechanism which explains these experimental observations is one involving ^1D oxygen atoms. The responsible reactions would be

In dry ozone: $O(^1D) + O_3 \rightarrow 2\,O_2'(^3\Sigma_g^-) + 138\,\text{kcal}$ (III-17)

In moist ozone: $O(^1D) + H_2O \rightarrow 2\,OH + 27\,\text{kcal}$ (III-18)

Additional reactions are postulated by McGrath and Norrish to provide the chains necessary to explain the high quantum yields, but these need not concern us here.

Of the three primary processes leading to the formation of $O(^1D)$, the most likely would appear to be (III-15). Reaction (III-14) probably involves a multiplicity change, and the suppression by water vapor of the absorption due to vibrationally excited $O_2(^3\Sigma_g^-)$, observed by McGrath and Norrish, rules against their being formed by this process. Reaction (III-16) is endothermic by an amount corresponding to the einstein at 2680 A, which rules out this reaction as far as the solar radiation region is concerned.

The long-wave limit of radiation which could produce reaction (III-14) is 3140 A, which falls in, but does not include, all of the solar ultraviolet region absorbed by ozone. Heidt[190] found that the ozone photolysis occurs at 3130 A with much the same quantum yield as at shorter wavelengths, indicating that whatever the chain carrier may be it is produced up to at least this wavelength. Whether this is equally true over the remainder of the solar absorption region, i.e., 3130–3500 A (Fig. 19) has not been determined. It may be that reaction (III-14) occurs in this region.

There is no direct evidence regarding the value of the primary quantum yield ϕ of the ozone photodissociation in air at atmospheric pressure. On the one hand, the lack of fine structure in absorption suggests a rapid dissociation with ϕ essentially unity, and this is supported by the fact that no fluorescence of ozone has been observed. On the other hand, Volman[434] has pointed out that the effects of oxygen and foreign gases on the quantum yield of ozone photolysis in the ultraviolet suggest that collisional deactivation is important. In fact, if the effects noted by Volman are due to deactivation, the value of ϕ in air at 1 atm must be quite small; around 0.03 to 0.04.

Returning to the reaction produced by visible radiation, the observed maximum quantum yields of around 2 are what would be expected if the primary photochemical process is the dissociation (III-10) with ϕ of unity, followed by the secondary reaction $O + O_3 \rightarrow 2\,O_2$. This suggests that collisional deactivation cannot, in this case, be very important.

The photodissociation of ozone by visible light has been questioned by Ogg and Sutphen[320] on the basis of observations of the rate of the isotope scrambling reaction

$$O^{16}O^{16} + O^{18}O^{18} \rightarrow 2\,O^{16}O^{18} \qquad \text{(III-19)}$$

When mixtures of ozone and O^{18} enriched oxygen were exposed to visible light, no significant increase in the scrambling rate over the thermal value was observed, but exposure to ultraviolet light gave a "relatively enormous" increase. Since the scrambling reaction is catalyzed by oxygen atoms, this might be evidence that ozone is dissociated by ultraviolet but not by visible light. However, Ogg and Sutphen did not correlate the scrambling rate with the absorption rate, and the difference they observed may well have been due to the difference in absorption rates in the two regions.

In summary, the weight of evidence indicates that the primary photochemical process following absorption by ozone in both the visible and ultraviolet regions is a photodissociation into an oxygen molecule and atom. Following absorption in the visible these products are both in their normal electronic states, while absorption in the solar ultraviolet probably produces electronically excited oxygen atoms, $O(^1D)$. Some electronically excited oxygen molecules, $O_2(^1\Delta_g)$, may also be produced in the ultraviolet. The primary quantum yields for these photodissociation processes in air are unknown, and the absorption rates in Table 13, therefore, represent only upper limits, under the conditions for which they were calculated, for the rates of production of ^3P and ^1D oxygen atoms by the photodissociation of ozone by solar radiation in the lower atmosphere. These limits are, however, quite substantial. At an ozone concentration of 10 pphm and $z = 45°$, they are about 10 pphm hr^{-1} for the rate of production of ^3P oxygen atoms (visible absorption region), and about 3 pphm hr^{-1} for the rate of production of ^1D oxygen atoms (ultraviolet absorption region).

5. NITROGEN DIOXIDE

Nitrogen dioxide absorbs over virtually the entire visible and ultraviolet range of the solar spectrum in the lower atmosphere. Through the visible region the absorption spectrum consists of a multitude of bands, in many of which sharp vibrational structure may be observed. In the ultraviolet, at about 3700 A, the bands become noticeably diffuse, and this diffuseness continues to below the limit of solar radiation.

The absorption coefficients of nitrogen dioxide have been measured over the range 4000–7000 A by Dixon,[103] and from 3000 to 5000 A by Hall and Blacet.[178] Dixon used a pressure range, calculated for NO_2 at 0°C, of 1 to 70 mm, a path length of 5 cm, and spectrophotometer slit widths of 15 and 40 A. Hall and Blacet used NO_2 pressures, at 25°C, of 32.7, 126, and 307 mm, with path lengths of 10, 2.5, and 1 cm, respectively, and an average spectrophotometer slit width of about 4 A. Owing to this narrower slit width, Hall and Blacet obtained greater resolution of the band maxima and minima (Fig. 21) than did Dixon, but neither of the investigators resolved the vibrational structure. Nevertheless, in both cases Beer's law was found to hold, and a plot of the two sets of data gives a smooth intersection at 4600–4800 A. Resulting values, aver-

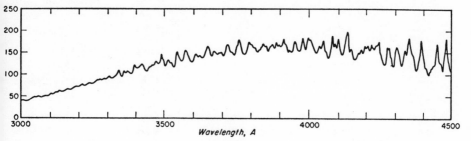

Fig. 21. Absorption coefficients of nitrogen dioxide in the region 3000–4500 A.

aged over 100-A intervals centered on the wavelengths shown, are given in Table 14, while Fig. 22 shows the estimated fraction of the NO_2 which will absorb photons per second in each 100-A bandwidth of solar radiation in the lower atmosphere.

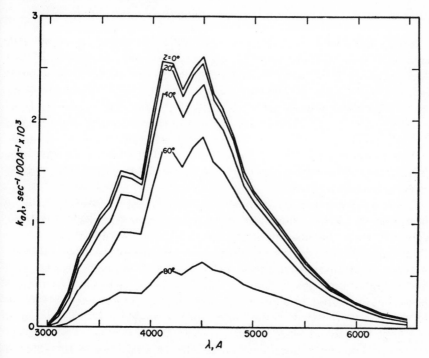

Fig. 22. Absorption of solar radiation by nitrogen dioxide.

TABLE 14

ABSORPTION COEFFICIENTS OF NO_2 AND N_2O_4

λ (A)	α_λ NO_2 (l mole^{-1} cm^{-1})	α_λ N_2O_4 (l mole^{-1} cm^{-1})	λ (A)	α_λ NO_2 (l mole^{-1} cm^{-1})
2900	26	106	4200	163
3000	37	84	4300	154
3100	57	84	4400	145
3200	78	111	4500	136
3300	98	154	4600	117
3400	119	195	4700	106
3500	136	152	4800	92
3600	149	84	4900	80
3700	158	33	5000	69
3800	163	15	5250	50
3900	167	3.7	5500	31
4000	171		5750	19
4100	167		6000	12
			6250	7
			6500	4.1
			6750	2.6
			7000	1.7

Since equilibrium concentrations of N_2O_4 are always present with gaseous NO_2, in the ultraviolet both substances will absorb. Hall and Blacet separated the absorption coefficients by means of a differential analyzer, and Table 14 includes their values for N_2O_4. From these we may estimate the amount which N_2O_4 will absorb at the concentrations to be expected in polluted air. By the equilibrium constant expression of Verhoek and Daniels,[431] at an NO_2 concentration of 10 pphm, the equilibrium concentration of N_2O_4 at 25°C is 7×10^{-14} atm. At this concentration the absorption rate of the N_2O_4 will be less than 10^{-6} that of the NO_2. This is negligible.

Evidence regarding the primary photochemical processes following absorption by nitrogen dioxide may be drawn from a number of sources, beginning with the absorption spectrum. The observation of a sharp vibrational structure in the visible region indicates excited molecule production; the diffuseness observed below ~3700 A indicates dissociation. Confirming this, on absorption of visible radiation nitrogen dioxide fluoresces, but on going to shorter wavelengths the fluorescence fades out. Norrish[304] reported that while fluorescence is produced by absorption at 4358 A, it is weak at 4047 A and is practically absent at 3660 A. Neuberger and Duncan[299] observed fluorescence on excitation with ~3950 A and longer wavelengths, but found none at 3660 A. The fluorescence is strongly quenched, both by increasing nitrogen dioxide pressure[299,313] and by adding nitrogen or oxygen,[26] indicating collisional deactivation of the excited molecules from which it originates.

The photochemical properties of nitrogen dioxide conform with its photophysical behavior. Most carefully studied with respect to the effects of wavelength is the photodecomposition of pure nitrogen dioxide into nitric oxide and oxygen. The over-all quantum yields for this reaction are reduced both by the accumulation of products and the addition of foreign gases. However, the initial or limiting quantum yields (Table 15) gradually increase with decreasing wavelength, from virtually zero at 4358 A to nearly unity at 3130 A.

TABLE 15

LIMITING QUANTUM YIELDS OF O_2 PRODUCTION IN THE PHOTOLYSIS OF NO_2

	Φ_{O_2}				
λ (A)	Dickinson and Baxter (1928)[101]	Norrish (1929)[304]	Holmes and Daniels (1934)[203]	Hall (1953)[177]	Weighted average
4358	0.004	0.000	0.00	—	0.00
4047	0.36	0.37	0.25	0.36	0.36
3660	0.77	1.05	0.92	—	0.92
3130	—	1.04	0.96	0.96	0.97
2700	—	1.04	1 (est.)	—	1.0

Other observations on the effects of wavelength on reactions initiated by nitrogen dioxide absorption agree in general, but not in detail, with those on the direct photolysis. Thus, in mixtures of nitrogen dioxide and O^{18} enriched oxygen, Hall [177] found that isotope scrambling [reaction (III-19)] was produced by exposure to radiation at 3130 A, but on exposure to 4047 A no scrambling occurred. Another observation, of even greater significance, came out of these experiments in the following manner. After exposing the NO_2–O^{18} enriched O_2 mixture at each wavelength, the mixture was passed through a cold trap to remove the NO_2 before examining the O_2 for isotope scrambling. A large part of the O^{18} remained behind with the material condensed in the cold trap after exposure to 3130 A, but none remained behind after exposure to 4047 A. This indicates that exposure to 3130 A resulted in transfer of O^{18} atoms from the O_2 to the NO_2, but exposure to 4047 A did not.

Different results were obtained by Sato and Cvetanović[371] in a study of the effect of wavelength on the photooxidation of 1-butene by nitrogen dioxide. The major products observed were n-butyraldehyde and butene oxide; these products were obtained on irradiation by 4047 A and shorter wavelengths, but not by 4358 A. In a set of experiments with equal amounts of irradiation (intensity $\times$ time), it appeared that 4047 A yielded roughly as much or possibly even more of the products as did 3660 A. However, these experiments were conducted with filters which did not fully separate the different lines, and the results are only semi-quantitative.

The various observations regarding wavelength effects are summarized in Table 16. Taken as a whole, they overwhelmingly indicate that

TABLE 16

EFFECTS OF WAVELENGTH ON PHENOMENA ASSOCIATED WITH NO₂ ABSORPTION

Observation	Wavelength (A)			
	3130	3660	4047	4358
Structure in absorption spectrum	Diffuse	Diffuse	Sharp	Sharp
Fluorescence	None	Little if any	Weak	Strong
Quantum yield of photolysis	0.97	0.92	0.36	0.00
Isotope scrambling and transfer of O¹⁸ from O₂ to NO₂	Yes	—	No	—
Photooxidation of 1-butene by NO₂	—	Yes	Yes	No

somewhere between 4358 A and 3660 A the primary processes following absorption by nitrogen dioxide change from excited molecule production, with fluorescence and collisional deactivation, to dissociation. The photochemical products and the observation of isotope scrambling both suggest that the dissociation yields an oxygen atom. In agreement with this is the fact that the bond dissociation energy of nitrogen dioxide into normal NO ($^2\Pi$) and O (^3P) is probably between 71 and 72 kcal/mole,[371] corresponding to the energy of the einstein at around 4000 A.

Before attempting to specify the processes which compete with the dissociation in the changeover region, it is necessary to consider the fluorescence of nitrogen dioxide in greater detail. Neuberger and Duncan[299] traced the decay of the fluorescence on an oscillograph, after irradiating nitrogen dioxide with flashes of 5-μsec duration from a condenser discharge. For fluorescence excited by bands centered at 3950, 4300, and 4650 A in pure nitrogen dioxide at pressures of 0.6 to 12 μ, the decay was found to be exponential. A plot of $1/t_f$, where t_f is the mean life, against pressure yielded a straight line, from which, if P is the pressure of NO₂ in mm Hg,

$$\frac{1}{t_f} = 2.25 \times 10^4 + 2 \times 10^6 \, P \, \text{sec}^{-1} \qquad \text{(III-20)}$$

The intercept at $P = 0$ gives a mean life in the absence of collisions of 4.45×10^{-5} sec, approximately the same value being obtained for each of the exciting wavelengths listed above.

When excited by 5461 A, the fluorescence was weaker, and no lifetime trace was observable, indicating a much shorter lifetime than when excited by shorter wavelengths. These observations suggest that the fluorescence excited by 5461 A originates in a different excited state of the NO_2 molecule than does that excited by 3950–4650 A.

Neuberger and Duncan postulate a second state lying near the one first produced by absorption, to which resonance transfer can occur, and from which the optical transition probability is smaller than from the first state. Absorption of 5461 A produces only the first state, hence the resulting fluorescence is short lived. Absorption by 3950–4650 A may lead to fluorescence from both states; one short lived and one long lived. The experimental method used would have detected only the longer lived fluorescence.

The processes indicated by the experimental evidence taken as a whole are

$$NO_2 + h\nu \rightarrow NO_2' \qquad \text{(III-21)}$$
$$NO_2' \rightarrow NO(^2\Pi) + O(^3P) \qquad \text{(III-22)}$$
$$NO_2' + A \rightarrow \text{products} \qquad \text{(III-23)}$$
$$NO_2' \rightarrow NO_2'' \qquad \text{(III-24)}$$
$$NO_2'' \rightarrow NO_2 + h\nu' \qquad \text{(III-25)}$$
$$NO_2'' + M \rightarrow NO_2 + M \qquad \text{(III-26)}$$

also possibly

$$NO_2' \rightarrow NO_2 + h\nu' \qquad \text{(III-27)}$$
$$NO_2' + M \rightarrow NO_2 + M \qquad \text{(III-28)}$$

An alternate possibility is that the second excited state, NO_2'', is also produced by absorption rather than by resonance transfer.

At wavelengths above 4350 A, the absence of any known photochemical reactions of nitrogen dioxide indicates that the excited molecules initially produced, NO_2', react entirely by processes (III-24), (III-27), or (III-28), and the primary yields of the chemical steps (III-22) and (III-23) are zero. At 4350 A some observers have reported very small amounts of reaction while others have reported none, and, if the primary chemical steps occur at all, the yields must be correspondingly small.

At 4047 A, the absorption spectrum of nitrogen dioxide still shows sharp vibrational structure, and it still fluoresces, although less so than at 4350 A. The weakening of the fluorescence might indicate some dissociation. However, the observation by Hall of no detectable O_2 isotope scrambling and no oxygen atom exchange between O_2 and NO_2 would indicate that the primary dissociation yield must be small. Further, if the bond dissociation energy of nitrogen dioxide is between 71 and 72 kcal mole^{-1}, the energy absorbed at 4047 A, 70.6 kcal mole^{-1}, is not sufficient to produce dissociation without some contribution of thermal energy. Yet photochemical reactions of nitrogen dioxide indubitably occur at 4047 A, and the products obtained are the same as at shorter wavelengths. The limiting quantum yield of the nitrogen dioxide photolysis at 4047 A is around $\frac{1}{4}$ to $\frac{1}{3}$ as great as it is at 3660 A, while Sato and Cvetanović's observations on the photooxidation of 1-butene by NO_2 suggest that the rates at these two wavelengths are roughly equal.

It may be that with more quantitative observations these experimental discrepancies will be resolved, and the chemical reactions at 4047 A will prove to be due to dissociation, but at the moment the explanation which best fits the reported facts is that the amount of dissociation is small at this wavelength and the primary chemical process involves direct reaction of excited NO_2 molecules [reaction (III-23)].

At 3660 A and shorter wavelengths, the diffuse absorption spectrum and absence of fluorescence would indicate a primary yield of unity for the dissociation process. On the other hand, the fact that the limiting quantum yield of the photolysis of pure nitrogen dioxide (Table 15) continues to increase with decreasing wavelength would suggest that even at 3660 A the primary dissociation yield may not have reached unity.

The changeover from excited molecule reactions to dissociation as the dominant process following absorption by nitrogen dioxide thus appears to occur between 4047 and 3660 A. It is unfortunate that there is no photochemical information upon which to base an estimate of primary yields in this region, but it may be surmised that the changeover occurs gradually, with a mid-point probably in the vicinity of 3850 ± 100 A. On this basis, the rate of production of nitric oxide and ^3P oxygen atoms by the photodissociation of nitrogen dioxide in the lower atmosphere will be approximately equal to its rate of absorption of solar radiation at wavelengths below the mid-point. Such absorption rates, derived from the data of Fig. 22 for solar radiation below 3850 A, are given in Table 17. A change of ±100 A in the estimated mid-point of 3850 A would change these absorption rates by about ±20%.

The rate of production of excited molecules which may react by process (III-23) is even more speculative than the dissociation. The absorption rates of nitrogen dioxide over the range of 3850–4150 A are included in Table 17 as an indication of what these production rates might be. In view of the importance of nitrogen dioxide in photochemical smog formation, it is apparent that its primary dissociation yields and its possible excited molecule reactions in the changeover region deserve further investigation.

TABLE 17

RATES OF ABSORPTION OF SOLAR RADIATION BY NITROGEN DIOXIDE

Solar zenith angle (z)	k_a (2900–3850 A)		k_a (3850–4150 A)	
	sec⁻¹	hr⁻¹	sec⁻¹	hr⁻¹
0	7.3×10^{-3}	26	6.0×10^{-3}	22
20	7.0×10^{-3}	25	5.8×10^{-3}	21
40	6.1×10^{-3}	22	5.2×10^{-3}	19
60	4.2×10^{-3}	15	3.9×10^{-3}	14
80	1.2×10^{-3}	4.5	1.2×10^{-3}	4.3

In air, the possible effects of pressure, as well as those of wavelength, on the primary yields must be considered. If the only processes competing with dissociation are the resonance transfer (III-24) and fluorescence (III-27), the yield will be independent of pressure. Collisional deactivation of the second excited state, NO_2'', will not affect the dissociation yield, but, if collisional deactivation by reaction (III-28) or direct reaction by (III-23) are important, the yield will be pressure dependent. Foreign gases, including oxygen and nitrogen, do reduce the over-all yield of the nitrogen dioxide photolysis, but these effects appear to be due to secondary reactions (Chapter V). Rate constants derived by Ford and Endow[136] are compatible with a primary dissociation yield of unity for nitrogen dioxide irradiated at 3660 A in the presence of an atmosphere of nitrogen. Thus, no pressure effect at and below 3660 A is indicated. At 4047 A, the sharp structure in the absorption spectrum indicates a longer lived initially excited state than at 3660 A, and whether the primary process is (III-22) or (III-23), some pressure effects not found at shorter wavelengths might be anticipated. However, there is currently no evidence that such effects exist.

From the absorption rates in Table 17 for λ 2900–3850 A, and assuming a primary yield of unity, at a nitrogen dioxide concentration of 10 pphm and $z = 45°$, the rate of production of nitric oxide and ^3P oxygen atoms by the NO_2 photolysis will be approximately 200 pphm hr⁻¹. This is by far the fastest of all known photochemical primary processes in polluted air.

6. SULFUR DIOXIDE

Gaseous sulfur dioxide shows absorption consisting of bands with sharp rotational structure, beginning at about 3950 A and increasing to

TABLE 18

APPROXIMATE ABSORPTION COEFFICIENTS
FOR SULFUR DIOXIDE

λ (A)	α_λ (l mole^{-1} cm^{-1})
2900	156
3000	121
3100	46
3200	13
3300	3.7
3400	1.1

a maximum at about 2850 A. Above about 3400 A the absorption is very weak. Detailed absorption coefficients have not been reported and, owing to the sharp rotational structure, would be difficult to obtain. The approximate absorption coefficients in Table 18, averaged over 100-A

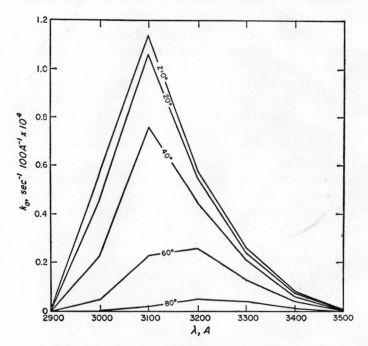

FIG. 23. Absorption of solar radiation by sulfur dioxide.

intervals, have been estimated from spectrophotometer measurements by Hall [177] of the transmission of a 10-cm layer of SO_2 at 5 mm pressure. Corresponding estimates of $k_{a\lambda}$ and k_a for solar radiation are presented in Fig. 23 and Table 19. The possibilities of error noted in Chapter II, Sec. 11, apply to these estimates.

TABLE 19

APPROXIMATE RATES OF ABSORPTION OF SOLAR
RADIATION BY SULFUR DIOXIDE

Solar zenith angle (z)	k_a	
	sec^{-1}	hr^{-1}
0	2.6×10^{-4}	0.94
20	2.4×10^{-4}	0.86
40	1.7×10^{-4}	0.62
60	0.7×10^{-4}	0.26
80	0.1×10^{-4}	0.04

In water solutions of sulfur dioxide, the absorption coefficients over the range 3200–3900 A are higher than in the gas and would lead to values of k_a about an order of magnitude larger than those in Table 18. However, in polluted air, the fraction of the total sulfur dioxide which will be in solution in liquid water droplets will be very small. Thus, at a gaseous sulfur dioxide concentration of 10 pphm the equilibrium concentration in water solution will be, by Henry's law, 1.2×10^{-7} M at 25°C. The liquid water content of most fogs is below 1 g m^{-3}, and in such fogs the fraction of the sulfur dioxide which is in solution, at 25°C, will be less than 3×10^{-5}. The absorption rate of that portion of the sulfur dioxide which is dissolved in water droplets in polluted air may therefore be regarded as negligible.

The sharp rotational structure in the absorption spectrum of sulfur dioxide is evidence that the molecule is not photodissociated by solar radiation, and this is confirmed by the energy requirements of the possible dissociation processes. The estimated bond dissociation energy[177,281] for the reaction

$$SO_2 \rightarrow SO + O \quad -135 \text{ kcal} \qquad \text{(III-29)}$$

corresponds to the einstein at 2100 A. Dissociation into a sulfur atom and an oxygen molecule would also require 135 kcal mole^{-1}, and dissociation into a sulfur atom and two oxygen atoms requires 253 kcal mole^{-1} of energy. The energy of the einstein in the region of solar radiation which is absorbed by sulfur dioxide is $\sim$85–95 kcal mole^{-1}, hence it falls short of the requirement to produce any of these dissociations. The primary photochemical processes following absorption of solar radiation by sulfur dioxide must therefore involve excited sulfur dioxide molecules rather than dissociation. Such processes do occur, but the photochemistry involved is such that a discussion which does not also include the subsequent secondary reactions will scarcely be profitable. For this reason, further consideration of the reactions of sulfur dioxide will be deferred to Chapter IX.

7. Nitric Acid and Alkyl Nitrates

Nitric acid and the organic nitrates show continuous absorption which extends to some extent into the solar ultraviolet. A curve of the

TABLE 20

APPROXIMATE ABSORPTION COEFFICIENTS
OF NITRIC ACID AND ETHYL NITRATE

λ (A)	α (l mole^{-1} cm^{-1})	
	HNO$_3$	C$_2$H$_5$ONO$_2$
2900	1.8	2.2
3000	1.2	0.9
3100	0.8	0.4
3200	0.4	0.2
3300	0.1	0.1

absorption coefficients of nitric acid vapor from 2200 to 3000 A has been published by Dalmon,[92] and extrapolating this curve to 3300 A gives the very rough values in Table 20. The absorption coefficients of ethyl nitrate vapor, which appear to be typical of the alkyl nitrates, are from the data of Goodeve.[161] Resultant absorption rates are given in Table 21.

TABLE 21

APPROXIMATE RATES OF ABSORPTION OF SOLAR RADIATION
BY NITRIC ACID AND ETHYL NITRATE

Solar zenith angle (z)	k_a (sec^{-1}) × 10^6		k_a (hr^{-1}) × 10^2	
	HNO$_3$	C$_2$H$_5$ONO$_2$	HNO$_3$	C$_2$H$_5$ONO$_2$
0	5.1	3.0	1.8	1.1
20	4.7	2.8	1.7	1.0
40	3.5	2.1	1.3	0.7
60	1.6	1.0	0.6	0.3
80	0.3	0.2	0.1	—

Reynolds and Taylor[355] have reported that while exposure of liquid HNO_3 in a quartz vessel to sunlight resulted in no visible change, exposure of the vapor above the liquid led to the immediate formation of NO_2. The continuous absorption indicates dissociation with a primary yield of unity, and the only dissociation process which appears to be energetically possible in solar radiation is

$$HNO_3 + h\nu \rightarrow \dot{O}H + NO_2 \ (-\sim 53 \text{ kcal})$$ (III-30)

The alkyl nitrates are also decomposed by ultraviolet radiation with the production of nitrogen dioxide and a variety of other products. Thus, in the photolysis of ethyl nitrate, Gray and Style[165] observed the formation of NO_2, NO, N_2O, CO_2, CO, H_2O, H_2, nitromethane, and aldehydes. Here again, the continuous absorption indicates a primary dissociation with yield of unity, and for this Gray and Style propose the reaction

$$C_2H_5ONO_2 + h\nu \rightarrow C_2H_5\dot{O} + NO_2$$ (III-31)

Some support of this as the primary process was obtained by Style and Ward [410] from a study of the fluorescence produced when ethyl nitrate is exposed to radiation in the Schumann region. The fluorescent radiation is composed of two systems, one in the visible and the other in the ultraviolet. The visible fluorescence appears to correspond with that of nitrogen dioxide, while the ultraviolet fluorescence corresponds to that obtained on irradiation of methyl and ethyl nitrites, diethyl peroxide, and other compounds which might be expected to yield alkoxyl radicals. From this, Style and Ward conclude that absorption in the Schumann region dissociates $RONO_2$ molecules into excited $R\dot{O}$ and NO_2.

The variety of products observed is not incompatible with a simple primary dissociation of the alkyl nitrates, as a variety of secondary reactions would be expected, particularly if some of the products, such as NO_2 and aldehydes, absorb and are photolyzed by radiation in the same region. There is thus no evidence to oppose, and some to support, the conclusion that for both nitric acid and the organic nitrates the primary photochemical process may be represented by the general equation

$$RONO_2 + h\nu \rightarrow R\dot{O} + NO_2$$ (III-32)

However, the case for this is not to be regarded as wholly proven, and other processes are possible, such as dissociation to yield alkyl radicals

$$RONO_2 + h\nu \rightarrow \dot{R} + NO_3$$ (III-33)

or dissociation with internal rearrangement

$$RCH_2ONO_2 + h\nu \rightarrow RCHO + HNO_2$$ (III-34)

Whatever the primary process or processes in nitric acid and the alkyl nitrates may be, their rates cannot exceed the absorption rates, and in solar radiation these are small. From the data of Table 21, at $z = 45°$ and concentrations of 10 pphm, the absorption rate of nitric acid will be about 0.1 pphm hr^{-1}, while that of ethyl nitrate will be only ~0.05 pphm hr^{-1}. Little is known of the concentrations which nitric acid and the organic nitrates actually attain in urban air. Chemical methods have indicated a substantial amount of nitrate in the air, but infrared absorption failed to reveal nitric acid, even under conditions such that 10 pphm could have been detected.[383] It scarcely seems likely, therefore, that the concentration of nitric acid will be high enough to make its photolysis of more than marginal significance, and the same is probably true of the organic nitrates.

8. NITROUS ACID, ALKYL NITRITES, AND NITRO COMPOUNDS

In an investigation of the absorption spectra of mixtures of NO, NO_2, and H_2O, Melvin and Wulf [286] observed a series of well separated bands, beginning at about 3850 A and extending to shorter wavelengths, which they attributed to gaseous nitrous acid, HNO_2. The bands appear to occur in two progressions, one of strong bands with a separation of 700–800 cm^{-1}, and the other of weak bands with a 250 cm^{-1} separation. At the long wavelength end of the series, the bands were very diffuse, but at shorter wavelengths they noticeably sharpened.

Somewhat similar bands, spaced 900–1000 cm^{-1} apart in the region 3000–4000 A, were observed by Thompson and Purkis[418] in the absorption spectra of methyl, ethyl, and amyl nitrites. In these spectra the bands appear to be completely diffuse. There is no evidence of sharpening at shorter wavelengths, and the bands overlap to such an extent that Goodeve[161] in measuring the absorption coefficients of ethyl nitrite vapor observed only continuous absorption.

The absorption of the nitro compounds lies at shorter wavelengths than does that of the nitrites, and appears to be wholly continuous. The long wavelength limit and strength of this absorption in the solar radiation region is uncertain. Thus Thompson and Purkis[417] reported the absorption of nitroethane to be very weak at 3000 A, and found none above ~2700 A for nitromethane, while Goodeve measured the nitroethane absorption up to about 3300 A and found it to be stronger in this region than that of ethyl nitrate.

The absorption coefficients of ethyl nitrite and nitroethane, estimated from Goodeve's data, are listed in Table 22, while Fig. 24 compares the wavelength distribution of the solar energy that would be absorbed by

TABLE 22

ABSORPTION COEFFICIENTS OF ETHYL NITRITE
AND NITROETHANE

λ (A)	α (l mole^{-1} cm^{-1})	
	C_2H_5ONO	$C_2H_5NO_2$
2900	41	12
3000	22	8.4
3100	19	5.5
3200	19	3.4
3300	22	2.0
3400	30	1.2
3500	39	0.7
3600	40	—
3700	37	—
3800	28	—
3900	17	—
4000	5.6	—
4100	1.3	—

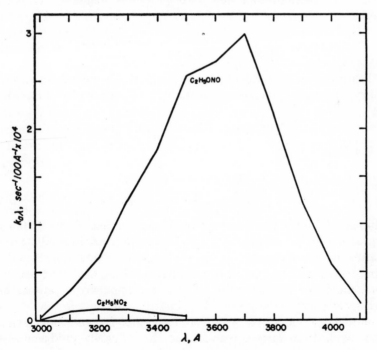

FIG. 24. Absorption of solar radiation by ethyl nitrite and nitroethane.

each of these compounds at a solar zenith angle of 40°, and Table 23 gives their over-all absorption rates at different zenith angles.

TABLE 23

RATES OF ABSORPTION OF SOLAR RADIATION BY ETHYL NITRITE AND NITROETHANE

Solar zenith angle (z)	k_a (sec^{-1}) $\times 10^4$		k_a (hr^{-1})	
	C_2H_5ONO	$C_2H_5NO_2$	C_2H_5ONO	$C_2H_5NO_2$
0	19.7	0.61	7.1	0.22
20	19.0	0.57	6.8	0.21
40	16.4	0.45	5.9	0.16
60	11.3	0.25	4.1	0.09
80	3.4	0.06	1.2	0.02

Little is known of the photochemistry of gaseous nitrous acid. Its absorption rates may be comparable with those of the alkyl nitrites. The diffuseness of the bands in the solar radiation region suggests a primary dissociation, and here two processes might be energetically possible:

$$HNO_2 + h\nu \rightarrow \overset{\bullet}{O}H + NO \ (-\sim 60 \text{ kcal}) \tag{III-35}$$
$$HNO_2 + h\nu \rightarrow H + NO_2 \ (-\sim 80 \text{ kcal}) \tag{III-36}$$

Absorption by the organic nitrites results in photolysis, and three primary processes have been postulated: an intramolecular rearrangement

$$RCH_2ONO + h\nu \rightarrow RCHO + HNO \tag{III-37}$$

and the dissociations

$$RONO + h\nu \rightarrow R\overset{\bullet}{O} + NO \tag{III-38}$$

$$RONO + h\nu \rightarrow \overset{\bullet}{R} + NO_2 \tag{III-39}$$

Process (III-37) was proposed by Thompson and Purkis[418] to explain the products of photolysis of methyl and ethyl nitrites. Using the full radiation of the mercury arc, they observed as products from methyl nitrite, paraformaldehyde, nitrogen, nitrous oxide, and small amounts of carbon monoxide and hydrogen. The paraformaldehyde presumably resulted from polymerization of the primarily produced formaldehyde, the carbon monoxide and hydrogen from its photolysis, and the nitrogen and nitrous oxide from further reactions of the primarily produced nitroxyl, HNO.

In a reinvestigation of the photolysis of methyl nitrite vapor, using

3660 A as the exciting radiation, Gray and Style[165] identified formaldehyde, nitrous oxide, and nitric oxide among the products, but found
little or no nitrogen. The NO/N_2O ratio increased with temperature
from about 1.1 at 30°C to 12.7 at 156°C. While recognizing that process
(III-37) is capable of explaining their results, Gray and Style note that
a number of investigations[398] of the pyrolysis of alkyl nitrites suggest
that the primary thermal process is

$$RONO \rightarrow \dot{R}O + NO \qquad \text{(III-40)}$$

The fact that, with increasing temperature, the photolysis products
approach those of the pyrolysis led these authors to conclude that the
photochemical and thermal primary processes are similar, hence that
reaction (III-38) is the photochemical process.

Process (III-39) is suggested by some of the products obtained
when the alkyl nitrites are photolyzed in air. Thus, ozone is rapidly
formed when butyl nitrite is photolyzed in the presence of air[173,174] or
oxygen.[405] In this case, ozone could result either from reaction of the
alkyl radicals with oxygen or from subsequent photolysis of the nitrogen
dioxide. Similarly, small concentrations of olefins in air are photo-
oxidized by alkyl nitrites in much the same manner as by nitrogen
dioxide, an observation which would appear to favor (III-39).

There is, however, substantial evidence against (III-39). Thus, in
the photolysis of t-butyl nitrite vapor, Coe and Doumani[81] found that
the initial products were acetone and nitrosomethane. These products
might be formed either directly from a primary process similar to
(III-37),

$$(CH_3)_3CONO + h\nu \rightarrow (CH_3)_2CO + CH_3NO \qquad \text{(III-41)}$$

or via secondary reactions following primary process (III-38), for example,

$$(CH_3)_3CONO + h\nu \rightarrow (CH_3)_3C\dot{O} + NO \qquad \text{(III-42)}$$

$$(CH_3)_3C\dot{O} \rightarrow (CH_3)_2CO + \dot{C}H_3 \qquad \text{(III-43)}$$

$$\dot{C}H_3 + NO \rightarrow CH_3NO \qquad \text{(III-44)}$$

It would be difficult to account for acetone and nitrosomethane formation
in this case if the primary process were (III-39).

In the photolysis of methyl nitrite in the presence of nitric oxide,
Hanst and Calvert[179] have reported that no detectable amounts of
nitrosomethane or formaldoxime were formed. This would indicate that
for methyl nitrite (III-39) is not important, since if it were, in the
presence of nitric oxide, reaction (III-44) would be expected to follow.

Direct physical evidence of the production of HNO molecules during the photolysis of nitrites and nitro compounds was first obtained by Dalby.[91] After the flash photolysis of nitromethane, nitroethane, and isoamyl nitrite, he observed two systems of sharp absorption bands in the products, centered at 7550 A, the structure of which indicated that the carrier was a nonlinear triatomic molecule of the type H—x—x or H—x—y, where x, y might be C, N, or O. The fact that the same bands are produced on flash photolysis of nitric oxide–ammonia mixtures eliminates carbon as being part of the molecule and leaves HN_2, HO_2, HNO, and HON as the possible structures. There is no chemical evidence for the existence of the HN_2 radical, it has not been observed by mass spectroscopy, and if it did exist it would be expected to be linear. The O—O bond length necessary to account for the absorption with HO_2 as the carrier is improbably small, and the bands are not produced by photolysis of oxygen–ammonia mixtures. The N—O bond length and stretching frequency necessary to explain the bands diverge widely from expectations for the structure HON, but agree with predictions for HNO. Thus of the four possible structures for the carrier, the evidence favors HNO.

For the lower electronic state involved in the absorption bands, Dalby derived 1.21 A for the N—O and 1.06 A for the H—N bond lengths, with a bond angle of 108.5°. From the rate of disappearance of the absorption bands, he estimated a lifetime of about 0.1 sec for the HNO molecule when the initial pressure of the compounds photolyzed was about 2 cm, in a 5 × 50-cm quartz cell. This is about 1000 times greater than the lifetime of NH_2 or HCO radicals under similar conditions.

While Dalby's observations are consistent with the primary formation of HNO in the photolysis of nitrites and nitro compounds, he emphasizes that they do not prove this to be the case, but rather show only that HNO is found within about 40 μsec from the start of the photolysis flash.

One of the most penetrating studies of the primary processes in the methyl nitrite and nitromethane photolyses is that of Brown and Pimentel.[58] These authors conducted the photolyses in an argon matrix at 20°K, observing the infrared spectra of the products. At this temperature the cis and trans rotational isomers of methyl nitrite are thermally stable and possess separate absorption frequencies; bands at 1619, 995, 985, and 840 cm^{-1} are assigned to the cis isomer and at 1670, 1185, 1043, and 810 cm^{-1} to the trans form. On photolysis of methyl nitrite, using unfiltered radiation from a medium pressure (AH-4) mercury arc, the bands assigned to the cis form disappeared rapidly, while those of the trans form remained almost constant until the cis form was depleted.

A number of product absorption bands appeared, including frequencies assigned to H_2O, H_2CO, NO, N_2O, CO, CO_2, HNCO, and new bands at 3300, 1570, 1125, and 1110 cm^{-1} which were assigned to HNO. A normal coordinate analysis of HNO, using Dalby's data, confirmed these assignments.

Brown and Pimentel propose, as consistent with these observations, the primary mechanism

$$cis\text{-}CH_3ONO + h\nu \rightarrow H_2CO + \overset{\bullet}{H}NO \qquad \text{(III-45)}$$

$$trans\text{-}CH_3ONO + h\nu \rightarrow CH_3\overset{\bullet}{O} + NO \qquad \text{(III-46)}$$
$$cis\text{-}CH_3ONO + h\nu = trans\text{-}CH_3ONO \qquad \text{(III-47)}$$

Reaction (III-46) accounts for the formation of NO, but must be slower than (III-45), and this with (III-47) explains the relative constancy of the trans isomer as long as the cis is present. The other observed products arise from secondary reactions.

Brown and Pimentel point out that these postulated reactions are consistent with earlier data on the gas phase photolysis of methyl nitrite. At ordinary temperatures the cis-trans equilibrium is probably maintained thermally; for the similar isomerization in nitrous acid Pimentel [329] estimates an energy barrier of only 1.5 kcal mole^{-1}. If this is the case, and if all three reactions result from absorption of the same wavelength, at ordinary temperatures the chief effect of reaction (III-47) would be to reduce the primary yields of the photolytic steps, (III-45) and (III-46). Also in this case reaction (III-47) must occur through an excited molecule-deactivation mechanism, and some pressure effects might be anticipated. Still further, the distribution between the three processes may be a function of wavelength as well as pressure. In Brown and Pimentel's experiments, the photolysis was apparently produced chiefly by short wavelengths, and whether the same processes would follow absorption in the solar radiation region (Fig. 24) remains to be determined.

An alternate mechanism which might be capable of explaining the experimental observations, both in solid argon and in the gas phase at room temperature with methyl nitrite, is that of (III-38) as the sole primary photochemical process, followed by partial reaction between the "hot" products to yield formaldehyde and HNO. Under conditions which would favor this reaction, such as flash photolysis or photolysis in a solid matrix, HNO formation is observed; under conditions which would favor rapid diffusion and other reactions of the methoxyl and nitric oxide, it might not be.

The nitromethane photolysis in argon at 20°K was also studied by Brown and Pimentel. When irradiated with a high pressure (AH-6) mercury arc and a $CoSO_4 - NiSO_4$ filter which limited the effective radiation chiefly to $\lambda > 2650$ A, the infrared bands assigned to *trans*-methyl nitrite, but not those due to the cis form, appeared in the products. When the light source was changed to an unfiltered medium pressure arc, the bands due to methyl nitrite were depressed, while those due to the same products as in the nitrite photolysis appeared strongly. To account for this behavior, Brown and Pimentel propose that, in solid argon at 20°K, the primary process in nitromethane is an intramolecular rearrangement to *trans*-methyl nitrite

$$CH_3NO_2 + h\nu \rightarrow trans\text{-}CH_3ONO \tag{III-48}$$

which is then followed by photolysis of the nitrite. The absence of NO_2, CH_4, and C_2H_6 among the products rules against the direct split

$$CH_3NO_2 + h\nu \rightarrow \overset{\bullet}{C}H_3 + NO_2 \tag{III-49}$$

as an important process at 20°K in argon.

Here again, process (III-48) is consistent with the data on the gas phase photolysis of nitromethane at ordinary temperatures, although under these conditions it may be that the subsequent splitting of the methyl nitrite does not require the absorption of a second photon.

In summary, the evidence suggests that one or both of two primary photochemical processes, the intramolecular rearrangement (III-37) or (III-45) and the dissociation (III-38) or (III-46), may be involved in the photolysis of the alkyl nitrites. If either process may occur in a given molecule, the distribution between the two may be a function of wavelength, and the primary yields may be reduced by deactivation, as evidenced by the low temperature reaction (III-47). The nitro alkanes, if nitromethane is typical, apparently yield the same primary products as do the nitrites, probably through a rearrangement prior to dissociation.

Nitrites are probably formed in the atmosphere by the combination of alkoxyl radicals, $R\overset{\bullet}{O}$, with nitric oxide. Their rate of absorption of solar radiation and resultant photolysis rates are so high that even if they were formed at a substantial rate they would reach no more than a trace concentration. For example, at $z = 45°$ and a concentration of only 1 pphm, the absorption rate of ethyl nitrite (Table 23) is over 5 pphm hr^{-1}. If the over-all primary photolysis yield of the nitrite approaches unity and it is formed at a rate of 5 pphm hr^{-1} in air, at solar altitudes of above 45° it would not even reach 1 pphm.

The nitrites may be regarded, therefore, as intermediates which are photolyzed almost as fast as they are formed, and it is interesting to inspect the primary processes with regard to the question of whether or not they promote photochemical smog formation. The photolysis of the nitrites, both alone and in the presence of olefins in air, would indicate that they do. Such promotional effects might be produced either by the conversion of nitric oxide to nitrogen dioxide or by the formation of new radicals which lead to an oxidation chain. From this point of view the dissociation into alkoxyl radicals and nitric oxide (III-38) and (III-46) merely reverses the probable process of nitrite formation and hence serves no promotional function unless the alkoxyl radicals so formed contain excess energy which leads them into new reactions. Nitrite formation from alkoxyl radicals and nitric oxide, followed by dissociation into alkyl radicals and nitrogen dioxide (III-39), would both convert nitric oxide into nitrogen dioxide and furnish chain carrying radicals, but the current evidence indicates that this dissociation does not occur. The sole remaining primary processes which might serve a promotional function are the rearrangements (III-37) and (III-45), and if this is the case the promotional effects must lie either in subsequent photolysis of the aldehyde or in the reactions of nitroxyl.

9. ALDEHYDES AND KETONES

Compounds containing a carbonyl group all show absorption in the solar radiation region. The absorption is rather weak, indicating a forbidden transition, and its position and characteristics with regard to structure depend on the remainder of the molecule.

In the simplest case, formaldehyde, absorption begins at about 3720 A and continues with increasing intensity to beyond the limit of solar radiation. The absorption shows clearly resolved rotational structure throughout this region.[192,195,375]

Replacement of one of the hydrogens of formaldehyde with an alkyl group (the aliphatic aldehydes) displaces the absorption somewhat toward shorter wavelengths and decreases the amount of observable structure. Thus, with acetaldehyde, absorption begins at 3484 A, and although bands are observed to below 2700 A,[253] only at above ~3300 A do they show distinct structure. Below this wavelength the structure grows gradually more diffuse and disappears entirely around 3100 A. In addition, either a continuous absorption underlies the whole region or the bands are so closely superimposed as to give a continuous background. With propionaldehyde and n-butyraldehyde, the structure is progressively less marked, and with isobutyraldehyde very little structure is observable at any wavelength.[34]

Replacement of both formaldehyde hydrogens with alkyl groups (the aliphatic ketones) displaces the absorption still further to shorter wavelengths and all but eliminates observable structure. For instance, with acetone, the long-wavelength limit of absorption is about 3270 A, and

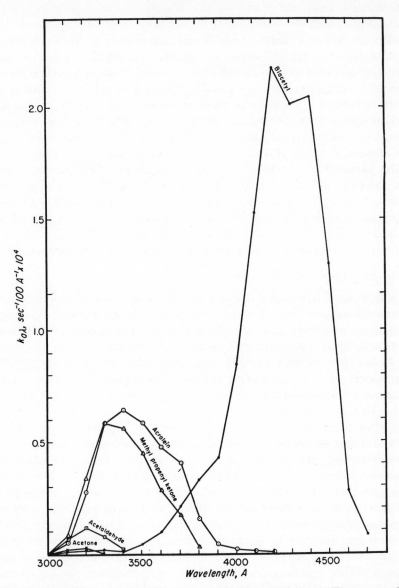

FIG. 25. Absorption of solar radiation by aldehydes and ketones. The curves show the fractions of the molecules which will absorb photons per second over 100-A bandwidths of solar radiation in the lower atmosphere at $z = 60°$.

although a number of investigations of its absorption spectrum had been made prior to 1934, it was not until then that it was shown that its absorption is not completely continuous. In that year, faint bands, extending from about 3270–3020 A, were reported by Norrish et al.,[307] and confirmed by Noyes et al.[311] No structure has been observed in the absorption of the higher aliphatic ketones.[108]

Introduction of an olefinic double bond conjugated with the carbonyl bond produces a bathochromic shift to longer wavelengths and increases the amount of structure, relative to the aliphatic aldehydes. For instance, the absorption of acrolein and crotonaldehyde extends slightly into the visible region.[38,44] As with the aliphatic aldehydes, the structure gradually becomes less distinct in going to shorter wavelengths and finally below ~3100 A, disappears entirely. The absorption of the aromatic aldehydes, relative to that of the aliphatic aldehydes, shows a slight bathochromic shift and an increase in structure. For example, the absorption of benzaldehyde begins about 3750 A and shows distinct structure to below 3000 A.[7]

With diketones the absorption is displaced toward longer wavelengths to an extent dependent on the proximity of the carbonyl groups within the molecule; with adjacent carbonyl groups the absorption extends up to 4500 or 5000 A.[191] Thus the absorption of biacetyl begins at 4670 A. From 4670 to 4400 A it shows bands with fine structure, but below this wavelength the bands become increasingly diffuse and merge into an apparent continuum. A second absorption region occurs below 3350 A. With glyoxal the bands are sharper, and, in hexane solution at least, the absorption coefficients appear to be smaller than in the case of biacetyl.[262]

While the photochemistry of the aldehydes and ketones has been widely studied, absorption coefficients in the gaseous state have been determined in only a few cases. Representative values, as far as available, averaged over 100-A intervals of the solar radiation region are given in Table 24. With the exception of the diketones, the coefficients for the members of a given class, such as the aliphatic aldehydes, do not appear to vary greatly. Among different classes also the peak absorption coefficients do not vary greatly; the chief difference is in the wavelengths absorbed. This, however, leads to large differences in the rate of absorption of solar radiation, as shown in Fig. 25 and Table 25. In judging these figures it should be remembered that the absorption rate is equal to $k_a c$, and while the total aldehydes found in urban air quite often exceed 10 pphm, the concentrations of some specific substances, such as biacetyl, may be very much smaller than this and may even be zero.

Evidence regarding the primary photochemical processes in aldehydes

TABLE 24

ABSORPTION COEFFICIENTS OF ALDEHYDES AND KETONES

	α_λ (l mole^{-1} cm^{-1})				
λ (A)	Acetone[337]	Acetaldehyde[393]	Methyl propenyl ketone[420]	Acrolein[38,44]	Biacetyl[113,262,294]
2900	10	19	9	4	12
3000	7	16	12	7	7
3100	4	12	15	10	3
3200	1.5	6	17	14	1
3300	0.1	2.2	16	16	0 5
3400	—	0.6	14	16	0 5
3500	—	—	10	13	1
3600	—	—	6	10	2
3700	—	—	3	7	4
3800	—	—	0.6	2.8	6
3900	—	—	—	0.3	8
4000	—	—	—	0.1	11
4100	—	—	—	—	15
4200	—	—	—	—	19
4300	—	—	—	—	18
4400	—	—	—	—	17
4500	—	—	—	—	10
4600	—	—	—	—	2
4700	—	—	—	—	0.5

and ketones has been drawn from the absorption spectra, fluorescence, careful analyses of the products under various conditions, use of metallic mirrors as radical detectors, and the effects of adding iodine in sufficient amount to act as a "trap" for primarily produced radicals and atoms.

For example, formaldehyde shows pronounced fluorescence on exposure to 3530 A and shorter wavelengths, with progressively decreasing intensity.[197] The fluorescence consists of a series of bands extending from ~3700–5700 A. Simultaneously, the formaldehyde is photochemically decomposed. At 3130 and 2537 A the products, in the absence of other gases, are H_2 and CO. In the presence of iodine, however, the products are almost exclusively HI and CO.[162] This indicates that, at these wavelengths at least, the primary formation of H_2 + CO by intramolecular rearrangement is unimportant. The formation of HI in the presence of iodine indicates the primary formation of hydrogen atoms, and the presence of free radicals or hydrogen atoms during the photolysis has been demonstrated by the Paneth method, using tellurium mirrors.[437]

A direct primary split into two H atoms and a CO molecule is energetically possible at 2537 A but not at 3130 A. This leaves dissociation into a hydrogen atom and a formyl radical as the sole possibility for the primary production of H atoms at 3130 A, and since the quantum

TABLE 25

RATES OF ABSORPTION OF SOLAR RADIATION BY ALDEHYDES AND KETONES

Solar zenith angle (z)	Acetone		Acetaldehyde	
	k_a (sec^{-1}) $\times$ 10^5	k_a (hr^{-1})	k_a (sec^{-1}) $\times$ 10^5	k_a (hr^{-1})
0°	2.1	0.08	8.4	0.30
20°	1.9	0.07	7.8	0.28
40°	1.4	0.05	6.0	0.22
60°	0.6	0.02	2.9	0.10
80°	0.1	0.003	0.6	0.02

Solar zenith angle (z)	Methyl propenyl ketone		Acrolein		Biacetyl	
	k_a (sec^{-1}) $\times$ 10^5	k_a (hr^{-1})	k_a (sec^{-1}) $\times$ 10^5	k_a (hr^{-1})	k_a (sec^{-1}) $\times$ 10^5	k_a (hr^{-1})
0°	50	1.8	62	2.2	170	6.1
20°	48	1.7	58	2.1	160	5.8
40°	41	1.5	51	1.8	150	5.4
60°	26	0.9	33	1.2	120	4.3
80°	7	0.25	9	0.3	40	1.4

yield and other features of the reaction at 2537 A do not differ significantly from those at 3130 A, it appears probable that this is the primary photochemical process at both wavelengths. The processes thus indicated for formaldehyde are

$$H_2CO + h\nu \rightarrow H_2CO' \qquad \text{(III-50)}$$
$$H_2CO' \rightarrow H_2CO + h\nu' \qquad \text{(III-51)}$$
$$H_2CO' + M \rightarrow H_2CO + M \qquad \text{(III-52)}$$

$$H_2CO' \rightarrow H + H\dot{C}O \qquad \text{(III-53)}$$

The sharp rotational structure and fluorescene of formaldehyde indicate an excited state with a life much greater than one vibrational period, which in turn suggests that the dissociation process must be rather slow, hence that the primary quantum yield may be substantially below unity. An indication that this is the case may be obtained from the results of Gorin,[162] given in Table 26.

TABLE 26

PHOTOLYSIS OF FORMALDEHYDE–IODINE MIXTURES AT 100°C

λ (A)	P_{H_2CO} (mm)	P_{I_2} (mm)	H_2/HI	HI/CO	Φ_{HI}
3130	85	4	0.008	1.8	0.97
3130	115	2	0.006	1.9	0.96
3130	215	1	0.005	1.7	0.84
2537	96	2	0.000	1.7	0.95
2537	157	5	0.005	1.7	0.86
2537	246	8.6	0.012	1.65	0.85
3650	154	3	0.42	1.1	—
3650	240	1	0.75	1.1	—

The observed HI/CO ratio of nearly 2 may be accounted for if the major secondary reactions are[39]

$$H + I_2 \rightarrow HI + I \tag{III-54}$$
$$HCO + I_2 \rightarrow HI + I + CO \tag{III-55}$$

If this is the case, the primary yield [reaction (III-53)] will be half the quantum yield of HI formation, which means that under the experimental conditions of Table 26 the primary quantum yield of formaldehyde dissociation is between 0.4 and 0.5.

Unless the fluorescence efficiency of formaldehyde differs markedly from that of other aldehydes, not more than a few per cent of the excited molecules will lose their excitation by fluorescence, and if the primary yield of dissociation is less than 0.5, deactivation by collision, reaction (III-52), must be rather important. This would suggest that the primary dissociation yield may decrease with increasing pressure, and hence be materially less than 0.4 at atmospheric pressure. An indication of such a decrease, in Φ_{HI}, with increasing pressure is seen in the data of Table 26.

The greatly increased H_2/HI ratio and the smaller HI/CO ratio obtained by Gorin at 3650 A (Table 26) suggest a change in the nature of the primary process at this wavelength; possibly by an increase in the amount of intramolecular rearrangement to yield $H_2 + CO$ directly, although there is evidence[248] that at 300°C at least part of the photodissociation of formaldehyde occurs by (III-53).

For the aliphatic aldehydes evidence of similar nature obtained by Blacet and his collaborators[37,39,42] indicates that the act of absorption is followed by several primary processes, which vary in importance with wavelength. First are the general processes of absorption, fluorescence, and deactivation:

$$RCHO + h\nu \rightarrow RCHO' \qquad \text{(III-56)}$$
$$RCHO' \rightarrow RCHO + h\nu' \qquad \text{(III-57)}$$
$$RCHO' + M \rightarrow RCHO + M \qquad \text{(III-58)}$$

Next are the photochemical processes, which are of four types:

I. Dissociation into alkyl and formyl radicals.

$$RCHO' \rightarrow \dot{R} + H\dot{C}O \qquad \text{(III-59)}$$

II. Intramolecular rearrangement to yield a saturated hydrocarbon and carbon monoxide.

$$RCHO' \rightarrow RH + CO \qquad \text{(III-60)}$$

III. Intramolecular rearrangement to yield ethylene and an aldehyde of two fewer carbon atoms.

Propionaldehyde: $C_2H_5CHO' \rightarrow C_2H_4 + H_2CO$ (III-61)
n-Butyraldehyde: $C_3H_7CHO' \rightarrow C_2H_4 + CH_3CHO$ (III-62)

IV. Dissociation into methyl and formyl-alkyl radicals.

Propionaldehyde: $C_2H_5CHO' \rightarrow \dot{C}H_3 + \dot{C}H_2CHO$ (III-63)

n-Butyraldehyde: $C_3H_7CHO' \rightarrow \dot{C}H_3 + \dot{C}H_2CH_2CHO$ (III-64)

Isobutyraldehyde: $(CH_3)_2CHCHO' \rightarrow \dot{C}H_3 + CH_3\dot{C}HCHO$ (III-65)

The primary quantum yields for these processes at different wavelengths, from Blacet and Heldman, Calvert, and Pitts,[37,39,42,71] are given in Table 27.

It is seen that in the solar radiation region (3130 A), with the exception of process III for n-butyraldehyde, by far the most important photochemical primary process is the dissociation into alkyl and formyl radicals.

Acetaldehyde and propionaldehyde show marked fluorescence at 3130 A, which weakens at shorter wavelengths and disappears entirely below about 2650 A. In the case of acetaldehyde at least, the fluorescence closely resembles that of biacetyl [285] and may be largely due to this compound, which is formed in small amounts via secondary reactions.[36] In any case, the intensity of the fluorescence is small compared with that of the absorbed radiation. The fluorescence of n-butyraldehyde is weak at 3130 A and absent at shorter wavelengths, while isobutyraldehyde shows no fluorescence at any wavelength.[254]

The sum of the primary photochemical yields for each specific aldehyde at 3130 A, from Table 27, varies from a lower limit of 0.21 for acetaldehyde to 0.76 for isobutyraldehyde. Since the balance cannot be accounted for by fluorescence alone, it is evident that a significant portion of the photoactivated molecules must be deactivated by collision.

TABLE 27

PRIMARY QUANTUM YIELDS FOR THE ALIPHATIC ALDEHYDES
(Aldehyde pressures, 100–200 mm; temperatures 20–170°C.)

Process		ϕ		
		3130 A	2804 A	2654 A
I	Acetaldehyde	0.2–0.8	0.39	0.36
	Propionaldehyde	0.48	0.53	0.28
	n-Butyraldehyde	0.35	0.28	0.28
	Isobutyraldehyde	0.72	—	0.43
II	Acetaldehyde	0.013	0.15	0.28
	Propionaldehyde	0.022	0.125	0.34
	n-Butyraldehyde	0.017	0.11	0.25
	Isobutyraldehyde	0.03	—	0.40
III	Propionaldehyde	0.003	0.011	0.013
	n-Butyraldehyde	0.164	0.27	0.38
IV	Propionaldehyde	0.000	0.007	0.012
	n-Butyraldehyde	0.005	0.006	0.010
	Isobutyraldehyde	0.006	0.012	0.036

The two figures given for the primary yield of process I for acetaldehyde are of particular interest in this connection. The value of $\phi = 0.2$ was obtained by Blacet and Heldman[39] on the basis of the rate of formation of CH_3I when acetaldehyde was photolyzed in the presence of sufficient iodine to react with essentially all of the methyl radicals produced. At $P_{I_2} > 1$ mm this rate was insensitive to iodine concentration and over the range of 60–170°C it was insensitive to temperature. The value of $\phi = 0.8$ was derived by Calvert, Pitts, and Thompson[71] on the basis of the rate of hydrogen production from the photolysis at low light intensities and temperatures high enough (300°–350°C) to decompose rapidly the formyl radicals into carbon monoxide and hydrogen atoms.

The difference between the two values is probably due to collisional deactivation of photoactivated acetaldehyde molecules by iodine. To explain the fact that the value obtained on the basis of CH_3I formation is insensitive to iodine concentration above $P_{I_2} = 1$ mm, Calvert, Pitts, and Thompson suggest that at least two excited states are formed on absorption of 3130 A by acetaldehyde. One of these states is short lived and dissociates so rapidly that it is not quenched by iodine; the value of $\phi = 0.2$ applies to this state. The other excited state or states are long lived and are quenched by iodine. The value of $\phi = 0.8$ is then the over-all uninhibited dissociation yield from all the excited states.

The reduction of the primary yield of acetaldehyde photolysis by iodine immediately raises the question of whether, in air, oxygen or nitrogen exert a similar effect. Evidence that oxygen does so, but nitrogen does not has been obtained by Calvert and Hanst.[69] In their experiments, 42.5 mm of acetaldehyde in an oxygen–nitrogen mixture to a total pressure of ~740 mm were photolyzed by radiation of 3000–3300 A at room temperature, and the initial rates of product formation determined by infrared spectrometry. As the partial pressure of oxygen in the mixture was increased, the initial rates of formation of carbon dioxide, methyl alcohol, and peroxyacetic acid all decreased, finally leveling off at values about $\frac{1}{4}$ as great as those at low oxygen pressure. Calvert and Hanst interpret this as due to a decrease in the primary yield of radical formation, and the fact that the magnitude of the effect is almost identical to that obtained with iodine suggests that the same deactivation mechanism is involved. The maximum decrease in yield was obtained with oxygen partial pressure of 247 mm and higher, whereas with iodine it was obtained with pressure down to 1 mm, indicating that oxygen is a less efficient deactivator than iodine.

Calvert and Hanst's curves of initial rate vs. oxygen pressure show that at the partial pressure of oxygen in air, ~150 mm, the rates are probably close to their minimum values. If their interpretation is correct, it follows that for the photolysis of acetaldehyde in air the primary yield of dissociation into radicals will not be far from that observed in the presence of iodine, or $\phi = 0.2$.

The other values of ϕ for process I in Table 27 were all obtained by the iodine inhibition technique, and by analogy they should also apply in air. For acetaldehyde at other wavelengths than 3130 A and for propionaldehyde, these values probably reflect similar quenching. For the butyraldehydes, however, the limiting values of ϕ estimated by iodine inhibition and by high-temperature hydrogen formation are the same,[37] suggesting that in these cases deactivation of excited molecules is unimportant.

The polymerization observed on photolysis of the aliphatic aldehydes is probably brought about by secondary free radical reactions, rather than by primary reaction between excited and normal molecules.[34]

The primary process of the aliphatic ketones will be discussed only briefly, first because their absorption rates in solar radiation are so low as to be of doubtful significance, and second, because several excellent discussions are available.[96,300,315,398] At low pressures, acetone[100,170,310] is photodissociated almost exclusively to yield methyl and acetyl radicals. With increasing pressure, either of acetone itself or of added carbon dioxide, the products obtained at high light intensities[361] suggest two additional dissociation processes, both induced by collision, one to yield two methyl radicals and carbon monoxide, the other to split off a hydrogen atom.

Methyl ethyl ketone[115,294,331] and diethyl ketone[251] also appear to dissociate chiefly to yield alkyl and acyl radicals, but ketones with larger alkyl groups, such as methyl n-propyl ketone,[300] di-n-propyl ketone,[284] and methyl n-butyl ketone[98] react to a significant extent by an intramolecular rearrangement to yield an olefin and a lower ketone. Methyl neopentyl ketone[283] dissociates primarily, not only by both of these processes, but also by the rupture of a C—C bond to yield $(CH_3)_3C$ and CH_2COCH_3 radicals. Among the cycloalkyl ketones, Pitts and his collaborators have obtained evidence that methyl cyclopropyl ketone[333] dissociates but little into mono radicals, the major primary process being an intramolecular rearrangement, possibly via the biradical $CH_3CO\dot{C}HCH_2\dot{C}H_2$, to yield methyl propenyl ketone. However, methyl cyclobutyl ketone[303] appears to dissociate almost exclusively into methyl and cyclobutyryl or cyclobutyl and acetyl radicals in the manner characteristic of the simple aliphatic ketones.

In the case of acetone at least the processes leading up to and competing with the primary dissociation are not simple. Studies of the quenching of acetone fluorescence[170,237] indicate that at least two excited states are involved, both of which are capable of fluorescing. The mean lives of the two states in the absence of collisions are quite different, one being 2×10^{-4} sec and the other less than 8×10^{-6} sec (the flash duration of the experiments) at 25°C. The long-lived fluorescence is strongly quenched by oxygen and by high temperatures, but the short-lived component is unaffected. This suggests that the two states are formed by independent paths, i.e., that the molecules in one state are not transformed to the other. The effect of oxygen on the primary dissociation yield cannot be stated with certainty, but several observations indicate it is probably negligible.[210,269] If this is the case, little of the dissociation would come from the long-lived state. There is no evidence that oxygen reacts with the excited acetone molecules; its effect seems to be limited to collisional deactivation of one of the excited states.

The primary quantum yield of acetone dissociation into methyl and acetyl radicals, following absorption of 3130 A, has been estimated as 0.7 at 25–50°C and 0.99 at 300°C.[170,310] In the presence of iodine the yield, based on CH_3I production, drops to 0.12 at 80° and 0.28 at 177°C.[332] This indicates that iodine is capable of changing the primary yield, probably by collisional deactivation of the excited state, or at least one of the excited states, from which most of the dissociation occurs. Primary yields for the other aliphatic ketones are probably of the same order as that of acetone. The yield of methyl cyclopropyl ketone rearrangement into methyl propenyl ketone is 0.31 at 2654–2537 A and 25–120°C.[333] If a one step process, this is the primary yield.

Aldehydes and ketones containing an olefinic double bond conjugated with the carbonyl group appear to be remarkably stable with respect to photodecomposition. Thus Blacet and collaborators found no fluorescence and no measurable gaseous products on exposure at room temperatures of crotonaldehyde[43] and acrolein[38] to wavelengths from 3660 to 2399 A, while Tolberg and Pitts[335,420] report a similar result for methyl propenyl ketone. Only at temperatures approaching the pyrolysis region (>150°C) was any significant photolysis observed for any of these compounds, and that only at wavelengths beyond the solar radiation region. Crotonaldehyde showed a slow polymerization with quantum yield of 0.02 at 3600 A but not at shorter wavelengths, while acrolein showed a sharply increasing polymerization yield at wavelengths below 3000 A. The only significant reaction observed by Tolberg and Pitts for methyl propenyl ketone at 3130 A and temperatures up to 275°C was an intramolecular rearrangement of the trans to the cis isomer.

Crotonaldehyde did, however, react with oxygen, presumably to give crotonic acid. The over-all quantum yields, calculated by Blacet and Volman[44] on the basis of oxygen used to quanta absorbed, at 30°C and wavelengths down to 2537 A, are given in Table 28.

It is seen from the figures that in the solar radiation region the quantum yield is small and shows relatively little change with oxygen pressure. The values reached at 2537 A indicate a chain mechanism. It is not known whether the primary process is a dissociation of the crotonaldehyde into free radicals or a direct reaction of activated crotonaldehyde and oxygen molecules. The absence of fluorescence and the products of photolysis at higher temperatures favor the former, while the lack of photolysis at room temperature and the effect of nitrogen on the quantum yield of the reaction with oxygen favor the latter.

Among the diketones, photochemical investigations have been centered on glyoxal and biacetyl, largely because these compounds are known to be produced in the photolysis of several aldehydes and ketones. Glyoxal is photolyzed at wavelengths at least as long as 3660 A, and probably 4350 A. Carbon monoxide, hydrogen, and a polymerized product, possibly a polymeride of glycerosone[308] have been identified among the products. A CO/H_2 ratio of 32 was found by Blacet and Moulton[41] at room temperature and 3660 A, and of 7.7 by Calvert and Layne[70] at 3130 A and temperatures of 100–300°C. Several items of evidence indicate that

TABLE 28

REACTION OF CROTONALDEHYDE WITH OXYGEN

λ (A)	Oxygen pressure (mm)	Crotonaldehyde pressure (mm)	Φ_{O_2}
3660	1.03	39.0	0.026
3130	1.24	38.8	0.076
	3.23	38.3	0.086
	6.87	37.6	0.12
2809	1.02	37.5	0.21
	3.23	36.8	0.35
	10.8	36.7	0.40
	12.5	36.5	0.39
2537	1.19	39.6	0.39
	3.88	39.2	0.45
	10.0	38.8	1.45
	10.7	36.5	1.20
	13.5	37.0	3.22
	13.8	37.2	3.16
	10.2 (+ 40 mm N$_2$)	38.0	0.89

the primary process, in the solar radiation region at least, does not involve the fracture of the C—C bond to give formyl radicals. First, tellurium mirror experiments gave no evidence of free radical formation when glyoxal was exposed to the full radiation of the mercury arc.[437] Second, no methane was formed when mixtures of glyoxal and acetaldehyde were exposed to 3660 A; whereas formyl radicals would be expected to lead to at least some methane in such a mixture.[41] Third, energetic estimates indicate that such a dissociation could not be produced by wavelengths longer than ~2940 A.[70]

The experimental evidence is consistent with the primary mechanism:

$$HCOCOH + h\nu \rightarrow HCOCOH' \qquad (III-66)$$

$$HCOCOH' + M \rightarrow HCOCOH \qquad (III-67)$$

$$H_2 + 2CO \qquad (III-68)$$

$$HCOCOH'$$

$$H_2CO + CO \qquad (III-69)$$

$$HCOCOH' + HCOCOH \rightarrow polymeride, possibly via CO + C_3H_4O_3 \quad (III-70)$$

The CO/H$_2$ ratio of 32 obtained by Blacet and Moulton indicates that at 3660 A and room temperature not more than ~3% of the molecules which react do so by process (III-68); 97% must react by either (III-69) or (III-70). On the other hand, Calvert and Laynes' observations, particularly their CO/H_2 ratio of 7.7 and quantum yields of $\Phi_{CO} = 1.2$ and $\Phi_{H_2} = 0.13$, suggest that at 3130 A and temperatures above 100°C the only processes of importance are (III-68) and (III-69), with primary yields of 0.15 and 0.85, respectively.

The photolysis of biacetyl at 3660 A and shorter wavelengths has been investigated by Roof and Blacet[365] and Bell and Blacet,[29] while preliminary results at 4358 A have been reported by Coward and Noyes.[83] The results at and below 3660 A are compatible with a primary dissociation into acetyl radicals, with possibly a small amount of intramolecular rearrangement into acetone and carbon monoxide. At room temperature the primary quantum yield of the dissociation was estimated by Bell and Blacet to be 0.06 at 3130 A and 0.37 at 2654 A.

Coward and Noyes point out the following differences in behavior of biacetyl at 3660 and 4358 A:

1. At 4358 A the quenching of the fluorescence is almost independent of pressure, while at 3660 A the fluorescence efficiency increases with pressure.

2. At room temperature the photochemical quantum yields are independent of intensity at 3660 A but are roughly proportional to intensity at 4358 A.

3. The ratio CO/C_2H_6 in the products decreases with increasing pressure at 3660 A but is virtually independent of pressure at 4358 A.

These facts strongly suggest a fundamental difference in the photochemical primary process at 4358 A as compared with 3660 A and shorter wavelengths; the process suggested at 4358 A is either a collision between two activated molecules or between activated molecules and free radicals.

Studies of the quenching of biacetyl fluorescence[8-10,83,169,238] indicate a situation resembling that in acetone, with at least two excited states, one short and one long lived, both of which contribute to the fluorescence. The mean life of the fluorescence from the long-lived state is estimated at 2×10^{-3} sec at 25°C, while that from the short-lived state is probably less than 8×10^{-6} sec.[238] The long-lived component, which is responsible for most of the fluorescence, is strongly quenched by oxygen and disappears at high temperatures, whereas the short-lived component appears to be unaffected by oxygen and is still present at 200°C. The quantum yield of fluorescence on exposure to 4047 or 4358 A was reported by Almy and Gillette[10] to be 0.14 and approximately independent of pressure, while at 3660 A the yield was zero at zero pressure, rising to about 0.08 at 50 mm pressure.

While it is obvious that no detailed primary mechanism may be specified without further information, the steps required to explain the observations to date would appear to be (B = biacetyl):

Absorption: $B + h\nu \rightarrow B'$ (III-71)

$B (+M)$ (III-72)

Deactivation or transfer: $B' (+M) \rightarrow B^* (+M)$ (III-73)

$B^{**} (+M)$ (III-74)

Fluorescence: $B^* \rightarrow B + h\nu^*$ (III-75)

$B^{**} \rightarrow B + h\nu^{**}$ (III-76)

Quenching by O_2: $B^{**} + O_2 \rightarrow ?$ (III-77)

Photochemical
at and below 3660 A:

$2CH_3CO$ ($\phi = 0.06$ at 3130 A; 0.37 at 2654 A)   (III-78)

B' (or B*)

$(CH_3)_2CO + CO$ (slight)   (III-79)

at 4358 A: (B' or B*) + (B' or B* or R) $\rightarrow ?$ (III-80)

While some points are still obscure, for example why the absorption spectrum should apparently be diffuse at 4358 A while the photochemical evidence indicates no dissociation at this wavelength, taken altogether the available information suggests strongly that the photodissociation of biacetyl is a short wavelength process, confined chiefly to the absorption region below 3350 A, with perhaps a small amount (low primary yield) in the short wavelength part of the region above 3350 A.

The disclosure of a complex primary mechanism in the cases of acetaldehyde, acetone, and biacetyl immediately raises the question as to whether similar mechanisms exist for other aldehydes and ketones. Even when little or no fluorescence is observed, as in the case of the butyraldehydes, the existence of several competing primary processes, with total yield well below unity, indicates a complex mechanism, and it is doubtful if any of these mechanisms are fully understood.

Aldehydes are contributed to the air by organic combustions,[397] and they are formed in the atmosphere by such reactions as that of ozone with the olefins, of oxygen atoms with the olefins, and the photolysis of nitrites. Atmospheric analyses quite often show midday aldehyde concentrations of 20 to 30 pphm, or even higher, in the air of the Los Angeles basin.[351] At these concentrations, if the absorption rates of acetaldehyde in Table 25 are representative and the primary yields in Table 27 are maintained in air, the rate of production of alkyl and formyl radicals by aldehyde photolysis at $z = 45°$ will be $k_a\phi c \approx 1$ to 4 pphm hr^{-1}. While not startling, this range of rates is definitely high enough to be significant.

For that fraction of the aldehyde which is formaldehyde, the dissociation products will be hydrogen atoms and formyl radicals. In air and sunlight the absorption rate of formaldehyde should be greater than that of acetaldehyde, as it absorbs at longer wavelengths, but the primary yield of dissociation relative to this absorption might be, as in the case of biacetyl, quite small.

The processes which contribute aldehydes apparently do not contribute ketones in comparable amounts to urban air, and there is no evidence that the ketone concentrations approach those of the aldehydes in the air. Moreover, even at equal concentrations the aliphatic ketones absorb less solar radiation than do the aldehydes, about $\frac{1}{4}$ to $\frac{1}{5}$ as much at $z = 45°$. Taking acetone as an example, if the primary yield of $\phi = 0.7$ for the dissociation into alkyl and acyl radicals is maintained in air, the rate of their formation at a ketone concentration of 5 pphm, which is probably high, would be only $k_a \phi c \approx 0.1$ to 0.2 pphm hr^{-1}. The alternate dissociations observed for the higher ketones would probably be even slower than this. It is doubtful, therefore, that the ketones are more than minor contributors to free radical formation in urban air.

The diketones absorb solar radiation so strongly that they must be considered as a possible free radical source even though their concentrations in air, if they occur at all, are almost certainly small. Of the two diketones for which experimental evidence on the primary processes is available, in the solar radiation region glyoxal apparently does not photodissociate into free radicals at all, while biacetyl may dissociate to some extent into acetyl radicals. The primary yields reported for this process decrease with increasing wavelength, from 0.37 at 2654 A to 0.06 at 3130 A and zero at 4358 A. It is uncertain whether the dissociation is confined to the absorption region below 3350 A or whether it extends partially into the region above this wavelength.

We may estimate the over-all primary yield for biacetyl dissociation in solar radiation on the basis of two assumptions, which probably bracket the actual situation. First assume the dissociation process is limited to the region below 3350 A, with a primary yield of $\phi = 0.06$ as found by Bell and Blacet at 3130 A, and second, assume the dissociation process occurs up to 4000 A with the same primary yield as at 3130 A. As Fig. 25 shows, in sunlight most of the biacetyl absorption lies above 4000 A. Under normal radiation conditions at $z = 45°$ fewer than 0.5% of the photons absorbed will lie below 3350 A and fewer than 14% will lie below 4000 A. The over-all primary yields in solar radiation will therefore be $\phi < 0.06 \times 0.005 < 3 \times 10^{-4}$ for the first assumption and $\phi < 0.06 \times 0.14 < 0.01$ for the second assumption.

If the diketones occur in urban air at all it is unlikely that they do so at concentrations much greater than 1 pphm. At this concentration the rate of acetyl radical production in sunlight, $2k_a\phi c$, would be $<3 \times 10^{-3}$ pphm hr^{-1} in the first case and <0.1 pphm hr^{-1} in the second case. Therefore, unless other diketones are found to differ markedly from glyoxal and biacetyl, it may be judged that they do not constitute a significant source of free radicals in urban air.

10. PEROXIDES

The ultraviolet absorption of the peroxides is wholly continuous, and increases without a maximum from its beginning in the solar region to below 2000 A.[204]

The absorption coefficients in the solar radiation region of hydrogen peroxide vapor, from Urey et al.,[427] and of several organic peroxides and hydroperoxides in the liquid state, from Rieche,[358] are given in Table 29. Resulting absorption rates, calculated for hydrogen peroxide, diethyl peroxide, and allyl hydroperoxide, are shown in Table 30.

TABLE 29

ABSORPTION COEFFICIENTS OF PEROXIDES IN THE SOLAR RADIATION REGION

α_λ (l mole^{-1} cm^{-1})

λ (A)	Hydrogen peroxide	Dimethyl peroxide	Diethyl peroxide	Hydroxymethyl peroxide (in hexane)	Methyl hydroperoxide (in heptane)	Allyl hydro- peroxide
2900	3.9	1.2	3.2	2.0	0.0	3.2
3000	2.6	0.0	2.3	1.6	—	1.6
3100	1.8	—	~1	0.0	—	~1
3200	1.3	—	—	—	—	—
3300	1.0	—	—	—	—	—
3400	0.8	—	—	—	—	—
3500	0.5	—	—	—	—	—
3600	0.3	—	—	—	—	—
3700	0.2	—	—	—	—	—

Several studies of the photochemistry of the peroxides[106,427,433,436] indicate that the primary photochemical process following absorption in the ultraviolet is almost certainly a dissociation of the O—O bond,

$$\text{ROOR} + h\nu \rightarrow 2\text{R}\dot{\text{O}} \qquad \text{(III-81)}$$

The wholly continuous absorption and absence of fluorescence attributable to the parent molecule indicates a primary yield of unity.

Of the absorption rates listed in Table 30, only those of hydrogen peroxide are based on absorption coefficients determined in the vapor

TABLE 30

RATES OF ABSORPTION OF SOLAR RADIATION BY PEROXIDES

Solar zenith angle (z)	Hydrogen peroxide		Diethyl peroxide		Allyl hydroperoxide	
	k_a (sec^{-1}) $\times 10^5$	k_a (hr^{-1})	k_a (sec^{-1}) $\times 10^5$	k_a (hr^{-1})	k_a (sec^{-1}) $\times 10^5$	k_a (hr^{-1})
0°	3.3	0.12	0.33	0.012	0.31	0.011
20°	3.1	0.11	0.32	0.011	0.30	0.011
40°	2.5	0.09	0.21	0.008	0.20	0.007
60°	1.5	0.05	0.06	0.002	0.06	0.002
80°	0.4	0.01	0.002	0.0007	0.002	0.0007

state. The resultant values show it to be a somewhat stronger absorber of solar radiation than the aliphatic ketones, and the rate of hydroxyl radical formation by its photolysis will be twice its absorption rate. Thus at $z = 45°$ under normal radiation conditions the rate of formation of hydroxyl radicals at a hydrogen peroxide concentration of 1 pphm would be $2k_a\phi c = 0.16$ pphm hr^{-1}. This rate is scarcely significant, but at a concentration much larger than 1 pphm it would become so.

The absorption coefficients for the organic peroxides and hydroperoxides (Table 29), if applicable to the vapor, show that these substances absorb solar radiation only very slightly, with values of k_a at $z = 45°$ of less than 0.01 hr^{-1} (Table 30). The corresponding rate of free radical formation, $2k_a\phi c$, would be less than $0.02c$ pphm hr^{-1}.

The presence of hydroperoxides in the air of the Los Angeles basin was reported by Haagen-Smit[172] on the basis of the peroxidase-guaiac test, with relative concentrations paralleling that of ozone. However, the test gave no evidence of the absolute concentrations, nor did it indicate how much of the response, if any, was due to hydrogen peroxide. There is, in fact, no positive evidence on the concentrations or even the presence of hydrogen peroxide per se in urban air. Peroxides have been detected among the products of the reactions of high concentrations of ozone with the olefins (Chapter VI), but not when these reactants are at concentrations approaching those in the atmosphere. Infrared and chromatographic analyses of the photolysis products of low concentrations of nitric oxide, nitrogen dioxide, and olefins in air[377] show little or no organic peroxide. Combining this evidence with the low absorption rates of the organic peroxides, it may be judged that their photolysis rate in urban air is probably unimportant, but a revision of this judgment might be necessary if their absorption coefficients in the vapor state should be found to resemble those of hydrogen peroxide.

11. ACYL AND PEROXYACYL NITRITES AND NITRATES

In 1955, during a study of the infrared spectra of the photolysis products obtained from low concentrations of nitrogen dioxide and various organic compounds in air or oxygen, Stephens, Scott, Hanst, and Doerr,[405] using a long path absorption cell, first observed several prominent absorptions which could not be identified, but which apparently all belonged to one compound or class of compounds. The chief absorption bands involved were at 5.4, 5.75, 7.7, 8.6, and 12.6 μ, and the unknown product responsible was referred to as compound X. It has since been demonstrated that the same absorption bands are formed on irradiation of dilute automobile exhaust[379] as well as on irradiation of alkyl nitrites alone in air, and the bands have been observed in the air of the Los Angeles basin during periods of photochemical smog.[383]

The infrared absorption bands of compound X give some indications of its structure. The band at 5.75 μ resembles that due to the carbonyl group in aldehydes and ketones. A band near 5.4 μ arises from the N—O stretching vibration in nitric oxide, nitrogen tetroxide, and nitrosyl chloride, one near 7.7 μ is found in alkyl nitrates and nitrogen tetroxide, and one near 12.6 μ occurs with the alkyl nitrites.

In an effort to obtain further information on the structure of compound X, Stephens, Scott, Hanst, and Doerr prepared it by irradiating 100 ppm each of nitrogen dioxide and biacetyl in an atmosphere of oxygen, and partially separating the products by a cold trap. Mass spectra of the material thus prepared showed major peaks at 15 and 43, indicating an acetyl group, and at 30, suggesting NO, among its decomposition fragments. The material decomposed slowly at room temperature, and on standing for one week in oxygen the infrared spectrum of the products showed only carbon dioxide and a small amount of organic nitrate. On photolysis of the material in oxygen, ozone was produced. In contact with water, it yielded an acid solution which liberated iodine from KI, decolorized potassium permanganate, and gave a brown ring test for nitrite and nitrate. On one occasion a two-drop sample exploded with extreme violence.

Stephens, Scott, Hanst, and Doerr concluded that taken altogether, the evidence indicated that compound X had one of the structures:

$$\underset{\text{I}}{\overset{\displaystyle\text{O}}{\underset{\|}{\text{R—C—NO}}}} \qquad \underset{\text{II}}{\overset{\displaystyle\text{O}}{\underset{\|}{\text{R—C—ONO}}}} \qquad \underset{\text{III}}{\overset{\displaystyle\text{O}}{\underset{\|}{\text{R—C—NO}_2}}} \qquad \underset{\text{IV}}{\overset{\displaystyle\text{O}}{\underset{\|}{\text{R—C—ONO}_2}}} \qquad \underset{\text{V}}{\overset{\displaystyle\text{O}}{\underset{\|}{\text{R—C—OONO}}}}$$

Of these possibilities they further concluded that structure V, which could be called an acyl pernitrite, nitrosyl peracylate, or peroxyacyl nitrite, was the most likely. Such a compound might be formed in air by the reaction of peroxyacyl radicals with nitric oxide,

$$\begin{bmatrix} O \\ \| \\ R\dot{C}O\dot{O} \end{bmatrix} + NO \rightarrow R\overset{O}{\overset{\|}{C}}OONO \qquad \text{(III-82)}$$

The infrared spectrum of compound X, its observed chemical properties, and the formation of ozone on its photolysis, all appeared to be consistent with this structure. Seeking confirmatory evidence, Scott, Stephens, Hanst, and Doerr[383] found that compound X was produced by the reaction of solid silver nitrite with 40% peracetic acid, presumably through the metathesis

$$CH_3\overset{O}{\overset{\|}{C}}OOH + AgONO \rightarrow CH_3\overset{O}{\overset{\|}{C}}OONO + AgOH \qquad \text{(III-83)}$$

In a study reported in 1958, of the photolyses of formaldehyde and biacetyl in oxygen, Hanst and Calvert[179] found formic and acetic acids, but no peroxyacids, among the products. From this and other evidence they concluded that peroxyformyl and peroxyacetyl radicals are rapidly converted to formate and acetate radicals, possibly by the reaction

$$R\overset{O}{\overset{\|}{C}}O\dot{O} + O_2 \rightarrow R\overset{O}{\overset{\|}{C}}\dot{O} + O_3 \qquad \text{(III-84)}$$

If this is the case, the formula to be expected for compound X would be that of structure II or IV, an acyl nitrite or nitrate, formed by the reaction

$$R\overset{O}{\overset{\|}{C}}\dot{O} + NO \quad \text{or} \quad NO_2 \rightarrow R\overset{O}{\overset{\|}{C}}ONO \quad \text{or} \quad R\overset{O}{\overset{\|}{C}}ONO_2 \qquad \text{(III-85)}$$

To account for the formation of an acyl nitrite or nitrate by the silver nitrite–peracetic acid reaction, Hanst and Calvert postulated that the silver nitrite dissolves in the peracetic solution to yield nitrous acid, which rapidly decomposes into $NO + NO_2$. These oxides then react with acetate radicals from the thermally decomposing peracetic acid, the possible products being

$$CH_3\overset{O}{\overset{\|}{C}}\dot{O} + NO \rightarrow CH_3\overset{O}{\overset{\|}{C}}ONO \cdot \qquad \text{(III-86)}$$

$$CH_3\overset{O}{\overset{\|}{C}}\dot{O} + NO_2 \rightarrow CH_3\overset{O}{\overset{\|}{C}}OONO \qquad \text{(III-87)}$$

$$CH_3\overset{O}{\overset{\|}{C}}\dot{O} + NO_2 \rightarrow CH_3\overset{O}{\overset{\|}{C}}ONO_2 \qquad \text{(III-88)}$$

The ultraviolet absorption spectrum of acetyl compound X in pentane solution was compared by Scott, Stephens, Hanst, and Doerr with that of ethyl nitrite and *n*-butyl nitrate. The results showed that the absorption of compound X more nearly resembles that of the alkyl nitrates than it does the nitrites. In agreement with this, the photolysis of compound X in air, produced by sunlight or artificial radiation approaching sunlight, has been observed to be much slower than that of the nitrites.

In 1959 Pimentel [330] reported the formation of an unstable dimer, an isomer of nitrogen tetroxide, when nitrogen dioxide is diffused through solid nitrogen under conditions which permit aggregation. The dimer showed infrared absorption at 5.4, 6.1, 7.7, and 12.9 μ. Three of these absorption bands are strikingly similar to those of compound X, suggesting a similarity in structure. The dimer structure might be either ONOOONO, corresponding to acyl pernitrite, or ONONO$_2$, corresponding to an acyl nitrate.

These observations led Schuck and Doyle[377] to synthesize acetyl nitrate by the reaction of acetic anhydride with nitrogen pentoxide.[84]

$$CH_3\overset{\overset{O}{\|}}{C}O\overset{\overset{O}{\|}}{C}CH_3 + N_2O_5 \rightarrow 2CH_3\overset{\overset{O}{\|}}{C}ONO_2 \qquad \text{(III-89)}$$

The product showed an infrared spectrum which at least superficially resembled that of the compound X generated by the nitrogen dioxide–olefin photolyses in air, and it also showed about the same photolysis rate on irradiation. On the basis of these resemblances, Schuck and Doyle suggested that compound X is composed of acyl nitrates, or structure IV of those proposed by Stephens, Scott, Hanst, and Doerr.

In the meantime, Stephens and his co-workers[401] had succeeded in isolating one member of the compound X series in pure form. To accomplish this, the compound X was synthesized by irradiating mixtures of about 1000 ppm of 2-butene and 220 ppm of nitrogen dioxide in air, using a flow reactor with a residence time of about 30 min. The effluent was condensed at dry-ice temperature, and the condensate, after re-evaporation, passed at room temperature through a 4 ft chromatographic column packed with C-22 firebrick coated with 20% of polyethylene glycol (Carbowax 600), using helium as the carrier gas. The stream of gas emerging from the column was split, so that about 10% passed through a thermal conductivity detector and the balance through a trap which, when the detector showed compound X to be emerging, was chilled in dry ice–acetone. The other major components of the photochemical condensate, acetaldehyde and methyl nitrate, emerged from the column ahead of the compound X, which showed an elution time of 40–60 min. This procedure yielded about 30 mg of product, which could be passed through the column a second and third time without appreciable change.

The purified material so obtained was a colorless liquid with a vapor

pressure of about 10 mm at room temperature. At parts per million concentrations in air, it was both an eye irritant and a phytotoxicant, producing one type of underleaf "smog oxidant" damage. It was highly explosive and required extreme care in handling, both as vapor and liquid.
On the other hand, vapor samples, when left undisturbed at room temperature showed no appreciable decomposition over periods of many
hours, but did decompose slowly at around 50°C. During this decomposition the major infrared peaks all decreased by the same proportionate
amount, indicating that the purified material was a single compound.

The mass spectrum of this compound, labeled PAN by Stephens and
his co-workers, showed major peaks at mass/charge ratios of 46, 43, 30,
and 15, corresponding respectively to NO_2^+, CH_3CO^+, NO^+, and CH_3^+.
No peaks greater than 46 could be detected. Two experiments in which
samples of PAN vapor were treated with 2% KI solution showed the
oxidation of approximately one mole of iodide ion per mole of vapor.

The infrared spectrum of PAN, and the absorption coefficients for the
major peaks, obtained by Stephens, are shown in Fig. 26 and Table 31.

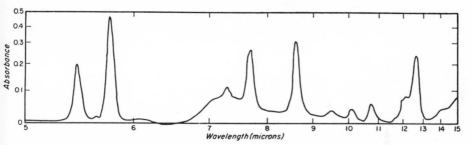

FIG. 26. Infrared absorption spectrum of PAN. From Stephens *et al.* (Ref. 401).

These are in good agreement with the spectra of the compound X obtained earlier from biacetyl and nitrogen dioxide, indicating that the
two materials were identical.

A comparison of the infrared spectra of PAN and the acetyl nitrate
(containing also acetic acid) prepared by Schuck and Doyle (Fig. 27)
shows definitely that they are not the same compound. While the peaks
at 5.75 and 8.6 μ are the same, the PAN peak at 5.44 μ falls at over 5.5 μ
in the spectrum of acetyl nitrate, the 7.7 μ peak of PAN is almost absent
for acetyl nitrate, the 12.6 μ peak shows different shape and structure,
and acetyl nitrate shows a peak at 13.9 μ which is absent in the PAN
spectrum. In addition, Stephens found other differences between the two
compounds. Thus, acetyl nitrate is hydrolyzed almost instantly by liquid
water and fumes in moist air, while PAN persists as a separate phase in

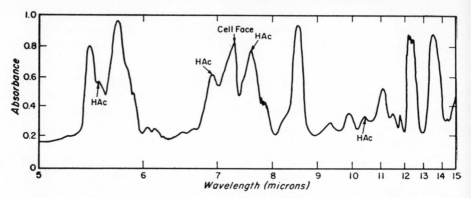

FIG. 27. Infrared absorption spectrum of acetyl nitrate. From Stephens *et al.* (Ref. 401).

contact with water and does not fume in air. The vapor pressure of acetyl nitrate was higher than that of PAN, and it did not emerge from the chromatographic column under the conditions used to purify PAN.

While acetyl nitrate thus may be ruled out as the structure of PAN, a new structure is suggested by the products of its slow thermal decomposition. These were found by Stephens and co-workers to consist chiefly

TABLE 31

INFRARED ABSORPTION COEFFICIENTS OF PAN

Wavelength (μ)	α (mm Hg^{-1} m^{-1})
5.44	0.62
5.76	1.45
7.68	0.78
8.60	0.89
12.61	0.70

of methyl nitrate and carbon dioxide. Small amounts of nitromethane, corresponding to 5 to 10% of the methyl nitrate, were also produced, but no carbon monoxide or other products could be detected. Formation of methyl nitrate and carbon dioxide in stoichiometric yield would indicate that the original molecule contained five oxygen atoms, whereas none of the proposed structures contain more than four. This has led Stephens *et al.*,[401] to propose that PAN may be peroxyacetyl nitrate, with the structure

$$\text{CH}_3\overset{\displaystyle O}{\overset{\|}{\text{C}}}\text{OONO}_2$$

VI

This structure, which might also be called acetyl pernitrate or nitro-peracetate, is consistent with the ultraviolet absorption spectrum of PAN (Fig. 28), and its formation during the photolysis of mixtures of biacetyl and nitrogen dioxide in air is readily explained by the combination of peroxyacetyl radicals with NO_2. Less readily explained is its formation, and particularly its exclusive formation among the possible acyl-nitrogen structures, during the photolysis of ethyl nitrite in air or by the reaction of peracetic acid with silver nitrite (III-83). Several attempts to obtain the empirical formula of PAN by conventional microanalysis have failed owing to explosion of the samples before they could be weighed, and a definitive answer to the question of its structure remains for the future.

The ultraviolet absorbance of PAN in a 10-cm layer at 10 mm pressure was found by Stephens to be virtually immeasurable above about 3000 A. Absorption coefficients estimated from his data are compared in Fig. 28

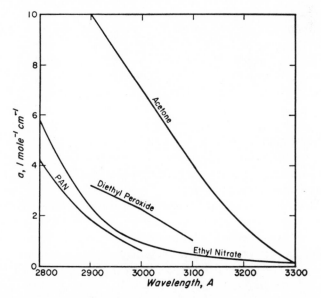

FIG. 28. Ultraviolet absorption coefficients of PAN compared to those of ethyl nitrate, diethyl peroxide, and acetone.

with those reported earlier in this chapter for ethyl nitrate, diethyl peroxide, and acetone. The experimental uncertainties in all of the values shown are such that except in the case of acetone little importance should be attached to the apparent differences. Stephens' measurements indicate that the absorption rate of PAN for solar radiation will be even less than that of ethyl nitrate (Table 21) and hence that its photolysis rate at the concentrations it might attain in polluted air will be very small. Thus at $z = 45°$ the indicated value of k_a is $< 5 \times 10^{-3}$ hr^{-1}; the corresponding photolysis rate with a primary yield of unity and a concentration of 10 pphm would be less than 0.05 pphm hr^{-1}.

It is not impossible that several acyl-nitrogen structures may be formed in varying amounts during the nitric oxide–nitrogen dioxide organic photolyses in polluted air. For example, both acylate and peroxyacyl radicals may be formed during these photolyses, and the possible combinations of these radicals with nitric oxide and nitrogen dioxide yield the four structures which have been discussed; acyl nitrite, nitrate, pernitrite, and pernitrate.

For each of these structures a homologous series of varying reactivity is possible. The acyl nitrates and pernitrates, if formed and if thermally stable in air, would absorb so weakly and be photolyzed so slowly that they would be expected to build up in concentration and appear among the observed products. The absence of any appreciable amount of compound X among the products of the nitrogen dioxide–ethylene photolysis in air suggests that the formyl members of these two series are either not stable or are not formed. The evidence which has been discussed indicates that the acetyl members are stable enough to exist for some time in air and that at least one, acetyl pernitrate, is formed. The acyl nitrites and pernitrites, even if formed and thermally stable in air, would be expected to absorb so strongly and be photolyzed so rapidly that, like the alkyl nitrites, they would have no opportunity to build up a large concentration and hence would act chiefly as reaction intermediates. In this manner, these compounds might play a considerable part in the over-all photochemical reactions which occur.

There is no evidence on the nature of the primary photochemical processes which might take place with the acyl nitrites and pernitrites, and for each structure several photodissociation processes, as well as primary rearrangements, are possible. For instance, acyl nitrites might dissociate at the O—N or C—O bond to yield a radical plus NO or NO$_2$, they might undergo a ketone-like dissociation at the R—C bond, or they might rearrange in a manner resembling that postulated for the alkyl nitrites:

$$\begin{array}{ll} R\overset{\text{O}}{\overset{\|}{\text{C}}}\dot{\text{O}} + \text{NO} & \text{A} \\ R\dot{\text{C}}\text{O} + \text{NO}_2 & \text{B} \\ \dot{\text{R}} + \cdot \overset{\text{O}}{\overset{\|}{\text{C}}}\text{ONO} & \text{C} \\ \text{CO}_2 + \text{RNO} & \text{D} \end{array}$$

$$R\overset{\text{O}}{\overset{\|}{\text{C}}}\text{ONO} + h\nu \qquad \text{(III-90)}$$

For the acyl pernitrites the corresponding processes would be

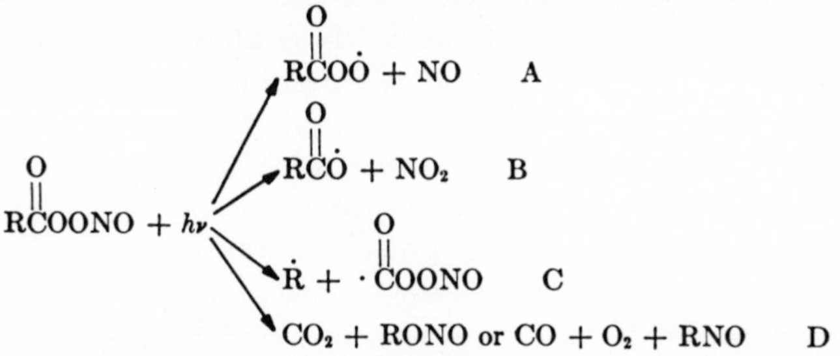

$$
RCOONO + h\nu
\begin{cases}
RCOO\cdot + NO & \text{A} \\
RC\dot{O} + NO_2 & \text{B} \\
\dot{R} + \cdot COONO & \text{C} \\
CO_2 + RONO \text{ or } CO + O_2 + RNO & \text{D}
\end{cases}
\qquad (III\text{-}91)
$$

These processes are wholly speculative, and while some are intuitively more acceptable than others, nothing definite may be said at this time regarding their relative probability. Several of the processes indicated might be followed by a rapid breakup of the complex radical into a simpler radical and a stable molecule. For example, the acetate radical appears to decompose rapidly into methyl radicals and carbon dioxide, and the benzoate radical into phenyl radicals and carbon dioxide.[116,236,350,442] Such a breakup would be favored if the radical produced by the initial photodissociation contains excess internal energy. Thus if one of the initial steps in the acyl nitrite photolysis were (III-90A), and this were followed by rapid breakup of the hot acylate radical, the effective dissociation process might be, at least in part

$$
RCONO + h\nu \rightarrow \dot{R} + CO_2 + NO \qquad (III\text{-}92)
$$

A primary split by (III-90C), followed by breakup of the

$$
\cdot CONO
$$

radical, could also lead to (III-92) as the effective dissociation process

For the acyl pernitrites a similar breakup, either of the acylate radical formed in (III-91B) or of the complex radical in (III-91C), would lead to

$$
RCOONO + h\nu \rightarrow \dot{R} + CO_2 + NO_2 \qquad (III\text{-}93)
$$

as an effective dissociation process.

The formyl compounds

$$
HCONO \quad \text{and} \quad HCOONO
$$

if produced in the air, would probably be photolyzed in a manner similar to the acyl compounds. In this case, if the effective dissociation process resembles (III-92) or (III-93), hydrogen atoms will be produced.

As with the alkyl nitrites, if any of these photolyses serve a promotional function in photochemical smog formation, the reaction involved will probably be the conversion of nitric oxide to nitrogen dioxide or the formation of radicals which lead to an oxidation chain. A primary dissociation which simply reverses the process of formation serves no promotional function. On this basis process A in reactions (III-90) and (III-91) is not promotional unless the radicals formed contain excitation energy which causes them to undergo new reactions. Possibilities here would be a radical breakup or a rapid reaction of the hot radical with oxygen, as by (III-84). The other dissociations are probably promotional in all cases, while any promotional effects of a primary rearrangement would depend on the nature and reactions of the molecules formed. This is an uninvestigated field.

12. REACTIONS FOLLOWING ABSORPTION BY PARTICULATE MATTER

It has been known for some time that finely divided zinc oxide,[23-25,113,160] and titanium dioxide[242,440,441] are capable of acting as photosensitizers for a number of chemical reactions. For instance, on exposure to ultraviolet radiation of zinc oxide surfaces in contact with oxygen, water, and an organic compound (sodium formate, potassium oxalate, phenol, toluene, acetanilide), the organic compound is oxidized and hydrogen peroxide is formed.

Several quantitative studies of these reactions[280,367,428,432] indicate an electronic mechanism similar to that originally proposed by Baur and Neuwiler,[24] in which the initial effect of light absorption is the displacement of electrons from certain sites in the crystal lattice of the metal oxide:

$$ZnO + h\nu \rightarrow (ZnO)^+ + e^- \tag{III-94}$$

The organic compound present is oxidized at the electron-deficient site, and the mobile electrons reduce either oxygen or water, with formation of hydrogen peroxide.

Calvert and his colleagues[73] have shown by use of O^{18} as a tracer that all the oxygen in the hydrogen peroxide comes from the molecular oxygen present. This favors, as the primary reduction process, the reaction

$$O_2 \text{ (ads)} + e^- \rightarrow O_2^- \text{ (ads)} \tag{III-95}$$

Supporting this, rather than the reduction of water, as the primary process are the facts that molecular oxygen apparently easily captures electrons ($O_2 + e^- \rightarrow O_2^- + 15.8$ kcal mole^{-1} in the gas phase),[118] oxygen quenches the fluorescence of zinc oxide but water does not,[146] and in the absence of oxygen no hydrogen is produced.[73] The primary oxidation process is not known; it will probably vary with the organic compound present. Several possible secondary reactions have been discussed by Calvert.[68]

With zinc oxide–water–sodium formate systems, a reaction is produced at all wavelengths from slightly above 4000 A to below 2500 A. The quantum yield of H_2O_2 formation at 3130 A, with zinc oxide suspended in water saturated with oxygen, sodium formate at 0.1 to 0.6 M, and hydrogen peroxide concentrations below 10^{-3} M, was found by Rubin, Calvert, Rankin, and MacNevin[367] to be nearly 0.5. Since the reduction of one molecule of oxygen to hydrogen peroxide requires two electrons, this indicates that under the above experimental conditions the primary quantum yield of reaction (III-95) was nearly unity.

Photosensitized surface reactions of similar nature have been observed with a number of other metallic oxides and sulfides, chiefly those of the transition elements.[68] These solids absorb very strongly in the solar ultraviolet and usually show photoconductivity in the same wavelength region which produces photosensitization. In most cases it appears that the mechanism consists of the formation of photoconduction electrons by light absorption in the solid, followed by electron transfer processes involving material adsorbed on the surface.

The particulate material in urban atmospheres has been found to contain appreciable quantities of at least two metals, lead and iron. For instance, over the period August–November 1954 the range of daily averages, with samples collected over 24-hr periods, in the Los Angeles atmosphere was 1.7 to 16.4 μg m^{-3} for lead and 1.3 to 22.0 μg m^{-3} for iron.[351] The lead content is of particular interest, as both PbO and Pb_3O_4 act as photosensitizers, while Fe_2O_3 shows little or no such effect. The chemical nature of the lead-containing particulate matter is not known; its chief source is probably automobile exhaust and it may enter the air either as oxide, halide, oxyhalide, or oxysulfate.[68]

An upper limit to the absorption rate by particulate matter in the atmosphere is set by the amount of radiation it intercepts. For spherical particles of density ρ in g cm^{-3} and radius r in microns, at concentrations c in μg m^{-3}, the average fraction of the incident radiation intercepted per centimeter of path length will be 7.5×10^{-9} $c/r\rho$ cm^{-1}. The number of photons intercepted per cubic centimeter per second may be obtained by multiplying this fraction by the sum of the values of J_λ (Table 8) over the photochemically effective region.

As an illustration, for particles of density 10, radius 0.25 μ and concentration 10 μg m^{-3}, 3×10^{-8} of the incident radiation will be intercepted per centimeter of light path. At $z = 45°$, over the solar ultraviolet

3000–4000 A, the number of photons intercepted will be about 4×10^8 cm^{-3} sec^{-1}. The equivalent gaseous absorption rate for this number of photons is about 6 pphm hr^{-1}. The actual absorptoin rate by the lead containing particulate matter in urban air may vary in either direction from this, depending on its particle size and density, on the wavelength range absorbed, and on its absorption coefficients over that range. The figure does suggest, however, that a significant absorption rate is possible.

No photosensitized surface reactions have been demonstrated, either in urban air itself or in laboratory experiments on photochemical smog formation. On the contrary, the irradiation of nitrogen dioxide–olefin mixtures in air produces the symptoms of oxidant formation, eye irritation, and plant damage in the almost complete absence of particulate matter. Addition of sulfur dioxide to such systems leads to the rapid formation of particulates, but apparently with no positive effect on the other symptoms and again without benefit of metal-containing particles. The mechanism of particulate formation in this instance will be discussed in Chapter IX; it is undoubtedly photochemical in nature but there is no evidence that light absorption by the particles themselves has any part in the process. Finally it should be noted that the wavelength variation in attenuation coefficient of solar radiation (Fig. 15) indicates relatively little absorption, compared to the amount of diffusion, by the particulate matter in photochemical smog.

We must conclude that while the rates of interception of radiation are sufficient to permit significant rates, there is no direct evidence that photoactivated surface reactions, or reactions of any other sort involving absorption by particulate matter, take any important part in photochemical smog formation.

13. Other Absorbers

In addition to the classes of compounds we have discussed, the possibility of the presence in polluted air of still other substances which might absorb solar radiation must be considered. Among such substances are free radicals, unstable molecules such as nitroxyl and nitrogen trioxide, and a large number of organic compounds, including ozonides, epoxides, dienes, nitroso compounds, peroxidic compounds, benzpyrene, and related substances. The existence of these compounds at significant concentrations in polluted air is for the most part a matter of surmise, and with a few exceptions, their absorption coefficients are unknown and their photochemistry little explored. More information is required, therefore, before the photochemical contribution of any of these substances to smog formation may be assessed.

14. SUMMARY

The specific absorption rates which have been estimated in this chapter are compared in Fig. 29. Particularly noteworthy in this comparison are the commanding position of nitrogen dioxide, the great difference between ethyl nitrite and nitrate, the differences between carbonyl compounds, from biacetyl to acetone, and the approximate location of PAN on the scale.

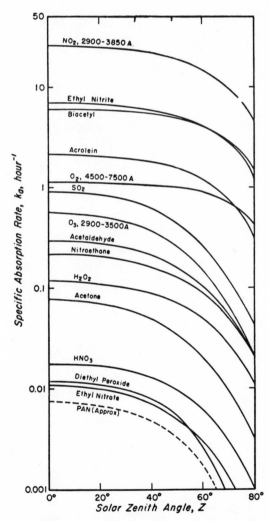

FIG. 29. Summary of specific absorption rates.

TABLE 32

SUMMARY OF PHOTOCHEMICAL PRIMARY PROCESSES IN URBAN AIR

Absorber	Primary photochemical process in air	k_a at $z = 45°$ (hr^{-1})	Probable primary yield ϕ	Estimated rate at $z = 45°$ and unit conc. (pphm hr^{-1})
NO$_2$	NO$_2'$ → NO + O(^3P)	21	0.9 to 1.0	~20
O$_3$ 4500–7500 A	O$_3'$ → O$_2$ + O(^3P)	1	1	1
O$_3$ 2900–3500 A	O$_3'$ → O$_2$ + O(^1D)	0.3	1	0.3
SO$_2$	Probably SO$_2'$ + O$_2$ → SO$_4'$ (see Chapter IX)	0.5	<1, possibly <10^{-2}	<0.5, possibly <0.005
Alkyl nitrites	RCH$_2$ONO' → RCH$_2$Ȯ + NO ; → RCHO + HNO	5.5	Not known, may be <1	≦5.5
Acyl and peroxyacyl nitrites	Not known (see text)	Not known	Not known	Not known
Nitroalkanes	Same as alkyl nitrites	0.15	Probably <1	≦0.15
Alkyl nitrates	RONO$_2'$ → RȮ + NO$_2$	0.006	1	0.006
Diketones (glyoxal, biacetyl)	(RCO)$_2'$ → 2RĊO ; → R$_2$CO + CO	5	0 to ~0.01	0 to 0.05
	(RCO)$_2'$ + X → ?		Not known	Not known
Olefinic aldehydes (acrolein, crotonaldehyde)	RCH = CHCHO' + O$_2$ → ?	~1.5	~0.1	~0.15

Formaldehyde	$HCHO' \nearrow^{H + H\dot{C}O}_{\searrow_?} H_2 + CO$	~0.5	~0.4	~0.2
Aliphatic aldehydes	$RCHO' \rightarrow \dot{R} + H\dot{C}O$	0.2	0.2 to 0.7	0.04 to 0.14
Aliphatic ketones	$RR\dot{C}O' \rightarrow \dot{R} + R\dot{C}O$	0.04	~0.7	~0.03
Nitrous acid	$HONO' \nearrow^{\dot{O}H + NO}_{?} \searrow_? H + NO_2$	Not known	Not known	Not known
Nitric acid	$HONO_2' \rightarrow \dot{O}H + NO_2$	~0.01	Not known	≤0.01
Hydrogen peroxide	$H_2O_2' \rightarrow 2\,\dot{O}H$	0.08	1	0.08
Organic peroxides and hydroperoxides	$ROOR' \rightarrow R\dot{O} + \dot{O}R$	<0.01	1	<0.01

The primary processes resulting from these absorptions are summarized in Table 32. Perhaps the most striking feature of this summary is the number of uncertainties and unknowns, which await further investigation. To these unknowns must be added the photolyses of speculative compounds, such as acyl nitrites and pernitrites, of unstable intermediates such as free radicals or nitroxyl, and of the minor organic constituents which may be present in the air. It will be noted that several of the products listed in Table 32 are formed by more than one reaction. Thus, oxygen atoms are a product of both the nitrogen dioxide and ozone photolyses, alkoxyl radicals a product of the nitrite, nitrate, and peroxide photolyses, and so on. It is illuminating, therefore, to consider the primary photochemical processes in polluted air in terms of products rather than absorbers. This is done in Table 33.

The speculative absorbers, such as the acyl and peroxyacyl nitrites, and the absorbers for which the primary processes are unknown, such as nitrous acid, have not been included in Table 33; the photolyses of some of these absorbers may substantially contribute to the rates of formation of some of the products listed in the table. Thus, the absorption rates of the acyl and peroxyacyl nitrites are probably comparable with those of the alkyl nitrites ($k_a > 5$ hr^{-1} at $z = 45°$), and their photolysis products might include nitrogen dioxide and alkyl or acyl radicals, as well as some products not listed in Table 33, such as acylate radicals or nitroso alkanes.

During periods of photochemical smog formation, as represented by the morning hours of smoggy days in the Los Angeles basin, the concentrations of known absorbers show wide variations. Typical concentrations for such periods are 5 to 30 pphm of nitrogen dioxide, ozone, aldehydes, and sulfur dioxide. Other absorber concentrations during these periods are uncertain; probably those of the ketones, nitric acid, the alkyl nitrates, and the acyl nitrates are generally below 10 pphm, while the concentrations of peroxides, nitrous acid, the alkyl nitrites, and the speculative absorbers such as acyl nitrites and pernitrites are probably of the order of 1 pphm or lower.

At these absorber concentrations, during the midmorning hours in sunlight, the rates of primary photochemical production of oxygen atoms and nitric oxide will each be in the range of 100 to 500 or more pphm hr^{-1}, the rates of primary formation of nitrogen dioxide, of alkyl, alkoxyl, formyl, and acyl radicals, of hydrogen atoms, aldehydes, and possibly of nitroxyl will be of the order of 1 to 10 pphm hr^{-1}, while that of hydroxyl radicals and of SO_4 will probably be below ~1 pphm hr^{-1}. Barring the possibility that unknown photochemical primary processes

TABLE 33

PRODUCTS OF PHOTOCHEMICAL PRIMARY PROCESSES IN URBAN AIR

Product		Absorber possibly forming the product	Estimated rate of formation at $z = 45°$ and unit absorber conc. (pphm hr^{-1})
Name	Formula		
Oxygen atoms	O	NO_2	~20
		O_3	1.3
Nitric oxide	NO	NO_2	~20
		Alkyl nitrites	≤ 5
		Nitroalkanes	≤ 0.15
Nitrogen dioxide	NO_2	Nitric acid	≤ 0.01
		Alkyl nitrates	0.006
Alkyl radicals	$\dot{R}$	Aldehydes	0.04 to 0.14
		Ketones	0.03
Alkoxyl radicals	$R\dot{O}$	Alkyl nitrites	≤ 5
		Alkyl nitrates	0.006
		Nitroalkanes	≤ 0.15
		Organic peroxides	< 0.01
Formyl radicals	$H\dot{C}O$	Formaldehyde	~0.2
		Aliphatic aldehydes	0.04 to 0.14
Acyl radicals	$R\dot{C}O$	Diketones	0 to 0.1
		Ketones	~0.03
Hydroxyl radicals	$\dot{O}H$	Hydrogen peroxide	0.06
		Hydroperoxides	< 0.01
		Nitric acid	≤ 0.01
Hydrogen atoms	H	Formaldehyde	~0.2
Aldehydes	RCHO	Alkyl nitrites	≤ 5.5
		Nitroalkanes	≤ 0.15
Nitroxyl	HNO	Alkyl nitrites	≤ 5.5
		Nitroalkanes	≤ 0.15
	SO_4	SO_2	< 0.5, possibly < 0.005

occur at a significant rate, the foregoing are the primary products (with approximate rates of their formation) which are responsible for photochemical smog formation.

Chapter IV

The Kinetics of Photochemical
Secondary Reactions in Air

In the preceding chapters the problems of solar radiation and its absorption in the lower atmosphere, and of the photochemical primary processes which result from that absorption, have been examined. These primary processes will be followed by secondary reactions and it will be the objective of most of the remaining chapters to review and correlate existing information which has a bearing on such secondary reactions.

1. APPLICABILITY OF LABORATORY DATA

Most of the information which will be found applicable to this problem has come from experimental laboratory studies, carried out under conditions quite different from those in the atmosphere. In particular, polluted urban air presents an environment which is far more complex, with a far greater range of reactants and concentrations, than is normally encountered in, or considered profitable for, laboratory investigation. While the differences in conditions and environment must be taken into account, there is no reason to suppose that there is any microscopic difference in character between the individual elementary reactions which occur in a laboratory reaction vessel and those which occur in urban air. The same kinetic behavior and the same elementary rate constants will apply, and the terminology and methods of treatment of data which have been found useful in the one case will also be found useful in the other.

2. RATE CONSTANTS AND UNITS

The kinetic laws, theories, and methods which will be found useful in considering photochemical secondary reactions in polluted air are for the most part elementary and will be reviewed here only with respect to special points which will arise in their application.

The majority of photochemical secondary reactions are elementary bimolecular processes. Such a process, and its rate law, may be represented by

$$A + B \rightarrow C + D \qquad \frac{-d\,(A)}{dt} = \frac{+d\,(C)}{dt} = S_1 = k_1\,(A)(B) \qquad \text{(IV-1)}$$

In laboratory studies of reactions it is customary to express concentrations in terms of moles liter^{-1} or moles cc^{-1}, and time in seconds. In studies of polluted air it has become customary to express concentrations in terms of parts per million (ppm), or better, parts per hundred million (pphm), generally referred to air at 1 atmosphere pressure and 25°C, while reaction times may conveniently be expressed in terms of minutes or hours. In the former case the dimensions of the bimolecular rate constant k_1 will be 1 mole^{-1} sec^{-1} or cc mole^{-1} sec^{-1}, while in the latter case its dimensions will be pphm^{-1} min^{-1} or pphm^{-1} hr^{-1}. In similar fashion, the dimensions of a termolecular rate constant will be liter^2 mole^{-2} sec^{-1}, cc^2 mole^{-2} sec^{-1}, pphm^{-2} min^{-1}, or pphm^{-2} hr^{-1}. The conversion factors, assuming the perfect gas laws, for ppm or pphm relative to air at 1 atm 25°C, are given in Table 34.

TABLE 34

CONVERSION FACTORS
(Based on concentration in ppm and pphm relative
to air at 1 atm, 25°C.)

Concentrations

moles l^{-1} × 2.445 × 10^9 = pphm
moles cc^{-1} × 2.445 × 10^{12} = pphm
pphm × 4.09 × 10^{-10} = moles l^{-1}
pphm × 4.09 × 10^{-13} = moles cc^{-1}

Rate constants, k

Bimolecular

1 mole^{-1} sec^{-1} × 2.45 × 10^{-6} = ppm^{-1} min^{-1}
cc mole^{-1} sec^{-1} × 2.45 × 10^{-9} = ppm^{-1} min^{-1}
1 mole^{-1} sec^{-1} × 1.47 × 10^{-6} = pphm^{-1} hr^{-1}
cc mole^{-1} sec^{-1} × 1.47 × 10^{-9} = pphm^{-1} hr^{-1}

Termolecular

l^2 mole^{-2} sec^{-1} × 1.005 × 10^{-13} = ppm^{-2} min^{-1}
cc^2 mole^{-2} sec^{-1} × 1.005 × 10^{-19} = ppm^{-2} min^{-1}
l^2 mole^{-2} sec^{-1} × 6.03 × 10^{-16} = pphm^{-2} hr^{-1}
cc^2 mole^{-2} sec^{-1} × 6.03 × 10^{-22} = pphm^{-2} hr^{-1}

3. EXTRAPOLATION OF RATE CONSTANT DATA

In some cases the rate constants of reactions which may be of importance in smog formation have been determined at temperatures and pressures quite different from those of urban air, and it is necessary in employing these data to extrapolate from the laboratory conditions. For most elementary processes the rate constant over a limited temperature range is given to a good approximation, and is most conveniently expressed, by the integrated form of the Arrhenius equation

$$k = Ae^{-(Q/RT)} \qquad \text{(IV-2)}$$

Ordinarily, the pre-exponential factor A and the activation energy Q are assumed to be temperature independent, but actually both may vary with temperature. Over a limited experimental temperature range these variations are usually slight and no important error is introduced by neglecting them. But when it becomes necessary to extrapolate beyond this range, the error introduced by assuming A and Q to be temperature independent may be substantial.

Another source of uncertainty in using the Arrhenius equation for temperature extrapolations lies in the fact that when the experimental temperature range is small the statistical uncertainty in the combination of values of A and Q which serves to best fit the data may be quite large. An error in A or Q alone will have the same proportionate effect on k at all temperatures, but an error in A, compensated by an error in Q such as to give the correct value of k at the mid-point of the experimental temperature range, will result in increasing errors in k with increasing departure from this temperature.

Laboratory studies of reaction rates are often conducted at reactant partial pressures, with the exception of free atoms and radicals, in the range of 1 mm to 1 atm. The partial pressures of the pollutants which may serve as reactants in urban atmospheres are commonly of the order of 10 pphm, or $\sim 7 \times 10^{-5}$mm. The application of laboratory data to pollutant reactions may therefore involve extrapolation over a concentration range of four to seven orders of magnitude. The concentrations of the free radicals and atoms involved in photochemical reactions in polluted air may also differ by several orders of magnitude from those existing in laboratory studies. Extrapolation over such ranges should be valid if the reaction in question is elementary, but may not be valid if it is complex. In a few instances rate constants have been obtained both in the "laboratory" concentration range of 1 mm or higher and in the "pollutant" range of $\sim$10 pphm; these will be discussed later.

4. Frequency Factor and Collision Yields

By the simple collision theory the rate constant for a bimolecular reaction is given by

$$k = pZe^{-E/RT} \tag{IV-3}$$

where p is a probability or steric factor, Z a frequency factor based on the number of kinetic theory binary collisions between reactant molecules, and E the minimum relative kinetic energy which the two molecules must have to react on collision.

The frequency factor Z, sometimes called the kinetic theory collision constant, is proportional to the square root of the absolute temperature and for normal simple gas molecules at ordinary temperatures its value is of the order of 10^{14} to 10^{15} cc mole^{-1} sec^{-1}, or 10^{11} to 10^{12} liter mole^{-1} sec^{-1}. An order of magnitude figure for bimolecular reactions is $Z \approx 3 \times 10^{14}$ cc mole^{-1} sec$^{-1} \approx 3 \times 10^{11}$ liter mole^{-1} sec$^{-1} \approx 4 \times 10^{5}$ pphm^{-1} hr^{-1}.

Similarly, for termolecular reactions the frequency factor, based on the number of kinetic theory ternary collisions between reactant molecules, is $Z \approx 10^{16}$ cc^2 mole^{-2} sec$^{-1} \approx 10^{10}$ liter^2 mole^{-2} sec$^{-1} \approx 6 \times 10^{-6}$ pphm^{-2} hr^{-1}.

The collision frequency sets a hypothetical upper limit to the possible rate of any bimolecular or termolecular reaction. To achieve it, the steric factor must be unity and the activation energy zero; in other words, the reaction must occur at every kinetic theory binary or ternary collision between the reacting molecules.

For any reaction the ratio of the actual rate to the hypothetical upper limit for the rate may be expressed as the collision yield, y. From equation (IV-3),

$$y = \frac{k}{Z} = pe^{-E/RT} \tag{IV-4}$$

For reactions in which no special orientation is necessary, such as atomic recombinations, the value of the steric factor p may approach unity. For radical-molecule reactions, or for reactions between simple molecules, p may be $\sim 10^{-2}$ to 10^{-6}, while for reactions between complex molecules it may be as small as 10^{-7} to 10^{-10} (Ref. 398). In addition, at 25°C the collision yield will be reduced by one order of magnitude for each 1360 cal of activation energy.

In applying kinetic theory values of Z to the estimate of upper limits for reaction rates or collision yields, it must be remembered that these values are highly approximate. We will, for example, encounter instances of rate constants expressed in terms of the Arrhenius equation in which the pre-exponential factor A exceeds the kinetic theory value of Z by an order of magnitude or more. In such instances, it may be that the reaction is complex, it may be that the effective collision diameter for the reaction is greater than the kinetic theory diameter, or it may be that the process should more properly be considered in terms of a transition state theory which does not explicitly involve collisions.[314]

5. Third Body Reactions

When two particles combine or associate to form a single product, and the process is exothermic, a collision with a third body will sooner or later be required to stabilize the product by removal of part of the energy released. Denoting the third body by M, a process of this type may be represented by the equation

$$A + B + M \rightarrow C + M \tag{IV-5}$$

At atmospheric pressures, the rate law for the reaction may or may not reflect the requirement of a third body. To illustrate, the process may be divided into two steps; the meeting of the two particles which are to combine and the stabilization of the product by a third particle:

$$A + B \underset{2}{\overset{1}{\rightleftharpoons}} C^* \qquad S_1 = k_1(A)(B), \quad S_2 = k_2(C^*) \tag{IV-6}$$

$$C^* + M \overset{3}{\rightarrow} C + M \qquad S_3 = k_3(C^*)(M) \tag{IV-7}$$

Assuming a stationary state with regard to C^* gives

$$S_1 = S_2 + S_3 \quad \text{or} \quad k_1(A)(B) = k_2(C^*) + k_3(C^*)(M) \tag{IV-8}$$

from which

$$(C^*) = \frac{k_1(A)(B)}{k_2 + k_3(M)} \tag{IV-9}$$

Substituting this in the rate equation for reaction (IV-7) gives for the rate of formation of the stable product C

$$\frac{+d(C)}{dt} = S_3 = \frac{k_1 k_3(A)(B)(M)}{k_2 + k_3(M)} \tag{IV-10}$$

By this equation, if k_2 is large compared to $k_3(M)$ the reaction will be first order with respect to each of the three reactants, or third order altogether. If k_2 is small compared to $k_3(M)$, the rate becomes second order and independent of the concentration of the third body, M. The kinetic importance of the third body thus depends on the natural life, $1/k_2$, of the unstabilized molecule C^*, on the rate constant, k_3, of the stabilization step, and on the concentration of M.

In air at atmospheric pressure and ordinary temperatures, the upper limit for the value of $k_3(M)$ will be $\sim 10^{10}$ sec^{-1}. For an atomic association, such as $H + H + M \rightarrow H_2 + M$, the life of the unstabilized complex formed by the collision of two atoms will scarcely be longer than one vibrational period, or $\sim 10^{-13}$ sec. In such a case the value of k_2 will be $\sim 10^{13}$ sec^{-1}, and as this is large compared to the upper limit for $k_3(M)$ in air, the rate equation for the reaction in air will be essentially third order and the upper limit to be expected for its rate constant will be $k_1 k_3/k_2 \approx 3 \times 10^{11} \times 3 \times 10^{11}/10^{13} \approx 10^{10}$ liter^2 mole^{-2} sec^{-1}, i.e., the limiting rate of a termolecular reaction. Rate constants approximating this figure have been observed for several atomic associations[79,341,399] while others, particularly the oxygen atom association,[114] fall short of the limiting rate.

In the association of radicals to form a polyatomic molecule in which a number of normal modes of vibration may interact to receive the association energy, the life of the association complex may be sufficiently large to make k_2 smaller than $k_3(M)$. The rate equation in this case will be essentially second order, the rate constant will approach k_1, and its upper limit will be that of a bimolecular reaction, $\sim 3 \times 10^{11}$ liter mole^{-1} sec^{-1}.

One of the most interesting characteristics of third body associations lies in their behavior with respect to temperature. In some cases it is found that the observed rate decreases with increasing temperature, and in such cases, expressing the observed rate constant in terms of the Arrhenius equation leads to an apparent negative activation energy. An explanation of this behavior is provided by equations (IV-6) and (IV-7). With increasing temperature, reactants A and B will collide with greater thermal energy, hence the unstabilized product C* will have greater internal energy. If the life of C* decreases (i.e., if k_2 increases) sufficiently with increasing internal energy, while k_3 remains little affected, the result will be to decrease the stationary concentration of C*, hence to decrease S_3 with increasing temperature. Atomic associations do not show this effect, probably because the life of the association complex is already only one vibrational period, hence it is not much affected by temperature.

6. STATIONARY STATES

When an intermediate, be it an unstabilized complex, a free atom or radical, or a stable molecule, is being formed by one set of reactions at the same rate at which it is being removed by another, the intermediate is said to be in a stationary state, and its concentration in this state is called the stationary concentration. By equating the rates of formation and removal, it is possible to obtain an over-all rate equation for the whole series of reactions, and when the rate constants are known it is possible to calculate the concentration of the intermediate. The application of this procedure in equations (IV-8), (IV-9), and (IV-10) of the preceding section is a good illustration of the method.

In view of its usefulness, it is appropriate to inquire into the extent to which the assumption of a stationary state is valid for reaction intermediates in polluted air. For this purpose, consider a simple case in which an intermediate B is formed by a photochemical primary process and removed by a secondary reaction which is first order with respect to the intermediate:

$$A + h\nu \xrightarrow{f} B + \ldots S_f = \phi I_a \qquad \text{(IV-11)}$$

$$B + C \xrightarrow{r} D + \ldots S_r = k_r(B)(C) \qquad \text{(IV-12)}$$

The rate of change in concentration of B will be equal to the difference between the rates of its formation and removal, or

$$\frac{d(B)}{dt} = S_f - S_r = \phi I_a - k_r(B)(C) \qquad \text{(IV-13)}$$

Integrating this equation over the limits $t = 0$ to $t = t$, with the assumption that ϕI_a and $k_r(C)$ remain constant and $(B) = 0$ at $t = 0$, gives

$$(B)_t = \frac{\phi I_a(1 - e^{-k_r(C)\cdot t})}{k_r(C)} \qquad \text{(IV-14)}$$

At the stationary state $S_f = S_r$, hence

$$(B)_s = \frac{\phi I_a}{k_r(C)} \qquad \text{(IV-15)}$$

Combining these two equations, the fraction F of the stationary concentration at time t, also the ratio of the rates of the removing and forming reactions at time t will be

$$F_t = \frac{(B)_t}{(B)_s} = \frac{S_{rt}}{S_f} = 1 - e^{-k_r(C)t} \qquad \text{(IV-16)}$$

The term $k_r(C)$ with (C) constant is the pseudounimolecular rate constant for the removal reaction and its reciprocal is the average life of B. If there are several forming and removing reactions, S_f and S_{rt} in equation (IV-16) become ΣS_f and ΣS_{rt}, and $k_r(C)$ becomes $\Sigma k_r(X)$; the sum of the pseudounimolecular rate constants for the removal processes.

If the removal process is second order with respect to the intermediate,

$$A + h\nu \xrightarrow{f} B + \dots S_f = \phi I_a \qquad \text{(IV-17)}$$

$$B + B \xrightarrow{r} D + \dots S_r = k_r(B)^2 \qquad \text{(IV-18)}$$

A similar derivation gives

$$F_t = \frac{1 - \exp(-2t\sqrt{S_f k_r})}{1 + \exp(-2t\sqrt{S_f k_r})} \qquad \text{(IV-19)}$$

At a true stationary state, or course, the value of F must be unity. By equations (IV-16) and (IV-19), as long as S_f, k_r, and (C) remain constant, F_t will approach unity asymtotically and will become unity only at infinite time. The time required for F to reach the value 0.99, hence for the concentration of the intermediate to reach 99% of its stationary value, will be $4.6/k_r(C)$ for the first-order removal, and $2.65/\sqrt{S_f k_r}$ for the second-order removal process. If S_f, k_r, and (C) are not constant the situation becomes much more complex, but, in general, while changes in these parameters are occurring F will approach a limiting value other than unity, and the more rapid these changes or the slower the rate at which F approaches the limit, the greater the departure of this limiting value from unity will be.

Similar conclusions apply to all cases involving the formation and removal of an intermediate. In any reaction system, therefore, the assumption of a stationary state with regard to an intermediate will be valid only if two requirements are satisfied. First, the time required for F to approach to within a negligible fraction of unity must be small compared to the total reaction time, and second, the effect on F of changes in the rates of the forming or removing reactions must be negligible.

In the atmosphere, changes in reaction rates may be brought about by changes in light intensity, pollutant concentrations, and temperature. The rate of change in light intensity with time of day under constant atmospheric conditions is predictable and is illustrated in Fig. 13. Around sunrise and sunset, the rate of change is very large, but during the middle of the day it is well below 1% per min. However, changing atmospheric conditions, both in and above the polluted layer, may lead to changes of ±5% per min or more in light intensity, even under a cloudless sky at midday.[395] As to pollutant concentrations, continuous recorder curves for oxidant and oxides of nitrogen in urban air show that during about 10% of the time between sunrise and sunset the rate of change in concentration is above ±2% per minute, and occasional sharp changes may exceed ±5% per min. Changes in reaction rates due to changes in air temperature will in general be smaller than those due to light intensity or concentration, and in fact are not likely to exceed ±0.5% per min.

In summary, changes of ±5% per min or more in the rates of photochemical secondary reactions in polluted air may be expected at any time of day. The greatest rates of change may be expected near sunrise and sunset, when light intensity is changing rapidly, and near sources of pollution, where concentrations and possibly temperatures are changing rapidly.

To illustrate the effect of such changes on stationary state conditions, Fig. 30 shows the limits between which the value of F will lie, and the rate at which these limits will be approached, for a case in which the removal process is first order with respect to the intermediate [equations (IV-11) to (IV-16)], with $1/k_r(C) = 1$ min, and in which the rate of the forming reaction may vary by ±5% per min. Bearing in mind the many uncertainties regarding reaction rates in polluted air, a departure of F from unity within the limits shown by the horizontal dashed lines in Fig. 30 will not in general be too important, and may be neglected. Moreover, the time required for F to approach to within a negligible fraction of these limits is small compared to the reaction times generally involved in polluted air. This case, therefore, may be judged to meet the requirements for a valid application of the method of stationary states. On the other hand, if the rate of the forming reaction should vary by

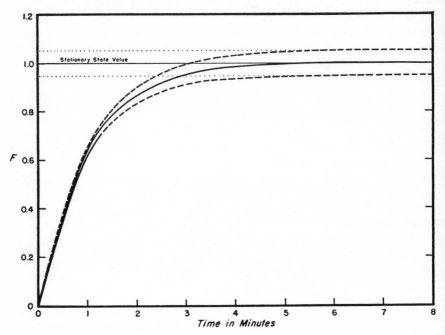

FIG. 30. Rate of approach to a stationary state. Solid line shows fraction F of stationary state concentration at time t starting from $F = 0$ at $t = 0$, if rate of forming reaction is constant and if removal of intermediate is first order with $k_r(C) = 1 \text{ min}^{-1}$. Dashed lines show limits within which F will lie if rate of forming reaction varies by $\pm 5\%$ during time $1/k_r(C)$.

much more than $\pm 5\%$ per min, or if $1/k_r(C)$ should be much longer than 1 min, the assumption of a stationary state would not be valid.

Similar considerations apply to other cases, and on the basis of these considerations the following may be stated as approximate working rules applicable to reaction intermediates in polluted air:

1. With the exceptions of times near sunrise and sunset, locations near sources of pollution, and other situations where rapid changes or short reaction times are involved, if $1/k_r(C)$ or its equivalent for the reaction concerned, or $1/\sqrt{S_f k_r}$, depending on whether the removal

process is first or second order with respect to the intermediate, is less than 1 min the assumption of a stationary state will in general be valid. If $1/k_r(C)$ or its equivalent, or $1/\sqrt{S_f k_r}$, is greater than 1 min, the assumption of a stationary state may not be valid and the case must be considered in detail.

2. For exceptional times and places, the assumption of a stationary state will be valid if both of the following are fulfilled:

a. That $1/k_r(C)$ or $1/\sqrt{S_f k_r}$, or their equivalents for the removal process concerned, are small compared with the reaction time involved.

b. Changes in reaction rates due to changes in light intensities, concentrations other than the concentration of the intermediate, or temperature, over an interval of time equal to $1/k_r(C)$ or $1/\sqrt{S_f k_r}$, are small.

7. ESTIMATES OF SIGNIFICANCE BASED ON RATE

Some of the secondary reactions which occur in polluted air will be important, and others will not. Of the criteria which determine the importance of a given reaction, one of the most incisive is its rate. With this in mind, whenever data are available the rate of each reaction will be calculated for reactant concentrations which are representative for polluted air. As a basis of reference, pollutant concentrations in urban air are for the most part in the range of 1 to 100 pphm, and quite commonly change at rates of 1 to 10 or more pphm per hr. Relative to these concentrations and observed rates of change, and with the exception of special cases such as reactions which initiate chains, it may be judged in general that if the calculated rate of a given reaction is below 1 pphm per hr it is not likely to be of major importance, and if it is below 0.1 pphm per hr it is probably insignificant.

8. REACTIONS TO BE CONSIDERED

A number of the substances listed as absorbers in Tables 32 and 33 undergo nonphotochemical or thermal reactions in addition to their primary photochemical reactions in the atmosphere. An example of this is the reaction of nitrogen dioxide with water vapor. Further, some of the primary products listed are also formed to some extent by thermal reactions or contributed by sources of pollution, and the reactions of these products will be, to this extent, independent of solar radiation. An example here is given by nitric oxide and its reaction with molecular oxygen. Still further, in some instances the primary products initiate a series of consecutive reactions, the final steps of which involve an entirely different set of substances. In this case an example is provided by the reaction of oxygen atoms with molecular oxygen to form ozone, which in turn reacts with olefin hydrocarbons.

In these instances, there is no sharp boundary between reactions which are distinctly "secondary photochemical," and reactions which are distinctly "nonphotochemical." All are thermal, and where a common reactant is involved all are mutually related, as simultaneous or consecutive reactions. For these reasons, all must be considered.

Chapter V

Reactions of Oxygen Atoms

1. THE PRODUCTION OF OXYGEN ATOMS IN POLLUTED AIR

Two, and only two, reactions in polluted urban atmospheres are known to lead to oxygen atoms. These are the primary photochemical dissociations of nitrogen dioxide and of ozone. The oxygen atoms produced by the nitrogen dioxide photodissociation and by the dissociation of ozone by visible radiation are in the normal or ^3P electronic state, while those produced by the dissociation of ozone by ultraviolet radiation are probably in the excited ^1D state.

From the absorption rates estimated in Chapter III, at concentrations of 10 pphm each of nitrogen dioxide and ozone, under normal radiation conditions at a solar zenith angle of $z = 45°$, the rate of production of ^3P oxygen atoms by these two reactions will be approximately 220 pphm hr^{-1}, and the upper limit to the rate of production of ^1D oxygen atoms will be about 3 pphm hr^{-1}. In other words, under these conditions nearly 99% of the oxygen atoms produced will be in the ^3P state. While these rates will of course vary with the solar radiation intensity and with the concentrations of nitrogen dioxide and ozone, on the basis of evidence now available it appears doubtful that any other radical or atom is produced at rates equalling or even approaching the rate of formation of ^3P oxygen atoms in urban atmospheres. In terms of rate of production, therefore, ^3P oxygen atoms unquestionably must be considered as one of the major if not the major molecular fragment resulting from photochemical primary processes in polluted air.

When written to include the initial act of absorption, the two primary processes yielding ^3P oxygen atoms are

$$NO_2 + h\nu \rightarrow NO + O \quad S_1 = \phi_1 I_{a_{NO_2}} = \phi_1 k_{a_1}(NO_2) \quad \text{(V-1)}$$

$$O_3 + h\nu_{vis} \rightarrow O_2 + O \quad S_2 = \phi_2 I_{a_{O_3}} = \phi_2 k_{a_2}(O_3) \quad \text{(V-2)}$$

Here S_1, S_2 are the rates of oxygen atom production, ϕ_1 and ϕ_2 the respective primary quantum yields, and $I_{a_{NO_2}}$, $I_{a_{O_3}}$, the rates of absorption. For weak absorption one may write to a good approximation $I_{a_{NO_2}} = k_{a_1}(NO_2)$ and $I_{a_{O_3}} = k_{a_2}(O_3)$, where k_{a_1} and k_{a_2} are the fractions of the NO_2 and O_3 molecules receiving photons per unit of time (Chapter II). An expression similar to (V-2) may be written for the rate of production of ^1D oxygen atoms.

Normal ^3P oxygen atoms react with a number of substances known or reported to be in urban atmospheres. They react with molecular oxygen, with ozone, and with themselves. They react with at least two oxides of nitrogen, NO and NO_2, with carbon monoxide, with hydrogen, and possibly with nitrites. Finally, they react with organic molecules, including hydrocarbons. Because of variations in rate constants and reactant concentrations, some of these reactions will be important in polluted atmospheres, and some will not. To evaluate these possibilities each reaction must be considered in turn. While differences in rate constants, and possibly even some differences in products, may be expected between the ^3P and ^1D states, in most cases there is no evidence on such differences, and in the following discussion when no distinction is made it may be assumed that the oxygen atoms are in the ^3P state.

2. The Reaction of Oxygen Atoms with Molecular Oxygen

When oxygen atoms are formed in the presence of molecular oxygen, ozone is produced.[133,185,186,435] The reaction is

$$O + O_2 + M \rightarrow O_3 + M + 24.6 \text{ kcal} \quad S_3 = k_3(O)(O_2)(M) \tag{V-3}$$

Rate equations derived from studies of the kinetics of both the photochemical [32,191,381,434] and thermal [30,155,411] decompositions of ozone indicate that, in agreement with theoretical expectations, reaction (V-3) is third order at pressures up to at least 1 atm.[155,411]

Until 1956 one could do little more than guess at the rate of this reaction, and estimates by different investigators varied by more than three orders of magnitude. In that year, Benson and Axworthy[30] disclosed the results of a kinetic study of the thermal decomposition of ozone, yielding rate constant values for the reactions concerned, which the authors considered to be reliable within ±5 to 7% in the temperature range of their measurements.

Benson and Axworthy's analysis was based on the long recognized fact that, except at high temperatures or high ozone concentrations, the kinetics of the thermal decomposition of ozone are capable of explanation by a first step consisting of the reverse of reaction (V-3),

$$O_3 + M \rightarrow O_2 + O + M - 24.6 \text{ kcal} \quad S_4 = k_4(O_3)(M) \tag{V-4}$$

This is followed by a competition between molecular oxygen and ozone for oxygen atoms:

$$O + O_2 + M \rightarrow O_3 + M + 24.6 \text{ kcal} \quad S_3 = k_3(O)(O_2)(M) \tag{V-3}$$

and

$$O + O_3 \rightarrow 2 O_2 + 93 \text{ kcal} \quad S_5 = k_5(O)(O_3) \tag{V-5}$$

Assuming a stationary concentration of oxygen atoms,

$$S_4 = S_3 + S_5$$

and

$$\frac{-d(O_3)}{dt} = S_4 + S_5 - S_3 = 2S_5 \tag{V-6}$$

Substituting the specific rate laws in these two equations and eliminating (O), yields the expression

$$\frac{-d(O_3)}{dt} = \frac{2k_4k_5(O_3)^2(M)}{k_3(O_2)(M) + k_5(O_3)} \tag{V-7}$$

This may be written in the form

$$\frac{(M)}{k_5(O_3)} = \frac{k_3(O_2)(M)}{2k_4k_5(O_3)} + \frac{1}{2k_4} \tag{V-8}$$

By plotting $(M)/k_5(O_3)$ against $(M)(O_2)/(O_3)$ for 44 runs of Glissman and Schumacher[155] over the temperature range 78–110°C and 4 runs of their own at 99.8°C, Benson and Axworthy found the best fit for

$$(M) = (O_3) + 0.44(O_2) + 0.41(N_2) + 1.06(CO_2) + 0.34(He) \tag{V-9}$$

Using these values for (M), from the intercepts and slopes of the resulting graphs, they obtained

$$k_4 = 4.61 \pm 0.25 \times 10^{12}e^{-24000/RT} \text{ liter mole}^{-1} \text{ sec}^{-1} \tag{V-10}$$

and

$$\frac{k_4k_5}{k_3} = 2.28 \pm 0.16 \times 10^{15}e^{-30600/RT} \text{ sec}^{-1} \tag{V-11}$$

From the known thermal data[297]

$$\frac{k_4}{k_3} = K_{eq} = 7.7 \times 10^4e^{-24600/RT} \text{ moles liter}^{-1} \tag{V-12}$$

Combining equations (V-10) and (V-12) gives

$$k_3 = 6.00 \times 10^7e^{+600/RT} \text{ liter}^2 \text{ mole}^{-2} \text{ sec}^{-1} \tag{V-13}$$

and

$$k_5 = 2.96 \times 10^{10}e^{-6000/RT} \text{ liter mole}^{-1} \text{ sec}^{-1} \tag{V-14}$$

The positive sign of the exponent in equation (V-13) is notable. Formally, this means that reaction (V-3) has an apparent negative activation energy of −600 cal. Practically, it means that the reaction of oxygen atoms with molecular oxygen has a negative temperature coefficient, hence the rate of the reaction will decrease with increasing temperature. Support for this is found in the observation years ago by

Eucken[117] that the rate of photochemical ozone formation from oxygen at very low pressures also has a negative temperature coefficient. An explanation for this type of behavior was given in Chapter IV. Specifically, in this case the reaction may be supposed to occur in steps:

$$O + O_2 \xrightarrow{3a} O_3{}^* \qquad S_{3a} = k_{3a}(O)(O_2) \qquad (V\text{-}15)$$

$$O_3{}^* \xrightarrow{3b} O + O_2 \qquad S_{3b} = k_{3b}(O_3{}^*) \qquad (V\text{-}16)$$

$$O_3{}^* + M \xrightarrow{3c} O_3 + M \qquad S_{3c} = k_{3c}(O_3{}^*)(M) \qquad (V\text{-}17)$$

Assuming a stationary state with respect to the intermediate $O_3{}^*$ gives for the rate of formation of ozone

$$S_3 = \frac{k_{3a}k_{3c}(O)(O_2)(M)}{k_{3b} + k_{3c}(M)} \qquad (V\text{-}18)$$

The observed dependence on (M) indicates that at atmospheric pressures $k_{3c}(M)$ is small relative to k_{3b}, and equation (V-18) approaches the form

$$S_3 = \frac{k_{3a}k_{3c}(O)(O_2)(M)}{k_{3b}} \qquad (V\text{-}19)$$

With increasing temperature, if k_{3b} increases more rapidly than the product $k_{3a}k_{3c}$, the rate S_3 will decrease, as is observed. By this hypothesis, $k_3 = (k_{3a}k_{3c})/k_{3b}$.

It should be noted that when (M) is calculated by equation (V-9) it is not a true concentration, but is a sum of concentrations times relative efficiency factors. By this method of calculation, the value of k_3 is made independent of the nature of (M), but part of the steric factor is included in (M) rather than in the value of k. In air, taken as 21% O_2 and 79% N_2, the value of this factor, from equation (V-9), is (M) = 0.416 (air). For our purposes, for reaction (V-3) in air, it will be more convenient to take (M) = (air), in which case the appropriate values of k_3 are 0.416 of those given by equation (V-13). These values, for temperatures in the atmospheric range, are given in Table 35.

Since the concentrations of oxygen and nitrogen in air at constant temperature and pressure are essentially constant, the rate of reaction (V-3) in air at any given temperature and pressure may be expressed in terms of a pseudobimolecular constant, $k_3(M)$, or a pseudounimolecular constant, $k_3(O_2)(M)$. These values, for (M) = (air) at 1 atm, are also given in Table 35.

On the basis of a hypothetical triple collision frequency factor of

RATE CONSTANTS FOR THE REACTION $O + O_2 + M \rightarrow O_3 + M$ IN AIR[a]

Temp. (°C)	k_3 (l^2 mole^{-2} sec^{-1})	Air at 1 atm			
		k_3(M)		k_3(O$_2$)(M)	
		l mole^{-1} sec^{-1}	pphm^{-1} hr^{-1}	sec^{-1}	hr^{-1}
0	7.5×10^7	3.4×10^6	5.0	3.2×10^4	11.4×10^7
10	7.3×10^7	3.1×10^6	4.6	2.8×10^4	10.2×10^7
20	7.0×10^7	2.9×10^6	4.3	2.5×10^4	9.1×10^7
25	6.9×10^7	2.8×10^6	4.2	2.4×10^4	8.7×10^7
30	6.7×10^7	2.7×10^6	4.0	2.3×10^4	8.3×10^7
40	6.5×10^7	2.5×10^6	3.8	2.1×10^4	7.5×10^7

[a] From the data of Benson and Axworthy, with (M) = (air).

$Z \approx 10^{10}$ liter^2 mole^{-2} sec^{-1}, the collision yield for reaction (V-3) in air at 25°C is

$$y_3 = \frac{k_3}{Z} \approx 7 \times 10^{-3} \qquad (V\text{-}20)$$

In view of the importance of the figures in Table 35 to the interpretation of atmospheric reactions, it is appropriate to consider some of the assumptions and uncertainties involved in their derivation. In the first place, they involve the assumption that the thermal decomposition of ozone does in fact proceed by reactions (V-4), (V-3), and (V-5). While the extent of agreement between the predictions of this assumption and the experimental data is good evidence in its favor, there is still no definitive proof that it is so. Moreover, this may not be the only path by which ozone thermally decomposes. For instance, the decomposition is known to be sensitive to surface effects and catalysts, and again, at fast reaction rates, produced either by high pressures or high temperatures, the observed decomposition rate is higher than would be predicted from reactions (V-4), (V-3), and (V-5).

By use of all-glass reaction systems and by obtaining consistent results in reaction vessels of different sizes, it would appear that in the experimental work upon which Benson and Axworthy based their analysis, surface and catalytic effects have been minimized.

The excess rate at high pressures or temperatures has been explained in several ways. It has been proposed that it is due to a thermal chain,[359] involving a reaction between ozone molecules and energy rich oxygen molecules from reaction (V-5); $O_3 + O_2^* \rightarrow 2\ O_2 + O$. It has also been proposed [155,411] that it is due to a direct reaction between ozone molecules; $O_3 + O_3 \rightarrow 3 O_2$. Benson and Axworthy present arguments against both of these reactions and propose, instead, that the excess rate is due to thermal gradients within the reaction vessel. With this explanation, no reactions other than (V-4), (V-3), and (V-5) are required to fit the experimental data for the homogeneous thermal decomposition of ozone.

Another source of uncertainty in the values in Table 35 lies in the fact that they represent a considerable extrapolation from the temperature range in which the experimental data were obtained. The nature of the uncertainty introduced by temperature extrapolations was discussed in Chapter IV. Still further, the derivation of k_3 is dependent on the thermal data for the equilibrium constant K_{eq} [equation (V-12)], and any uncertainty in this constant will be reflected in k_3.

Uncertainty with regard to the value of (M) in air is probably of second order importance. For example, water vapor will probably be more effective than nitrogen or oxygen as the third body, but even if it were as effective as carbon dioxide its presence in air would increase k_3 by only a few per cent.

Taken as a whole, it would not be surprising if these factors might lead to an uncertainty of as much as an order of magnitude in the values of k_3 in Table 35. It is reassuring, therefore, that two more recent and more direct investigations, by Kaufman,[240] and by Elias et al.[114] have yielded room temperature estimates of k_3 which within this limit of uncertainty are in agreement with, although somewhat higher than, those derived from Benson and Axworthy's equations.

Kaufman produced oxygen atoms by subjecting oxygen, in a flow system, to a microwave discharge. A small amount of nitric oxide was fed into the oxygen–oxygen atom mixture, and the rate of disappearance of oxygen atoms was determined by measuring the intensity, at varying distances down a 2×150-cm flow tube, of the luminescence due to the reaction[148,412] $O + NO \rightarrow NO_2 + h\nu$. Owing to the fast reaction $O + NO_2 \rightarrow O_2 + NO$, the nitric oxide was regenerated and remained at essentially constant concentration, and also due to this reaction the oxygen atom concentration could be titrated by adding NO_2 until the luminescence just disappeared.

With a knowledge of the velocity of flow down the tube, rate constants are obtained for the first-order disappearance of oxygen atoms by this method, with $k = (2.3/t_{xy})\log_{10}(I_x/I_y)$. Where I_x, I_y are the luminescent intensities at positions x and y, and t_{xy} is the flow time between the two positions. To be reasonably valid several corrections must be applied and the limitations kept in mind. These include the effects of viscous pressure drop along the tube, wall effects, temperature effects,

effects of radial distribution of flow, and of other gas phase reactions which compete for oxygen atoms.

Taking account of the first three of these effects, at oxygen pressures of 0.57 to 1.55 mm and oxygen atom pressures of 0.025 to 0.035 mm, Kaufman obtained a first-order removal rate of oxygen atoms corresponding to a rate constant for reaction (V-3), with $M = O_2$, of $k_3 = 4 \times 10^8$ liter^2 mole^{-2} sec^{-1}. The actual value of k_3 would be less than this, owing to the competing reactions $O + O + M \to O_2 + M$ and $O + O_3 \to 2\,O_2$. From the fact that the observed decay rate in the presence of added nitrogen and argon was entirely explained by the pressure drop correction and wall effects, plus the fact that with varying reactant concentrations the rate constants calculated on the basis of $O + O_2 + M$ remained nearly constant while those calculated on the basis of $O + O + M$ did not, it was concluded that the contribution of the recombination reaction is unimportant. On the other hand, the reaction of oxygen atoms with ozone is important, and Kaufman estimates that allowance for this reaction would reduce the value of k_3 to something between 2 and 4×10^8 liter^2 mole^{-2} sec^{-1}.

Elias, Ogryzlo, and Schiff also used a room temperature flow method, producing oxygen atoms by an electrodeless discharge in oxygen and streaming the mixture down a 1.75×35-cm tube, in which the oxygen atom concentration could be measured by a movable spiral of platinum wire coated with silver oxide to catalyze the surface recombination reaction. In each experiment, normal oxygen was first passed through the system, and the resistance of the detector wire was measured with a known current passing through. The discharge was then activated and the current through the wire reduced to yield the same resistance, hence the same temperature. If the two currents are i_0 and i, the resistance R, the heat of atom recombination ΔH, and if the detector removes all the atoms from the gas stream, the flow rate of atoms F_0 is given by $F_0 = R(i_0^2 - i^2)/\Delta H$. Experiments with two successive detectors, and with added NO to produce luminescence, showed that at wire temperatures of up to 100°C the detector did remove all the atoms, and the same value of F_0 was obtained at different wire temperatures. Other temperature effects were shown to be unimportant.

Elias, Ogryzlo, and Schiff compared the oxygen atom concentrations measured by their wire detector with those measured by a Wrede gauge, and by the NO_2 titration method of Kaufman. The Wrede gauge gave concentrations about 10% lower, and the NO_2 titration gave values about 25% lower, than those obtained by the detector. After conducting a number of experiments, using different oxide coatings on the wire, mercury mirrors on the tube walls, and added ethylene sufficient to remove all the oxygen atoms, the authors concluded that the difference between the wire detector and the NO_2 titration was due to the presence in the gas stream of excited O_2 molecules, possibly in the $^1\Delta_g$ state, which liberated heat on the detector but did not react with NO_2. During these experiments it was found that a freshly prepared silver oxide detector surface would remove all the atoms but deactivate only a negligible amount of the excited molecules, and such surfaces were thereafter employed.

Using pressures of 0.5 to 5 mm, with $(O_2)/(O) \sim 20$, and taking wall removal and the reaction $O + O_3 \rightarrow 2\ O_2'$ into account, but neglecting the effects of pressure drop and radial distribution of flow, Elias, Ogryzlo, and Schiff obtained the value of $k_3 = 1.0 \times 10^8$ liter^2 mole^{-2} sec^{-1} for reaction (V-3) at room temperature, with $M = O_2$. Several runs at $-60°C$ indicated a small negative temperature coefficient, corresponding to a negative activation energy of about 0.7 ± 0.2 kcal mole^{-1}, for reaction (V-3), in agreement with that estimated by Benson and Axworthy [equation (V-13)]. In agreement with Kaufman, no effects resulting from the recombination reaction $O + O + M \rightarrow O_2 + M$ were observed (cf. Section 5).

In summary, the three values which have been discussed for the rate constant of reaction (V-3) at ordinary temperatures are shown in the tabulation.

	k_3 (l^2 mole^{-2} sec^{-1})
Benson and Axworthy, M = air	0.7×10^8
Kaufman, M = O_2	2 to 4×10^8
Elias, Ogryzlo, and Schiff, M = O_2	1.0×10^8

While various corrections might bring these values closer together, considering the inherent uncertainties in each case and the almost total difference in origin between Benson and Axworthy's value and the other two, the agreement must be regarded as remarkably good.*

There is no evidence on the rate of combination of ^1D oxygen atoms with molecular oxygen. Since the latter will be in its normal $^3\Sigma_g^-$ state, by the correlation rules[196,450] the formation of a singlet or ground-state ozone molecule is permitted with ^3P, but not with ^1D oxygen atoms. The

* A re-evaluation of the thermal ozone data by Zaslowsky, J. A., et al. [J. Am. Chem. Soc., 82, 2682 (1960)], and new discharge experiments by Kaufman, F., and Kelso, J. R., (Proc. Intern. Symposium on Chem. Reactions in the Upper and Lower Atmospheres, San Francisco, 1961) both suggest that the value of k_3 in air may be only about 60% as large as that estimated from Benson and Axworthy's data. If true, the estimated oxygen atom concentrations (Section 3) and values of other rate constants based on k_3 (Sections 7, 8) will be correspondingly changed.

formation of a triplet or electronically excited ozone molecule would be permitted by the selection rules, and the weak absorption of ozone in the visible (Chapter III) shows that it does possess an excited state, possibly a triplet, with excitation energy roughly corresponding to that of a ^1D oxygen atom (45.2 kcal). However, the absence of fluorescence from this state and its photodissociation with an apparent quantum yield of unity indicate that it is short lived. Two paths for the reaction of ^1D oxygen atoms with molecular oxygen are thus suggested: collisional deactivation of the ^1D atoms to the ^3P state, which would then react with oxygen in the normal manner, or direct reaction of the ^1D atoms with the O_2, followed or accompanied by collisional deactivation of the electronically excited product. There is some evidence that collisional quenching of ^1D oxygen atoms to the ^3P state does occur,[371] but its rate is not known.

3. THE CONCENTRATION OF OXYGEN ATOMS IN POLLUTED AIR

The reaction of oxygen atoms with molecular oxygen sets an upper limit to the stationary concentration which these atoms will attain in polluted air. From equations (V-1), (V-2), and (V-3) this concentration will be given by

$$(O) = \frac{S_1 + S_2}{k_3(O_2)(M)} = \frac{\phi_1 k_{a_1}(NO_2) + \phi_2 k_{a_2}(O_3)}{k_3(O_2)(M)} \tag{V-21}$$

Since $1/k_3(O_2)(M) = 4 \times 10^{-5}$ sec, the assumption of a stationary state is valid, and since it appears (*vide infra*) that the great majority of the oxygen atoms react with molecular oxygen rather than by other processes, their true concentration will probably be close to the values predicted by equation (V-21).

It is seen at once that the concentration of oxygen atoms in polluted air is very small. Thus, if the rate of photochemical production of oxygen atoms, $S_1 + S_2$, is 100 pphm per hr, by equation (V-21) the stationary concentration at 25°C will be $100/9 \times 10^7 \cong 1.1 \times 10^{-6}$ pphm, or about 1 part per hundred trillion.

During the day, this concentration will vary with the light intensity, the concentrations of the light absorbers (nitrogen dioxide and ozone), and the temperature. The diurnal variations calculated from observed data for three single days are shown in Fig. 31, while those calculated from data averaged over periods of time at two different locations are shown in Figs. 32 and 33. The figures illustrate not only the nature of the diurnal variation, but also its wide variation with time and location. The values were estimated with the assumption that ϕ_1 and ϕ_2 are both unity, and Benson and Axworthy's values of k_3 were employed. Adjustments in both of these parameters, as well as allowance for other reac-

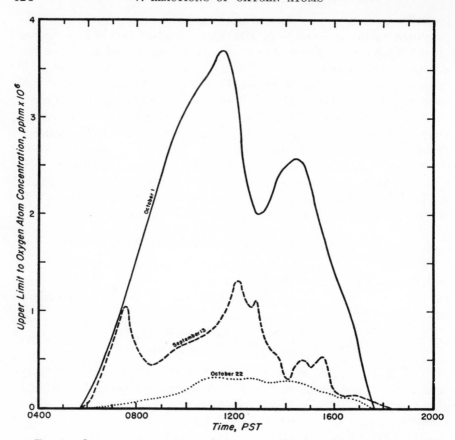

FIG. 31. Oxygen atom concentrations on specific days. The curves represent oxygen atom concentrations calculated from equation (V-21) using observed nitrogen dioxide and oxidant concentrations at Pasadena, California on days of severe, moderate, and low smog) from records of Air Pollution Foundation, San Marino, California). The dates and peak oxidant concentrations were:

Date	Peak oxidant conc.	
	Time	Amount pphm
October 1, 1955	1130	67
September 13, 1955	1145	45
October 22, 1955	1430	17

tions consuming oxygen atoms, might produce some alteration in the estimated concentrations, but it is doubtful that this would exceed 30 to 40%, and in any event, it would be small relative to the day-to-day and place-to-place variations.

From these figures, it appears that an oxygen atom concentration of ~1 to 3×10^{-6} pphm may be accepted as a representative "order of magnitude" value for polluted air during photochemical smog forming periods. It will be convenient to use this figure to estimate the rates of

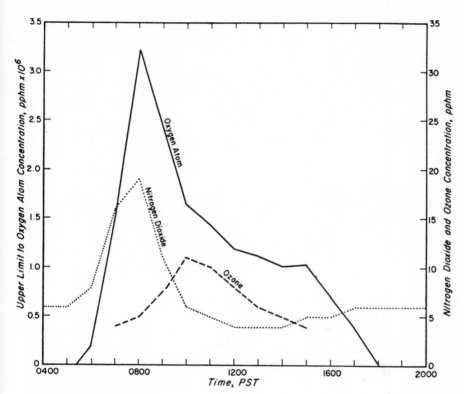

FIG. 32. Averaged diurnal oxygen atom concentrations in downtown Los Angeles. Oxygen atom concentrations from equation (V-21) using nitrogen dioxide and ozone concentrations (from records of the Air Pollution Control District, Los Angeles, California) measured in downtown Los Angeles during September 1958.

reactions of oxygen atoms with pollutants during such periods. For this purpose, if the rate constant k for the reaction between oxygen atoms and a pollutant P is known and expressed in parts per hundred million per hour, the representative rate will be

$$S = k(P) \times 1 \text{ to } 3 \times 10^{-6} \text{ pphm hr}^{-1} \qquad (V\text{-}22)$$

where (P) is the concentration of the pollutant in pphm. If only the collision yield y of the reaction has been estimated, the corresponding estimate of the representative rate will be $yZ(P) \times 1$ to 3×10^{-6}, or taking

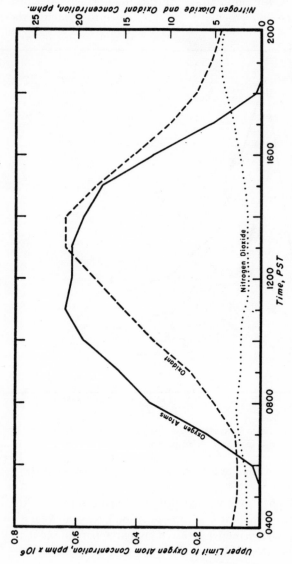

FIG. 33. Averaged diurnal oxygen atom concentrations in Pasadena. Oxygen atom concentrations from equation (V-21) using nitrogen dioxide and oxidant concentrations (from records of the Air Pollution Foundation, San Marino, California) at Pasadena, California averaged over September–October–November, 1955.

$Z \cong 4 \times 10^5$ pphm^{-1} hr^1 (Chapter IV), the order of magnitude rate will be

$$S \approx y(P) \text{ pphm hr}^{-1} \tag{V-23}$$

These equations impose a severe restriction with respect to the significance of the reactions of oxygen atoms with pollutants in urban air. Thus, by equation (V-23), in order for the rate of the reaction to equal 1 pphm per hr, the product $y(P)$ must be of the order of unity. If the pollutant concentration is below 100 pphm, the collision yield will have to exceed 10^{-2} in order to achieve this rate.

4. THE REACTION OF OXYGEN ATOMS WITH OZONE

$$O + O_3 \rightarrow 2 O_2 + 93 \text{ kcal} \quad S_5 = k_5(O)(O_3) \tag{V-5}$$

We have just seen the function of this reaction in the thermal decomposition of ozone. It serves a similar function in the photochemical decomposition,[314] and by removing ozone, retards the photochemical synthesis of ozone from oxygen.[32,190,381] Values of the rate constant k_5, calculated from equation (V-14) for temperatures in the atmospheric range, are given in Table 36.

TABLE 36

RATE CONSTANTS FOR THE REACTION $O + O_3 \rightarrow 2 O_2$
[Based on equation (V-14).]

Temp. (°C)	k_5		$\dfrac{k_5}{k_3(O_2)(M)}$ in air at 1 atm (pphm^{-1})
	l mole^{-1} sec^{-1}	pphm^{-1} hr^{-1}	
0	4.6×10^5	0.67	5.9×10^{-9}
10	6.8×10^5	1.00	1.0×10^{-8}
20	9.8×10^5	1.44	1.6×10^{-8}
25	11.5×10^5	1.7	2.0×10^{-8}
30	13.5×10^5	2.0	2.4×10^{-8}
40	19.1×10^5	2.8	3.7×10^{-8}

In air, ozone must compete with molecular oxygen for oxygen atoms, and the relative rates of the two reactions will be given by

$$\frac{S_5}{S_3} = \frac{k_5(O)(O_3)}{k_3(O)(O_2)(M)} = \frac{k_5(O_3)}{k_3(O_2)(M)} \tag{V-24}$$

From the values of k_5 given in Table 36, and the values of $k_3(O_2)$ (M) from Table 34, it is seen that even at high ozone concentrations the ratio

S_5/S_3 will be very small in air. For example, at 25°C and $(O_3) = 50$ pphm, equation (V-24) gives $S_5/S_3 = 10^{-6}$. This means that at an ozone concentration of 50 pphm in air at 25°C, only one oxygen atom per million produced will react with the ozone. If the oxygen atoms are being photochemically produced at a rate of 100 pphm per hr, the rate of reaction (V-5), at an ozone concentration of 50 pphm in air at 25°C would be 10^{-4} pphm per hr. Values of the same order are given by equation (V-22). This rate is negligible, and this reaction may therefore be excluded from further consideration.

5. THE RECOMBINATION OF OXYGEN ATOMS

$$O + O + M \rightarrow O_2 + M + 117.7 \text{ kcal} \quad S_{25} = k_{25}(O)^2(M) \tag{V-25}$$

Oxygen atoms appear to recombine much more slowly in the gas phase than do other atoms such as hydrogen, iodine, or bromine. We have already noted that both Kaufman[240] and Elias et al.[114] found no indication of this reaction during their experiments on the reaction of oxygen atoms with molecular oxygen (Section 2). The latter authors obtained straight lines, corresponding to a first-order removal of oxygen atoms, when log (O) was plotted against distance down the flow tube. They estimate that if as much as 10% of the removal had occurred by reaction (V-25), which is second order with respect to oxygen atoms, a noticeable curvature would have been produced in these plots, and that this would have been the case if the value of k_{25} were as high as 4×10^8 liter^2 mole^{-2} sec^{-1}. Since no curvature was found they conclude that $k_{25} \leq 4 \times 10^8$. This has been confirmed by Ruehrwein and Hashman[368] through a study of the relative rates of the $O + O + M$ and $O + O_2 + M$ reactions. From the amount of ozone produced they obtained the ratio $k_{25}/k_3 = 1.3$. Introducing Benson and Axworthy's value of k_3 (Table 35) this ratio yields $k_{25} \sim 1 \times 10^8$ liter^2 mole^{-2} sec^{-1}, or 6×10^{-8} pphm^{-2} hr^{-1}.

Using this value, the rate of reaction (V-25) in air, with an atomic oxygen concentration of 3×10^{-6} pphm (Figs. 31–33) and $(M) = 10^8$ pphm, would be

$$S_{25} = 6 \times 10^{-8} \times (3 \times 10^{-6})^2 \times 10^8 = 5 \times 10^{-11} \text{ pphm hr}^{-1}$$

It is evident from this that the rate of recombination of oxygen atoms in polluted air is wholly negligible.

6. THE REACTION OF OXYGEN ATOMS WITH MOLECULAR NITROGEN

Groth and Schierholz[171] have reported the formation of small amounts of nitrous oxide upon irradiation of a mixture of nitrogen and oxygen with light of wavelengths (1470 and 1295 A) which are known to photodissociate the oxygen. The authors believe this to be due to the reaction

$$O + N_2 + M \rightarrow N_2O + M - 12 \text{ to } 13 \text{ kcal} \qquad \text{(V-26)}$$

In a mixture of 419 mm N_2 and 7 mm O_2 about 10^{-4} of the oxygen atoms reacted with nitrogen to form N_2O. Since the experiments were performed in a circulating system with a liquid oxygen trap which would remove both N_2O and O_3, it may be assumed that the major competing reaction was $O + O_2 + M \rightarrow O_3 + M$. On this basis the fraction of the oxygen atoms reacting with nitrogen in ordinary air should be still smaller than 10^{-4}, since the ratio of nitrogen to oxygen is smaller in air than it was in the experimental mixture. The N_2/O_2 ratio in the experimental mixture was about 60; in air it is about 4. Assuming that the fraction of the oxygen atoms reacting with nitrogen is directly proportional to this ratio, its value in air would be $10^{-4} \times 4/60 \cong 7 \times 10^{-6}$. If oxygen atoms were being produced at a rate of 100 pphm per hr, the rate of their reaction with the molecular nitrogen in air would be, on this basis, $\sim 7 \times 10^{-4}$ pphm hr^{-1}. It may be concluded that this reaction is negligible in polluted air.

7. THE REACTIONS OF OXYGEN ATOMS WITH NITRIC OXIDE AND NITROGEN DIOXIDE

The reactions postulated [136] are

$$O + NO + M \rightarrow NO_2 + M + 72 \text{ kcal} \qquad S_{27} = k_{27}(O)(NO)(M) \qquad \text{(V-27)}$$
$$O + NO_2 \rightarrow NO + O_2 + 45 \text{ kcal} \qquad S_{28} = k_{28}(O)(NO_2) \qquad \text{(V-28)}$$
$$O + NO_2 + M \rightarrow NO_3 + M + 49.5 \text{ kcal} \qquad S_{29} = k_{29}(O)(NO_2)(M) \qquad \text{(V-29)}$$

Evidence for these reactions is provided by several studies of the photolysis of nitrogen dioxide under various conditions.[133,136,177,183,309,403] Although the kinetic behavior disclosed by these studies is satisfactorily explained by the rate laws as written in the foregoing, it is probable that none of the three reactions proceeds exactly as shown. For instance, at low pressures the reaction of nitric oxide with oxygen atoms is accompanied by chemiluminescence.[148,241,338,412,449] This luminescence, coupled with the known collisional quenching of the fluorescence of nitrogen dioxide[299] indicates that reaction (V-27) proceeds through the intermediate formation of an electronically excited NO_2 molecule, which is then stabilized by collision:

$$NO + O \rightleftharpoons NO_2' \qquad \text{(V-27a,b)}$$
$$NO_2' \rightarrow NO_2 + h\nu \qquad \text{(V-27c)}$$
$$NO_2' + M \rightarrow NO_2 + M \qquad \text{(V-27d)}$$

Depending on the life of the intermediate NO_2', the rate of reaction (V-27) thus may or may not show a dependence on (M). The photochemical studies permit no decision on this point, but the kinetics of the thermal decomposition of nitrous oxide[241] provide evidence that at ordinary pressures reaction (V-27) is termolecular.

Similarly, the luminescence produced when nitric oxide is released in the upper atmosphere[338] and the absorption spectrum of the immediate products when nitrogen dioxide is decomposed by flash photolysis[309] indicate that the O_2 molecule produced by reaction (V-28) is vibrationally if not electronically excited. It is possible[177] that reactions (V-28) and (V-29) have as a common first step the association of a nitrogen dioxide molecule with an oxygen atom to form an activated complex, NO_3^*, which may either decompose spontaneously to $NO + O_2$ or be stabilized on collision to form NO_3.

During the photolysis of nitrogen dioxide, the primary dissociation, reaction (V-1), will be followed not only by (V-27), (V-28), and (V-29), but by several other processes as well. Ford and Endow[136] have shown that the observed products, the quantum yields, and the kinetic behavior of the photolysis, at concentrations approaching those in polluted air, all appear to be in accordance with the reactions:

$$
\begin{array}{lll}
NO_2 + h\nu \rightarrow NO + O & \phi I_a & \text{(V-1)} \\
O + NO + M \rightarrow NO_2 + M & k_{27}(O)(NO)(M) & \text{(V-27)} \\
O + NO_2 \rightarrow NO + O_2 & k_{28}(O)(NO_2) & \text{(V-28)} \\
O + NO_2 + M \rightarrow NO_3 + M & k_{29}(O)(NO_2)(M) & \text{(V-29)} \\
O + O_2 + M \rightarrow O_3 + M & k_3(O)(O_2)(M) & \text{(V-3)} \\
NO + NO_3 \rightarrow 2NO_2 & & \text{(V-30)} \\
NO + O_3 \rightarrow NO_2 + O_2 & & \text{(V-31)}
\end{array}
$$

If the latter two reactions are sufficiently fast, and as we shall see later, this appears to be the case, the over-all products of the photolysis will be, as observed, simply nitric oxide and oxygen. In this case, assuming a stationary state with respect to oxygen atoms and a primary quantum yield of unity for reaction (V-1) leads to the expression, where Φ_{NO_2} and Φ_{O_2} are the quantum yields of nitrogen dioxide disappearance and oxygen formation,

$$
\frac{2}{\Phi_{NO_2}} = \frac{1}{\Phi_{O_2}} = 1 + \frac{k_{29}(M)}{k_{28}} + \frac{k_{27}(NO)(M)}{k_{28}(NO_2)} + \frac{k_3(O_2)(M)}{k_{28}(NO_2)} \quad \text{(V-32)}
$$

Each of the terms of this equation is supported by experimental evidence. Thus, on adding CO_2, C_2H_6, and C_3H_8, at pressures up to 1500 mm, to NO_2 at 6 mm, Hall [177] found that a plot of $1/\Phi_{O_2}$ vs. the pressure of the added gas showed a linear relation, beginning at $1/\Phi_{O_2} = 1.04$ when the added gas pressure was zero and increasing with a different slope for each gas. Since both (NO) and (O_2) were small under Hall's conditions, these results substantiate the first two terms of the equation and provide the evidence that reaction (V-29) requires a third body. The different slopes with different gases indicate that the efficiency as a third body varies with the gas, being least for CO_2, greatest for C_3H_8.

Evidence in support of each of the last two terms of equation (V-32), as well as of a constant corresponding to the first two terms, and an estimate of the rate constants involved, have been obtained by Ford and Endow[136] through a study of the photolysis of low concentrations of nitrogen dioxide, with and without added nitric oxide and oxygen, in nitrogen at atmospheric pressure. The photolysis was initiated by light of 3660 A in a stirred flow reactor at room temperature. Nitrogen dioxide concentrations were from 0.3 to 5.3 ppm, the $(NO)/(NO_2)$ ratio was varied from 0.25 to 200, and the $(O_2)/(NO_2)$ ratio from nearly zero to over 8000. Ford and Endow found that $1/\Phi_{NO_2}$ increased linearly with each of these ratios, and from the slopes and intercepts of the resulting lines and equation (V-32) they obtained the values, where M is nitrogen at one atmosphere,

$$\frac{k_{29}(M)}{k_{28}} = 1.9, \quad \frac{k_{27}(M)}{k_{28}} = 0.36, \quad \text{and} \quad \frac{k_3(M)}{k_{28}} = 1.33 \times 10^{-3}$$

Inserting Benson and Axworthy's value (Table 35) of $k_3(M) = 2.8 \times 10^6$ liter mole^{-1} sec^{-1} leads to the following values at 25°C, if M is nitrogen at atmospheric pressure:

$$k_{27}(M) = 7.5 \times 10^8 \text{ liter mole}^{-1} \text{ sec}^{-1} = 1.1 \times 10^3 \text{ pphm}^{-1} \text{ hr}^{-1}$$
$$k_{28} = 2.1 \times 10^9 \text{ liter mole}^{-1} \text{ sec}^{-1} = 3.1 \times 10^3 \text{ pphm}^{-1} \text{ hr}^{-1}$$
$$k_{29}(M) = 4.0 \times 10^9 \text{ liter mole}^{-1} \text{ sec}^{-1} = 5.9 \times 10^3 \text{ pphm}^{-1} \text{ hr}^{-1}$$

Setting $(M) = 4 \times 10^{-2}$ liter mole^{-1} gives

$$k_{27} = 1.9 \times 10^{10} \text{ liter}^2 \text{ mole}^{-2} \text{ sec}^{-1}$$
$$k_{29} = 1 \times 10^{11} \text{ liter}^2 \text{ mole}^{-2} \text{ sec}^{-1}$$

Several independent determinations of k_{27}, summarized in Table 37, have yielded values close to that derived by Ford and Endow. In these determinations Kaufman,[240] Harteck et al.,[187] and Orgyzlo and Schiff [321] all used flow systems, with oxygen atoms produced by microwave or electric discharges in molecular oxygen, and the methods of measuring oxygen atoms described in Section 2. The third body, M, in each case was essentially O_2. The agreement between these values and that of Ford and Endow provides support for two of the parameters used by the latter, namely Benson and Axworthy's value of k_3 (Table 35), and a primary yield of unity for reaction (V-1) at 3660 A.

The high temperature values of Kaufman et al.,[241] for k_{27} were derived from a study of the thermal decomposition of nitrous oxide. These values, as do those of Orgyzlo and Schiff at 6 and 20°C, indicate a small negative temperature coefficient for reaction (V-27).

TABLE 37

RATE CONSTANTS FOR REACTIONS OF OXYGEN ATOMS WITH NITRIC OXIDE AND NITROGEN DIOXIDE

Reaction	Ford and Endow (25°C)	Kaufman (room temp.)	Orgyzlo and Schiff	Harteck, Reeves, and Mannella (room temp.)	Kaufman, Gerri, and Bowman	Kistiakowsky and Volpi (room temp.)
$O + NO + M \rightarrow NO_2 + M$, k_{27}, l^2 mole^{-2} sec^{-1}	1.9×10^{10}	$\sim 2.5 \times 10^{10}$	2×10^{10} at 6°C 1.85×10^{10} at 20°C	2.7×10^{10}	7.2×10^9 at 700°C 5.2×10^9 at 758°C	—
$O + NO_2 \rightarrow NO + O_2$ k_{28}, l mole^{-1} sec^{-1}	2.1×10^9	$> 10^8$	—	—	—	$\geq 10^9$
$O + NO_2 + M \rightarrow NO_3 + M$ k_{29}, l^2 mole^{-2} sec^{-1}	1×10^{11}	—	—	—	—	—

Ford and Endow's value of k_{28} is in line with two estimates of the lower limit for this rate constant. From the approximate dimensions of the mixing region and reaction zone when nitrogen dioxide was introduced into a stream of oxygen and oxygen atoms (Section 2), Kaufman estimated that $k_{28} \geq 10^8$ liter mole^{-1} sec^{-1}. In a study of the flash photolysis of NO₂, using a time-of-flight mass spectrometer for identification of the products, Kistiakowsky and Kydd[245] observed that the mass 32 peak had already reached its full magnitude within 100 μsec after the flash. For this to be so, they concluded that the collision efficiency of the oxygen producing reaction, (V-28), must be of the order of or larger than 10^{-2}. From this, together with the fact that no NO₂ was observed when nitrogen atoms reacted with nitric oxide in a stirred flow reactor, Kistiakowsky and Volpi[247] concluded that $k_{28} \geq 10^9$ liter mole^{-1} sec^{-1}. The assumed mechanism in this case was $N + NO \rightarrow N_2 + O$, followed by (V-27 a, b), (V-27d), and (V-28).

The rate constants reported here are much higher than earlier estimates.[88,148,159] In fact, the values of k_{27} are about equal to, while the value of k_{29} is an order of magnitude larger than, the hypothetical termolecular collision frequency factor, $Z \approx 10^{10}$ liter^2 mole^{-2} sec^{-1}. This would suggest that neither reaction (V-27) or (V-29) requires any appreciable activation energy, a suggestion which is supported for reaction (V-27) by the fact that the values of k_{27} indicate a negative temperature coefficient.

High though the rate constants of these reactions may be, they are still not enough to attach any importance to these reactions in polluted air. Thus, at nitric oxide and nitrogen dioxide concentrations of 10 pphm and an oxygen atom concentration of 3×10^{-6} pphm, the resulting rates of reactions (V-27), (V-28), and (V-29) will be, respectively, 0.03, 0.09, and 0.18 pphm hr^{-1}.

Under exceptional conditions, to be sure, the rates of these reactions may be substantially greater than this. For example, at 11 A.M. on October 6, 1958, a day of smog alert in the Los Angeles basin, the nitrogen dioxide concentration at Pasadena was 18 pphm. Under these conditions the oxygen atom concentration would have been about 5×10^{-6} pphm and the rates of (V-28) and (V-29) would have been approximately 0.3 and 0.5 pphm hr^{-1}. Even these rates are not high enough to be significant, since, by them, over a period of one hour, reaction (V-28) would have reduced 0.3 pphm out of a total of 18 pphm of NO₂ to NO, while at the same time reaction (V-29), if followed by $NO + NO_3 \rightarrow 2NO_2$, would have oxidized 0.5 pphm of NO back to NO₂. Compared to the rate of photochemical dissociation of NO₂, which would have been about 400 pphm hr^{-1} at this concentration, these changes are negligible.

8. THE REACTIONS OF OXYGEN ATOMS WITH HYDROCARBONS

In every case which has been investigated thus far, oxygen atoms have been found to react with hydrocarbons, and it appears unlikely that there are any exceptions. At the same time, substantial differences have been found in both mechanism and rate of the reaction, not only between the different classes of hydrocarbons, but also among the members of a given class.

Considering mechanism first, by far the most complete investigations are those of Cvetanović and his collaborators[87-89,220,371,372] on the reactions of oxygen atoms with olefins. In order to produce oxygen atoms in the absence of molecular oxygen, Cvetanović used the mercury sensitized decomposition of nitrous oxide

$$Hg(^3P_1) + N_2O \rightarrow Hg + N_2 + O \qquad (V-33)$$

This method has the added advantage that the amount of nitrogen formed is a measure of the number of oxygen atoms produced. The products of the reaction of these oxygen atoms with a hydrocarbon were separated by gas-liquid chromatography (GLC) and identified by mass spectrometer and infrared spectroscopy.

With oxygen atoms and ethylene, at 25°C and in the absence of molecular oxygen, Cvetanović[88] found that the products were chiefly carbon monoxide, paraffin hydrocarbons (CH_4, C_2H_6, and C_3H_8), and aldehydes (CH_3CHO, C_2H_5CHO, and C_3H_7CHO), together with small amounts of hydrogen, ethylene oxide, and possibly ketene. The effect of pressure on the relative amounts of these products appeared to be small, although there was some indication that with increasing pressure the yields of aldehyde and ethylene oxide increased while that of carbon monoxide decreased. On the addition of a small amount of molecular oxygen ($\sim$2 mm O_2 in 100 mm N_2O with 3 to 85 mm of C_2H_4) there was a large increase in the amount of carbon monoxide produced, while ethane and hydrogen were completely suppressed and methane and aldehydes were drastically reduced. While the new products resulting from the presence of molecular oxygen were not completely identified, the evidence indicates that organic acids, alcohols, and water were formed in important quantities. At a higher temperature, 123°C, substantial amounts of formaldehyde were produced.

With propylene, in the absence of molecular oxygen, the major products were propylene oxide, propionaldehyde together with some acetone, and carbon monoxide. Minor products included ethane, acetaldehyde, methane, hydrogen, and ethylene. In this case a pronounced pressure effect occurred, with the observed variations shown in Fig. 34. The propionaldehyde and acetone were not resolved by the chromatographic column used in these experiments, but one separation carried out with a column which did resolve the two gave an aldehyde to

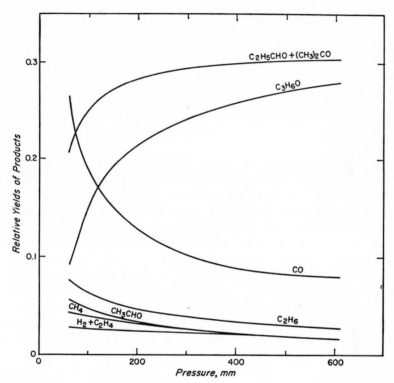

FIG. 34. Effect of pressure on products of the reaction of oxygen atoms with propylene.

acetone ratio of about 9:1, and this predominance of the aldehyde was supported by infrared and mass spectra.

In the reaction of oxygen atoms with the butenes, in the absence of molecular oxygen, the only major products found by Cvetanović[88] were the epoxides and their carbonyl isomers, in the relative amounts shown in Table 38. The amounts of these products which were recovered by chromatography accounted for about 70 to 80% of the oxygen atoms consumed, but owing to the difficulty in obtaining complete recovery this figure is probably not quantitative. The minor products formed accounted for some 5 to 15% of the oxygen atoms

TABLE 38

ADDITION PRODUCTS OF REACTIONS OF OXYGEN ATOMS WITH BUTENES[a]

	Epoxides				Carbonyl compounds		
	α-Butene oxide	Iso-butene oxide	β-Butene oxide		n-Butanal	Iso-butanal	Methyl ethyl ketone
			cis	trans			
1-Butene	0.53	—	—	—	0.43	—	0.04
Isobutene	—	0.54	—	—	—	0.43	0.03
cis-2-Butene	—	—	0.25	0.26	—	0.23	0.26
trans-2-Butene	—	—	0.15	0.33	—	0.21	0.31

[a] The fractions are calculated from chromatographic peak areas and are relative to all addition compounds as unity.

consumed, and included carbon monoxide, ethane, traces of methane and ethylene, and small amounts of other products shown by minor chromatographic peaks which were not identified, but in the case of 1-butene seemed to consist largely of acetaldehyde and propionaldehyde. In the experiments with oxygen atoms from nitrous oxide, which were carried out over the pressure range of 50 to 600 mm, very little change of any sort with pressure was observed. But in experiments with oxygen atoms produced by the photolysis of nitrogen dioxide,[371] in which it was possible to go to lower pressures, over the range from about 2 to 30 mm, obtained by varying the amount of nitrogen present, the products from 1-butene and isobutene showed much the same behavior as did those from propylene at pressures more than an order of magnitude higher (Fig. 34).

On the addition of molecular oxygen at pressures of 3 to 40 mm in the presence of 7 to 15 mm of olefin and 500 mm of N_2O, in the case of 1-butene and isobutene there was little or no inhibition of the formation of addition products, although the yields of aldehydes appeared to be slightly lowered and some new products, possibly alcohols and ketones, were formed. With cis-2-butene the yields of epoxide and methyl ethyl ketone were unaffected by oxygen, but the yield of ethane was rapidly suppressed, that of isobutyraldehyde was reduced to about 20 to 25% of its value in the absence of oxygen, and appreciable amounts of methyl alcohol were formed.

The two higher olefins which have been investigated, cis-2-pentene and tetramethyl ethylene, resemble the butenes in that the major products of the oxygen atom reactions were the epoxides and their carbonyl isomers, with carbon monoxide and simpler hydrocarbons and aldehydes as minor products. The specific substances and amounts obtained by Sato and Cvetanović[372] from *cis*-2-pentene in the absence and presence of molecular oxygen are given in Table 39. Other analyses[88] also showed small amounts of carbon monoxide and ethane.

TABLE 39

PRODUCTS OBSERVED BY CHROMATOGRAPHIC ANALYSIS
FROM THE REACTION OF OXYGEN ATOMS WITH *cis*-2-PENTENE
(Amounts expressed as chromatographic peak areas in arbitrary units;
temperature = 25 ± 2°C.)

Product	N_2O = 245 mm olefin = 2.7 mm O_2 = 0	N_2O = 245 mm olefin = 2.9 mm O_2 = 4.4 mm
trans-β-Pentene oxide	642	604
cis-β-Pentene oxide	462	435
2-Methyl butyraldehyde	364	100
Methyl propyl ketone	505	499
n-Butane	53	Not determined
Acetaldehyde	5	535
Propionaldehyde	25	240
Isobutyraldehyde	87	0
2-Ethyl butyraldehyde	63	0
Methyl alcohol	0	129
Ethyl alcohol	0	249
Water	0	Indication

It is apparent that the observed products of the oxygen atom–olefin reactions fall into two general categories: addition products, consisting of epoxides and carbonyl compounds which are mutually isomeric and of molecular weight equal to that of the olefin plus an oxygen atom; and fragmentation products, consisting of carbon monoxide, hydrocarbons, and aldehydes with a smaller number of carbon atoms than the original olefin. The formation of carbonyl isomers of the epoxides shows that the addition may be accompanied by a rearrangement consisting of the migration of a hydrogen atom or alkyl radical from the carbon atom carrying the oxygen atom to the other carbon atom of the original double bond. In the case of the unsymmetrical olefins, the relative amounts of the different carbonyl products, e.g., the predominance of propionaldehyde over acetone in the case of propylene, of *n*-butyraldehyde over methyl ethyl ketone in the case of 1-butene, and of isobutyraldehyde over methyl ethyl ketone in that of isobutene (Table 38) shows that the oxygen atom adds predominantly to the less substituted carbon atom of the double bond.

Cvetanović has shown that the observed products can be explained in general by assuming that the initial product is a triplet biradical, which either decomposes or degrades to a singlet product, with or without the migration of a particle. Taking propylene as an example, the postulated reactions, which with minor modifications will fit the other olefins as well, would be

$$
\begin{array}{ccc}
& & \overset{\displaystyle H}{\underset{\displaystyle \underset{\displaystyle \dot{O}}{|}}{CH_3\dot{C}}}{-}CH_2 & (V\text{-}34) \\
CH_3CH = CH_2 + O & & \\
& & \overset{\displaystyle H}{\underset{\displaystyle \underset{\displaystyle \dot{O}}{|}}{CH_3\dot{C}}}{-}CH_2 & (V\text{-}35)
\end{array}
$$

$$
CH_3CH_2CHO* \begin{cases} \overset{(M)}{\longrightarrow} CH_3CH_2CHO & (V\text{-}36) \\ \longrightarrow \text{decomposition} & (V\text{-}37) \end{cases}
$$

$$
\underset{\displaystyle \underset{\displaystyle \dot{O}}{|}}{\overset{\displaystyle H}{CH_3\dot{C}}}{-}CH_2 \longrightarrow \underset{\displaystyle O}{\overset{\displaystyle H}{CH_3\overset{|}{C}}}\underset{\displaystyle \diagdown\diagup}{}CH_2* \begin{cases} \overset{(M)}{\longrightarrow} \underset{\displaystyle O}{\overset{\displaystyle H}{CH_3C}}\underset{\displaystyle \diagdown\diagup}{\;\;\;}CH_2 & (V\text{-}38) \\ \longrightarrow \text{decomposition} & (V\text{-}39) \end{cases}
$$

decomposition   (V-40)

$$
CH_3\underset{\displaystyle \underset{\displaystyle O}{\|}}{C}{-}CH_3* \begin{cases} \nearrow (CH_3)_2CO & (V\text{-}41) \\ \searrow \text{decomposition} & (V\text{-}42) \end{cases}
$$

$$
\underset{\displaystyle \underset{\displaystyle \dot{O}}{|}}{\overset{\displaystyle H}{CH_3C}}{-}CH_2 \longrightarrow \underset{\displaystyle O}{\overset{\displaystyle H}{CH_3\overset{|}{C}}}\underset{\displaystyle \diagdown\diagup}{}CH_2* \begin{cases} \nearrow \underset{\displaystyle O}{\overset{\displaystyle H}{CH_3C}}\underset{\displaystyle \diagdown\diagup}{\;\;\;}CH_2 & (V\text{-}43) \\ \searrow \text{decomposition} & (V\text{-}44) \end{cases}
$$

decomposition   (V-45)

The apparent leveling off of the yields of fragmentation products from propylene at finite values with increasing pressure (Fig. 34), and the fact that some decomposition products are obtained from the butenes and higher olefins (Table 39) even in the range where no further pressure effects are observed, suggest two fragmentation processes, one dependent on and one independent of the pressure. In the preceding mechanism, the pressure dependent processes are (V-37), (V-39), (V-42), and (V-44), while those independent of pressure are (V-40) and (V-45). The products of the pressure dependent fragmentation, as characterized by propylene and to some extent by ethylene, resemble those to be expected from the thermal and photochemical decompositions[159] of the addition products and are consistent with the assumption that these are initially formed in an energy rich state. Indeed, the addition reactions are quite exothermic, about 115 kcal mole^{-1} for the carbonyl compounds and probably about 90 kcal mole^{-1} for the epoxides, so some form of competition between decomposition and stabilization, either by collision or by internal degradation of the excess energy, is to be expected. Likewise, with increase in the number of internal degrees of freedom over which the energy may be degraded, the lifetime of the "hot" addition product may be expected to increase and the pressure required for its stabilization to decrease, as observed in going from propylene to the butenes.

The relative amounts of addition and fragmentation are a matter of primary interest with respect to the participation of these reactions in the process of photochemical smog formation. Over the investigated pressure range (up to about 600 mm) the simplest olefin, ethylene, appears to undergo almost exclusive fragmentation on reacting with oxygen atoms, although to explain the products it is necessary to postulate that this occurs by several different paths. Cvetanović[88] considers that a stoichiometric balance of the likely processes involved may be written as follows:

$$O + C_2H_4 \rightarrow \begin{cases} 0.03 \ C_2H_4O \text{ and polymer} \\ 0.05 \ H_2 + CH_2 + CO \\ 0.04 \ H_2 + CH_2CO \\ 0.10 \ H + C_2H_3O \\ 0.75 \ \dot{C}H_3 + H\dot{C}O \end{cases} \qquad (V\text{-}46)$$

The resulting radicals then react further to give the observed products. While this is speculative there is at least a strong indication that the major products of the reaction of oxygen atoms with ethylene are methyl and formyl radicals.

With the higher olefins, the large yields of addition products indicate that, in the pressure range of about 50 to 600 mm at least, the fragmentation is much less important than in the case of ethylene. However, the actual amount of fragmentation is difficult to establish. In most cases the amount of addition products observed by chromatography accounted for only some 70 to 80% of the oxygen atoms consumed, but for several reasons this is not a satisfactory indicator. Thus, with *cis*-2-butene, experiments with a partially deuterated mixture showed that the ethane is formed by combination of free methyl radicals. This, together with the suppression of ethane formation and marked reduction in the yield of isobutyraldehyde on addition of oxygen to *cis*-2-butene suggests that when the internal rearrangement of the biradical involves the migration of a methyl radical, this radical becomes momentarily detached, sufficiently so, at least, to react to some extent with other methyl radicals and to a greater extent with oxygen. The effects of oxygen on the products from *cis*-2-pentene (Table 39) suggest a similar detachment on the part of migrating ethyl radicals. On the other hand, oxygen has little effect on the yields of those products which involve the migration of a hydrogen atom, suggesting in this case a lesser degree of detachment. The formation of nitromethane and methyl nitrate in the photolysis of mixtures of nitrogen dioxide and isobutene, of ethyl nitrate from mixtures of nitrogen dioxide with 1-butene, and of all three of these products from the photolysis of nitrogen dioxide with *cis*-2-pentene,[371] confirm this view.

The pressure independent fragmentation thus appears to consist predominantly of a splitting off of alkyl radicals which would otherwise migrate. For the terminal olefins, where most of the migration involves hydrogen atoms, free radical formation by this process is not very important, possibly amounting to not more than 10% of the total molecules reacting. For the nonterminal olefins, it apparently assumes greater importance; Cvetanović estimates the extent of such fragmentation at about 30 to 35% for *cis*-2-pentene and probably as much as 60% for tetramethyl ethylene.[88]

There is some evidence of a different reaction mechanism for ^1D oxygen atoms as compared with that of ^3P atoms with olefins. Using the photolysis of nitrogen dioxide at different wavelengths as a source of oxygen atoms, Sato and Cvetanović[371] found, with 1-butene, an abrupt change in the ratios of reaction products between 2288 and 2537 A. About three times as much α-butene oxide as *n*-butyraldehyde was formed at 2288 A, while at the longer wavelengths the amounts of these two products were almost equal. The photodissociation of nitrogen dioxide by absorption in its diffuse absorption region in the longer ultraviolet, to yield ^3P oxygen atoms, has already been discussed (Chapter III). Near 2450 A, a second diffuse region begins, absorption in which may produce ^1D oxygen atoms.[314] The observed difference in products at 2288 A and longer wavelengths may be explained by the production of ^1D vs. ^3P oxygen atoms and the spin conservation rules. Since the olefin is originally in a singlet state, addition of a ^3P oxygen atom should yield a triplet activated complex, i.e., the biradical already assumed. Addition of a ^1D oxygen atom to an olefin, on the other hand, should yield an activated complex in a singlet state. Sato and Cvetanović suggest that this singlet state is probably a stage in the formation of the epoxide,

$$
\begin{array}{ccc}
R_1 \diagdown \\
\diagdown \\
C{=}C \\
\diagup \\
R_2 \diagup \\
R_4
\end{array}
+ O(^1D) \rightarrow
\begin{array}{ccc}
R_1 \diagdown \\
C\!-\!\!-\!\!-\!\!C \\
R_2 \diagup \\
O R_4
\end{array}
\,R_3{}^* \qquad \text{(V-47)}
$$

Aside from the work of Cvetanović on olefins, information on the mechanism of oxygen atom–hydrocarbon reactions is sparse. With the paraffins, the initial reaction has not been established, but the experimental observations[398] are compatible with a hydrogen abstraction.

$$\text{RH} + \text{O} \rightarrow \text{R} + \text{OH} \qquad \text{(V-48)}$$

If RH is methane, or if the hydrogen is abstracted from a primary carbon atom, this reaction will be nearly thermoneutral. It will be ~5 to 10 kcal exothermic for secondary, and ~10 to 15 kcal exothermic for tertiary hydrogens.

With acetylene and oxygen atoms at liquid air temperature, Geib and Harteck[149] obtained an addition product of empirical formula $C_2H_2O_2$. As with the olefins, the first step may be

$$C_2H_2 + O \rightarrow C_2H_2O \qquad \text{(V-49)}$$

but this cannot be regarded as established.

With benzene, Harteck and Kopsch[186] observed OH, CH, and CC bands emitted as luminescence during the reaction with oxygen atoms, while the main over-all products were carbon monoxide, carbon dioxide, hydrogen, and water. At low temperatures, Geib and Harteck[149] found that addition products were formed, and phenol has also been reported [15] as a major product of the reaction. This evidence is not sufficient to determine whether the primary reaction is a hydrogen abstraction or an addition; both may occur.

With the experimental technique employed by Cvetanović, it is possible to evaluate the ratio of rate constants for two compounds competing for oxygen atoms, and by this technique he has determined the relative rates, given in Table 40, of the reactions of oxygen atoms with a number of hydrocarbons.[87,89] Estimates of the absolute rates in the cases of 1-butene and isobutene were obtained by Sato and Cvetanović from the data of their experiments on the photolysis of nitrogen dioxide–olefin mixtures.[371] Using the rate of formation of bu-

TABLE 40

RATES OF REACTION OF OXYGEN ATOMS WITH HYDROCARBONS
(All at 25 ± 5°C.)

	Relative rates from Cvetanović	Rate constants, k				
		l mole⁻¹ sec⁻¹			pphm⁻¹ hr⁻¹	
		Cvetanović[a]	Ford and Endow	Kaufman	a	b
n-Butane	0.0016	7.3×10^6	—	—	1.1×10^1	2.9×10^1
3-Methyl heptane	0.019	8.7×10^7	6.5×10^7	—	1.3×10^2	3.4×10^2
Ethylene	0.038	1.7×10^8	—	$>5 \times 10^7$	2.5×10^2	6.8×10^2
Propylene	0.23	1.05×10^9	—	—	1.5×10^3	4.1×10^3
1-Butene	0.24	1.1×10^9	—	—	1.6×10^3	4.3×10^3
Isobutene	1.00	4.6×10^9	—	—	6.8×10^3	1.8×10^4
cis-2-Butene	0.84	3.9×10^9	—	—	5.7×10^3	1.5×10^4
trans-2-Butene	1.13	5.2×10^9	—	—	7.6×10^3	2.0×10^4
1-Pentene	—	—	2.8×10^9	—	—	4.1×10^3
cis-2-Pentene	0.90	4.1×10^9	1.1×10^{10}	—	6.0×10^3	1.6×10^4
Cyclopentene	1.20	5.5×10^9	—	—	8.1×10^3	2.2×10^4
Tetramethylethylene	4.18	1.9×10^{10}	—	—	2.8×10^4	7.5×10^4

[a] Based on Cvetanović's value for 1-butene and the relative rates in column 1.
[b] Based on Ford and Endow's value for cis-2-pentene and the relative rates in column 1.

tyraldehyde (n-butyraldehyde from 1-butene, isobutyraldehyde from iso-butene) as an index of the rate of reaction of oxygen atoms with the olefin, and assuming that at small conversions all of the oxygen atoms formed react either with the nitrogen dioxide or the olefin, the relationship which should apply is

$$\frac{\alpha\phi I_a(NO_2)}{R_A} = 1 + \frac{k_{28}(NO_2)}{k_{Bu}(Bu)}\left(1 + \frac{k_{29}(M)}{k_{28}}\right) \tag{V-50}$$

Here R_A is the rate of formation of the butyraldehyde, α the ratio of molecules of aldehyde formed to oxygen atoms reacting with the butene, k_{Bu} the rate constant for the oxygen atom–butene reaction, and k_{28}, k_{29} the rate constants for reactions (V-28) and (V-29), of oxygen atoms with nitrogen dioxide.

It is seen that at a constant rate of light absorption and constant (M), a plot of $1/R_A$ against $(NO_2)/(Bu)$ should be linear, and from the slope/intercept ratio of this plot the function

$$\frac{k_{28}}{k_{Bu}}\left(1 + \frac{k_{29}(M)}{k_{28}}\right)$$

may be evaluated without requiring a knowledge of $\alpha\phi I_a(NO_2)$. Using the GLC aldehyde peak areas yielded at constant irradiation time by mixtures of 3.1 mm of NO_2, ~1 to 30 mm of olefin, and nitrogen to give an approximately constant total pressure of 40–50 mm, Sato and Cvetanović obtained such linear plots, from which they derived the values

$$\frac{k_{28}}{k_{(1\text{-Bu})}}\left(1 + \frac{k_{29}(M)}{k_{28}}\right) = 2.1 \tag{V-51}$$

$$\frac{k_{28}}{k_{(iso\text{-Bu})}}\left(1 + \frac{k_{29}(M)}{k_{28}}\right) = 0.38 \tag{V-52}$$

Introducing Ford and Endow's figures for k_{28} and k_{29} (Section 7) yields $k_{(1\text{-Bu})} = 1.1 \times 10^9$ and $k_{(iso\text{-Bu})} = 6.2 \times 10^9$ liter mole^{-1} sec^{-1}. This involves the assumption that nitrogen dioxide and the butenes are equally as effective as nitrogen in serving as the third body in reaction (V-29). However, under the experimental conditions of Sato and Cvetanović reaction (V-29) is probably slow relative to (V-28), and any error resulting from this assumption should be small.

Of the two rate constant values given in the preceding paragraph, Cvetanović[89] considers that for 1-butene to be slightly more reliable. Accordingly, this value has been combined with his relative rates to give the absolute rate constants for other oxygen atom–hydrocarbon reactions in Table 40. Several values reported by other investigators are also included in this table. Those of Ford and Endow[136] were obtained by introducing small amounts, mostly 10 to 100 pphm, of hydrocarbon vapor into their nitrogen dioxide photolysis system (Section 7) and by measuring its concentration in the influent and effluent gas streams by chromatography. The rate of disappearance of hydrocarbon during the photolysis was obtained from these concentrations, the flow rate, and the equations for a stirred flow reactor. Assuming, except in the case of 1-pentene, that this removal was accomplished solely through a bimolecular reaction with oxygen atoms which competed with the other oxygen atom reactions occurring during the NO_2 photolysis, and using their rate constants for these other reactions, by an iterative method Ford and Endow were able to calculate the rate constants given in Table 40. If the oxygen atom reaction produces free radicals which in turn react with olefin, the constants as estimated would be, of course, too high. However, in the experiments with cis-2-pentene the reactant concentrations were varied over a rather wide range (3.9×10^{-9} to 370×10^{-9} mole liter^{-1} for cis-2-pentene and 11×10^{-9} to 376×10^{-9} mole liter^{-1} for NO_2) with virtually no effect on the value of k. With 1-pentene a dark reaction between nitrogen dioxide and the hydrocarbon was observed, with an apparent bimolecular rate constant of $k = 1.3 \times 10^3$ liter mole^{-1} sec^{-1}, this was taken into account in calculating the rate of the photochemical reaction.

The value of Kaufman[240] for the rate constant of the oxygen atom–ethylene reaction was obtained by the flow method, using the extinguishment of the glow from the $O + NO$ reaction as a measure of the rate of removal of oxygen atoms, as described in Section 2. In order to obtain a measurable rate for the oxygen atom–ethylene reaction, it was necessary to keep the ethylene concentration down to only 0.1 to 0.3 of that of the oxygen atoms, and under these conditions the number of oxygen atoms consumed was considerably greater than the amount of ethylene, indicating that part of the atoms were being removed by secondary reactions. For this reason his estimate of the rate constant is probably a lower limit.

The rate constants in Table 40 indicate that the oxygen atom–olefin reactions may in fact be fast enough to have some importance in polluted air, especially if they are a source of free radicals which initiate chains (Chapter X). The over-all rate in air will depend on the concentration and composition of the olefins present. Information on this subject leaves much to be desired, and probably the best approximation which may be made at this time is to assume that the types and relative amounts of different olefins in the air resemble those in automobile exhaust. While exhaust compositions themselves show wide variations, a representative range of olefin distribution would appear to be 50 to 70% ethylene, 15 to 25% propylene, 5 to 15% butenes, of which the majority will be 1-butene and isobutene, and 5 to 15% of other olefins, chiefly pentenes and diolefins.[211,379] In air at a total concentration of 50 to 100 pphm with an oxygen atom concentration of 1 to 3×10^{-6} pphm, the over-all rate of reaction of such a mixture with oxygen atoms would probably be in the range of 0.1 to 0.5 pphm hr^{-1}. While this estimate involves many assumptions of questionable validity, it at least suggests the order of magnitude to be expected.

For the rates of reaction of oxygen atoms with paraffin hydrocarbons, in addition to the values given in Table 40 a number of rough estimates are available. Such estimates, expressed as collision yields, are given in Table 41. This information shows that the rates of reaction of oxygen

TABLE 41

ESTIMATED COLLISION YIELDS FOR REACTIONS OF OXYGEN ATOMS WITH PARAFFIN HYDROCARBONS

Hydrocarbon	Est. collision yield at 25°C	Ref.
Methane	10^{-5} to 10^{-6}	88, 159, 186
Ethane	$\sim 10^{-5}$	186
n-Butane	$\sim 10^{-5}$	212
Pentane	$\sim 10^{-4}$	186
Hexane	$\sim 10^{-4}$	186

atoms with the paraffins are much slower than those with the olefins. Thus the rate of reaction with n-butane (Table 40) is less than 1% of that with 1-butene and only 1/600 of that with isobutene. In fact, the indicated rates are so small that even with the most generous figures the resultant rates of reaction in the atmosphere will be negligible. For example, at a methane concentration of 250 pphm and an oxygen atom concentration of 3×10^{-6} pphm, even at the highest estimated collision yield of 10^{-5}, the rate of reaction will be little over 10^{-3} pphm hr^{-1}. For the higher paraffins, if the concentration be taken as 25 pphm and the collision yield 10^{-4}, the rate of reaction will again be little over 10^{-3} pphm hr^{-1}.

Oxygen atoms appear to react more rapidly with acetylene and with aromatic hydrocarbons than they do with paraffins. Harteck and Kopsch[186] obtained complete reaction of oxygen atoms with both acetylene and benzene at room temperature, as compared to 2–5% reaction with ethane and 10 to 25% reaction with hexane. Complete reaction, under their experimental conditions, indicates a collision yield of $\sim 10^{-3}$ or higher. The observation by Geib and Harteck[149] of a fast reaction of oxygen atoms with acetylene and benzene at liquid air temperature would suggest a very small activation energy for the process, but this might have been a surface reaction.

Thus, while there is some indication that the reactions of oxygen atoms with acetylene and aromatic hydrocarbons may be as fast as those with the olefins, at present it cannot definitely be said that this is the case. Since the concentration of these compounds in urban air is almost certainly smaller than that of the olefins,[277,402] it does not appear likely that their reactions with oxygen atoms will be fast enough to be significant, although the possibility that this is so cannot be excluded until more accurate information on concentrations and rates is available.

9. OTHER REACTIONS OF OXYGEN ATOMS

With aldehydes, oxygen atoms react, probably by abstraction of the aldehyde hydrogen:

$$RCHO + O \rightarrow R\dot{C}O + \dot{O}H \quad S_{53} = k_{53}(RCHO)(O) \qquad (V\text{-}53)$$

The rate constant for the reaction of oxygen atoms with acetaldehyde, from the work of Cvetanović,[88,90] is 1.2×10^8 liter mole^{-1} sec^{-1}, or 1.7×10^2 pphm^{-1} hr^{-1} at 25–27°C. The corresponding collision yield is between 10^{-3} and 10^{-4}. At an aldehyde concentration of 25 pphm and an oxygen atom concentration of 3×10^{-6} pphm, this would correspond to a reaction rate of about 10^{-2} pphm per hr. If this may be taken as representative, it does not appear that the reaction of oxygen atoms with aldehydes will be significant in polluted air.

Undoubtedly, all other organic compounds present in polluted urban air, such as alcohols, acids, peroxides, and nitrites, react to some extent with oxygen atoms. With methyl and ethyl alcohol, for example, Harteck and Kopsch[186] obtained complete reaction, indicating a collision yield of $\sim 10^{-3}$ or higher. While the possibility that some of these reactions may occur at significant rates cannot be excluded, in view of the restrictions imposed by equations (V-22) and (V-23), this does not seem likely.

At ordinary temperatures, the reactions of ^3P oxygen atoms with carbon monoxide, hydrogen, and water are all slow.

With carbon monoxide the reaction to be expected is

$$CO + O + M \rightarrow CO_2 + M \quad S_{54} = k_{54}(CO)(O)(M) \qquad (V\text{-}54)$$

Jackson[218] attempted to determine the rate of this reaction, relative to that of $O + O_2 + M \rightarrow O_3 + M$, by exposing mixtures of carbon monoxide and oxygen to ultraviolet radiation in the oxygen photodissociation region, and determining the effect of the carbon monoxide on the rate of ozone production. At room temperature he was unable to detect any effect, even when the carbon monoxide was present in 15 fold excess over the oxygen. Granting that a reduction of as much as 10% in the ozone yield might have escaped attention through experimental error, Jackson concluded that the reaction of oxygen atoms with carbon monoxide at room temperatures must be more than 150 fold slower than their reaction with molecular oxygen. Lewis and von Elbe[261] have concluded that the difference between the two reactions at ordinary temperatures must be at least 500 fold, probably because normal $CO_2(^1\Sigma)$ cannot be formed from normal $CO(^1\Sigma)$ and $O(^3P)$ without electronic rearrangement. Garvin[147] from a study of the effect of carbon monoxide on the ozone decomposition at 150–300°C concluded that the reaction of oxygen atoms with carbon monoxide has no activation energy and occurs with a triple collision efficiency of about 10^{-3}. Kaufman[240] found that the rate of removal of oxygen atoms by CO + NO mixtures in his flow system was only slightly faster than that by corresponding A + NO mixtures. It was not possible to determine whether this was due to the O + CO reaction or to the increased effectiveness of carbon monoxide over argon as the third body in the $O + O_2 + M$ and $O + O + M$ reactions, and he concluded that if reaction (V-54) occurs at all, its rate constant must be less than about 5×10^8 liter^2 mole^{-2} sec^{-1}.

These various estimates, summarized in Table 42, show a wide

TABLE 42

ESTIMATED RATE CONSTANTS FOR THE REACTION
$O(^3P) + CO + M \rightarrow CO_2 + M$

Author	k_{54} (l^2 mole^{-2} sec^{-1})
Jackson	$<4.6 \times 10^5$
Lewis and von Elbe	$<1.4 \times 10^5$
Garvin	$\sim 10^7$
Kaufman	$<5 \times 10^8$

range, but even the highest values do not assign any importance to reaction (V-54) in urban air. Thus at a carbon monoxide concentration of 10 ppm[351] and an oxygen atom concentration of 3×10^{-6} pphm in air, Garvin's estimate would lead to a rate of $\sim 10^{-3}$ pphm hr^{-1}, and Kaufman's to a rate of <0.1 pphm hr^{-1}, for this reaction.

Contrary to the case with ^3P oxygen atoms, the reaction

$$O(^1D) + CO(^1\Sigma) + M \rightarrow CO_2(^1\Sigma) + M \tag{V-55}$$

is permitted by the spin conservation rules, and might on this account be considerably faster than (V-54). Even so, it is doubtful that it has any significance in air.

The reaction of oxygen atoms with hydrogen is probably

$$O + H_2 \rightarrow OH + H - 1.7 \text{ kcal} \quad S_{56} = k_{56}(O)(H_2) \tag{V-56}$$

In their experiments with oxygen atoms produced in the electric discharge, Harteck and Kopsch[186] found that this reaction is very slow at room temperature, the observed rate corresponding to a collision yield [185] of $\sim 10^{-7}$, or a rate constant of $k_{56} \sim 3 \times 10^4$ liter mole^{-1} sec^{-1}. In his more refined experiments using similar technique Kaufman[240] obtained $k_{56} = 2$ to 4×10^4 liter mole^{-1} sec^{-1}, a value virtually identical with that of Harteck and Kopsch. These low values are confirmed by the conclusion of Schumacher,[380] based on experiments involving the photodissociation of nitrogen dioxide in the presence of hydrogen, that reaction (V-56) is at least 10^4 times slower than $O + NO_2 \rightarrow O_2 + NO$ [reaction (V-28)]. At the normal atmospheric hydrogen concentration of 50 pphm,[156,264,324] the resulting rate of reaction, with oxygen atoms at 3×10^{-6} pphm, would be $<10^{-5}$ pphm hr^{-1}.

The reaction of oxygen atoms with water molecules to form two hydroxyl radicals,

$$O + H_2O \rightarrow 2\,\dot{O}H - 18 \text{ kcal} \tag{V-57}$$

has occasionally been postulated as a source of free radicals in polluted air. Although the reaction with ^3P atoms probably does occur at elevated temperatures, the indicated endothermicity of 18 kcal would require that its collision yield at ordinary temperatures be less than 10^{-13}. In agreement with this, Harteck and Kopsch[185,186] found no reaction between ^3P oxygen atoms and water vapor at room temperature. On the other hand, with ^1D oxygen atoms the reaction with water to form hydroxyl radicals is some 27 kcal exothermic, and evidence suggesting a rapid reaction has been obtained by McGrath and Norrish[275,306] through their experiments on the flash photolysis of moist ozone (Chapter III). Unfortunately, no rate constants for either reaction are available.

Since the products are presumably hydroxyl radicals, the possibility of a significant rate of reaction between oxygen atoms and water in polluted air is of particular interest. With ^3P oxygen atoms at 3×10^{-6} pphm, water vapor at 2×10^6 pphm (corresponding to 60% RH at 25°C), and a collision yield of 10^{-13}, the rate of reaction (V-57) would be less than 10^{-6} pphm hr^{-1}, which quite definitely rules it out. With ^1D oxygen atoms only speculation is possible. If ^1D oxygen atoms are formed at all in the lower atmosphere, the rate of their formation is not large (Section 1), and in order to compete significantly with the other reactions of these atoms, such as collisional deactivation and reaction with oxygen, it would be necessary that the rate of their reaction with water be comparable with or higher than that of these other processes. Since the concentration of water molecules in air is normally about 1/10 that of oxygen and 1/50 of the total, this would require that the bimolecular collision yield of the reaction with water be at least an order of magnitude higher than that of the reaction with oxygen, and two orders of magnitude higher than that of the collisional deactivation. Even though doubtful, this is a possibility which should be investigated.

The reaction of oxygen atoms with sulfur dioxide is probably

$$O + SO_2 + M \rightarrow SO_3 + M \quad S_{58} = k_{58}(O)(SO_2)(M) \tag{V-58}$$

Kaufman,[240] using the technique previously described, has obtained for this reaction, at 25°C, the value $k_{58} = 3 \times 10^{10}$ liter^2 mole^{-2} sec^{-1}, or 1.8×10^{-5} pphm^{-2} hr^{-1}. As with Ford and Endow's rate constant for $O + NO_2 + M \rightarrow NO_3 + M$ (Section 7), this is larger than the hypothetical termolecular frequency factor but does not, even so, assign any importance to this reaction in urban air. Thus at a sulfur dioxide concentration of 20 pphm and an oxygen atom concentration of 3×10^{-6} pphm, with the foregoing value of the rate constant, the rate of reaction (V-58) will be only 0.1 pphm hr^{-1}.

In addition to reactions with gaseous pollutants, the possibility of a reaction between oxygen atoms and particulate material in urban air must be considered. Although nothing is known of such reactions, their rates cannot exceed the rate at which oxygen atoms reach the particulate surface, and this can be estimated.

The distance from a surface at which diffusion thereto will become appreciable will be of the order of magnitude of the root-mean-square displacement, $\bar{X}$, during the life of the oxygen atoms τ. By Smoluchowsky's formula this is

$$\bar{X} = \left(\frac{\bar{\mu}l\tau}{3\pi}\right)^{1/2} \tag{V-59}$$

where $\bar{\mu}$ is the root-mean-square velocity, and l the mean free path. The average life of the oxygen atoms with respect to their reaction with molecular oxygen is $\tau = 1/k_3(O_2)(M)$, which, from Table 35 is about 4×10^{-5} sec at ordinary temperatures. Taking $\bar{\mu} = 5 \times 10^4$ cm sec^{-1}, $l = 5 \times 10^{-6}$ cm, and $\tau = 4 \times 10^{-5}$ sec, equation (V-59) gives $\bar{X} = 10^{-3}$ cm.

If the air contains 1 mg m^{-3} of particulate matter[351] of mass median diameter 0.5 μ and density 1, the number of particles per cubic centimeter will be 1.5×10^4. The volume within a distance of 10^{-3} cm from each particle will be 4.5×10^{-9} cm^3, and the volume within this distance of all the particles in 1 cc of air will be $4.5 \times 10^{-9} \times 1.5 \times 10^4 = 7 \times 10^{-5}$ cm^3. Assuming the oxygen atoms are formed uniformly throughout the air, only this fraction, 7×10^{-5}, will be formed within the distance $\overline{X}$ of a particulate surface, and the fraction reaching that surface will be smaller still. If the oxygen atoms were being formed in the air at the rate of 100 pphm hr^{-1}, they would reach the surface of suspended particles, under the conditions of the foregoing calculation, at a rate of less than 0.01 pphm hr^{-1}. From this, it may be concluded that any reactions of atomic oxygen with the particulate matter in urban air will be negligible.

10. SUMMARY OF OXYGEN ATOM REACTIONS

Under conditions of air pollution which lead to photochemical smog formation, ^3P oxygen atoms may be formed at a rate well in excess of 100 pphm hr^{-1} by the photolyses of nitrogen dioxide and ozone. Some ^1D oxygen atom formation, possibly at a rate of the order of 1 to 10 pphm hr^{-1}, may also result from the photolysis of ozone.

The conclusions of this chapter regarding relative rates of the reactions of ^3P oxygen atoms under such conditions are summarized in Table 43. On the basis of the reactions and reactant concentrations listed in this table, over 99.7% of the ^3P oxygen atoms will react with molecular oxygen, and less than 0.3% will react by all of the other processes added together. These figures will, of course, change with concentration, and they may also be changed as more accurate information on individual reaction rates becomes available. But, unless there exists some unknown and very fast reaction of ^3P oxygen atoms, the conclusion seems inescapable that in polluted air these atoms react almost exclusively with molecular oxygen to form ozone. Of the minor reactions of ^3P oxygen atoms, the most important is that with the olefins, which may achieve an over-all rate in the range of 0.1 to 1 pphm hr^{-1}, followed by the reactions with nitrogen dioxide and sulfur dioxide, which may reach rates in the vicinity of 0.1 pphm hr^{-1}. On the basis of present information all other reactions of ^3P oxygen atoms in polluted air are negligible.

The fate of any ^1D oxygen atoms formed in the air is unknown. Again the most likely process is reaction with molecular oxygen to form ozone, either directly or preceded by collisional deactivation to the ^3P state. Other reactions, of unknown though doubtful importance, include that of ^1D oxygen atoms with carbon monoxide to form carbon dioxide, and with water to form hydroxyl radicals.

The overwhelming importance of the reaction with molecular oxygen

TABLE 43

SUMMARY OF ESTIMATED RELATIVE RATES OF ^3P OXYGEN ATOM REACTIONS IN AIR

Reaction	Concentration of reactant other than O (pphm)	Estimated relative rate at 25°C
$O + O_2$	2×10^7	100
$O + O_3$	50	10^{-4}
$O + O$	—	6×10^{-10}
$O + N_2$	8×10^7	7×10^{-4}
$O + NO$	10	0.01
$O + NO_2 \rightarrow NO + O_2$	10	0.02
$O + NO_2 \rightarrow NO_3$	10	0.07
$O + CH_4$	250	0.001
O + higher paraffins (estimated av. collision yield $\sim 10^{-4}$)	25	0.001
$O + C_2H_4$	50	0.014
O + higher olefins (estimated av. collision yield $\sim 10^{-2}$)	25	0.1
$O + C_2H_2$	10	~ 0.01
$O + C_6H_6$	10	~ 0.01
$O + CH_3CHO$	25	0.005
$O + CO$	1000	$< 10^{-3}$
$O + H_2$	50	$< 10^{-5}$
$O + H_2O$	2×10^6	$\sim 10^{-7}$
$O + SO_2$	20	0.04
O + particulates	1 mg/m^3	< 0.01

leads to two corollary conclusions. First, the photodissociation of ozone will increase the stationary oxygen atom concentration but will not result in the disappearance of any substantial amount of ozone. Second, the net rate of ozone formation via the oxygen atom–molecular oxygen reaction will be virtually equal to the rate of photochemical dissociation of nitrogen dioxide.

Chapter VI

Reactions of Ozone

1. The Thermal Decomposition of Ozone in Air

The experimental evidence, as noted in Chapter V, indicates that the homogeneous thermal decomposition of gaseous ozone to molecular oxygen occurs in steps:

$$O_3 + M \rightarrow O_2 + O + M \qquad \text{(V-4)}$$
$$O + O_2 + M \rightarrow O_3 + M \qquad \text{(V-3)}$$
$$O + O_3 \rightarrow 2\,O_2 \qquad \text{(V-5)}$$

The observed rate of the decomposition, over the temperature range 78–110°C and at ozone pressures of 8 to 400 mm, is expressed by equations (V-7) to (V-14), which need not be repeated here. Assuming that an extrapolation from the experimental temperatures and pressures is valid, these equations indicate that under the conditions existing in polluted air the rate of thermal decomposition of ozone will be very slow. For example, at low concentrations in air at 1 atm, 25°C, the half-life of ozone relative to the first step in the decomposition, reaction (V-4), will be 1.6×10^3 hr, and the half-life relative to the over-all decomposition to molecular oxygen will be $3.7 \times 10^{10}/(O_3)$ hr, where (O_3) is the ozone concentration in pphm. The corresponding rates, at an ozone concentration of 50 pphm, will be 0.03 pphm hr^{-1} for the first step and 7×10^{-8} pphm hr^{-1} for the over-all decomposition. On the basis of these figures, it is evident that the homogeneous thermal decomposition of ozone is of no importance in polluted air.

2. The Reaction of Ozone with Nitric Oxide

$$NO + O_3 \rightarrow NO_2 + O_2 + 48 \text{ kcal} \qquad S_1 = k_1(NO)(O_3) \qquad \text{(VI-1)}$$

This reaction was studied by Johnston and Crosby[228] using the method of Johnston and Yost[230] for the study of fast reactions. Dilute ozone and nitric oxide, each in nitrogen as a carrier gas, were mixed and led through an 0.8×10-cm stainless steel reaction cell, the ends of which were equipped with quartz windows. After a steady state was reached (about 3 sec), the flow into and out of the cell was cut off by needle valves, and the rate of disappearance of ozone therein was followed by light absorption, using 2537 A. The delay time from the mixing chamber to the reaction cell was 0.1 sec, and the needle valves could be closed somewhat faster than this. The amount of light absorption was measured with a photocell-electron multiplier tube and an oscilloscope with a sweep frequency of 0.2 to 2 sec. The absorption coefficient of ozone at 2537 A was taken as $\alpha = 6.3 \times 10^3$ liter mole^{-1} cm^{-1}, and corrections were made for absorption by nitrogen tetroxide, for which the absorption coefficient at 2537 A was taken as $\alpha = 0.27 \times 10^3$ liter mole^{-1} cm^{-1}.

The stoichiometry of the reaction was established at concentrations and temperatures at which the rate was too fast to follow, but chosen to improve the precision of making up known amounts of nitric oxide. In a few runs at room temperature the amount of nitrogen dioxide formed was determined by absorption of 4360 A. With excess ozone it was found that one ozone molecule immediately disappeared for each nitric oxide originally present, and with excess nitric oxide one nitrogen dioxide molecule (corrected for nitrogen tetroxide) was immediately produced for each ozone originally present. Subsequent slower reactions of ozone with nitrogen dioxide and of oxygen with nitric oxide disturb these ratios, but do not disturb the conclusion that stoichiometrically the reaction of ozone with nitric oxide is as written in equation (VI-1).

The rate of the reaction was followed at ~ -75 and ~ -43°C, at initial nitric oxide concentrations of 0.17×10^{-8} to 1.85×10^{-8} mole cc^{-1}, and initial ozone concentrations of 0.27×10^{-8} to 2.13×10^{-8} mole cc^{-1}. For comparative purposes, relative to air at 25°C, these would correspond to 4.1×10^3 to 4.5×10^4 pphm of nitric oxide and 6.6×10^3 to 5.2×10^4 pphm of ozone. The nitrogen pressure varied from about 130 to 650 mm.

As the nitric oxide concentration could not be accurately determined at these concentrations and temperatures, the runs were made with a slight excess of ozone, and the difference between the ozone present at any time and that remaining at the end of the run was assumed to be equal to the nitric oxide present.

The order of the reaction was determined by comparing the curves of concentration versus time with the various integrated rate expressions. It was found to be second order, with the rate law given in equation (VI-1). The rate constants from individual runs and a line found by least squares are shown in Fig. 35. This line yields the expression

$$k_1 = 8.0 \times 10^8 e^{-(2500\pm300)/RT} \text{ liter mole}^{-1} \text{ sec}^{-1} \qquad \text{(VI-2)}$$

Values for k_1 in the atmospheric temperature range, calculated from this expression, are given in Table 44. The factor of uncertainty in these values is approximately two.

An independent value for k_1, obtained by Ford, Doyle, and Endow[135] under conditions approximating those in polluted air, is also included in Table 44. This value was obtained by measuring the stationary ozone

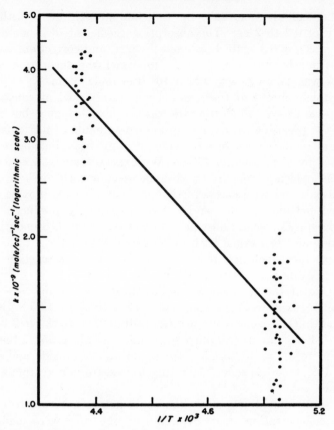

FIG. 35. Rate constant data for the nitric oxide–ozone reaction. From H. S. Johnston and H. J. Crosby (Ref. 228).

TABLE 44

RATE CONSTANTS FOR THE REACTION $NO + O_3 \rightarrow NO_2 + O_2$

Temp. °C	k_1, from Johnston and Crosby [equation (VI-2)]		k_1, from Ford, Doyle, and Endow	
	l mole^{-1} sec^{-1}	pphm^{-1} hr^{-1}	l mole^{-1} sec^{-1}	pphm^{-1} hr^{-1}
0	7.9×10^6	11.7	—	—
10	9.3×10^6	13.7	—	—
20	1.09×10^7	16.0	—	—
25	1.17×10^7	17.2	—	—
30	1.25×10^7	18.4	2.8×10^7	41
40	1.43×10^7	21.0	—	—

concentration produced during the photolysis of nitrogen dioxide at concentrations of 5 to 160 pphm in pure dry air at 1 atm. The measurements of ozone concentration were made in a separate photometer cell, and ozone decay in transit to the photometer had to be taken into account. In view of the uncertainties attached to both investigations, and particularly in view of the fact that at 30°C the value of k_1 obtained from Johnston and Crosby's data represents an extrapolation of 75°C from the nearest experimental temperature, the difference between the two values has little if any significance.

In air, the reaction of nitric oxide with ozone is complementary to the photolysis of nitrogen dioxide, followed by the reaction of oxygen atoms with molecular oxygen:

$$NO_2 + h\nu \rightarrow NO + O \qquad \phi k_a(NO_2) \qquad (V\text{-}1)$$
$$O + O_2 + M \rightarrow O_3 + M \qquad (V\text{-}3)$$
$$NO + O_3 \rightarrow NO_2 + O_2 \quad k_1(NO)(O_3) \qquad (VI\text{-}1)$$

In the absence of other competing reactions, and in the absence of rapid changes in light intensity or reactant concentrations, the rates of these two processes must approach equality. Setting them equal gives

$$\frac{(NO)(O_3)}{(NO_2)} = \frac{\phi k_a}{k_1} \qquad (VI\text{-}3)$$

Values of the ratio k_a/k_1, estimated for Los Angeles air, are shown in Fig. 36.

All of the available evidence indicates that over most of the daylight hours in polluted urban air the nitrogen dioxide photolysis and the nitric oxide–ozone reaction occur at higher rates than do any other known reactions involving the same substances. If this is the case, the rates of the two must tend to approach equality, and the product ratio $(NO)(O_3)/(NO_2)$ will tend to approach the values given by equation (VI-3), or taking $\phi = 1$, the values given in Fig. 36.

These values severely limit the concentrations at which nitric oxide and ozone can coexist in air. To illustrate by two specific examples, if the nitrogen dioxide and ozone concentrations are both 10 pphm and $k_a/k_1 = 1.0$ (the approximate conditions at 9 to 10 A.M. from Figs. 32 and 36), the rate of the nitric oxide–ozone reaction will equal the rate of the nitrogen dioxide photolysis at a nitric oxide concentration of 1 pphm. If $(NO_2) = 2$ pphm and $(O_3) = 20$ pphm with $k_a/k_1 = 1.0$ (the approximate noon conditions from Figs. 33 and 36), the upper limit to the nitric oxide concentration permitted by equation (VI-3) is only 0.1 pphm.

For a number of reasons, however, this equation should be regarded as yielding only an approximation to the actual $(NO)(O_3)/(NO_2)$ product ratio in air. In the first place, there are the uncertainties regard-

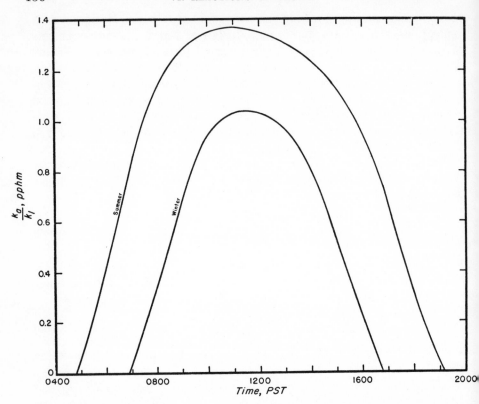

Fig. 36. Diurnal variation in the ratio k_a/k_1. The upper curve is based on values of k_a for NO_2 during representative summer solstice radiation conditions over Los Angeles, and on values of k_1 from Johnston and Crosby (Table 44), estimated for a diurnal temperature range of 60–90°F. The lower curve is similarly estimated for the winter solstice, with a diurnal temperature range of 40–70°F.

ing the values of ϕ, k_a, and k_1, upon which the estimated "equal rates" product ratio is based. Next, the equal rates relation in effect assumes a stationary state with respect to all three of the reactants involved, the approach to this stationary state will be disturbed by changes in light intensity and reactant concentrations, and the criteria of validity discussed in Chapter IV, Section 6 will apply to both reactions.

In relation to these criteria, by rule 1 (p. 112, the assumption of a stationary state in air may, in general, be considered valid if $1/k_r(C)$ or its equivalent for the reaction concerned is less than 1 min. The value of $1/k_a$ when the sun is halfway to the zenith ($z = 45°$) is about 3 min, and one hour after sunrise or one hour before sunset, it is about 10 min. The value of $1/k_1(C)$, where (C) is the concentration of either nitric oxide or ozone, will be less than 1 min only if (C) is greater than ~ 3 pphm. This must, therefore, be regarded as a borderline case insofar as the validity of a stationary state assumption is concerned, and substantial departures from the equal rates product ratio may occur at times when either k_a or the reactant concentrations are changing rapidly, especially when the reactant concentrations are low.

Third, the stationary state concentrations, and hence the $(NO)(O_3)/(NO_2)$ product ratio, will be disturbed by other reactions. An example of this is provided by the reactions, which will be discussed subsequently,

$$NO_2 + O_3 \rightarrow NO_3 + O_2$$
$$NO + NO_3 \rightarrow 2NO_2$$

These reactions, taken together, accomplish the same result as the nitric oxide-ozone reaction and will in effect make the actual $(NO)(O_3)/(NO_2)$ product ratio slightly smaller than the value calculated from equation (VI-3).

3. The Reaction of Ozone with Nitrogen Dioxide

$$NO_2 + O_3 \rightarrow NO_3 + O_2 \ (+\sim 25 \text{ kcal}) \quad S_4 = k_4(NO_2)(O_3) \qquad \text{(VI-4)}$$

This reaction was studied by Johnston and Yost[230] in the temperature range 13–29°C, at NO_2 and O_3 partial pressures of roughly 2×10^{-3} to 2×10^{-2} atm. The reactants, each carried in a stream of oxygen gas, were mixed in about 0.01 sec, and the mixture passed through a 2×37-mm reaction cell. When a steady state had been reached the flow was stopped by cut-off valves and the disappearance of NO_2 was followed by light absorption, using a chopped light beam, photomultiplier tube, and oscilloscope.

Although the stoichiometric equation for the reaction was found to be

$$2NO_2 + O_3 \rightarrow N_2O_5 + O_2$$

the rate equation obtained was that of a simple bimolecular process, first order with respect to both NO_2 and O_3, with a rate constant given by the expression

$$k = 5.9 \times 10^9 e^{-(7000\pm600)/RT} \text{ liter mole}^{-1} \text{ sec}^{-1} \qquad \text{(VI-5)}$$

The authors concluded that the reaction occurs in two steps, with (VI-4) as the first and rate determining step, followed by the fast reaction

$$NO_2 + NO_3 \ (+M) \rightarrow N_2O_5 \ (+M)$$

On this basis, the experimentally determined rate constant would be that of reaction (VI-4).

The rate constant for this reaction at low reactant concentrations in pure air at 1 atm, and 25°C has been determined by Ford et al.,[135] using a 50-liter reaction flask and a flow system. The nitrogen dioxide steady-state concentration range was from 15 to 50 pphm, and that of the ozone was from 30 to 160 pphm. The ozone was determined in situ by light absorption, and the nitrogen dioxide in the effluent stream was followed with a continuous recorder.[362] The mean value thus obtained for the rate constant, as well as values calculated from equation (VI-5), are given in Table 45.

TABLE 45

RATE CONSTANTS FOR THE REACTION $NO_2 + O_3 \rightarrow NO_3 + O_2$
(Factor of uncertainty ~3.)

Temp. °C	From Johnston and Yost [equation (VI-5)]		From Ford, Doyle, and Endow	
	l mole^{-1} sec^{-1}	pphm^{-1} hr^{-1}	l mole^{-1} sec^{-1}	pphm^{-1} hr^{-1}
0	1.4×10^4	0.021	—	—
10	2.3×10^4	0.034	—	—
20	3.5×10^4	0.051	—	—
25	4.3×10^4	0.063	2×10^4	0.03
30	5.1×10^4	0.075	—	—
40	7.5×10^4	0.10	. —	—

Comparing these values with Table 44, it is seen that, at equal concentrations, the reaction of ozone with nitrogen dioxide is from 300 to 1000 fold slower than is its reaction with nitric oxide. Nevertheless, the reaction is still fast enough to be important in air. For example, at 25°C, with nitrogen dioxide and ozone concentrations of 10 pphm each, the rate of the reaction, based on the figures in Table 45, will be from 3 to 6 pphm hr^{-1}

4. THE REACTIONS OF OZONE WITH OLEFIN HYDROCARBONS

Studies of the reactions between ozone and the olefins provide ample evidence that a complex over-all process is involved, with stoichiometry, kinetics, and products all dependent on experimental conditions. For this reason it is not surprising that reported results show wide variations, and it becomes the task of the reviewer to attempt to correlate those variations.

The first quantitative studies to be reported on the kinetics of the gas phase reactions were those of Cadle and Schadt.[63,65,66] Two reaction systems were used; in one system the reaction cell consisted of a 10-cu m air-filled galvanized iron chamber, to which known amounts of reactants were added and mixed with an electric fan, and from which samples were withdrawn for analysis of oxidant by titration with neutral KI. Apparently no attempt was made to purify the air in the chamber, although its relative humidity was varied from 40 to 12% by use of drying agents. The temperatures in the chamber were from 8 to 27°C, and the reactant concentrations from 1 to 10 ppm. The results obtained from this system suffered from the facts that only the initial concentration of the hydrocarbon was known and that any product capable of oxidizing iodide ion would interfere with the ozone analysis.

In the second system, used only for the ozone–ethylene reaction, ozone in tank oxygen as a carrier and ethylene in tank nitrogen as a carrier were passed through a mixing chamber similar to that used by Johnston and Yost,[230] and thence immediately into the previously evacuated 3×10-cm absorption cell of an infrared spectrometer. The ethylene concentration in this cell was followed by its absorption at 10.5 μ, and the ozone by absorption at 9.6 μ. The reaction products interfered with the ozone absorption and made its determination increasingly uncertain as the reaction progressed. In order to obtain sufficient absorption it was necessary to use reactant concentrations around a thousand-fold higher than those used in the large chamber; the initial partial pressures were from 0.3 to 2.8 mm of ozone and 0.14 to 1.6 mm of ethylene. The pressure of the nitrogen–oxygen mixture in the cell was from 150 to 620 mm, and the temperatures were from 30 to 50°C.

The results obtained from both reaction systems were in agreement in indicating that the over-all reaction is nonstoichiometric and that more olefin than ozone is consumed. The apparent ratio of olefin to ozone consumed varied both with the starting concentrations and with the extent to which the reaction had proceeded. Values deduced from the data varied from 1:1 to over 3:1. However, in the experiments based on iodimetric titration the apparent deficiency in ozone consumed may have been due, in part at least, to oxidizing products.

On extrapolating concentrations and rates back to the time of mixing, and comparing the resultant figures for different runs, it was found that, for a given olefin, the initial rates for all starting mixtures conformed to a simple bimolecular equation

$$S_i = k_i(\mathrm{O_3})(\text{olefin}) \tag{VI-6a}$$

The initial rate constants k_i were determined in two ways, with essentially identical results; by extrapolating the observed rates to the initial reactant concentrations and by extrapolating rate constants to zero time. The initial rate constants so obtained appeared to be independent of the

TABLE 46

RATE CONSTANTS FOR OZONE–OLEFIN REACTIONS[a]

Olefin	k (l mole^{-1} sec^{-1}) $\times 10^{-3}$				
	Cadle and Schadt, k_i based on O_3	Hanst, Stephens, Scott, and Doerr, based on O_3	Saltzman and Gilbert, based on O_3	Schuck and Doyle, based on olefin	Vrbaški and Cvetanović, relative rates based on carbonyl products
Ethylene	1.8	0.8	—	—	2.4
Propylene	3.7	4.9	—	—	6.7
1-Butene	—	—	—	—	5.1
Isobutene	—	3.7	—	8.5	4.8
cis-2-Butene	—	2.9	—	—	17.6
trans-2-Butene	—	—	—	100	21.8
1-3 Butadiene	—	4.9	—	—	—
1-Pentene	3.2	4.5	—	~6	5.1
cis-2-Pentene	—	—	—	—	13.5
trans-2-Pentene	—	98 (cis-trans)	—	—	16.7
2-Methyl 1-butene	—	—	—	—	5.3
3-Methyl 1-butene	—	—	—	—	4.0
2-Methyl 2-butene	—	—	—	—	15.5
1-Hexene	6.1	6.1	5.5	6.9	6.1 (assumed)
Tetramethylethylene	—	—	—	—	18.2
Cyclohexene	35.4	—	—	—	17.9
1-Heptene	4.9	—	—	—	—
3-Heptene (cis-trans)	—	53	—	—	—
1-Octene	4.9	—	—	—	—
1-Decene	6.6	—	—	—	—

[a] Values are for an assumed bimolecular reaction with $S = k(O_3)(olefin)$.

pressure and relative humidity of the carrier gas, and in the case of the
ozone–ethylene reaction both reaction systems gave the same value of k_i.
Resultant values are reported in Table 46.

In order to illustrate the extent to which, with progress of the reaction, the rates observed by Cadle and Schadt departed from simple
bimolecular behavior, in Fig. 37 the observed ozone concentration vs. time

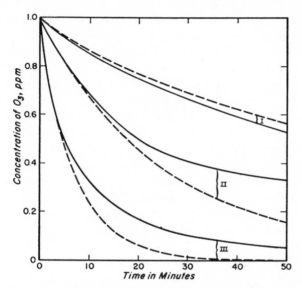

FIG. 37. Ozone concentration vs. time curves for ozone–olefin reactions. Solid lines
are observed oxidant concentrations; dashed lines are calculated ozone concentrations for a bimolecular reaction with $k = k_i$.

Curve no.	Starting mixture
I	1 ppm O_3 + 1 ppm 1-hexene
II	1 ppm O_3 + 10 ppm ethylene
III	1 ppm O_3 + 10 ppm 1-hexene

curves for three typical runs are compared with the calculated curves for
a bimolecular reaction with $k = k_i$. In this case the departure from bimolecular behavior is negligible in the case of starting concentrations of
1 ppm each of ozone and 1-hexene (curve I) but when an excess of hexene
was used the difference becomes significant after the ozone concentration
has dropped below about half its original value (curve III). Experiments
with ethylene (curve II) and other olefins showed similar behavior, with
the apparent ozone concentration decreasing less rapidly with time than
would be estimated on the basis of a bimolecular reaction. As already

noted, this effect may have been due at least in part to interference of oxidizing products with the iodimetric titration used for ozone determination.

Two attempts were made by Cadle and Schadt to determine the activation energy of the initial reactions, one with ozone and 1-hexene in the large chamber, and one with the ozone–ethylene reaction in the small cell. In the former case, the temperature was varied from 8 to 27°C, and in the latter from 30 to 50°C. In neither case was any statistically significant change in k_i with temperature observed, although with the ozone–ethylene reaction the results suggest a temperature coefficient corresponding to an activation energy of ~6 kcal.

The rate constants of Hanst et al. [184] were obtained by using the 640-liter cell of their long-path infrared spectrometer[403,405] as the reaction vessel, and following reactant and product concentrations by infrared absorption. All experiments were carried out at 1 atm total pressure, in most cases using untreated air containing the normal amounts of water and carbon dioxide. Olefin was added by diluting the desired quantity with cylinder oxygen in a side-bulb and sweeping the mixture into the large cell with additional oxygen. Ozone was prepared in a discharge tube and swept into the reaction cell with cylinder oxygen. The mixture was stirred by a blower operated, circulating system which took the air–reactant mixture from one end of the cell and reintroduced it at the other. When desired, fresh air and reactants could be introduced into the circulating mixture as it entered the cell, and an equivalent volume exhausted from the other end. The system could thus be operated as either a batch or a stirred flow reactor, the former being more suitable for slow and the latter for fast reactions. The infrared bands used for following reactant concentrations were 9.6 μ for ozone, 11.0 μ for 1-olefins, 11.2 μ for isobutene, and 10.4 μ for 2- and 3-olefins. For calibration purposes the absorptivity of ozone was determined with some care, the value obtained

TABLE 47

STOICHIOMETRY OF OZONE–OLEFIN REACTIONS
(From Hanst, Stephens, Scott, and Doerr.)

Olefin	Amount of olefin (ppm)		Amount of ozone (ppm)		Ratio of olefin/ozone consumed
	Initial	Reacted	Initial	Reacted	
Ethylene	20	5.2	20	5.5	0.95
Propylene	40	12.7	11.9	11.9	1.07
2-Pentene	6.2	6.2	13.1	5.6	1.11
3-Heptene	5.8	5.8	13.4	5.8	1.0

for its decadic absorption coefficient at 9.48 μ was $\alpha = 3.74 \times 10^{-4}$ ppm^{-1} m^{-1}.

The stoichiometry of the reaction was investigated by Hanst, Stephens, Scott, and Doerr for four olefins, with the results given in Table 47. Within experimental error, a 1:1 ratio of olefin to ozone consumed was obtained. The simple bimolecular rate law which these results would indicate was verified for 1-pentene and *cis*-2-butene by following the disappearance of ozone in static reactions. Integrating the rate equation

$$\frac{-d(O_3)}{dt} = k(O_3)(\text{olefin}) \qquad \text{(VI-6b)}$$

with the assumption of a 1:1 stoichiometry gives

$$\log\left(1 + \frac{e}{(O_3)}\right) - \log\left(1 + \frac{e}{(O_3)}\right)_0 = \frac{ekt}{2.303} \qquad \text{(VI-7)}$$

where e is the excess of olefin concentration over that of the ozone. If this equation holds, a plot of $\log\ [1 + e/(O_3)]$ against time should yield a straight line; the results, shown in Fig. 38, confirm the second-order

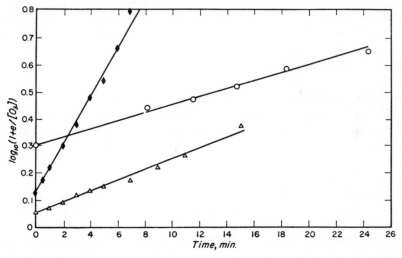

FIG. 38. Test of second-order rate law for ozone–olefin reactions. From Hanst *et al.* (Ref. 184).

kinetics of the reaction. The rate constants obtained on this basis are included in Table 46.

The value of Saltzman and Gilbert[370] for the rate constant of the ozone-1-hexene reaction (Table 46) was derived from measurements of the rate of ozone consumption in a 10-liter turbulent flow reactor. Ozone concentrations ranged from 0.3 to 80 ppm and hexene from 1.4 to 37 ppm, with air at 1 atm and 22 to 28°C, containing 0.9 to 3.0 mole % of water vapor, as the carrier. Total oxidant was measured by titration with neutral KI, and ozone by introducing an excess of nitric oxide, allowing it just time to react with the ozone, and titrating the resulting nitrogen dioxide with Griess-Saltzman reagent. In this manner it was found that products capable of oxidizing neutral KI are formed during the reaction, in amount corresponding to 0.17 to 0.25 of the ozone consumed. The amount of hexene consumed was not measured, but calculations by an indirect method gave, except for one atypical experiment, hexene/ozone ratios of 0.9 to 1.3. In estimating the rate constant the reaction was assumed to be first order with respect to both ozone and hexene.

A few experiments by Schuck and Doyle[378] on the kinetics of ozone-olefin reactions at low concentrations in air have yielded results which partly agree and are partly at variance with those of Hanst, Stephens, Scott, and Doerr. The experiments were conducted in the 520-cu ft chamber previously used [376,377,379] for the irradiation of dilute automobile exhaust and of nitric oxide–nitrogen dioxide–olefin mixtures in air. Initial ozone concentrations were generally in the range of 0.5 to 1.0 ppm, and initial olefin concentrations 1 to 3 ppm. In some cases the initial ozone concentration was allowed to decrease with the reaction, in other cases it was maintained at or near a fixed value by slowly bleeding in an ozone–oxygen mixture from an ozonizer. Both ozone and olefin concentrations were followed by long-path infrared spectrometry, using the absorption at 9.5 μ for ozone, and ~3.4 and 11 μ for the olefin.

The ratios of olefin to ozone consumed, observed by Schuck and Doyle, were close to 1/1 for 1-hexene, but nearly 3/1 for isobutene. In both cases there appeared to be little change in these ratios with the course of the reaction. In accordance with this, the bimolecular rate constant, calculated from the instantaneous rates and concentrations, remained fairly steady in the case of 1-hexene, but decreased with time to less than half its initial value in the case of isobutene. This checks with the observations of Cadle and Schadt (Fig. 37), but not with those of Hanst, Stephens, Scott, and Doerr (Fig. 38). The cause of this variance cannot be pinpointed. All three groups of investigators used large reaction vessels, with reactant concentrations in the ppm range in air at room temperature. Hanst, Stephens, Scott, and Doerr, as well as Schuck and Doyle, used long-path infrared absorption to follow both the ozone and olefin concentrations. The two major differences are, first, that Hanst, Stephens, Scott, and Doerr used their infrared absorption cell itself as the reaction vessel, while Schuck and Doyle circulated the reaction mixture from the reaction chamber through the infrared cell, and second, that Schuck and

Doyle found the major departures from a 1:1 ratio and bimolecular behavior for isobutene, which Hanst, Stephens, Scott, and Doerr did not
investigate. Cadle and Schadt's results with 1-hexene approach those of
Hanst, Stephens, Scott, and Doerr when the olefin and ozone concentrations were equal (Fig. 37, curve I), but when the olefin was present in
excess (Fig. 37, curve III), they depart in the direction of Schuck and
Doyle's observations on isobutene. The observed departures from simple
second-order behavior, if real, indicate that secondary reactions, including either additional attack on the olefin or regeneration of ozone, are
partially governing the rate, and that as a result a more complex rate law
is required to describe the over-all kinetics of the reaction. This raises
the question, which cannot be answered without further investigation, of
whether the initial second-order rate constant in such cases is really the
rate constant for the initial reaction, or whether it is the resultant of a
combination of the rate constants of two or more reactions.

A number of relative rates have been obtained by Vrbaški and
Cvetanović[439] for ozone–olefin reactions, using a technique similar to that
employed by Cvetanović and his collaborators in the study of oxygen
atom–olefin reactions (Chapter V). A mixture of two olefins was allowed
to react with ozone, and the amounts of the major carbonyl product from
each olefin were determined by gas–liquid chromatography. The reactions were carried out in a 188-cc reaction vessel, at 25°C. In most cases
the combined initial olefin pressure was 40 mm, with an initial 2.5 mm
of ozone and 78 to 96 mm of oxygen; in some experiments initial pressures of 20 mm of olefins, 1 mm of ozone, and 30 to 40 mm of oxygen
were used. The required amounts of the two olefins were first led into
the reaction cell, and the ozone–oxygen mixture was then slowly introduced. After the reaction was completed, the condensable products were
frozen in a liquid nitrogen trap and then transferred to a chromatographic column for analysis.

By the method of competing reactions, if the two reactions concerned
are

$$A_1 + O_3 \rightarrow a_1P_1 + \text{other products} \tag{VI-8}$$
$$A_2 + O_3 \rightarrow a_2P_2 + \text{other products} \tag{VI-9}$$

if the initial concentrations $(A_1)_i$, $(A_2)_i$ of the two olefins are sufficiently
high so that they remain essentially unaltered by the reaction, and if
ΔP_1, and ΔP_2 are the amounts of P_1 and P_2 formed by the reaction, the
ratio of the two rate constants should be given by

$$\frac{k_1}{k_2} = \frac{\Delta P_1}{\Delta P_2} \cdot \frac{a_2(A_2)_i}{a_1(A_1)_i} \tag{VI-10}$$

Vrbaški and Cvetanović determined the ratio $\Delta P_1/\Delta P_2$ from GLC peak areas, and obtained a_1/a_2 from the amounts of P_1 and P_2 formed from each olefin taken singly, using the same amount of ozone in each case. The method requires that ozone be consumed exclusively by the two competing reactions, and that first-order relationships exist between reactants and products. By equation (VI-10) a plot of $\Delta P_1/\Delta P_2$ against $(A_1)_i/(A_2)_i$ should yield a straight line with zero intercept and slope equal to $(k_1/k_2')(a_1/a_2)$. Vrbaški and Cvetanović found such lines, and from their slopes divided by the corresponding a_1/a_2 values obtained a ratio of k_1/k_2 for each pair of olefins investigated. By using overlapping pairs, a series of relative rate constants was obtained. The resulting values, relative to an assumed value of 6.1×10^3 liter mole^{-1} sec^{-1} for 1-hexene, are given in the last column of Table 46.

Regardless of the reservations expressed earlier concerning the significance of bimolecular rate constants for the ozone–olefin reactions, the values of Table 46 show some interesting relations. First, the values for propylene and the higher 1-olefins are from 2 to 5 times that for ethylene, but there is no clear evidence of any further increase in the rate beyond propylene. Next, the values for the internal olefins are from 3 to ∽20 times those for the corresponding terminal olefins. Third, the relative rates of Vrbaški and Cvetanović, based on the major carbonyl product from each olefin, while showing in general the same trends with changing olefin structure as the rates based on ozone or olefin consumption, disclose some marked differences as well. Especially noteworthy in this regard are the differences in the case of *trans*-2-butene and the 2-pentenes.

It is interesting to compare the relative rates of the ozone–olefin reactions for different olefins with those of the oxygen atom–olefin reactions and with the rates of photochemical consumption of the same olefins in the presence of nitrogen dioxide in air. This is done in Table 48 for the olefins for which all three values are available. In each column the olefins are listed in order of increasing rate, using for oxygen atoms the relative rates of Cvetanović from Table 40, for ozone those of Vrbaški and Cvetanović from Table 46 (both based on product formation), and for the nitrogen dioxide photolysis the rates of Schuck and Doyle.[377] In each case the rate shown is relative to that for isobutene as unity. A study of the three columns discloses several common features and several differences. In all three cases the slowest olefin to react is ethylene and the fastest are *trans*-2-butene and tetramethylethylene. Also in all three cases the internal olefins react more rapidly than the terminal, and *trans*-2-butene reacts more rapidly than its *cis* isomer. Among the differences, the most striking are the variations in the position of propylene and isobutene. These differences are chiefly in the order of reaction rates with

TABLE 48

ORDER OF INCREASING RATE OF REACTIONS OF OLEFINS WITH OXYGEN ATOMS,
OZONE, AND PHOTOCHEMICALLY WITH NITROGEN DIOXIDE

Oxygen atoms		Ozone		Nitrogen dioxide (photochemical)	
Olefin	Rel. rate	Olefin	Rel. rate	Olefin	Rel. rate
Ethylene	0.04	Ethylene	0.50	Ethylene	0.04
Propylene	0.23	Isobutene	1.00	1-Butene	0.39
1-Pentene	0.23	1-Pentene	1.06	1-Pentene	0.50
1-Butene	0.24	1-Butene	1.06	Propylene	0.55
cis-2-Butene	0.84	Propylene	1.40	Isobutene	1.00
				cis-2-Butene	2.3
Isobutene	1.00	cis-2-Butene	3.7		
trans-2-Butene	1.13	Tetramethyl- ethylene	3.8	trans-2-Butene	3.6
Tetramethyl- ethylene	4.18	trans-2-Butene	4.5	Tetramethyl- ethylene	6.4

ozone relative to those with oxygen atoms; the order of photochemical reaction with nitrogen dioxide falls between the two.

There is no doubt that the ozone–olefin reactions are fast enough to be of major importance with respect to photochemical smog formation. For example, at the representative midmorning ozone concentration of 10 pphm and the distribution and concentration of olefins postulated in the similar estimate for oxygen atoms (page 145), the over-all rate of reaction, on the basis of the rate constants in Table 46, would fall in the range of 2 to 20 pphm hr^{-1}. This is an order of magnitude greater than the estimated over-all rate of the oxygen atom–olefin reactions at the same time of day.

In addition to the kinetic studies, a number of investigations have been pointed specifically at the reaction products of the ozone–olefin reactions, and the results of these investigations are summarized in Tables 49 and 50. The most extensive product analyses are those of Vrbaški and Cvetanović,[439] summarized in Table 50. These were obtained by gas–liquid chromatography, using the batch technique with the reactor employed in their determination of relative rate constants. Initial concentrations were mostly 40 mm of olefin, 10 mm of ozone, and 310 to 380 mm of oxygen; in a few cases initial mixtures of 20 mm of olefin, 2.5 mm of ozone, and 80 to 100 mm of oxygen were used. The identity of the products eluted by GLC was confirmed by infrared and mass spectro-

TABLE 49

SUMMARY OF REPORTED PRODUCTS OF GAS PHASE OZONE–OLEFIN REACTIONS

Olefin and investigator	Experimental conditions	Reported products	
Ethylene (Briner and Schnorf[52])	Flow system. Ozone and olefin in air, with and without added water vapor. Products identified by chemical analysis	1. Formaldehyde 2. Formic acid 3. Intermediate product, which was nonexplosive, water soluble, decomposed dry into formaldehyde and formic acid, and upon hydrolysis was converted first into dihydroxy methyl peroxide, finally into formaldehyde, formic acid, and hydrogen. Over-all yields up to 85% based on O_3.	
Ethylene (Scott, Stephens, Hanst, and Doerr[383])	Ethylene and ozone, 32 ppm each in 1 atm of oxygen, reacted statically in 640-l absorption cell of long-path infrared spectrometer. Products observed by IR.		Moles product per mole of ozone
		Water	0.9 ± 0.3
		Formaldehyde	0.5 ± 0.1
		CO	0.9 ± 0.2
		CO_2	0.12 ± 0.03
		Formic acid	<0.03
Propylene (Briner and Schnorf[52])	Flow system, using 0.025 atm of ozone and from 0.012 to 0.075 atm of propylene in 1 atm of air. Temp. 48–78°C. Products by chemical analysis.	Intermediate product which on hydrolysis yielded: 1. Formaldehyde 2. Acetaldehyde 3. Formic acid 4. Acetic acid	
Propylene (Scott, Stephens, Hanst, and Doerr[383])	Propylene and ozone, 32 ppm each in 1 atm of oxygen. Product analysis by IR.		Moles product per mole of ozone
		Water	1.6 ± 0.12
		Formaldehyde	0.5 ± 0.12
		Acetaldehyde	0.37 ± 0.06
		CO	0.62 ± 0.16
		CO_2	0.28 ± 0.06
		Ketene	0.05 ± 0.02
		Acid	<0.06

TABLE 49 (Continued)

Olefin and investigator	Experimental conditions	Reported products
1-Butene 2-Butene Isobutene (Briner and Meier[50])	Flow system, O_2 carrier at 1 atm, flow rate 10 to 15 l hr^{-1}. Ozone conc. 0.03 atm, olefin 0.04 to 0.05 atm. Temp. 40°–70°C. Chemical analyses.	1. Stable products: aldehydes, acids, and acetone. Yields up to 72%, based on O_3. 2. Intermediate, nonexplosive, water soluble products, from which the peroxides of formaldehyde and acetone were isolated.
1-Pentene (Hanst and Stephens[180])	Reactants plus air mixed upon entering previously evacuated 1-m absorption cell of infrared spectrometer. Initial conc. from ~400 to 10,000 ppm in air at 1 atm. Products observed by IR absorption. Added water vapor and change in initial reactant conc. had no effect on products.	1. Butyraldehyde (estimated amount about ⅔ of theoretical yield, based on O_3). 2. CO_2 (amount about ⅛ that of butyraldehyde). 3. Formic acid. 4. Transitory product absorbing at 4.7 and 8.4μ. 5. No detectable formaldehyde.
1-Pentene (Scott, Stephens, Hanst, and Doerr[383])	1-Pentene, 64 ppm, and 32 ppm of ozone reacted in 1 atm of oxygen. Analysis by IR.	Moles product per mole of ozone Water 1.6 ± 0.6 Formaldehyde 0.44 ± 0.12 Butyraldehyde 0.50 ± 0.06 CO 0.47 ± 0.12 CO_2 0.2 ± 0.1 Acid <0.03 Little or no ozonide
1-Hexene (Eastman and Silverstein[112])	Ozone and 1-hexene in anhydrous carrier (80% O_2, 20% N_2) at 1 atm mixed in flow reactor. Used 3:1 excess of hexene, with ozone conc. ~3000–6000 ppm. Products identified by chemical methods, supplemented by UV and IR absorption.	1. Gas was chiefly formaldehyde (30% of theoretical yield, based on O_3) 2. Liquid and condensed aerosol showed OH and C=O absorption, but only weak aldehyde absorption. On hydrolysis it yielded chiefly valeric acid and valeraldehyde. 3. Products had no strong oxiding power.

TABLE 49 (Continued)

Olefin and investigator	Experimental conditions	Reported products
1-Hexene (Saltzman[369])	Flow system designed to study fast reactions. Ozone conc. 1500 ppm; 1-hexene conc. 800 ppm. Analysis by mass spectrometer. Some of the groups observed, particularly the free radicals, may have resulted from fragmentation in the mass spectrometer.	1. Butyraldehyde 2. Formaldehyde 3. Peracid or hydroperoxide, C_3H_7COOH or $C_3H_9CH_2OOH$. 4. Hydroperoxide, $C_3H_7CH_2OOH$. 5. Acetylene 6. CO_2, H_2O 7. Free radicals: C_4H_9CO, C_3H_7CO; $C_3H_7C(=\!\!O)\!-\!O\!-\!O$ or $C_4H_9CH_2OO$; CH_3O, CH_3O_2; C_3H_5, C_3H_3, C_2H_3. 8. No ozonide

1-Hexene (Hanst, Stephens, Scott, and Doerr[184])	Ozone and 1-hexene, 11 ppm each, in air at 1 atm
	Ozonides identified by IR absorption near 9μ.
		Moles
		             per mole
		             of ozone
		Terminal ozonide 0.11
		Internal ozonide 0.02
		Yields of both ozonides were increased (0.11 to 0.26 for terminal, 0.02 to 0.09 for internal) by addition of 12 ppm of butyraldehyde prior to reaction.

Cyclohexene (Eastman and Silverstein[63,112])	Ozone at 0.012 atm and cyclohexene at 0.02 atm in anhydrous carrier consisting of 80% O_2, 20% N_2 at 1 atm passed into flow reactor at 12 l hr^{-1}. Products identified by UV, IR, and chemical methods.	1. Gas contained small amounts of formic acie and cyclopentenealdehyde-1.
		2. Liquid and condensed aerosol showed OH and C=O, but no significant aldehyde or ketone absorption.
		Liquid yielded:
		  a. On distillation, about 10% formic acid.
		  b. On standing in air, up to 50% adipic acid.
		  c. On hydrolysis, cyclopentenealdehyde-1 and *trans*-1,2-cyclohexandiol.
		3. Products had no strong oxidizing power.

TABLE 49 (Continued)

Olefin and investigator	Experimental conditions	Reported products
Tetramethyl-ethylene (Eastman and Smith[390])	Ozone at 0.008 atm and olefin at 0.017 atm in anhydrous carrier consisting of 66% O_2, 32% N_2 at 1 atm passed into flow reactor at 47 l hr^{-1}. Temp. in reactor up to 240°C. Products collected by cold trap (-78°C), precipitron, and bubbler; identified by UV, IR, and chemical methods.	1. Infrared absn. of products indicated CO_2, formic acid, acetone, methanol, and an ester. 2. Aqueous soln. of gas yielded CO_2, formaldehyde, formic acid, acetic acid. 3. Aqueous soln. of condensate and aerosol yielded:

		% Comp. by wt.	
		Condensate	Aerosol
Formaldehyde		11	10
Formic acid		11	19
Acetone		27	33
Acetic acid		13	25
Total % recovery:		62	87

4. Alkaline hydrolysis of aqueous soln. indicated presence of an ester, probably methyl acetate.

Olefin and investigator	Experimental conditions	Reported products
Tetramethyl-ethylene (Hanst and Calvert[179])	Reaction flask (5-liter), room temp. Conc. not given. Analyses by IR.	Acetone, with yield of 1 mole per mole of ozone.
3-Heptene (Hanst, Stephens, Scott, and Doerr[184])	Ozone and 3-heptene, 11 ppm each, in air at 1 atm	Moles per mole of ozone

	Terminal ozonide	Internal ozonide
alone:	0.00	0.19
+11 ppm butyraldehyde:	0.00	0.20
+26 ppm formaldehyde:	0.18	0.06

scopy. The percentage of carbon atoms recovered, assuming a 1:1 ratio between ozone and olefin reacting, ran from 15 to 74%, as shown in the last column of Table 50. Among the products which were not determined were carbon monoxide and formaldehyde. The presence of formaldehyde in the case of some terminal olefins was shown qualitatively by chromotropic acid and infrared absorption, but on the whole the amount did not

TABLE 50

PRODUCTS OF OZONE-OLEFIN REACTIONS OBTAINED VIA CHROMATOGRAPHIC ANALYSIS BY VRBAŠKI AND CVETANOVIĆ

Moles of product per mole of ozone consumed

Olefin	Aldehydes				Ketones		HCOOH	CH₃OH	Hyds[a]	CO₂	% Recov.[b]
	Ac	Pr	n-Bu	Other	A	MEK					
Ethylene	0.019	—	—	—	—	—	0.25	—	n.d.	n.d.	15
Propylene	0.38	0.003	—	—	0.008	—	0.34	0.033	n.d.	0.32	50
1-Butene	0.133	0.48	0.006	—	—	—	0.24	0.014	0.089	0.40	64
Isobutene	—	—	—	0.005[c]	0.53	—	0.66	0.013	0.014	0.37	69
cis-2-Butene	1.02	—	—	—	—	—	0.20	0.152	0.023+	0.42	72
trans-2-Butene	1.06	—	—	—	—	—	0.23	pr.	0.014	0.35	69+
1-3-Butadiene	0.026	—	—	0.43[d]	—	—	0.18	—	0.136[f]	0.24	52
1-Pentene	0.061	0.161	0.32	—	—	—	0.20	—	0.175[g]	0.29	59
2-Me-1-butene	0.130	—	—	—	—	0.42	0.33	0.113	tr.	0.54	58
3-Me-1-butene	0.032	—	—	0.30[c]	0.074	—	0.25	0.015	0.213[g]	0.29	54
2-Me-2-butene	pr.	—	—	—	0.43	—	0.24	0.058	0.026+	0.29	40+
cis-2-Pentene	0.56	0.56	0.0003	—	—	0.001	0.20	0.013	0.014	0.30	67
trans-2-Pentene	0.56	0.56	n.d.	—	—	n.d.	0.16	0.012	0.117[h]	0.36	71
1-Hexene	0.005	—	0.056	0.118[e]	0.015	—	0.24	—	0.108	0.23	30
Cyclohexene	0.014	—	—	—	—	—	0.29	—	0.118[f]	0.59	19
Tetramethylethylene	0.010	—	—	—	1.49	—	0.22	pr.	tr.	0.40	74

Ac = Acetaldehyde, Pr = propionaldehyde, n-Bu = n-butyraldehyde, A = acetone, MEK = methyl ethyl ketone, n.d. = not determined, pr. = present, tr. = trace

[a] Hydrocarbons recovered included both olefins and paraffins of fewer carbon atoms than the original olefin.
[b] Percentage of carbon atoms recovered, assuming 1 mole of olefin consumed per mole of ozone.
[c] Isobutyraldehyde.
[d] Acrolein.
[e] n-Valeraldehyde.
[f] All or mostly ethylene.
[g] Propane and propylene.
[i] Chiefly ethane

appear to be too important. Some of the original reaction products were decomposed into the observed products during passage through the chromatographic column. This is particularly true of peroxides, which were shown by a positive KI test to be present in the original reaction products, for example from 1-butene, isobutene, and the 2-pentenes. The peroxides appeared to be reduced to the corresponding carbonyl compounds on passage through the column.

While the product studies show pronounced variance on certain points, there is general agreement that the major products include the aldehydes or ketones which would be produced by rupture of the olefin at the double bond and by addition of an oxygen atom to one of the fragments. Thus ethylene yields formaldehyde; propylene yields formaldehyde and acetaldehyde; 1-butene, formaldehyde and propionaldehyde; isobutene, acetone, and so on. In this respect the formation of acrolein from butadiene, reported by Vrbaški and Cvetanović, is noteworthy. There is not much evidence on the yields of these primary carbonyl products relative to the amount of olefin actually consumed, as in most cases the latter was not determined. Relative to ozone consumed, the reported yields range from 0.5 mole of formaldehyde in the case of ethylene to 1.12 moles of acetaldehyde and propionaldehyde from the 2-pentenes. There is also general agreement that carbon monoxide and dioxide are among the major products. The large amounts of water reported by Scott, Stephens, Hanst, and Doerr (Table 49) are also noteworthy; the analytical methods used by most of the other investigators did not permit its determination. The minor products reported include other aldehydes and ketones, acids, alcohols, peroxides, possibly peracids, ozonides, and hydrocarbons.

Perhaps the greatest source of variance among different observers concerning products of the ozone–olefin reactions has been with regard to transitory intermediates and ozonides. It now appears to be established, through the work of Hanst et al.,[184] that true ozonides of structure

are produced in significant amounts from the gas-phase reaction of ozone with 1-hexene and 3-heptene, but not from 1-pentene and smaller olefins. The unstable peroxidic intermediates observed by Briner and his associates among the products of the ozone–ethylene, propylene, and butene reactions, and by Hanst and Stephens from the ozone–1-pentene reaction, are apparently not ozonides. Thus, Briner found these intermediates to be nonexplosive and water soluble, while the liquid-phase ozonides are explosive and only slightly water soluble. Moreover, both Briner and Hanst and Stephens found the infrared absorption spectra of these intermediates to differ from those of the ozonides; the intermediate observed by Hanst and Stephens absorbed at 5.8 μ, the carbonyl absorption region, whereas Scott et al.[383] found no carbonyl type absorption in liquid-phase ozonides when prepared in pentane at dry-ice temperature.

The ozone and olefin concentrations used in much of the experimental work reported in Tables 49 and 50 ranged from 10^4 to 10^5 times larger than the concentrations at which these substances are present during photochemical smog forming periods in air, and there are several reasons to suspect that the products formed at the higher concentrations may not be representative of those formed at the lower. Thus, with ozone and olefin at pressures in the millimeter range, some of the products condense to form an aerosol, and in the early days this was proposed as one source of the particulate matter in photochemical smog. But more recently Hanst et al.[184] have shown that when the reactant concentrations are in the parts-per-million range, little or no aerosol is formed. Again, the ozone–olefin reactions are highly exothermic, so much so as to produce a substantial increase in temperature when the reaction is carried out at concentrations in the millimeter range. Thus Eastman and Smith,[390] during their study of the ozone–tetramethylene reaction, using a flow system with 6 mm of ozone and 13 mm of olefin in a carrier consisting of 66% O_2 and 32% N_2 at 1 atm total pressure, observed temperature increases near the mixing tip of over 200°C. Such a temperature increase would almost certainly affect the over-all reaction; indeed Vrbaški and Cvetanović found during their experiments that if the ozone and olefin were mixed too rapidly the temperature rise was sufficient to cause complete combustion. Still further, where competitive reactions are involved, as they very likely are in this case, the relative importance of different reactions may be a direct function of concentration. For such reasons, for our purposes greatest weight should probably be given to the experiments with reactant concentrations most nearly approaching those found in the atmosphere, namely those of Scott, Stephens, Hanst, and Doerr.

The mechanism most commonly proposed for the gas-phase ozone-olefin reactions closely follows that which has become generally accepted, through the work of Criegee and others,[19,85] for the liquid-phase reaction. With some vagueness as to detail, this mechanism may be written

$$
\begin{array}{c}
R_1 \\
\diagdown \\
C{=}C \\
\diagup \diagdown \\
R_2 R_4
\end{array}
+ O_3 \rightarrow
\begin{array}{c}
\text{initial} \\
\text{addition}
\end{array}
\rightarrow
\begin{array}{c}
R_1 \\
\diagdown \\
C{=}O \\
\diagup \\
R_2
\end{array}
+
\begin{array}{c}
R_3 \\
\diagdown \\
\overset{+}{C}\overset{-}{OO} \\
\diagup \\
R_4
\end{array}
\qquad \text{(VI-11)}
$$

The initial addition might involve one or two steps, possibly first forming a π-complex[19] which then forms either a four- or five-membered ring,

$$
\begin{array}{cc}
\underset{R_2}{\overset{R_1}{>}}C\!-\!C\underset{R_4}{\overset{R_3}{<}} & \underset{R_2}{\overset{R_1}{>}}C\!-\!C\underset{R_4}{\overset{R_3}{<}} \\
\quad | \quad | \quad & \quad \backslash \quad / \quad \\
\quad O\!-\!O^{+} \quad \text{or} \quad & O \quad \quad O \\
\quad \quad | \quad & \quad \backslash \quad / \\
\quad \quad O^{-} \quad & \quad O
\end{array}
$$

Conflicting views regarding the initial addition process and product have been discussed in detail by Bailey[19]; in any event it is unstable and is postulated to decompose, as shown in (VI-11), into an aldehyde or ketone and a zwitterion.

The zwitterion may enter into any of several reactions. It may combine with an aldehyde or ketone to form the ozonide

$$
\underset{R_2}{\overset{R_1}{>}}C\!=\!O + \underset{R_4}{\overset{R_3}{>}}\overset{+}{C}O\bar{O} \rightarrow \underset{R_2}{\overset{R_1}{>}}C\underset{\underset{O\longrightarrow O}{|}}{\overset{\overset{O}{\diagup\;\diagdown}}{}}C\underset{R_4}{\overset{R_3}{<}} \tag{VI-12}
$$

it may dimerize,

$$
2\;\underset{R_2}{\overset{R_1}{>}}\overset{+}{C}O\bar{O} \rightarrow \underset{R_2}{\overset{R_1}{>}}C\underset{O\!-\!O}{\overset{O\!-\!O}{}}C\underset{R_4}{\overset{R_3}{<}} \tag{VI-13}
$$
$$
\text{alkylidene peroxide}
$$

it may decompose by various paths,

$$
\underset{R_2}{\overset{R_1}{>}}\overset{+}{C}O\bar{O} \rightarrow R_1R_2 + CO_2 \tag{VI-14}
$$

$$
\underset{H}{\overset{R}{>}}\overset{+}{C}O\bar{O} \rightarrow ROH + CO \tag{VI-15}
$$

$$
\underset{H}{\overset{CH_3}{>}}\overset{+}{C}O\bar{O} \rightarrow H_2O + CH_2\!=\!C\!=\!O \tag{VI-16}
$$

$$
\underset{H}{\overset{CH_3CH_2}{>}}\overset{+}{C}O\bar{O} \rightarrow C_2H_4 + \underset{H}{\overset{H}{>}}\overset{+}{C}O\bar{O} \text{ or } HCOOH \tag{VI-17}
$$

or it may rearrange

$$\underset{H}{\overset{R}{>}}\overset{+}{C}O\bar{O} \rightarrow ROC\overset{O}{\underset{H}{\diagdown}} \quad \text{or} \quad HOC\overset{O}{\underset{R}{\diagdown}} \qquad \text{(VI-18)}$$

$$\underset{H}{\overset{CH_3CH_2}{>}}\overset{+}{C}O\bar{O} \rightarrow CH_3CH\underset{O-O}{-}CH_2 \rightarrow CH_3CHO + H_2CO \qquad \text{(VI-19)}$$

The major as well as many of the minor observed products may be accounted for by these reactions. The formation of aldehydes or ketones corresponding to addition of an oxygen atom to one end of the olefin, with yields approximating the amount of ozone consumed, observed by Scott, Stephens, Hanst, and Doerr for propylene and 1-pentene, and by Vrbaški and Cvetanović for the 2-butenes and 2-pentenes, is explained by (VI-11). Ozonide formation from 1-hexene and 3-heptene, together with the increased yields of ozonide produced by added aldehyde, and particularly the formation of terminal ozonide from 3-heptene in the presence of added formaldehyde, may all be explained by (VI-12). The absence of ozonides in the case of the smaller olefins may signify that the shorter chain length zwitterions are too unstable to form them. The peroxidic intermediates which have been observed may be explained by such reactions as (VI-13), while zwitterion decomposition reactions, such as (VI-14) to (VI-17), may be postulated to explain the formation of carbon monoxide and dioxide, water, hydrocarbons, alcohols, and ketene. Formic acid might result either from (VI-17) or from a rearrangement such as (VI-18).

Among the products observed by Vrbaški and Cvetanović (Table 50) were in some cases appreciable amounts of aldehydes of one or two fewer carbon atoms than those corresponding to a split of the olefin at the double bond. For example, from 1-butene the yield of acetaldehyde was about 28% of that of propionaldehyde, and both acetaldehyde and propionaldehyde were obtained from 1-pentene, the yield of the latter amounting to 50% of the yield of butyraldehyde. These might be explained in any of several ways; by decomposition following rearrangement of the zwitterion (VI-19), by secondary oxidation, or by an attack at the allylic carbon atom of the original olefin.

In addition to the foregoing, reactions between the zwitterions and other molecules present in air may also be postulated, for example, with oxygen,

$$\begin{array}{c} R_1 \\ \diagdown \\ \overset{+}{C}O\overset{-}{O} + O_2 \rightarrow \\ \diagup \\ R_2 \end{array} \quad \begin{array}{c} R_1 \\ \diagdown \\ CO + O_3 \\ \diagup \\ R_2 \end{array} \qquad \text{(VI-20)}$$

with nitric oxide

$$\begin{array}{c} R_1 \\ \diagdown \\ \overset{+}{C}O\overset{-}{O} + NO \rightarrow \\ \diagup \\ R_2 \end{array} \quad \begin{array}{c} R_1 \\ \diagdown \\ CO + NO_2 \\ \diagup \\ R_2 \end{array} \qquad \text{(VI-21)}$$

or with another molecule of olefin

$$\begin{array}{c} R_1 \\ \diagdown \\ \overset{+}{C}O\overset{-}{O} + \\ \diagup \\ R_2 \end{array} \begin{array}{c} R \\ \diagdown \\ C=C \\ \diagup \quad \diagdown \\ R \qquad R \end{array} \rightarrow \begin{array}{c} R_1 \\ \diagdown \\ CO + \\ \diagup \\ R_2 \end{array} \begin{array}{c} R \qquad R \\ \diagdown \quad \diagup \\ C-C \\ \diagup \quad | \quad \diagdown \\ R \quad O \quad R \end{array} \qquad \text{(VI-22)}$$

$$\begin{array}{c} R \qquad R \\ \diagdown \quad \diagup \\ C-C \\ \diagup \quad | \quad \overset{\cdot}{\diagdown} \\ R \quad \overset{\cdot}{O} \quad R \end{array} + O_2 \rightarrow \begin{array}{c} \text{addition} \\ \text{product} \end{array} \rightarrow \begin{array}{c} R \\ \diagdown \\ CO + \\ \diagup \\ R \end{array} \begin{array}{c} R \\ \diagdown \\ \overset{+}{C}O\overset{-}{O} \\ \diagup \\ R \end{array} \qquad \text{(VI-23)}$$

Either reaction (VI-20) or (VI-22) followed by (VI-23) might explain olefin/ozone ratios of greater than unity as well as departures from second-order kinetics in the ozone–olefin reactions, but there is no evidence that either of them occur. The biradical postulated in (VI-22) might be expected, as in the case of the oxygen atom–olefin reactions (Chapter V) to lead to some epoxide formation, which is not observed.

It is noteworthy that none of the zwitterion reactions thus far written lead to free radical formation, nor is it necessary to postulate free radical formation to explain the products of the ozone–olefin reactions. The only experiments thus far conducted capable of detecting free radicals during the gas-phase reactions are those of Saltzman, reported in Table 49. Here mass spectrographic peaks corresponding to a variety of radicals including hydrocarbon fragments, alkoxyl, and acyl radicals were found, but it is quite possible that these were not present in the reaction mixture, but rather were formed by fragmentation in the mass spectrometer. While there is thus no definitive evidence that any free radicals are formed during these reactions, their role in the nitrogen dioxide–olefin photolysis (Chapter X), and particularly the observation that in air containing nitrogen dioxide the reaction leads to the formation of PAN, even in the dark, strongly suggests that some radicals are produced.

Several *ad hoc* processes leading to free radical formation may be postulated, for example, by fragmentation of the biradical in (VI-22), or by zwitterion reactions such as

$$\underset{H}{\overset{R}{\diagdown}}\overset{+}{C}\overset{-}{OO} \rightarrow ROC\underset{H}{\overset{O^*}{\diagup}} \rightarrow R\dot{O} + H\dot{C}O \tag{VI-24}$$

or

$$\underset{H}{\overset{R}{\diagdown}}\overset{+}{C}\overset{-}{OO} + O_2 \rightarrow \dot{R} + CO_2 + H\dot{O}_2 \tag{VI-25}$$

While Criegee and his co-workers[19,85] have identified zwitterions as a relatively stable and long-lived species in solution, they have not been observed in the vapor phase, and the speculative status of the application of this mechanism to vapor-phase reactions should be recognized. Darley et al.[94] have reported the formation of a phytotoxicant by the ozone–olefin reactions in air, with a shorter life and a different effect than those of the toxicants ozone and PAN, and have suggested that it might be a zwitterion or an ozone-olefin addition complex. Arnold[14] has found that the half-life of this phytotoxicant was 3 min when produced from ozone and 2-pentene, and 15 min when produced from ozone and 3-heptene. While these half-lives are short relative to those of the other phytotoxicants which have been identified, they are long relative to that of the ozone–olefin reaction at the concentrations used in product studies. Thus at the initial ozone and 3-heptene concentrations of 11 ppm each used by Scott, Stephens, Hanst, and Doerr (Table 48), the half-life of the reaction, if the bimolecular rate constant in Table 46 holds, would be less than 1 sec and the reaction would be 90% complete in only 6.3 sec. If the zwitterion is formed with stoichiometric yield, as required by equation (VI-11), and has the half-life of 15 min observed by Arnold for the phytotoxicant, it should have reached a peak concentration nearly equal to that of the original ozone, and would almost certainly have been detected. Moreover, under such circumstances there should be a readily observable difference between the rate of appearance of the aldehyde or ketone formed by (VI-11), and the rate of appearance of the products of the zwitterion reactions. If the initial addition complex, or any other major intermediate, has an appreciable life there should be observable differences between the rates of olefin or ozone consumption and those of product formation. Such differences may exist, but have not been reported.

There thus remain a number of unanswered questions regarding both the kinetics and mechanism of the ozone–olefin reactions in air, and although much excellent work has been done, much remains to be done before the role of these reactions in photochemical smog formation becomes satisfactorily understood.

5. REACTIONS OF OZONE WITH HYDROCARBONS OTHER THAN OLEFINS

Reactions of ozone with saturated hydrocarbons, if they occur at all, are apparently too slow to be of any importance in air pollution. Thus Cadle and Johnston[64] reported that these reactions are too slow to measure, and Hanst and Stephens[180] reported that the reactions of ozone with 2-methyl pentane, hexane, and cyclohexane were all "very slow." For example, a mixture of 8 mm of 2-methyl pentane and 5 mm of ozone gave no observable reaction over a 1-hr period, and the addition of 9 ppm of hexane to a mixture of 1 ppm each of ozone and 1-hexene had no observable effect on the reaction of the latter two.[65]

Mixtures of ozone and acetylene are explosive and must be handled with caution.[54] The nonexplosive ozone–acetylene reaction was studied by Cadle and Schadt[66] at reactant partial pressures of 0.5 to 6.5 mm in an oxygen-nitrogen carrier at 280 to 630 mm and 30 to 50°C. The reactants were mixed in a 1-m infrared absorption tube, and the ozone and acetylene concentrations were followed by absorption at 9.6 and 13.6 μ, respectively. The initial reaction was first order with respect to both ozone and acetylene, its activation energy was 4.8 kcal, and at 30°C its rate constant was $4.6 \pm 1.6 \times 10^1$ liter mole^{-1} sec^{-1}. This is about 1/40 as large as the initial rate constant for the ozone–ethylene reaction (Table 46).

The products of the gas-phase ozone–acetylene reaction are unknown. Cadle and Schadt found that infrared absorption bands corresponding to $C=O$, but none corresponding to OH groups, appeared during the reaction. Briner and Wunenburger,[54] after experiencing several explosions in the gas phase, studied the reaction in CCl_4 solution and identified glyoxal, formic acid, and carbon dioxide as products.

The acetylene content of urban air has not been directly measured. Analyses of automobile exhaust[123,277] indicate that roughly 5% to 25% of the hydrocarbons emitted to the atmosphere from this source will be acetylene, and as this is the major known source, an order of magnitude acetylene concentration of ~10 pphm during smog forming periods would appear to be a reasonable expectation. On the basis of Cadle and Schadt's rate constant, at an acetylene concentration of 10 pphm and an ozone concentration of 10 pphm the rate of reaction between the two, at 30°C, will be 7×10^{-3} pphm hr^{-1}. Even at an acetylene concentration of 30 pphm and an ozone concentration of 50 pphm, the rate of reaction would be only 0.1 pphm hr^{-1}. It is probable, therefore, that the ozone–acetylene reaction is not of major importance in polluted air.

The reactions of ozone with aromatic hydrocarbons have not been quantitatively studied, and until such studies have been performed the importance of these reactions in urban air cannot be assessed. The concentrations of aromatic hydrocarbons in urban air are probably considerably smaller than those of the olefins, and for structural reasons one would expect their reactions with ozone to be slower.

6. Reactions of Ozone with Aldehydes and Ketones

In carbon tetrachloride solution, ozone reacts with aldehydes to form peroxyacids; the reaction may be used as a means of synthesis of these acids.[129]

In the gas phase, using the same flow system as in their study of the ozone-butylene reactions (Table 49), Briner and Meier[50] found no reaction between ozone and formaldehyde, probably because the flow conditions did not allow sufficient time. With acetaldehyde, acetone, and propionaldehyde some reaction was observed, the products showing evidence of formic groupings.

Hanst and Stephens[180] introduced mixtures of ozone with both propionaldehyde and butyraldehyde, at partial pressures of 1.4 to 13 mm in air at 1 atm, into a 1-m infrared absorption cell, and recorded the absorption spectra of the reaction products. The resulting spectra (Fig. 39) showed essentially complete reaction of the ozone; they showed carbon dioxide but not carbon monoxide, and they showed bands due to C—H and C=O groups. In addition, the products showed absorption bands at 3.05, 6.88, and 8.53 μ.

To identify the source of these bands, peroxypropionic and peroxybutyric acids were synthesized by the reaction of ozone with the corresponding aldehydes in carbon tetrachloride solution.[129] The vapors of these acids, introduced into the absorption cell at ~4 mm pressure in air at 1 atm showed the same three bands. In addition, the peroxy acids from the liquid-phase reaction and the products of the gas-phase reaction both oxidized iodide ion in 2% KI solution. This evidence indicates that peroxy acids are a product of the gas phase, as well as the liquid phase, ozone–aldehyde reactions.

In one experiment, with ozone and propionaldehyde, Hanst and Stephens separated the ozone from its parent oxygen and mixed the reactants in nitrogen instead of air. The amount of peroxy acid formed, as shown by the strength of the 3.05 μ band, was considerably reduced by this procedure. This indicates that molecular oxygen itself takes some part in the formation of peroxy acid; Hanst and Stephens suggest that

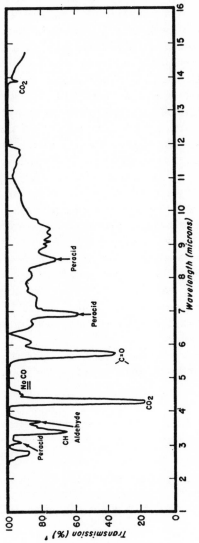

Fig. 39. Infrared spectrum of products of the reaction between ozone and butyraldehyde. Initial pressures of ozone and butyraldehyde each 1.4 mm in air at 1 atm in 1-meter absorption cell. From Hanst and Stephens; *Interim Rept. I-2372-2*, Project SF-7, The Franklin Institute, Philadelphia, Pennsylvania (1954).

the ozone reacts with the aldehyde to form acyl radicals which then form peroxy acid by reaction with molecular oxygen.

The peroxy acids were found to be unstable in air, the peroxy-propionic more so than the peroxybutyric. The infrared spectra of their decomposition products showed only butyric acid and carbon dioxide.

The kinetics of the ozone–aldehyde reactions have not been studied. The observations of Briner and Meier, as well as those of Hanst and Stephens, would indicate that they are slower than the ozone–olefin reactions, and that the reaction of ozone with formaldehyde is slower than its reactions with the higher aldehydes. In one of the Hanst and Stephens experiments, starting with a mixture of 0.8 mm each of ozone and formaldehyde, it was found that about $\frac{1}{4}$ of the formaldehyde had disappeared after 15 min. Assuming a rate law which is first order with respect to each reactant, this rate of disappearance of formaldehyde would correspond to a rate constant of the order of 10 liter mole^{-1} sec^{-1}. If the rates for the higher aldehydes lie between that of formaldehyde and those of the olefins, a similar assumption would indicate rate constants of somewhere between 10 and 10^3 liter mole^{-1} sec^{-1} for these reactions. If the ozone–aldehyde reactions are indeed first order with respect to each reactant, and if the rate constants approach the smaller of these two figures, they will be too slow to have any importance in polluted air. But if the rate constants approach the larger figure, they may have some importance. Kinetic studies must be made before any decision is reached on this point.

The ozone–ketone reactions have received little or no attention as to either kinetics or products. Briner and Meier's experiments would

TABLE 51

SUMMARY OF RATE CONSTANTS OF OZONE REACTIONS

Reactant other than ozone	k (1 mole^{-1} sec^{-1} at 25°C)	Representative rate in polluted air (pphm hr^{-1})
NO	1×10^7 to 3×10^7	~200
NO$_2$	2×10^4 to 4×10^4	3 to 6
Olefin hydrocarbons	10^3 to 10^5	2 to 20
Paraffin hydrocarbons	too small to measure	—
Acetylene	~46	~10^{-2}
Aromatic hydrocarbons	not known; probably small	probably <10^{-1}
Formaldehyde	possibly ~10	probably <10^{-2}
Aliphatic aldehydes and ketones	not known, possibly between 10^1 and 10^3	?

suggest rates which are comparable with those of the ozone–aldehyde reactions; if this is the case, these reactions should receive further study.

7. SUMMARY OF OZONE REACTIONS

The conclusions of this chapter regarding the rates of ozone reactions in polluted air are summarized in Table 51. In addition, it may be said that at atmospheric temperatures, ozone undergoes no reaction of importance with either carbon monoxide[456] or sulfur dioxide.[62] Reactions with such substances as nitrous acid, organic nitrites, nitroso compounds, other organic species, and with the particulate matter in polluted air, are unknown quantities.

It is evident from this that only three reactions of ozone, with nitric oxide, nitrogen dioxide, and the olefins, are definitely known to be fast enough to be of importance in air pollution.

Chapter VII

Reactions and Equilibria of the Oxides and Oxy Acids of Nitrogen

The reactions of nitric oxide and nitrogen dioxide with oxygen atoms and with ozone have been discussed in the preceding chapters, and their reactions with organic free radicals will be discussed in the chapter to follow. Before entering into a discussion of free radicals, however, there are still a number of reactions involving the oxides and oxy acids of nitrogen which should be examined. Some of these reactions are not, strictly speaking, photochemical secondary reactions. They must, nevertheless, be considered, as they occur simultaneously with the photochemical reactions of these substances, and through their effects on reactant concentrations the one will mutually affect the other.

1. The Reaction of Nitric Oxide with Molecular Oxygen

$$2NO + O_2 \underset{b}{\overset{a}{\rightleftharpoons}} 2NO_2 + 26.2 \text{ kcal} \quad S_{1a} = k_{1a}(NO)^m(O_2)^n \qquad \text{(VII-1)}$$

This reaction has been extensively studied over the past half century, and while some questions yet remain regarding its mechanism, both the equilibrium and the rate have been well established over a broad temperature range.

Values of the equilibrium constant, interpolated from the data of Giauque and Kemp,[154] are given in Table 52.

TABLE 52

EQUILIBRIUM CONSTANT FOR $NO + \frac{1}{2} O_2 \rightleftharpoons NO_2$

$(K = P_{NO_2}/P_{NO}P_{O_2}^{1/2} \text{ atm}^{-1/2})$

Temp. °C	K (atm$^{-1/2}$)
25	1.38×10^6
100	1.35×10^4
300	2.09×10^1
500	0.93
700	0.16
1000	0.03 (extrapolated)

From these values, the equilibrium ratio of nitrogen dioxide in air at 1 atm, 25°C, will be

$$\frac{P_{NO_2}(\text{equil})}{P_{NO}(\text{equil})} = 6.1 \times 10^5$$

From this equilibrium ratio it is evident that only the forward reaction need be considered. This reaction has been studied[45,47,51,271,391] at temperatures from −193 to +390°C, at nitric oxide pressures ranging from 0.02 to 125 mm, and oxygen pressures from 0.1 to 500 mm. Most investigators have reported that the reaction is third order, with m in equation (VII-1) equal to 2 and $n = 1$, and that it has a negative temperature coefficient which increases with temperature. The most extensive investigation, by Bodenstein and his collaborators[47] yields the data given in Table 53.

TABLE 53

RATE CONSTANTS FOR REACTION $2NO + O_2 \rightarrow 2NO_2$

$$(+d(NO_2)/dt = k_{1a}(NO_2)^2(O_2))$$

Temp. (°C)	From Bodenstein k_{1a} (l² mole⁻² sec⁻¹)	$k_{1a}(O_2)$ in air at 1 atm		From Treacy and Daniels k_{1a} (l² mole⁻² sec⁻¹)
		l mole⁻¹ sec⁻¹	pphm⁻¹ hr⁻¹ [a]	
0	17.9×10^3	168	24.7×10^{-5}	—
10	16.6×10^3	150	22.0×10^{-5}	—
20	15.2×10^3	133	19.5×10^{-5}	—
25	14.8×10^3	127	18.7×10^{-5}	8×10^3
30	14.1×10^3	119	17.5×10^{-5}	—
40	13.1×10^3	107	15.7×10^{-5}	—
90	9.0×10^3	63	9.3×10^{-5}	—
200	6.6×10^3	36	5.3×10^{-5}	—
390	5.1×10^3	20	2.9×10^{-5}	—

[a] For concentrations in pphm relative to air at 1 atm, 25°C.

Treacy and Daniels[422] have presented evidence that the reaction is much more complex than had previously been supposed. They found that the rate is dependent on the extent to which the reaction has progressed, being slower in the presence of NO_2. Moreover, they found that while m approaches 2 and n approaches 1 at higher pressures, in the pressure range of 1 to 10 mm the value of m is about 2.3, while n is slightly less than unity. Their value of the rate constant for less than 25% completion of the reaction is also given in Table 53.

On the basis of these values, in the temperature range of 0 to 40°C, and at a nitric oxide concentration of 10 pphm in air at 1 atm, the calculated rate of reaction (VII-1a) will be only ~0.01 pphm hr^{-1}, and the observations of Treacy and Daniels would indicate that the actual rate may be still smaller. From this it may be concluded that the reaction of nitric oxide with molecular oxygen does not occur at a significant rate in urban air.

In passing, it might be remarked that it is also difficult to see how the reaction could be significant during the combustion processes which contribute oxides of nitrogen to urban air. With increasing temperature, up to at least 390°C, the rate decreases (Table 53), and at still higher temperatures, while the temperature coefficient may become positive,[239] the equilibrium position becomes unfavorable (Table 52).

2. Association Reactions

$$NO + NO_2 \rightleftharpoons N_2O_3 + 10.3 \text{ kcal} \qquad \text{(VII-2)}$$
$$NO_2 + NO_2 \rightleftharpoons N_2O_4 + 14.6 \text{ kcal} \qquad \text{(VII-3)}$$

For the equilibrium constants of these reactions, Verhoek and Daniels[431] obtained the values in Table 54, where, if P is the partial

TABLE 54

DISSOCIATION CONSTANTS OF N_2O_3 AND N_2O_4
FROM VERHOEK AND DANIELS

Temp. (°C)	$K_{N_2O_3}$ atm	$K_{N_2O_4}$ atm
25	$2.105 - 45.63 \ C^{\circ}_{N_2O_3}$	$0.1426 - 0.7588 \ C^{\circ}_{N_2O_4}$
35	$3.673 - 78.11 \ C^{\circ}_{N_2O_3}$	$0.3183 - 1.591 \ C^{\circ}_{N_2O_4}$
45	$6.880 - 196.4 \ C^{\circ}_{N_2O_3}$	$0.6706 - 3.382 \ C^{\circ}_{N_2O_4}$

pressure of each species in atmospheres and $R = 0.082$ l atm deg.$^{-1}$,

$$\frac{P_{NO}P_{NO_2}}{P_{N_2O_3}} = K_{N_2O_3} \qquad \text{(VII-4)}$$

and

$$\frac{(P_{NO_2})^2}{P_{N_2O_4}} = K_{N_2O_4} \qquad \text{(VII-5)}$$

The values of C° are given by

$$C^{\circ}_{N_2O_3} = \frac{P_{NO} + P_{NO_2} + 2P_{N_2O_3}}{2RT} \qquad \text{(VII-6)}$$

and

$$C^{\circ}_{N_2O_4} = \frac{P_{NO_2} + 2P_{N_2O_4}}{2RT} \qquad \text{(VII-7)}$$

At the concentrations of nitric oxide and nitrogen dioxide found in urban air, the values of $C°$ are negligible and the concentrations of N_2O_3 and N_2O_4, calculated from these equations, are exceedingly small. For example, if $(NO_2) = 10$ pphm, at $25°C$ the equilibrium concentration of N_2O_4 will be 7×10^{-6} pphm, and if both $(NO) = 10$ pphm and $(NO_2) = 10$ pphm the equilibrium concentration of N_2O_3 at $25°C$ will be 5×10^{-7} pphm. These are negligible.

3. Reactions of Nitrogen Trioxide

The formation of nitrogen trioxide, NO_3, was first postulated more than seventy-five years ago by Hautefeuille and Chappuis[189] to explain the appearance of absorption bands in the region 5000–7000 A, other than those of ozone, when a mixture of nitrogen and oxygen was passed through a Siemens ozonizer. In 1906 the same bands, leading to a visually blue color, were observed by Warburg and Leithauser[445] in a reacting mixture of nitrogen pentoxide and ozone. Since then, this observation has often been repeated,[232,258,268,374,382,384,421] and the formation of nitrogen trioxide as an intermediate has frequently been postulated to explain the mechanisms of reactions of the oxides of nitrogen.[133–136,177,226,229,230,292, 318,319,374,382,392,394,422]

The success of these postulates in explaining a mass of otherwise uncorrelated experimental data,[134,226] and particularly the agreement between the observed intensity of the absorption bands attributed to NO_3 and its predicted concentration,[374,382,394] has led to the acceptance of the existence of nitrogen trioxide as more nearly established than hypothetical.

The reactions involving nitrogen trioxide which appear to be necessary to explain the major behavior of the oxides of nitrogen are

$$NO_2 + O_3 \rightarrow NO_3 + O_2 + 25.4 \text{ kcal} \qquad S_8 = k_8(NO_2)(O_3) \qquad \text{(VII-8)}$$

$$NO_3 + NO \rightarrow 2NO_2 + 22.4 \text{ kcal} \qquad S_9 = k_9(NO_3)(NO) \qquad \text{(VII-9)}$$

$$NO_3 + NO_2 \underset{b}{\overset{a}{\rightleftharpoons}} N_2O_5 + 21.0 \text{ kcal} \qquad K_{10} = \frac{k_{10a}}{k_{10b}} = \frac{(N_2O_5)}{(NO_3)(NO_2)} \qquad \text{(VII-10)}$$

$$NO_3 + NO_2 \rightarrow NO + O_2 + NO_2 - 3.8 \text{ kcal} \qquad S_{11} = k_{11}(NO_3)(NO_2) \qquad \text{(VII-11)}$$

$$NO_3 + NO_3 \rightarrow 2NO_2 + O_2 + 18.6 \text{ kcal} \qquad S_{12} = k_{12}(NO_3)^2 \qquad \text{(VII-12)}$$

The energetic values are $-\Delta E_{298}^°$, based on Schott and Davidson's estimate[374] of $\Delta E_{300}^° = -21.0$ kcal for reaction (VII-10), and $\Delta H_f = 3.6$ kcal for N_2O_5, 8.1 kcal for NO_2, and 21.5 kcal for NO.

All of these reactions are presumably elementary except (VII-10), which is assumed to be the resultant of the elementary steps

$$NO_3 + NO_2 \rightleftharpoons N_2O_5^* \qquad \text{(VII-13)}$$

$$N_2O_5^* + M \rightleftharpoons N_2O_5 + M \qquad \text{(VII-14)}$$

This is similar to the third body reaction discussed in Chapter IV and the same considerations apply; at low pressures the over-all rates of formation and decomposition of N_2O_5 are dependent on the concentration of the third body, M, but at high pressures they become independent of M, and the over-all reactions (VII-10a and 10b) behave as simple second- and first-order processes. This will be the case in air, and the "high pressure" values of k_{10a} and k_{10b} should therefore be used.

The reaction of oxygen atoms with nitrogen dioxide (V-29) will also contribute to some extent to the formation of nitrogen trioxide, but in air this contribution will generally be small relative to that of reaction (VII-8).

Values of the rate constants and activation energies for reactions (VII-8) to (VII-12) are given in Table 55. The figures for reaction

TABLE 55

RATE AND EQUILIBRIUM CONSTANTS FOR REACTIONS OF NITROGEN TRIOXIDE

	Value at 25°C		
Constant	l mole^{-1} sec^{-1} except as noted	pphm^{-1} hr^{-1} except as noted	Activation energy (kcal)
k_8	4×10^4	0.06	7.0 ± 0.6
k_9	5.6×10^9	8×10^3	1.4 ± 2.5
k_{10a}	1.8×10^9	2.6×10^3	0 ± 2.5
k_{10b}	0.24 sec^{-1}	8.6×10^2 hr^{-1}	21.0 ± 1
K_{10}	7.5×10^9 l mole^{-1}	3 pphm^{-1}	—
k_{11}	2.5×10^5	0.37	3.7 ± 1
k_{12}	1.2×10^4	1.8×10^{-2}	7.0 ± 2.5

(VII-8) are from Johnston and Yost[230] and have been discussed in Chapter VI. The remaining values were derived from the estimates of Schott and Davidson,[374] which in turn were deduced partly from their experiments on the shock wave pyrolysis of nitrogen pentoxide, partly from the kinetic studies of Mills and Johnston[292] and Hisatsune et al.,[199] and partly from the earlier estimates of Johnston.[226]

Since nitrogen pentoxide is known to react rapidly with water vapor, it cannot be assumed that reaction (VII-10) reaches equilibrium in urban air. On the contrary, it probably does not. The stationary concentration of nitrogen trioxide will depend on the extent of departure of (VII-10) from equilibrium. It must, however, fall between an upper limit corresponding to reaction (VII-10) at equilibrium, and a lower limit attained if reaction (VII-10b) is negligible. The stationary concentration of nitrogen trioxide for each of these limits, if (VII-12) and the direct photolysis of NO_3 be neglected, is, upper limit

$$(NO_3)_u = \frac{k_8(NO_2)(O_3)}{k_9(NO) + k_{11}(NO_2)} \qquad \text{(VII-15)}$$

lower limit

$$(NO_3)_l = \frac{k_8(NO_2)(O_3)}{k_9(NO) + k_{10a}(NO_2) + k_{11}(NO_2)} \qquad \text{(VII-16)}$$

From the values of the constants given in Table 55, and the reported concentrations of nitric oxide and nitrogen dioxide, it may be estimated that the denominators of equations (VII-15) and (VII-16), when applied to polluted air, will normally have a value of ~ 1 sec^{-1} or more. These equations should, therefore, be valid insofar as the ability of the stationary concentration of nitrogen trioxide to follow ordinary atmospheric changes is concerned (Chapter IV).

For nitrogen pentoxide, only an upper limit to the stationary concentration may be estimated from reactions (VII-8) to (VII-11). This upper limit, achieved if (VII-10) is at equilibrium, is

$$(N_2O_5)_{lim} = \frac{k_8 K_{10}(NO_2)^2(O_3)}{k_9(NO) + k_{11}(NO_2)} \qquad \text{(VII-17)}$$

These equations, together with the estimated rate constants in Table 55, indicate that the concentrations of nitrogen trioxide and pentoxide in urban air will be quite small. As an example, if $(O_3) = 10$ pphm, $(NO_2) = 10$ pphm, and $(NO) = 1$ pphm (page 155), the resultant values are $(NO_3)_u = 7.5 \times 10^{-4}$ pphm, $(NO_3)_l = 1.8 \times 10^{-4}$ pphm, and $(N_2O_5)_{lim} = 2.2 \times 10^{-2}$ pphm.

In order to explain the mechanism of the reaction of nitric oxide with molecular oxygen (Section 1), Treacy and Daniels[422] have postulated, in addition to (VII-9) and (VII-10), the reactions

$$NO + O_2 \underset{b}{\overset{a}{\rightleftharpoons}} NO_3 \qquad K_{18} = \frac{(NO_3)}{(NO)(O_2)} \qquad \text{(VII-18)}$$

$$NO_3 + NO \underset{b}{\overset{a}{\rightleftharpoons}} NO_3 \cdot NO \qquad \text{(VII-19)}$$

$$NO_3 \cdot NO + NO \rightarrow 2NO_2 + NO \qquad \text{(VII-20)}$$
$$NO_3 \cdot NO + NO_2 \rightarrow 2NO + O_2 + NO_2 \qquad \text{(VII-21)}$$

It is assumed that reaction (VII-18) reaches equilibrium, and the resulting rate law requires that $k_{1a} > 2k_9 K_{18}$. Inserting the values of k_{1a} and k_9 from Tables 53 and 55 gives $K_{18} < 1.3 \times 10^{-6}$ liter mole^{-1} or $<6 \times 10^{-16}$ pphm^{-1} at 25°C. At a nitric oxide concentration of 1 pphm in air the corresponding equilibrium concentration of NO_3, for reaction (VII-18), would be $<10^{-8}$ pphm. This would indicate that reaction (VII-18), if it exists, cannot be an important contributor to the stationary concentration of nitrogen trioxide in polluted air. On the contrary, if it has any effect at all, it would reduce the stationary concentrations estimated by equations (VII-15) to (VII-17).

The remaining reactions postulated by Treacy and Daniels, (VII-19) to (VII-21), are not necessary, as we have seen, to explain the experimental data for such processes as the thermal decomposition of nitrogen pentoxide and the reaction of ozone with nitrogen dioxide, even though the stationary NO_3 concentration reached during these processes would appear to be much higher than that resulting from (VII-18). It is possible that the NO_3 involved in reactions (VII-18) to (VII-21) is an isomer of that in reactions (VII-8) to (VII-12), and that the two forms react differently. Thus, the former might be a nitrate radical,

$$O-N\begin{smallmatrix} \nearrow O \\ \searrow O \end{smallmatrix}$$

and the latter a pernitrite, OONO. In any event, more information must be obtained before the existence of reactions (VII-18) to (VII-21) may be determined and the part they play in the atmosphere may be judged.

In view of the reactivity of nitrogen trioxide, the possibility that it may undergo other reactions of importance in polluted air cannot be wholly set aside. For instance, it may react with water vapor, or with organic species, such as olefins or aldehydes. Being a polyatomic molecule, however, it would probably have a low steric factor in its reactions with other polyatomic molecules.

4. Reactions Involving Water

Of the various reactions which the oxides of nitrogen may undergo with water vapor, only one, the reaction of nitric oxide and nitrogen dioxide with water to give nitrous acid, has been quantitatively studied. This reaction may be written

$$NO + NO_2 + H_2O \underset{b}{\overset{a}{\rightleftharpoons}} 2HNO_2 \quad K_{22} = \frac{(HNO_2)^2}{(NO)(NO_2)(H_2O)} \quad \text{(VII-22)}$$

The equilibrium constant was estimated by Wayne and Yost[446] to have the value, at 25°C

$$K_{22} = 1.65 \text{ atm}^{-1} = 1.65 \times 10^{-8} \text{ pphm}^{-1}$$

Wayne and Yost also measured the rate of the forward reaction, using the method of Johnston and Yost (page 157). A large excess of nitric oxide was used; nitrogen dioxide and water vapor at 0.5 to 2.4 mole % being mixed in nitric oxide at atmospheric pressure. Under these conditions they obtained, from the rate of disappearance of NO_2, at 25°C

$$k_{22a} = 4.3 \times 10^7 \text{ liter}^2 \text{ mole}^{-2} \text{ sec}^{-1} = 2.6 \times 10^{-8} \text{ pphm}^{-2} \text{ hr}^{-1}$$

Combining this with the above value for K_{22} gives

$$k_{22b} = \frac{k_{22a}}{K_{22}} = 1.1 \times 10^6 \text{ liter mole}^{-1} \text{ sec}^{-1} = 1.6 \text{ pphm}^{-1} \text{ hr}^{-1}$$

These values, when combined with the normally encountered NO, NO_2, and H_2O concentrations, indicate that the reaction is not particularly fast, nor is the equilibrium concentration of nitrous acid particularly high, in urban air. Letting $(NO_2) = 10$ pphm and $(NO) = 1$ pphm (page 155), setting $(H_2O) = 2 \times 10^6$ pphm (corresponding to 63% relative humidity at 25°C), and assuming that the rate law for the forward reaction agrees with (VII-22a), the rate of formation of nitrous acid by this reaction will be only 0.5 pphm hr^{-1}, and its equilibrium concentration will be only 0.6 pphm.

The equilibrium concentration of nitrous acid calculated in this manner probably has little meaning with respect to air pollution. The reaction is not fast enough to maintain the equilibrium concentration of HNO_2 as the NO and NO_2 concentrations change in the atmosphere; in fact, the value of $1/\sqrt{S_{22a} \, k_{22b}}$ will be of the order of 1 hr or more (Chapter IV). In addition, other reactions may and probably do affect the nitrous acid concentration.

One such reaction, which may consume nitrous acid in the atmosphere, is its photolysis (Chapter III). Another is the reverse of (VII-23). Little is known of these reactions, but it is obvious that the sum of the rates of the reactions consuming nitrous acid cannot, on the average, exceed the rates of the reactions producing it, and unless there are faster producing reactions than (VII-22a), none of the consuming reactions, including the photolysis, can be very important.

The gas-phase reaction of nitrogen dioxide with water to form nitric acid appears to be slow at atmospheric concentrations. In one experiment, Hanst and Stephens[182] found no nitric acid after 20 min irradiation, with carbon arc, of a mixture of 3.2 mm NO_2 and 9.5 mm H_2O in 860 mm of air. Infrared absorption was used as the analytical method, and as little as 0.2 mm of HNO_3 would have been detected. In other experiments, using 8 and 16 mm of NO_2 with 8 mm of H_2O in air at 860 mm, a slow dark reaction was observed. The rate of formation of nitric acid appeared to be first order with respect to nitrogen dioxide, and the pseudo-unimolecular rate constant, at the water vapor and oxygen concentrations used, was $k \approx 6 \times 10^{-3} \text{ hr}^{-1}$.

The mechanism which would lead to a first-order dependence on the nitrogen dioxide concentration is unknown. As nitrogen dioxide contains an odd number of electrons, one of the products of any elementary bimolecular reaction between it and water must be another odd molecule or free radical, which would presumably undergo further reactions. The over-all result might be

$$2NO_2 + H_2O \rightleftharpoons HNO_3 + HNO_2 \qquad\qquad\qquad (VII\text{-}23)$$

or combined with (VII-22),

$$3NO_2 + H_2O \rightleftharpoons 2HNO_3 + NO \quad \Delta F^\circ_{298} = +1765 \text{ cal} \qquad (VII\text{-}24)$$

From the free energy value the thermodynamic equilibrium constant for (VII-24) is, at 25°C,

$$\frac{(HNO_3)^2(NO)}{(NO_2)^3(H_2O)} = K_{24} = 0.05 \text{ atm}^{-1} = 5 \times 10^{-10} \text{ pphm}^{-1} \qquad (VII\text{-}25)$$

At the exemplary concentrations $(NO_2) = 10$ pphm, $(NO) = 1$ pphm, and $(H_2O) = 2 \times 10^6$ pphm, the equilibrium concentration of nitric acid, by this equation, is $(HNO_3) = 1.0$ pphm. The rate of its formation at these concentrations, from the data of Hanst and Stephens, together with the assumption that the rate is also first order with respect to water vapor, will be ~0.1 pphm hr^{-1}. From this it may be concluded that the reaction of nitrogen dioxide with water vapor is of only minor significance in polluted air. It appears to be too slow to produce nitric acid at a significant rate, and its reverse is probably too slow to permit its equilibrium to govern the nitric acid concentration.

Nitric acid is also formed by the gas-phase hydrolysis of nitrogen pentoxide:

$$N_2O_5 + H_2O \underset{b}{\overset{a}{\rightleftharpoons}} 2HNO_3 \quad \Delta F^\circ_{298} = -8600 \text{ cal} \qquad (VII\text{-}26)$$

The corresponding thermodynamic equilibrium constant at 25°C is

$$\frac{(HNO_3)^2}{(N_2O_5)(H_2O)} = K_{26} = 2 \times 10^6 \qquad\qquad (VII\text{-}27)$$

The mechanism, kinetics, and rate of this reaction have not been quantitatively determined, and until this is done its importance in air pollution cannot be fully specified. Some useful information may be obtained, however, by considering its relation to reactions (VII-8) to (VII-12). Neglecting the slow reaction (VII-12), combining the rate laws and equilibrium expressions yields, for the stationary concentration of nitric acid with respect to these reactions,

$$(HNO_3)_s = \left[\frac{k_8 K_{11} K_{26} (NO_2)^2 (O_3)(H_2O)}{k_9(NO) + k_{11}(NO_2)} \right]^{1/2} \qquad (VII\text{-}28)$$

Inserting the values of the constants from Table 55 and equation (VII-27), at the exemplary concentrations $(NO_2) = 10$ pphm, $(O_3) = 10$ pphm, $(NO) = 1$ pphm, and $(H_2O) = 2 \times 10^6$ pphm, the corresponding stationary concentration of nitric acid will be $(HNO_3)_s = 3 \times 10^5$ pphm.

Since this is far higher than any nitric acid concentrations which have been encountered in the atmosphere, it is obvious, first, that the stationary nitric acid concentration with respect to these reactions is not attained and, second, that the equilibrium of reaction (VII-26) does not determine the actual nitric acid concentrations in urban air.

Whether or not the rate of reaction (VII-26a) determines these concentrations is another matter. This reaction may be complex, and its mechanism and rate law are unknown. However, the maximum rate of nitric acid production by reactions (VII-8), (VII-10), and (VII-26) will be achieved if reaction (VII-26a), whatever its mechanism, is so fast as to consume virtually all of the nitrogen pentoxide produced by (VII-10a); i.e., if (VII-10b) is negligible. In this case the rate of nitric acid production will be twice the rate of reaction (VII-10a), or, using (VII-16) to eliminate (NO_3),

$$\frac{+d(HNO_3)_{lim}}{dt} = 2k_{10a}(NO_3)(NO_2)$$

$$= \frac{2k_8k_{10a}(NO_2)^2(O_3)}{k_9(NO) + k_{10a}(NO_2) + k_{11}(NO_2)} \qquad \text{(VII-29)}$$

Inserting the values of the constants from Table 55, this equation yields 9.2 pphm hr^{-1} as the upper limit for the rate of nitric acid production by reactions (VII-8), (VII-10), and (VII-20) at the exemplary concentrations $(NO_2) = 10$, $(O_3) = 10$, and $(NO) = 1$ pphm.

In order for the rate of nitric acid production to approach this limit, the rate of reaction (VII-26a) must be large relative to (VII-10b). As (VII-26a) is reported to be very fast, and the concentration of water vapor is some 10^8 fold greater than that of the N_2O_5, it is not impossible that this is the case. If so, the stationary concentration of nitrogen pentoxide will be smaller than the upper limit estimated by equation (VII-17), and the stationary concentration of nitrogen trioxide will approach the lower limit given by equation (VII-16). In any event, a substantial proportion of the nitrogen dioxide in polluted air may be converted to nitric acid by this series of reactions.

A reaction of nitrogen trioxide with water presents an interesting speculative possibility about which nothing is known. As with nitrogen dioxide, nitrogen trioxide is an odd molecule, so one of the initial products of such a reaction must also be an odd molecule or free radical. The hydrogen abstraction reaction

$$NO_3 + H_2O \rightarrow HNO_3 + \dot{O}H - \sim 15 \text{ kcal} \qquad \text{(VII-30)}$$

if 15 kcal endothermic, cannot have a collision yield greater than $\sim 10^{-11}$ at 25°C. In addition a low steric factor is to be expected. In spite of the concentration advantage, in air this reaction can scarcely compete with the reactions of nitrogen trioxide with nitric oxide and nitrogen dioxide, which have collision yields of the order of 10^{-2}.

5. REACTIONS INVOLVING HYDROCARBONS

Nitrogen dioxide reacts slowly with unsaturated hydrocarbons, even in the dark. On the other hand, pure nitric oxide can be stored in contact with liquid olefins for days without reaction, but if a trace of nitrogen dioxide is present, reaction occurs.[59]

Detailed studies of the products of these reactions have been conducted only in the liquid state and in the absence of any large amount of oxygen. Under these conditions addition products are formed. Thus, for the reaction between nitrogen tetroxide, N_2O_4, and liquid olefins at 0°C, Levy[260] found the first products were the dinitroparaffins and nitro nitrites which would be expected from direct addition; the nitro nitrites however were unstable and the final products he observed were dinitroparaffins, nitroalcohols, and nitroalkyl nitrates. With nitric oxide, containing a small amount of nitrogen dioxide, and liquid isobutene, Brown[59] obtained an unstable oil, probably a partially polymerized nitro nitroso adduct, as the major product, together with a number of minor products, including β-nitro isobutene, nitro-t-butanol, and nitrogen.

Brown postulates that the first step in these reactions is an addition of nitrogen dioxide at the double bond to form a nitroalkyl radical,

$$\text{(VII-31)}$$

This radical then undergoes further reactions, with nitrogen dioxide to form the dinitro compound or a nitro nitrite, or with nitric oxide to form a nitro nitroso compound. Most of these addition compounds are unstable and undergo further reactions.

The products of the dark reaction of nitrogen dioxide with olefins in air are unknown. If the first step is (VII-31), one might expect the nitroalkyl radical to add oxygen to form a nitroperoxyalkyl radical, which in turn might either spontaneously decompose or undergo further reaction, but this is pure speculation.

One interesting observation of a reaction involving oxygen was reported some time ago by Fulweiler.[144,145] During an investigation of gum formation in the presence of small amounts of nitric oxide (~1 to 3 ppm) in coal and water gas, he found that the oxidation of nitric oxide to nitrogen dioxide in the presence of oxygen was apparently catalyzed by some of the constituents of the gas. Gum formation either accompanied or followed this oxidation. Later Jordan, Smoker, Ward, and Fulweiler[234,235] identified diolefins as the responsible constituents and determined the relative activity of a number of individual diolefins. The results, in terms of the percentage of the nitric oxide oxidized under a standard procedure, are given in the tabulation. The nature of this reaction is not known,

1-3-Butadiene	65%
2-4-Hexadiene	48%
Isoprene	45%
2-3-Dimethyl-1-3-butadiene	35%
1-3-Pentadiene	30%
Cyclopentadiene	25%

nor has its rate been determined in a manner which would permit an estimate of its importance in polluted air. The process may, however, be partially responsible for the conversion of nitric oxide to nitrogen dioxide, particularly at night.

Returning to the reaction of nitrogen dioxide with olefins, in only one case, that of nitrogen dioxide and cyclohexene, has enough data been obtained to give some indication of the kinetics of the dark reaction in the presence of oxygen. In this case, Cadle et al.[63] found a possible negative temperature coefficient and, from the slopes of the log rate vs. log concentration curves, an apparent over-all order of ~1.2 to 1.3. These observations, which indicate a complex over-all reaction, were made at temperatures of 25 to 45°C and reactant partial pressures of ~1 to 35 mm in (from 160 to 630 mm of) oxygen as a carrier, using a 3 × 10-cm infrared absorption cell as the reaction vessel.

The initial rates of the dark reaction of nitrogen dioxide with 1-hexene, cyclohexene, and 1-3-butadiene at 30°C as reported by Cadle and collaborators,[63] and for the reaction with 1-pentene at 27 ± 3°C as reported by Ford and Endow[136] are given in Table 56. All of the values are reported as second-order rate constants.

The reactant and carrier gas concentrations used in these investigations are also given in Table 56. As additional data, Cadle and his collaborators followed the reaction in their 3 × 10-cm cell by the infrared absorption of either the nitrogen dioxide or the hydrocarbon. Ford and Endow passed the reactants, in 1 atm of nitrogen as a carrier, at a flow

TABLE 56

RATE CONSTANTS FOR THERMAL REACTIONS OF NITROGEN DIOXIDE
WITH UNSATURATED HYDROCARBONS AT ~30°C

| Hydrocarbon | Source | Reactant conc. (mm) | | Carrier | Total pressure (mm) | k (l mole^{-1} sec^{-1}) |
		NO_2	Hyd.			
1-Hexene	Cadle	3 to 52	6 to 60	O_2 or O_2-N_2	196–669	1.5×10^{-2}
Cyclohexene	Cadle	1.5 to 36	2 to 30	O_2-N_2	130–636	1.8
1-3-Butadiene	Cadle	0.9 to 6.5	0.4 to 12	O_2-N_2	130–668	76
1-Pentene	Ford and Endow	6×10^{-3} to 9×10^{-3}	3×10^{-4} to 4×10^{-4}	N_2	760	1.3×10^3

rate of 65 ml per second, through a 52-liter stirred reaction flask. The influent and effluent hydrocarbon concentrations were determined by gas chromatography, and the reaction rate was calculated as in these authors' work on oxygen atom–hydrocarbon reactions (Chapter V, Section 8).

In addition to the positive results listed in Table 56, Cadle, Eastman, Littman, and Benedict found that the reaction of nitrogen dioxide and ethylene was too slow to measure under their experimental conditions (a reaction with a rate constant of ~4 liter mole^{-1} sec^{-1} would have been detected), while Ford and Endow observed no reaction, in their stirred flow reactor, between nitrogen dioxide and *cis*-2-pentene.

Perhaps the most notable feature of the data in Table 56 is the fact that Ford and Endow's rate constant for the 1-pentene reaction is some 10^5 fold larger than that of Cadle and collaborators for 1-hexene. This difference may be due in part to a difference in reactivity of the two hydrocarbons, in part to differences in experimental conditions, and in part to a complex reaction with an apparent order of less than 2. If the latter were the case, expression of the data in terms of second-order rate constants, and particularly the comparison of such constants obtained at different concentration ranges, would not be valid.

Of the six unsaturated hydrocarbons for which observations have been reported, only one, 1-pentene, appears to react with nitrogen dioxide rapidly enough to give the reaction any possible significance in polluted air. At nitrogen dioxide and 1-pentene concentrations of 10 pphm each, the rate of this reaction, using Ford and Endow's constant, would be 0.2 pphm hr^{-1}. The next fastest reported rate, that of nitrogen dioxide with butadiene, using Cadle, Eastman, Littman, and Benedict's constant, would be 0.01 pphm hr^{-1} at the same concentrations, while that of the reaction with 1-hexene would be only 2×10^{-6} pphm hr^{-1}. It must be remembered, however, that if these reactions are complex the use of the reported second-order rate constants to calculate rates at atmospheric concentrations may not be valid. Since such calculations involve an extrapolation to lower concentrations, if the effective orders of the reactions are less than two the calculated rates will be too small.

With this reservation, the reported rate constants indicate that the over-all thermal reaction of nitrogen dioxide with the mixture of unsaturated hydrocarbons found in polluted urban air will be too slow to have any significance.

In this connection, it has sometimes been speculated that nitroolefins,

$$\underset{NO_2}{\overset{R}{\diagdown}} \underset{R}{\overset{R}{\diagup}} C{=}C \underset{R}{\overset{}{\diagdown}}$$

may be formed in small amounts by the nitrogen oxide–olefin reactions in air, and that these compounds may be at least partially responsible for the observed eye irritation. These compounds are highly toxic and are powerful irritants, not only to the eyes but also to the respiratory tract and to the skin,[99] so much so that their presence even at concentrations of a few parts per billion in air might produce noticeable symptoms. Accordingly, if nitroolefins were a product of the thermal nitrogen dioxide–olefin reactions, these reactions, even though slow, might be significant. But there is no evidence that they are such a product, nor has eye irritation ever been reported from nonirradiated nitrogen dioxide–olefin mixtures.

Nitric acid also reacts nonphotochemically with unsaturated hydrocarbons in air, and in one instance, that of the dark reaction between nitric acid and cyclohexene, the rate has been measured. For this reaction Cadle, Eastman, Littman, and Benedict obtained an initial rate constant of $k = 4.4$ liter mole^{-1} sec^{-1} = 6.5×10^{-6} pphm^{-1} hr^{-1} at reactant concentrations of ~1 to 4 mm in an O_2–N_2 carrier at total pressures of 340 to 670 mm. The rate at atmospheric concentrations on the basis of this constant would be less than 10^{-2} pphm hr^{-1}. Subject to the reservation that this reaction may also be complex and the extrapolation therefore invalid, and also the reservation that faster reactions may exist with other hydrocarbons, the evidence available indicates that the dark reaction between nitric acid and unsaturated hydrocarbons is too slow to be of any importance in air pollution.

6. OTHER REACTIONS

The reactions of oxides and oxy acids of nitrogen with aldehydes, organic acids, peroxy acids, and other organic compounds which may be present in polluted air offer an almost unlimited range of possibilities, but there is no evidence that any of these reactions is fast enough to be of any importance. Thus, the dark reactions of nitrogen dioxide with aldehydes and organic acids appear to be negligible. Hanst and Stephens[181] observed a dark reaction between peroxybutyric acid and nitrogen dioxide in air, with the formation of propyl nitrite and some propyl nitrate, but the rate of the reaction was not measured.

Sato and Cvetanović have reported[371] a rapid reaction between nitrogen dioxide and isobutene oxide, but again the rate was not measured.

The reaction of nitrogen dioxide with ammonia has sometimes been suggested as a possible means of reducing the concentration of nitrogen dioxide in polluted air. At room temperature the products of this reaction are NH_4NO_3, N_2, and H_2O, while at higher temperatures (300–500°C) they are chiefly NO, N_2, and H_2O. In the temperature range 150–200°C, Falk and Pease[127] found a third-order reaction, with the rate law.

$$-\frac{d(NO_2)}{dt} = k_{32}(NH_3)(NO_2)^2 \qquad \text{(VII-32)}$$

The reaction had an apparent negative activation energy of -12.5 kcal, and the rate constant obtained is given by

$$k_{32} = 4 \times 10^{-3}e^{+12500/RT} \text{ liter}^2 \text{ mole}^{-2} \text{ sec}^{-1} \qquad \text{(VII-33)}$$

Over the temperature range 325–525°C, Rosser and Wise[366] found a second-order reaction, with the rate law

$$\frac{d(NO_2)}{dt} = k_{34}(NH_3)(NO_2) \qquad \text{(VII-34)}$$

The activation energy observed by Rosser and Wise was 27.5 kcal and positive, and the rate constant was given by

$$k_{34} = 5 \times 10^9 e^{-(27500/RT)} \text{ liter mole}^{-1} \text{ sec}^{-1} \qquad \text{(VII-35)}$$

Extrapolation to ordinary atmospheric temperatures from either set of experimental data shows a wholly negligible rate for this reaction, at any concentrations which might be expected in urban air.

7. SUMMARY OF REACTIONS OF OXIDES AND OXY ACIDS OF NITROGEN

The thermal or dark reactions of the oxides and oxy acids of nitrogen thus far discussed are summarized in Table 57, with rates calculated for the exemplary concentrations

$(NO) = 1$ pphm $(O) = 2 \times 10^{-6}$ pphm
$(NO_2) = 10$ pphm $(H_2O) = 2 \times 10^6$ pphm
$(O_3) = 10$ pphm $(NO_3) = 7.5 \times 10^{-4}$ to 1.8×10^{-4} pphm

TABLE 57

SUMMARY OF REACTIONS OF OXIDES AND OXY ACIDS OF NITROGEN

Reaction no.	Reaction	k at 25°C in air at 1 atm, $pphm^{-1}\ hr^{-1}$ except as noted	Rate at exemplary conc. $(pphm\ hr^{-1})$
V-27	$NO + O + M \rightarrow NO_2 + M$	1.1×10^3	2×10^{-3}
V-28	$NO_2 + O \rightarrow NO + O_2$	3.1×10^3	6×10^{-2}
V-29	$NO_2 + O + M \rightarrow NO_3 + M$	5.9×10^3	0.12
VI-1	$NO + O_3 \rightarrow NO_2 + O_2$	17.2	172.
VI-4	$NO_2 + O_3 \rightarrow NO_3 + O_2$	0.06	6.
VII-1	$2NO + O_2 \rightarrow 2NO_2$	$9 \times 10^{-12}\ pphm^{-2}\ hr^{-1}$	1.8×10^{-4}
VII-9	$NO + NO_3 \rightarrow 2NO_2$	8×10^3	6 to 1.4
VII-10a	$NO_2 + NO_3 \rightarrow N_2O_5$	2.6×10^3	20 to 4.7
VII-10b	$N_2O_5 \rightarrow NO_2 + NO_3$	$8.6 \times 10^2\ hr^{-1}$	20 to 0
VII-11	$NO_2 + NO_3 \rightarrow NO + O_2 + NO_2$	0.37	3×10^{-3} to 7×10^{-4}
VII-12	$NO_3 + NO_3 \rightarrow 2NO_2 + O_2$	1.8×10^{-2}	1×10^{-8} to 6×10^{-10}
VII-22	$NO + NO_2 + H_2O \rightarrow 2HNO_2$	$2.6 \times 10^{-8}\ pphm^{-2}\ hr^{-1}$	0.5
VII-23 or 24	$NO_2 + H_2O \rightarrow ?$	$\sim 10^{-2}\ hr^{-1}$	~ 0.1
VII-26	$N_2O_5 + H_2O \rightarrow 2HNO_3$	Not known	0 to 4.7
—	$NO + O_2 + diolefin$	Not known	Not known
VII-31	$NO_2 + olefin$	2×10^{-8} to 2×10^{-3}	2×10^{-6} to 0.2
—	$NO_2 + NH_3$	$\sim 4 \times 10^{-9}\ pphm^{-2}\ hr^{-1}$	$\sim 10^{-7}$

These concentrations, which are believed to be fairly representative for photochemical smog forming periods (Fig. 32) correspond to a value of unity for the $[(NO)(O_3)]/(NO_2)$ product ratio (Chapter VI, Section 2).

Two limiting rate values are given for the reactions of nitrogen trioxide and pentoxide. For each reaction the first value would hold if the reaction of nitrogen pentoxide with water vapor (VII-26) is negligible and the stationary concentration of nitrogen trioxide is given by equation (VII-15). The second value results if the reaction with water vapor (VII-26) is so fast as to use all the nitrogen pentoxide produced by reaction (VII-10a), and the stationary concentration of nitrogen trioxide is given by (VII-16). While the rate of the nitrogen pentoxide–water vapor reaction is not known, it is probably fast enough to approach the second of these two limits.

Judging from these exemplary rates, the only reactions in the table which will be fast enough to be important during photochemical smog forming periods in air are (VI-1), (VI-4), (VII-9), (VII-10), and possibly (VII-26). These are the reactions of nitric oxide and of nitrogen dioxide with ozone, of the nitrogen trioxide, resulting from the latter reaction, with both nitric oxide and nitrogen dioxide, and possibly of nitrogen pentoxide with water. In addition, the reaction of nitric oxide, nitrogen dioxide, and water to form nitrous acid [(VII-22)] may have some significance in the event that the nitrous acid is rapidly photolyzed to yield free radicals or atoms.

Chapter VIII

Free Radical Reactions

Laboratory studies of individual members of some of the known classes of pollutants in urban air indicate that free radicals are very probably formed in this air during the daylight hours. But precise specification of the radicals formed, and the nature and rates of the reactions which they undergo, is another matter. For such a specification it would be necessary to know the individual compounds present in the air rather than the classes of compounds, such as aldehydes and olefins, which may be concerned with radical formation, it would be necessary to know the individual photochemistry of each of these compounds, and it would be necessary to know the reactions, with rate constants, which each of the resulting radicals might undergo in the air. Even though a vast literature is available, it is still not sufficient to permit such a detailed specification. Some useful information may nevertheless be gained by considering free radical reactions and their probable importance in air pollution generally in terms of classes of reactants and types of reactions, using the specific cases for which experimental data are available to indicate the general behavior of each class and type.

1. The Formation of Free Radicals in Polluted Air

The discussion of the preceding chapters has indicated that one of the important sources of free radicals in polluted air is the photochemical dissociation of molecules which absorb solar radiation. It was concluded (Chapter III, Section 14) that radicals of four types, alkyl, formyl, acyl, and alkoxyl may each be produced at rates of the order of 1 to 10 pphm hr^{-1} during periods of photochemical smog formation. Hydrogen atoms and hydroxyl radicals may also be produced by photodissociation processes, the former also possibly at a rate in the 1 to 10 pphm hr^{-1} range, but the latter at a rate probably below ~1 pphm hr^{-1}.

In addition, there is evidence that at least one class of secondary reactions, that of oxygen atoms with the olefins (Chapter V) may produce alkyl and formyl or acyl radicals to some extent. The over-all rate of these reactions for the mixture of olefins probably present in air was estimated (page 145) to lie in the range of 0.1 to 0.5 pphm hr^{-1}, and as only a fraction goes to radical formation, the rate of radical formation will be smaller still. The alkyl, formyl, or acyl radicals so formed will be added to those originating from photochemical dissociation. The reactions of ozone with the olefins have not been demonstrated to produce free radicals, although there are some indications that they may do so. With the possible exception of hydroperoxyl (VI-25), any radicals originating from this source are probably of the same classes as those produced photochemically.

Not only are radicals originated in air by photochemical and possibly by chemical reactions, they are also formed by the secondary reactions of these original radicals. The most important new types produced in this manner are the peroxyl radicals resulting from the reactions of alkyl, formyl, and acyl radicals with oxygen. These reactions will be discussed in the sections to follow.

2. REACTIONS OF ALKYL RADICALS

Five general or type reactions of alkyl radicals will be considered with respect to polluted air. These are the reactions of alkyl radicals with molecular oxygen, with ozone, with other alkyl radicals, with organic molecules, and with nitric oxide.

A rapid reaction between alkyl radicals and molecular oxygen to form peroxyalkyl radicals

$$\dot{R} + O_2 (+M) \rightarrow R\dot{O}O (+M) \tag{VIII-1}$$

has long been postulated in reaction mechanisms,[398] chiefly as one step of the Bodenstein-Bäckström-Ubbelohde chain[17,323,426] for organic oxidations at elevated temperatures, as well as in photochemical oxidations at room temperature.

Since this reaction is an association and is quite exothermic ($\sim$49 kcal when $\dot{R}$ is CH_3), it might be expected that with the smaller alkyl radicals, and especially with methyl radicals, the reaction would show a dependence on the concentration of the stabilizing molecule M, and hence be kinetically third order, up to pressures in the atmospheric range. Evidence that this is true has been derived from several studies of the pressure dependence of product yields; by Hoare and Walsh[201] using the acetone photolysis at 200°C, by Christie[78] using the methyl iodide photolysis, and by Sleppy and Calvert[387] using the azomethane photolysis, both at room temperature, as sources of methyl radicals. From their results Hoare and Walsh estimated for the third-order rate constant at 200°C, with $\dot{R} = CH_3$ and M = acetone, the value $k_1 = 5.8 \times 10^{10}$ liter^2 mole^{-2} sec^{-1}, while Sleppy and Calvert, with M = azomethane + neopentane, obtained $k_k = 3.8 \times 10^{10}$ liter^2 mole^{-2} sec^{-1} at 25°C. These values are consistent with earlier estimates[45,202,213,279] which indicated a bimolecular collision yield in the range of 10^{-4} to 10^{-3} for the reaction of methyl radicals with oxygen.

As these rate constants are larger than the hypothetical kinetic theory triple collision frequency factor of $Z \approx 10^{10}$ liter^2 mole^{-2} sec^{-1}, a large effective cross section is suggested for acetone, azomethane, and neopentane molecules when serving as the third body M in (VIII-1). In fact, there appears to be a great difference in the effectiveness of different molecules acting as M. Sleppy and Calvert noted a significant difference between azomethane and neopentane in this regard, while Hoare and Walsh and Christie found carbon dioxide to be only about one-tenth as effective as acetone or methyl iodide, respectively.

At low pressures Hoare and Walsh, and particularly Christie, observed deviations from the behavior which would be expected if the methyl radical–oxygen reaction is simply a third-order association competing with other methyl radical reactions which are second order. For instance, Christie obtained estimates at varying total pressures of the ratio k_{O_2}/k_{I_2}, the rate constants for the reactions $CH_3 + O_2 \rightarrow$ products, and $CH_3 + I_2 \rightarrow CH_3I + I$. If the $CH_3 + O_2$ reaction is entirely third order, i.e., if $k_{O_2} = k_1(M)$, this ratio should approach zero at zero pressure. Instead, it approached a finite value at zero pressure. This deviation is in the opposite sense from that which would occur in the normal changeover region where, with increasing pressure, the association rate becomes independent of the concentration of the third body, and suggests that in addition to the association there is also a second-order reaction between methyl radicals and oxygen.

At least two such reactions had already been postulated,

$$\dot{C}H_3 + O_2 \begin{cases} \nearrow & H\dot{C}O + H_2O \qquad\qquad \text{(VIII-2a)} \\ \searrow & H_2CO + \dot{O}H \qquad\qquad \text{(VIII-2b)} \end{cases}$$

The reaction to yield formyl radicals and water was assumed by Marcotte and Noyes[279] as one step in the photooxidation of acetone in the range of 120–225°C, while that to yield formaldehyde and hydroxyl has been postulated in connection with hydrocarbon oxidations.[323] Christie estimates that if such a reaction is responsible for the observed deviation its rate constant must lie in the range of $k_2 = 7 \times 10^6$ to 7×10^7 liter mole^{-1} sec^{-1}. It is quite possible, of course, that both the association and the metathetic reactions proceed through an initial energy rich association product, which may be stabilized or may decompose either into the original or into new products,

$$\dot{C}H_3 + O_2 \rightleftharpoons CH_3OO^* \xrightarrow{M} CH_3O\dot{O} \qquad\qquad (VIII-3)$$
$$\searrow$$
$$\text{metathetic products}$$

The effectiveness of oxygen and nitrogen as the third body in the methyl radical–oxygen reaction has not been determined, and for this reason an extension of any of the published results to air at atmospheric pressure must be regarded with caution. From the results of Christie it may be estimated that in carbon dioxide at room temperature and atmospheric pressure roughly 0.3 to 3% of the methyl radicals reacting with oxygen would do so by the second-order process, presumably to yield metathetic products, while 97% or better would yield peroxymethyl radicals. If oxygen and nitrogen are less efficient third bodies than carbon dioxide, the fraction yielding metathetic products in air would be greater, and that yielding peroxymethyl would be less, than these figures.

Similar estimates have not been made for the reactions of larger alkyl radicals with oxygen. On the one hand, one would expect the steric factor to become smaller, while on the other hand the dependence of the association reaction on a third body should diminish, as the alkyl radicals become larger. Certainly with ethyl radicals[312] and propyl radicals[131] the reaction appears to be quite fast at ordinary temperatures, and there is no good reason to suspect any products other than peroxyalkyl radicals. Lacking further information, it appears reasonable to assume an average collision yield of $y_1 \sim 10^{-4}$ for the alkyl radical–oxygen reaction in air, with peroxyalkyl radicals as the dominant product.

A rapid reaction between methyl radicals and ozone

$$\dot{C}H_3 + O_3 \rightarrow CH_3\dot{O} + O_2 \qquad\qquad (VIII-4)$$

has been suggested by Calvert and Hanst[69] to explain the low steady-state concentration of ozone which is reached during the photochemical decomposition of azomethane in the presence of a large excess of oxygen. Assuming that the ozone is formed in this system by (VIII-1) followed by (VIII-26), they conclude that the rate constant for (VIII-4) lies between 5×10^9 and 2×10^{11} liter mole^{-1} sec^{-1}, corresponding to a collision yield roughly between 10^{-2} and 1. The rates of reaction of the larger alkyl radicals with ozone are unknown, and the reactions are speculative.

Alkyl radicals react with each other in two ways. They may combine to form a single molecule

$$R_1\dot{C}H_2 + R_2CH_2\dot{C}H_2 \rightarrow R_1CH_2CH_2CH_2R_2 \qquad\qquad (VIII-5)$$

or disproportionate to yield one paraffin and one olefin molecule

$$R_1\dot{C}H_2 + R_2CH_2\dot{C}H_2 \rightarrow R_1CH_3 + R_2CH=CH_2 \qquad \text{(VIII-6)}$$

With methyl radicals at room temperature only the combination is observed. With ethyl [217,332,385] as well as n-propyl [448] from 0.1 to 0.2 of the radicals appears to disproportionate, and with butyl radicals the fraction which disproportionates appears to be about 0.3.[294]

The rate of the methyl radical combination has received a great deal of attention, and all investigators agree that the reaction is very fast. Ingold and Lossing[214] studied the combination by a mass spectrometric method, using methyl radicals produced by the thermal decomposition of mercury dimethyl. Over the total pressure range of 4.8 to 18.5 mm., the combination reaction was second order with respect to methyl radicals and independent of the total pressure, indicating that the association complex is sufficiently long lived to make the reaction kinetically independent of the third body, even at this pressure. The reaction also showed a negative temperature coefficient, corresponding to a negative activation energy of -2.2 kcal, which the authors regard as due to a decrease in the effective collision cross section of the radicals with increasing temperature. At $25°C$ they obtained for the recombination rate constant the value $k_5 = 4 \times 10^{10}$ liter mole^{-1} sec^{-1}.

Gomer and Kistiakowsky[158] and Kistiakowsky and Roberts[246] studied the methyl radical combination by application of a rotating sector technique to the photolyses of acetone and mercury dimethyl. Shepp[384] by a recalculation of the results of these authors obtained $k_5 = 2.2 \times 10^{10}$ liter mole^{-1} sec^{-1} for the combination rate constant at $125–175°C$. This, and the value of Ingold and Lossing, indicates a combination collision yield of about $y_5 = 0.1$ for methyl radicals. Other values which have been reported[423,424] fall within an order of magnitude of this figure.

The rates of combination and disproportionation of ethyl radicals were estimated by Ivin and Steacie[217] from an application of the rotating sector technique to the photolysis of mercury diethyl. Depending on whether the activation energy for the combination reaction is assumed to be zero or 0.65 kcal mole^{-1}, their results yield, at $25°C$, the values of $k_5 = 1.6 \times 10^{10}$ to 4×10^{10} liter mole^{-1} sec^{-1}, and $k_6 = 4.3 \times 10^9$ to 4.7×10^9 liter mole^{-1} sec^{-1}. A similar investigation by Shepp and Kutschke[385] applying the rotating sector method to the photolysis of diethyl ketone, yielded $k_5 = 1.5 \times 10^{10}$ liter mole^{-1} sec^{-1} at $50°C$, with an apparent activation energy of about 2 kcal, for the ethyl radical combination, and a ratio of disproportionation to combination of 0.12. The collision yields corresponding to these rate constants are about $y_5 = 0.1$ for the combination and $y_6 = 0.01$ for the disproportionation of ethyl radicals.

Again using the rotating sector technique, this time on the photolysis of di-n-propyl ketone, Whiteway and Masson[448] obtained, for the sum of the combination and disproportionation of n-propyl radicals, a measured rate even higher than the theoretical collision rate, with a ratio of combination to disproportionation of 8 to 1. While the measured rate may involve some experimental error, the results for methyl, ethyl, and n-propyl radicals give no indication, for the combination reaction, of any decrease in collision yield with increasing radical size. Furthermore, there is no cause for belief that the collision yields between unlike radicals, e.g., methyl and propyl, would be materially smaller than those between like radicals. Order of magnitude values of $y_5 \sim 10^{-1}$ and $y_6 \sim 10^{-2}$ may, therefore, be accepted as representative of the combination and disproportionation yields of alkyl radicals in general.

With organic molecules, alkyl radicals react in at least two ways, by hydrogen abstraction and by addition. The hydrogen abstraction reaction may be written

$$\dot{R} + XH \rightarrow RH + \dot{X} \tag{VIII-7}$$

It should be noted that if XH is a paraffin hydrocarbon, no net change in the number of alkyl radicals, but only a possible change in radical type, results from this reaction.

The activation energies and steric factors, hence the collision yields, have been determined for a large number of hydrogen abstractions by methyl radicals.[398] For the most part the activation energies lie between 7 and 10 kcal and the steric factors between 10^{-3} and 10^{-4}.

TABLE 58

RATES OF HYDROGEN ABSTRACTION BY METHYL RADICALS

$$\dot{CH}_3 + XH \rightarrow CH_4 + \dot{X}$$

Compound, XH	Estimated collision yield y, at 25°C.	Ref.
Ethane	10^{-11}	423, 424
n-Butane	2×10^{-10}	233
2-Methyl propane	10^{-9}	233
Ethylene	4×10^{-11}	424
1-Butene	2×10^{-9}	424
2-Butene	1.5×10^{-9}	424
2-Methyl propylene	1.7×10^{-9}	424
Acetone	7×10^{-11}	219
Formaldehyde	10^{-8}	408
Acetaldehyde	5×10^{-9}	55

Some representative values of the collision yields for hydrogen abstraction by methyl radicals, estimated for 25°C from the references given, are listed in Table 58. The abstraction yields for ethane, n-butane, and 2-methyl propane, which are in the ratio of 1:20:100, illustrate the successively greater reactivity of secondary and tertiary, relative to that of primary, hydrogen atoms. The values for the olefins show the relatively small effect of structure on the rate of hydrogen abstraction. With the exception of ethylene, this appears to be rather general for the olefins. Finally, the values for acetone and formaldehyde or acetaldehyde bring out the marked sensitivity of the aldehyde hydrogen to abstraction. Evidently the abstraction reaction with aldehydes is chiefly

$$\dot{R}_1 + R_2CHO \rightarrow R_1H + R_2\dot{C}O \qquad\qquad (VIII\text{-}8)$$

Information on the rates of hydrogen abstraction by the larger alkyl radicals is far less complete than it is for methyl radicals. Rates of abstraction of hydrogen from diethyl ether by ethyl radicals,[251] from di-n-propyl ketone by n-propyl radicals,[284] and from azoisopropane by isopropyl radicals[110] have been reported, and the results in all three cases lead to an estimated collision yield of $y \sim 10^{-9}$ at 25°C.

With unsaturated molecules, such as olefins, alkyl radicals may react by addition as well as hydrogen abstraction,

$$\dot{R}_1 + \underset{R_3}{\overset{R_2}{>}}C=C\underset{R_5}{\overset{R_4}{<}} \rightarrow R_1-\underset{\overset{|}{R_3}}{\overset{\overset{|}{R_2}}{C}}-\underset{\overset{|}{R_5}}{\overset{\overset{|}{R_4}}{C}}\cdot \qquad (VIII\text{-}9)$$

The larger alkyl radical thus formed may react with another olefin molecule, leading to polymerization, or it may break down, by something like the reverse of (VIII-9), into another alkyl radical and olefin molecule.

The over-all result of (VIII-9) followed by a breakdown of the larger radical is a displacement of one alkyl radical in the olefin by another, and it is possible that in some cases this may occur in a single step. With other unsaturated molecules than olefins, other radicals than alkyl may be displaced. Thus Pitts et al.[334] have obtained evidence of a reaction of methyl radicals with trans-methyl propenyl ketone to yield 2-butene and acetyl radicals, and of methyl radicals with crotonaldehyde to yield 2-butene and formyl radicals. Free radical displacement reactions have been observed thus far only at elevated temperatures, and it is not yet known whether they are important at ordinary temperatures.

Estimates of the rate of the addition process (VIII-9) at ordinary temperatures are not in agreement. Thus, Taylor and Jungers[414] estimated 1 to 2 kcal, while Mandelcorn and Steacie[278] obtained 7 ± 1.5 kcal, for the activation energy of the addition of methyl radicals to ethylene, both estimates being based on studies of the photolysis of acetone–ethylene mixtures. Some investigations[27,386] indicate that the addition of methyl radicals to propylene is slower than it is to ethylene, others[93,340] indicate that the rate of the two is about the same. Steacie[398] after reviewing the evidence, concludes that the activation energy of the methyl radical–propylene addition is low, probably of the order of 1 to 3 kcal.

If the activation energies for addition are indeed as low as 1 to 3 kcal, it is possible that they are much faster than the hydrogen abstractions, for which the activation energies are generally between 7 and 10 kcal. Given the same steric factors, this difference in activation energies would result in a difference of $\sim 10^4$ or 10^5 in collision yields at ordinary temperatures. However, Buckley et al.[60] have reported that in pentane solution the rate of addition of methyl radicals to isobutene is only about 17 times the rate of hydrogen abstraction, while with the 2-butenes the rates of addition and abstraction are about the same. If this is the case, and the activation energy of addition is indeed smaller than that of abstraction, then the steric factor must also be smaller.

Nitric oxide has been much used as an inhibitor of reactions which involve free radical chains, and the inhibiting effect is believed to be due to the removal of radicals by the reaction

$$\dot{R} + NO \rightarrow RNO \qquad \text{(VIII-10)}$$

Since nitric oxide is an odd electron molecule, the formation of a simple nitroso addition compound would be expected, at least as the first step, although it is still not clear that this is the case. Coe and Doumani[81] isolated colorless crystals of dimeric nitrosomethane as a product of the photolysis of t-butyl nitrite, and on gentle heating, to $\sim 125°C$, the crystals melted and yielded a bluish vapor which the authors believed to be monomeric CH_3NO. From this it would appear that nitrosomethane is fairly stable at ordinary temperatures, although with time, particularly at higher temperatures, it may rearrange to formaldoxime, CH_2NOH.[77,339,343,413]

As in the case of the reaction of methyl radicals with oxygen, it might be expected that the association of methyl radicals with nitric oxide would show a third-order dependence on stabilizing collisions extending to substantial pressures.[201] However, Sleppy and Calvert[387] have found that in the pressure region of 150–280 mm of azomethane or neopentane, while the $CH_3 + O_2$ reaction is third order, the $CH_3 + NO$ reaction is definitely second order, and shows no dependence on M. The authors suggest that this may be due to a difference in exothermicity of the two reactions, and estimate the values 49 kcal for $CH_3 + O_2$ vs. 25 kcal for

$CH_3 + NO$. Since the initial association products $CH_3O\dot{O}$ and CH_3NO have similar complexity, the product with smaller excess energy should be less dependent on stabilizing collisions, and thus should exhibit second-order behavior at lower pressures.

The rate of the reaction between methyl radicals and nitric oxide was first measured by Forsyth,[137] using the Paneth method. Methyl radicals were produced by the thermal decomposition of ethylene oxide and the products, with and without added nitric oxide, were passed over tellurium mirrors. From the rate of disappearance of methyl radicals, based on the rate of removal of the mirrors, Forsyth concluded that the collision efficiency of their reaction with nitric oxide was $y_{10} = 1.4 \times 10^{-5}$. Later, Durham and Steacie[110] repeated Forsyth's work, using di-t-butyl peroxide as the radical source, and obtained a room temperature collision yield of $y_{10} = 1.5 \times 10^{-4}$.

By photolyzing mercury dimethyl to produce methyl radicals in an apparatus in which nitric oxide was introduced at a continuous rate, thus allowing an approach to steady state conditions, and by measuring the rate of ethane formation and nitric oxide disappearance, Miller and Steacie[291] obtained, as an average value, the ratio $k_5^{1/2}/k_{10} = 3.1 \times 10^{-5}$ mole$^{1/2}$ cc$^{-1/2}$ sec$^{-1/2}$, where k_5 is the rate constant for methyl radical combination and k_{10} is that for the methyl radical–nitric oxide reaction. Combining this with Ingold and Lossing's value of $k_5 = 4 \times 10^{10}$ liter mole^{-1} sec^{-1} (page 205) gives $k_{10} = 2 \times 10^8$ liter mole^{-1} sec^{-1} at 25°C. This would correspond to a collision yield of $y_{10} \sim 6 \times 10^{-4}$. Miller and Steacie suggest that their value of the ratio $k_5^{1/2}/k_{10}$, used in this calculation, should be taken as an upper limit. If so, the values of k_{10} and y_{10} calculated from this ratio should be taken as a lower limit.

Sleppy and Calvert,[387] from an analysis of the results of the flash photolysis of mixtures of about 50 mm of azomethane with 97 to 233 mm of neopentane and 7 to 18 mm of nitric oxide, obtained the rate constant $k_{10} = 6.3 \times 10^8$ liter mole^{-1} sec^{-1} for the reaction $CH_3 + NO \rightarrow CH_3NO$ at 25°C. The corresponding collision yield, $y_{10} \sim 2 \times 10^{-3}$, is higher than any of the earlier estimates, probably because only in this work were the conditions such as to provide kinetic independence of stabilizing collisions. In extending the value of Sleppy and Calvert to air, it must be remembered that as in the case of the $CH_3 + O_2$ reaction, oxygen and nitrogen may be less effective than azomethane and neopentane in stabilizing the initially produced CH_3NO, and the collision yield calculated from their results should therefore be taken as an upper limit for that in air.

By determining the effect of nitric oxide on the concentration of methyl radicals produced by the pyrolysis of ethylene oxide, Lossing *et al.*[267] obtained the values $y_{10} = 1.4 \times 10^{-4}$ to 2.6×10^{-4} for the collision yield of the methyl radical–nitric oxide reaction at 950°C. The close agreement between these and the room temperature yields is good evidence that the activation energy of the reaction is small.

The rates of reaction of alkyl radicals other than methyl with nitric oxide have not been determined, but there is no indication that they differ substantially from that of methyl.

An addition reaction between alkyl radicals and nitrogen dioxide to yield the nitro compound

$$\dot{R} + NO_2 \rightarrow RNO_2 \qquad (VIII\text{-}11)$$

has been postulated, for example by Gray and Style[165] to account for the appearance of nitromethane as a product of the photolysis of ethyl nitrate, but these reactions have escaped quantitative study and their collision yields are unknown. A metathetic reaction

$$\dot{R} + NO_2 \rightarrow \dot{R}O + NO \qquad (VIII\text{-}12)$$

is also a possibility,[167] but again no kinetic data are available.

It has long been believed, and often stated, that any alkyl radicals formed in polluted air will react almost exclusively with oxygen to form peroxyl radicals, by reaction (VIII-1). From the rate constants and collision yields presented in this discussion we may arrive at an estimate of the extent to which this is true. In the case of methyl radicals at least, the reaction best able to compete with the oxygen reaction in polluted air appears to be that with ozone, (VIII-4). The rate of reaction of methyl radicals with ozone relative to that of their reaction with oxygen, assuming the same collision diameters, will be

$$\frac{S_4}{S_1} = \frac{y_4(O_3)}{y_1(O_2)} \qquad (VIII\text{-}13)$$

Taking $y_1 = 10^{-4}$ and $y_4 = 10^{-1}$, $(O_2) = 2 z 10^7$ pphm, and $(O_3) = 10$ pphm, yields the ratio

$$\frac{S_4}{S_1} = 5 \times 10^{-4}$$

A similar estimate for the reaction with nitric oxide, (VIII-10), using $y_{10} = 2 \times 10^{-3}$ and $(NO) = 1$ pphm yields the ratio

$$\frac{S_{10}}{S_1} = 10^{-6}$$

These fractions are negligible, and in like manner the fractions of alkyl radicals combining or reacting with other pollutants in air may also be shown to be negligible, even with the most optimistic assumptions regarding collision yields. While there is some question as to the extent to which peroxyalkyl radicals are the product, the conclusion that alkyl radicals will react almost exclusively with oxygen in polluted air is thus substantiated.

This being the case, if S_f is the rate of formation of alkyl radicals, their stationary concentration in air will be very nearly

$$(\dot{R}) = \frac{S_f}{k_1(O_2)} \qquad (VIII\text{-}14)$$

Taking $S_f = 5$ pphm hr^{-1}, probably a reasonable value for photochemical smog forming periods, and $k_1 = 40$ pphm^{-1} hr^{-1} (the value corresponding to a collision yield of 10^{-4}), gives

$$(\dot{R}) = 6 \times 10^{-9} \text{ pphm.}$$

This low stationary concentration of alkyl radicals, resulting from their rapid reaction with oxygen, is noteworthy.

3. REACTIONS OF FORMYL AND ACYL RADICALS

Formyl and acyl radicals, $H\dot{C}O$ and $R\dot{C}O$, undergo most of the same general reactions as do alkyl radicals, i.e., they react with oxygen, with other radicals, with organic molecules, and with nitric oxide. In addition, they thermally decompose.

The direct addition of oxygen to formyl and acetyl radicals to form peroxyformyl and peroxyacetyl radicals

$$HCO + O_2 \rightarrow H\overset{\overset{\displaystyle O}{\|}}{C}O\dot{O} \qquad (VIII\text{-}15)$$

$$CH_3\dot{C}O + O_2 \rightarrow CH_3\overset{\overset{\displaystyle O}{\|}}{C}O\dot{O} \qquad (VIII\text{-}16)$$

has been proposed and is in accordance with observed behavior in both the thermal and photochemical oxidations of formaldehyde and acetaldehyde.[74,181,272,274] While there is little information on the collision yields of these reactions at ordinary temperatures, a low activation energy is to be expected, and the collision yields probably will not vastly differ from those of the alkyl radical–oxygen reactions.

At higher temperatures, as with alkyl radicals, the reactions of formyl and acyl radicals with oxygen may lead to other products, either directly or through decomposition of the peroxyl radicals first formed by addition. For example, Marcotte and Noyes[279] assumed a mechanism containing the reaction

$$\dot{H}CO + O_2 \rightarrow \dot{O}H + CO_2 \qquad\qquad \text{(VIII-17)}$$

as well as (VIII-2) to explain their observations on the photochemical oxidation of acetone at temperatures of 120 to 225°C, and concluded from an analysis of the effects of temperature that if the assumed mechanism is correct the activation energy of (VIII-17) must be zero or close thereto.

Another reaction of formyl radicals with oxygen,

$$\dot{H}CO + O_2 \rightarrow H\dot{O}_2 + CO \qquad\qquad \text{(VIII-18)}$$

has been suggested by Ingold and Bryce[213] and Strong and Kutschke[408] as a possible step in the series of reactions which are initiated when methyl radicals are produced in the presence of oxygen. For example, during the photolysis of a starting mixture of ~82 mm of azomethane and ~11 mm of oxygen at 124°C, the latter authors found that one product, formaldehyde, approaches a rather low stationary concentration, while the rate of formation of another product, carbon monoxide, increases with time. This behavior could be explained by a hydrogen abstraction reaction $\dot{R} + H_2CO \rightarrow RH + \dot{H}CO$ followed by (VIII-18).

Reactions similar to (VIII-17) and (VIII-18) have also been proposed for acetyl radicals. Taylor and Blacet[415] in an investigation of the photochemical oxidation of biacetyl, found by using O_2 enriched with the O^{18} isotope that carbon dioxide produced by the reaction at 140°C contains one oxygen atom from the biacetyl and one from the molecular oxygen, while in at least part of the carbon monoxide produced the oxygen atom must have come from the biacetyl. To explain these observations Taylor and Blacet propose the reactions

$$CH_3\dot{C}O + O_2 \rightarrow CH_3\dot{O} + CO_2 \qquad\qquad \text{(VIII-19)}$$

$$CH_3\dot{C}O + O_2 \rightarrow CH_3O\dot{O} + CO \qquad\qquad \text{(VIII-20)}$$

At variance with this, Marcotte and Noyes concluded from their work on the acetone photooxidation that the reaction of acetyl radicals with oxygen does not produce CO or CO_2, and leads to the disappearance of two molecules of O_2 per $CH_3\dot{C}O$.

It is possible, of course, in all of this work that the initial product is a peroxyformyl or peroxyacetyl radical which subsequently decomposes. At ordinary temperatures, perhaps the best evidence that acetyl radicals do form peroxyacetyl radicals on reaction with oxygen is provided by the discovery of Stephens and his associates[401,405] that PAN, which at present writing appears to be peroxyacetyl nitrate (Chapter III), may be prepared by irradiating mixtures of biacetyl and nitrogen dioxide in the presence of oxygen. On the other hand, the corresponding peroxyformyl compound has not been observed, suggesting that either it or peroxy-formyl radicals are unstable, or that the latter are not formed by the reaction of formyl radicals with oxygen.

For the reactions of formyl and acyl radicals with themselves or with other radicals, additions and hydrogen abstractions of various types have been postulated,[35,74,272,451] but there is little or no information on the rates of these reactions at room temperature. The same must be said for the reactions of formyl and acyl radicals with organic molecules; a number have been postulated but little or nothing is known of their rates. In general, however, such reactions would be expected to be much slower than reactions between radicals.

The reaction of formyl and acyl radicals with nitric oxide is presumably an addition

$$R\dot{C}O + \dot{N}O \rightarrow R\overset{\overset{\displaystyle O}{\|}}{C}NO \qquad \text{(VIII-21)}$$

In the course of an investigation of the photolysis of mixtures of acetone and nitric oxide, Anderson and Rollefson[11] found that the formation of carbon monoxide was less inhibited by nitric oxide than was the formation of ethane. This would probably indicate that the collision yield of reaction (VIII-21), when RCO is an acetyl radical, is somewhat less than that of the reaction of methyl radicals with nitric oxide (VIII-10). On the basis of this evidence, an order of magnitude value of $y_{21} \sim 10^{-4}$ is reasonable for reaction (VIII-21).

With nitrogen dioxide the corresponding reaction would be

$$R\dot{C}O + NO_2 \rightarrow R\overset{\overset{\displaystyle O}{\|}}{C}ONO \text{ or } R\overset{\overset{\displaystyle O}{\|}}{C}NO_2 \qquad \text{(VIII-22)}$$

The collision yield of this reaction has not been established.

The decomposition reactions of formyl and acyl radicals are

$$H\dot{C}O \ (+M) \rightarrow \dot{H} + CO \ (+M) \qquad \text{(VIII-23)}$$

$$R\dot{C}O \ (+M) \rightarrow \dot{R} + CO \ (+M) \qquad \text{(VIII-24)}$$

These reactions have received much attention in connection with the photolysis of aldehydes and ketones, and several estimates of their activation energies have been reached through the study of these photolyses.

For the activation energy of the formyl radical decomposition, (VIII-23), an early estimate of 26 kcal by Gorin[162] was shown by Calvert and Steacie[72] to be almost certainly too high. Subsequently Klein and Schoen,[248] on the basis of evidence that at 300°C at least part of the photodissociation of formaldehyde by light of 3660 A occurs by the process

$$H_2CO = h\nu \rightarrow H + H\dot{C}O \qquad \text{(VIII-25)}$$

concluded that the activation energy of formyl radical decomposition must be at least 27 kcal. The argument was that the energy absorbed at 3660 A is 78 kcal/mole, and if it is able to produce this dissociation, the dissociation energy of (VIII-25) must be equal to or less than 78 kcal. Since the reaction $H_2CO \rightarrow 2H + CO$ is endothermic by 105 kcal, the dissociation energy of the formyl radical must be equal to the difference between these two, or ≥ 27 kcal. This argument has been questioned by Calvert et al.[71] on the basis that the photodissociation of formaldehyde at 3660 A and 300°C probably results from absorption by vibrationally excited molecules. In consequencee, the estimate of 78 kcal for the dissociation energy of (VIII-25) would be too low and the resulting figure of 27 kcal for the activation energy of (VIII-23) would be too high.

Other estimates of the activation energy of the formyl radical decomposition, based on analyses of the products of the photolysis of various aldehydes over a range of temperature, by Akeroyd and Norrish,[6] Style and Summers,[409] Blacet and Calvert,[37] Calvert and Steacie,[72] Blacet and Pitts,[42] Horner et al.,[205] and Calvert et al.,[71] all fall in the range of 12 to 16 kcal, and there appears to be little doubt but that the true value lies within this range.

Estimates of the activation energy of the acetyl radical decomposition are >17 kcal by Gorin,[162] ~18 kcal by Herr and Noyes,[193] 16 kcal by Benson and Forbes,[31] and 13.5 kcal by Volman and Craven.[436] Judging from these activation energies, the decompositions of formyl and acetyl radicals are rather slow at ordinary air temperatures. For the larger acyl radicals no similar estimates are available, but the propionyl radical, C_2H_5CO, seems to be sufficiently unstable to decompose appreciably, even at room temperature.[97,312]

The extent to which the reactions of formyl and acyl radicals with oxygen predominate over their other reactions in polluted air may only be surmised. Consider, for example, the relative rates of reaction of acetyl radicals with oxygen (VIII-16) and with nitric oxide (VIII-21). Such evidence as is available would suggest that the collision yields of these two reactions may be about the same. If this is the case the ratio of their rates in air will be equal to the ratio of the concentrations of oxygen and nitric oxide. As the value of this ratio is ordinarily $\sim 10^7$ during smog forming periods, on this basis it would not be expected that more than one acetyl radical in $\sim 10^7$ would react with nitric oxide.

Another comparison may be obtained between the rate of reaction of formyl and acetyl radicals with oxygen and the rate of their decomposition. If the reaction with oxygen has a collision yield of $y = 10^{-4}$ and the decomposition an activation energy of 14 kcal, then even if every activating collision should lead to decomposition only some 2×10^{-6} of the radicals formed in air would decompose, relative to those reacting with oxygen.

By similar arguments the other reactions of formyl and acetyl radicals appear to be negligible when compared with their reactions with oxygen in air. The larger acyl radicals, such as propionyl, might dissociate to an appreciable extent by (V-26) even in air, but the evidence available will not permit a decision on this.

Owing to their rapid reaction with oxygen, the stationary concentrations of formyl and acyl radicals in urban air will be very small, perhaps of the same order as that of alkyl radicals (Section 2).

4. REACTIONS OF PEROXYALKYL RADICALS

A rapid addition reaction between peroxyl radicals and oxygen would not be expected and there is no evidence that any such reaction occurs. In the case of the peroxyalkyl radicals, the reaction with oxygen

$$R\dot{O}O + O_2 \rightarrow R\dot{O} + O_3 \qquad \text{(VIII-26)}$$

has been proposed [64,227,415] to explain the formation of ozone on irradiation of aldehydes in air. Objection has been raised to this reaction on the grounds that it must be endothermic, but arguments in its support have been presented by Hanst and Calvert.[179]

These authors base their support of (VIII-26) on two observations made during a study of the photolysis of azomethane in the presence of oxygen. Azomethane is photolyzed to yield methyl radicals and molecular nitrogen, and in oxygen at atmospheric pressure, which Hanst and Calvert used, the methyl radicals would react almost exclusively with oxygen presumably to yield peroxymethyl, $CH_3O\dot{O}$. The peroxymethyl radicals in turn might react with each other by such a process as (VIII-27), they might abstract hydrogen from other molecules to yield methyl hydroperoxide, or they might react with oxygen by (VIII-26).

The first observation of Hanst and Calvert was that a major product was methanol, while no detectable amount of methyl hydroperoxide was formed. Assuming that the methanol was produced by hydrogen abstraction reactions of methoxyl radicals, and that the rates of hydrogen abstraction by methoxyl and peroxymethyl radicals are comparable, this observation suggests to them that peroxymethyl radicals have a much shorter lifetime in the system than do methoxyl radicals. They indicate that the apparent short lifetime of peroxymethyl radicals makes their disappearance by radical–radical reactions such as (VIII-27) seem improbable, and therefore a more likely possibility is the ozone forming reaction (VIII-26).

The second observation of Hanst and Calvert was that acetone appeared as a product when tetramethylethylene was added to the azomethane–oxygen photolysis system. The starting concentrations were 2.4 mm of azomethane, 748 mm of oxygen, and 13.5 mm of tetramethylethylene; during the 10-minute photolysis period approximately half of the azomethane was decomposed and 0.7 mm of acetone were produced. Acetone is a known product of the reaction of ozone with tetramethylethylene (Tables 48, 49), and in separate experiments Hanst and Calvert found a one-to-one stoichiometric ratio between the ozone and tetramethylethylene consumed and the acetone produced by this reaction. They accordingly suggest that the appearance of acetone on addition of tetramethylethylene indicates the formation of ozone during the azomethane–oxygen photolysis, and if ozone is indeed produced during this photolysis it is difficult to account for it by any other reaction than (VIII-26).

The reaction system studied by Hanst and Calvert was well chosen, their observations are important, and their suggestions are stimulating. Nevertheless several points remain to be demonstrated in establishing the bearing of their work on reaction (VIII-26). With regard to their observation that no detectable amount of methyl hydroperoxide was formed, the infrared absorption method used is not particularly sensitive for this substance; for instance with a starting mixture of 31.6 mm of azomethane in 1 atm of oxygen and photolysis sufficient to decompose about 20 mm of the azomethane, up to 1 mm of methyl hydroperoxide among the photolysis products might have escaped detection. The rates of the hydrogen abstraction reactions of peroxymethyl radicals are not known, and it is possible that they are not fast enough to have produced a detectable amount of methyl hydroperoxide under Hanst and Calvert's experimental conditions, even if the only competing processes were radical–radical reactions. Concerning their observation on the appearance of acetone when tetramethylethylene was added to the photolysis system, it remains to be demonstrated that there are no other reactions than that of ozone which could produce acetone under these conditions. One other possibility for acetone production, for example, would be through the reaction of peroxymethyl radicals with tetramethylethylene.

Returning to the question of the enthalpy of reaction (VIII-26), from the data of Walsh[444] the corresponding reaction $HO\dot{O} + O_2 \rightarrow \dot{O}H + O_3$ is endothermic by 52 kcal. On the other hand, assuming that the O—O bond dissociation energy in the $R O \dot{O}$ radical is the same as diethyl peroxide, namely 31.5 kcal,[348] makes reaction (VIII-26) endothermic by only

7 kcal. The true value probably lies between these two figures. An alternate possibility, suggested by Hanst and Calvert, is that (VIII-26) involves the thermally excited peroxyalkyl radicals formed by reaction (VIII-1). The latter reaction is estimated to be ~49 kcal exothermic,[387] and its apparent dependence on stabilizing collisions would not be inconsistent with a reaction, rather than stabilization, on collision of the newly formed peroxyalkyl radicals with oxygen. The thermal requirements for this reaction to be important in air will be discussed later.

Apparently peroxyalkyl radicals not only do not add to oxygen, but also they do not combine with each other to yield a stable association product. A reaction between peroxyalkyl radicals to yield alkoxyl radicals and oxygen,

$$\text{RO}\dot{\text{O}} + \text{RO}\dot{\text{O}} \rightarrow 2\text{R}\dot{\text{O}} + \text{O}_2 \qquad \text{(VIII-27)}$$

has been proposed by Vaughan and his collaborators[28,342] as one step in the mechanism of oxidation of hydrocarbons. Although Hanst and Calvert obtained no evidence in support of this reaction, their experimental setup did not yield proof of its absence.

The abstraction of hydrogen from organic molecules by peroxyalkyl radicals

$$\text{R}_1\text{O}\dot{\text{O}} + \text{R}_2\text{H} \rightarrow \text{R}_1\text{OOH} + \dot{\text{R}}_2 \qquad \text{(VIII-28)}$$

$$\text{R}_1\text{O}\dot{\text{O}} + \text{R}_2\text{CHO} \rightarrow \text{R}_1\text{OOH} + \text{R}_2\dot{\text{C}}\text{O} \qquad \text{(VIII-29)}$$

forms one step in the Bodenstein-Bäckström-Ubbelohde chain for organic oxidations (Section 2), which is about as well established as any mechanism in the whole of chemical kinetics. But being hydrogen abstractions, these reactions probably do not have a high collision yield at ordinary temperatures. Indeed, if they resemble the abstraction reactions of alkyl radicals their collision yields may be ~10^{-9} or lower (Table 58).

With olefins, direct addition of peroxyalkyl radicals is a possibility,

$$\text{R}_1\text{O}\dot{\text{O}} + \begin{array}{c} \text{R}_2 \\ \diagdown \\ \diagup \\ \text{R}_3 \end{array} \text{C}=\text{C} \begin{array}{c} \text{R}_4 \\ \diagup \\ \diagdown \\ \text{R}_5 \end{array} \rightarrow \text{R}_1\text{O}-\text{O}-\underset{\underset{\text{R}_3}{|}}{\overset{\overset{\text{R}_2}{|}}{\text{C}}}-\underset{\underset{\text{R}_5}{|}}{\overset{\overset{\text{R}_4}{|}}{\text{C}}}\cdot \qquad \text{(VIII-30)}$$

The resulting peroxide radical might add to oxygen, and this product in turn add to an olefin, forming a chain which could conceivably result in peroxy polymers.[61,406,419] A further possibility involves a split of the olefin at the double bond on reacting with peroxyalkyl radicals, with one end forming an aldehyde or ketone and the other an oxy radical.

A reaction between peroxyalkyl radicals and nitric oxide, to form either an association product (an alkyl pernitrite) or an alkoxyl radical and nitrogen dioxide,

$$\text{RO}\dot{\text{O}} + \text{NO} \begin{array}{c} \nearrow \text{ROONO} \\ \\ \searrow \text{R}\dot{\text{O}} + \text{NO}_2 \end{array} \qquad\qquad (\text{VIII-31})$$

has been proposed as a possible means of removal or reoxidation of nitric oxide in polluted air.[64,227] While an association reaction might be expected in view of other known reactions of nitric oxide, the product has not been observed, either in the air or in the laboratory. Further, there is no direct evidence for the reaction yielding alkoxyl radicals and nitrogen dioxide. Peroxyalkyl radicals might also add to nitrogen dioxide to yield an alkyl pernitrate, but again there is no eviednce that this occurs.

One or both of the decomposition reactions

$$\text{RCH}_2\text{O}\dot{\text{O}} \begin{array}{c} \nearrow \text{RCHO} + \dot{\text{O}}\text{H} \\ \\ \searrow \text{R}\dot{\text{C}}\text{O} + \text{H}_2\text{O} \end{array} \qquad\qquad (\text{VIII-32})$$

have been proposed by a number of investigators as steps in oxidation mechanisms, particularly for peroxymethyl, $\text{CH}_3\text{O}\dot{\text{O}}$,[28,119,213-4,282,342,373,443] and peroxyethyl, $\text{C}_2\text{H}_5\text{O}\dot{\text{O}}$,[312] radicals. However, Gray,[163] during a study of the mercury sensitized oxidation of methane and ethane, using a 50–50 hydrocarbon–oxygen mixture in a flow system at 1 atm total pressure and 25°C, found no formaldehyde and no water among the products. Starting with methane and oxygen, the condensable product was almost pure methyl hydroperoxide, while starting with ethane and oxygen it was ethyl hydroperoxide. The suggested mechanism is

$$\text{RH} + \text{Hg}(^3P_1) \rightarrow \dot{\text{R}} + \text{H} + \text{Hg}(^1S_0) \qquad\qquad (\text{VIII-33})$$

$$\dot{\text{R}} + \text{O}_2 \rightarrow \text{RO}\dot{\text{O}} \qquad\qquad (\text{VIII-1})$$

$$\text{RO}\dot{\text{O}} + \text{RH} \rightarrow \text{ROOH} + \dot{\text{R}} \qquad\qquad (\text{VIII-28})$$

If this mechanism is correct, the absence of aldehyde or water among the products definitely excludes the decomposition, in measurable amounts under the experimental conditions, of peroxyalkyl radicals by either of the paths of (VIII-32).

At present it is possible to do no more than speculate on the relative importance of reactions (VIII-26) to (VIII-32) in polluted air, and even to speculate it is necessary to make assumptions. For this purpose, assume a situation in air in which nitric oxide is present at 1 pphm, hydrocarbons are present at 50 pphm, and peroxyalkyl radicals are being produced from alkyl radicals at a rate of 5 pphm hr^{-1}. Further assume that a reaction between nitric oxide and peroxyalkyl radicals (VII-31) does occur, and that its collision yield is between $\sim 10^{-4}$, which is in the same range as the yields for the alkyl and acyl radical–nitric oxide reactions, and $\sim 10^{-2}$, which is of the same order as that of the nitric oxide–nitrogen trioxide reaction (VII-9).

In order for the rate of the reaction of peroxyalkyl radicals with oxygen (VIII-26) to equal the rate of their reaction with nitric oxide, it will be necessary that $y_{26} = y_{31} (NO)/(O_2)$, or inserting the assumed values, that $y_{26} \sim 10^{-11}$ to 10^{-9}. At 25°C, to achieve a collision yield in this range, the activation energy must be less than ~ 12 to 15 kcal. On the basis of these admittedly rough assumptions we may conclude that reaction (VIII-26) will not be important in polluted air unless (1) it is endothermic by less than ~ 12 to 15 kcal, or (2) it involves newly formed, energy rich peroxyalkyl radicals. As we have seen, both of these requirements are possible, but neither has been demonstrated.

In similar fashion, for the rate of hydrogen abstraction from hydrocarbons by peroxyalkyl radical (VIII-28) to equal that of their reaction with nitric oxide it is necessary that $y_{28} = y_{31} (NO)/(RH)$, or, inserting the assumed values, that $y_{28} \sim 10^{-6}$ to 10^{-4}. If these reactions resemble the hydrogen abstractions of alkyl radicals the yields to be expected are $y_{28} \sim 10^{-9}$ or lower. It follows that one of three things must be true; either reaction (VIII-28) is unimportant in polluted air, or peroxyalkyl radicals must abstract hydrogen far more efficiently than do alkyl radicals, or the starting assumptions are in error. The same considerations apply to reaction (VIII-29).

Returning to the starting assumptions, if the rate of formation S_f of peroxyalkyl radicals is 5 pphm hr^{-1}, $y_{31} \sim 10^{-4}$ to 10^{-2}, and $(NO) = 1$ pphm, the stationary concentration of peroxyalkyl radicals, if they are removed by reaction (VIII-31) only, will be

$$(R\dot{O}O) = \frac{S_f}{y_{31}Z(NO)} = \frac{5}{(\sim 10^{-4} \text{ to } 10^{-2}) \times 4 \times 10^5 \times 1}$$

$$\cong 10^{-3} \text{ to } 10^{-1} \text{ pphm} \qquad\qquad \text{(VIII-34)}$$

This result warrants attention. It means either that some reaction or reactions of peroxyalkyl radicals must remove them at a much higher rate than we have assumed for (VIII-31), or the concentration of these radicals in polluted air, when exposed to sunlight, must be far higher than that of alkyl, formyl, or acyl radicals, and might even approach that of some molecular pollutants. A collision yield higher than 10^{-2} for reaction (VIII-31) seems unlikely, but a yield higher than 10^{-9} for (VIII-26), the reaction with oxygen, is possible, especially if this reaction involves thermally excited peroxyalkyl radicals.

We have still to examine the reaction between peroxyalkyl radicals (VIII-27) and the decomposition (VIII-32). In order for the rate of reaction (VIII-27) to equal that of (VIII-31), it is necessary that $y_{27} = y_{31}$ (NO)/(ROȮ). If these are the only two reactions removing peroxyalkyl radicals, inserting the assumed values indicates that if y_{31} is $\sim 10^{-4}$, reaction (VIII-27) could compete equally if y_{27} is $\sim 10^{-3}$, but if y_{31} is $\sim 10^{-2}$, y_{27} would have to be greater than unity in order to compete.

The requirement for the decomposition reaction (VIII-32) to compete equally with reaction (VIII-31) is that $k_{32} = y_{31}Z$(NO). Inserting the assumed values of y_{31} and (NO) gives $k_{32} \sim 10^{-2}$ to 1 sec^{-1}. For a first-order reaction with a "normal" pre-exponential factor of $A \sim 10^{13}$ sec^{-1}, a rate constant of $k = 10^{-2}$ to 1 sec^{-1} corresponds to an activation energy of ~ 18 to 21 kcal. An activation energy this large would probably account for Gray's observation that, under his experimental conditions, the decomposition products were not formed in detectable quantities, and at the same time would permit the decomposition to occur at a competitive rate in air.

It is evident from these speculations that without further information no one of the reactions of peroxyalkyl radicals may be selected as predominant and none may be discarded as insignificant in polluted air. The most likely candidates for dominance would appear to be the reactions with oxygen and with nitric oxide, while the most likely to be insignificant are the hydrogen abstractions. The clearest thing to emerge is the unsatisfactory state of knowledge in the field.

5. REACTIONS OF PEROXYACYL AND ACYLATE RADICALS

A number of reactions of peroxyacyl radicals have been or may be postulated. These include reactions with oxygen,[181,274,397]

$$
\overset{\overset{\displaystyle O}{\|}}{CH_3C}OȮ + O_2 \rightarrow CH_2CO_3 + HȮ_2 \tag{VIII-35}
$$

$$
\overset{\overset{\displaystyle O}{\|}}{RC}OȮ + O_2 \rightarrow \overset{\overset{\displaystyle O}{\|}}{RC}Ȯ + O_3 \tag{VIII-36}
$$

with nitric oxide and nitrogen dioxide (Chapter III),[401,405]

$$
\overset{\overset{\displaystyle O}{\|}}{RC}OȮ + NO \Bigg\langle \begin{array}{l} \overset{\overset{\displaystyle O}{\|}}{RC}OONO \tag{VIII-37} \\[2ex] \overset{\overset{\displaystyle O}{\|}}{RC}Ȯ + NO_2 \tag{VIII-38} \end{array}
$$

$$\underset{\text{RCOO}}{\overset{\text{O}}{\|}}\cdot + NO_2 \rightarrow \underset{\text{RCOONO}_2}{\overset{\text{O}}{\|}} \qquad \text{(VIII-39)}$$

with other radicals,[49,272]

$$\underset{\text{RCOO}}{\overset{\text{O}}{\|}}\cdot + \underset{\text{RCOO}}{\overset{\text{O}}{\|}}\cdot \rightarrow \underset{\text{RCOOCR}}{\overset{\text{O}\ \ \text{O}}{\|\ \ \|}} + O_2 \qquad \text{(VIII-40)}$$

$$\underset{\text{RCOO}}{\overset{\text{O}}{\|}}\cdot + ROO\cdot \rightarrow \underset{\text{RCOOR}}{\overset{\text{O}}{\|}} + O_2 \qquad \text{(VIII-41)}$$

$$\underset{\text{RCOO}}{\overset{\text{O}}{\|}}\cdot + RO\cdot \rightarrow \underset{\text{RCOR}}{\overset{\text{O}}{\|}} + O_2 \qquad \text{(VIII-42)}$$

hydrogen abstractions,[49,74,272,301,438]

$$\underset{\text{RCOO}}{\overset{\text{O}}{\|}}\cdot + RCHO \rightarrow \underset{\text{RCOOH}}{\overset{\text{O}}{\|}} + R\dot{C}O \qquad \text{(VIII-43)}$$

polymerizations,

$$\underset{\text{RCOO}}{\overset{\text{O}}{\|}}\cdot + \text{olefins} \rightarrow \text{polymers} \qquad \text{(VIII-44)}$$

and decompositions,

$$\underset{\text{RCOO}}{\overset{\text{O}}{\|}}\cdot \rightarrow R\dot{O} + CO_2 \qquad \text{(VIII-45)}$$

As in the case of peroxyalkyl radicals, on the basis of present knowledge one may only speculate as to the relative importance of these reactions in polluted air. In this case, however, the evidence discussed in Chapter III that either peroxyacyl nitrites or nitrates (PAN), or both, are formed by the irradiation of mixtures of biacetyl and nitrogen dioxide in oxygen, by the irradiation of alkyl nitrites as well as of nitrogen dioxide–olefin mixtures in air or oxygen, and by the irradiation of polluted air itself, suggests that the reaction of peroxyacyl radicals with nitrogen dioxide, or nitric oxide, or possibly both, are important.

Assuming a collision yield of 10^{-4} to 10^{-2} for each of these reactions, at the representative concentrations of $(NO) = 1$ pphm and $(NO_2) = 10$ pphm, the reaction of peroxyacyl radicals with oxygen would be able to compete on an equal basis if its collision yield were in the range of $\sim 10^{-11}$ to 10^{-8}. Similarly, the hydrogen abstraction yields would have to be $\sim 10^{-6}$ to 10^{-3}, the radical–radical reactions will be unable to compete unless the collision yields of other reactions are on the low side, and the activation energy of the decomposition reaction would have to be less than ~ 17 to 21 kcal. These speculative estimates suggest that the hydrogen abstraction reactions of peroxyacyl radicals may be ruled out and that their reactions with other radicals are questionable, but the reaction with oxygen and the decomposition might be competitive with the nitrogen dioxide or the nitric oxide reaction.

In order to account for the observed rates of formation of PAN if it is formed from peroxyacyl radicals, the concentrations attained by these radicals must be far higher than those of the radicals which react rapidly with oxygen. For example, in the irradiation of a starting mixture of 1 ppm of nitrogen dioxide and 3 ppm of isobutene illustrated in Fig. 51, the rate of increase in PAN concentration at $t = 25$ min was close to 100 pphm hr^{-1}. The nitrogen dioxide concentration at this time was approximately 50 pphm. The nitric oxide concentration was not measured but from equation (VI-3) and the known photolysis rate and ozone concentration it could not have been more than $\sim$0.5 pphm. At collision yields of 10^{-4} to 10^{-2}, and these concentrations of NO$_2$ and NO, in order for reaction (VIII-39) to achieve a rate of 100 pphm hr^{-1} the peroxyacyl radical concentration would have to be from 5×10^{-4} to 5×10^{-2} pphm, while in order for reaction (VIII-37) to achieve this rate the required peroxyacyl radical concentration would have to be from 5×10^{-2} to 5 pphm.

The fact that the formyl equivalent of PAN has not been observed suggests, among other possibilities, that peroxyformyl radicals either are not formed, are unstable, react less rapidly with nitrogen dioxide than do peroxyacyl radicals, or that the products, peroxyformyl nitrate or nitrite, are unstable.

Acylate radicals, $R\overset{\overset{\displaystyle O}{\|}}{C}O$, might be formed in polluted air by reactions (VIII-36) or (VIII-38), or by processes such as (III-90A) or (III-91B). There is, however, no good evidence that they are produced in significant amounts by any of these reactions. Any acylate radicals that are produced might react in several ways,

$$R\overset{\overset{\displaystyle O}{\|}}{\overset{\displaystyle}{C}}\dot{O} + NO \nearrow R\overset{\overset{\displaystyle O}{\|}}{C}ONO \qquad \text{(VIII-46)}$$

$$\searrow R\dot{C}O + NO_2 \qquad \text{(VIII-47)}$$

$$R\overset{\overset{\displaystyle O}{\|}}{\overset{\displaystyle}{C}}\dot{O} + NO_2 \nearrow R\overset{\overset{\displaystyle O}{\|}}{C}ONO_2 \qquad \text{(VIII-48)}$$

$$\searrow RNO_2 + CO_2 \qquad \text{(VIII-49)}$$

$$R\overset{\overset{\displaystyle O}{\|}}{\overset{\displaystyle}{C}}\dot{O} + RCHO \rightarrow RCOOH + R\dot{C}O \qquad \text{(VIII-50)}$$

$$RCO + RO \nearrow \overset{O}{\underset{||}{R}COOR} \tag{VIII-51}$$

$$\underset{||}{\overset{O}{R}}CO + RO \searrow RCOOH + R'CHO \tag{VIII-52}$$

$$\overset{O}{\underset{||}{R}}CO \rightarrow \dot{R} + CO_2 \tag{VIII-53}$$

There is very little evidence regarding these reactions. The fact that nitro compounds and esters are apparently not formed in appreciable amounts in polluted air suggests that (VIII-49) and (VIII-51) are unimportant, and the questions concerning the formation of acyl nitrates cast doubt on (VIII-48). There is some evidence[116,236,350,442] that acetate and benzoate radicals decompose rapidly by (VIII-53), and it is possible that this is the major process for acylate radicals in air, particularly if they are formed with excess internal energy.

6. REACTIONS OF ALKOXYL RADICALS

There is no good evidence that alkoxyl radicals react with oxygen at ordinary temperatures. Reactions which have been postulated [213,261,415] are

$$\dot{RO} + O_2 \rightarrow \dot{R} + O_3 \tag{VIII-54}$$

$$CH_3\dot{O} + O_2 \rightarrow HCHO + H\dot{O}_2 \tag{VIII-55}$$

$$CH_3\dot{O} + O_2 \rightarrow CO + H_2O + \dot{O}H \tag{VIII-56}$$

The first of these (VIII-54) would probably be so endothermic that it would be extremely slow at ordinary temperatures. The second, while possibly more favorable energy-wise, is purely speculative. The third (VIII-56) involves such a drastic rearrangement that a low collision yield is to be expected at ordinary temperatures.

Hydrogen abstractions by alkoxyl radicals, from both hydrocarbons and aldehydes,

$$\dot{RO} + RH \rightarrow ROH + \dot{R} \tag{VIII-57}$$

$$\dot{RO} + RCHO \rightarrow ROH + R\dot{C}O \tag{VIII-58}$$

have been postulated as steps in oxidation mechanisms,[28,342] but there is no evidence on the collision yields of such reactions.

Alkoxyl radical–radical reactions of various types have been or may be postulated:[28,64,227,342,373]

$$\dot{R}O + \dot{R}O \rightarrow ROOR \qquad\qquad (VIII\text{-}59)$$

$$\dot{R}O + \dot{R}O \rightarrow ROH + R'CHO \qquad (VIII\text{-}60)$$

$$\dot{R}O + H\dot{C}O \rightarrow ROH + CO \qquad (VIII\text{-}61)$$

$$\dot{R}O + RO\dot{O} \rightarrow ROR + O_2 \qquad (VIII\text{-}62)$$

$$\dot{R}O + R\overset{\overset{O}{\|}}{C}O\dot{O} \rightarrow R\overset{\overset{O}{\|}}{C}OR + O_2 \qquad (VIII\text{-}63)$$

Of these, the direct combination to form a peroxide (VIII-59) would normally be expected to be the fastest, since the other processes involve transfer or rearrangement. However, the work of Vaughan and his collaborators[28,342] indicates that in hydrocarbon oxidations the usual chain-terminating step is (VIII-60). This reaction, a hydrogen transfer or disproportionation between two alkoxyl radicals to form an alcohol and an aldehyde, has also been suggested by Levy[259] to explain the products of the thermal decomposition of ethyl nitrite, by Calvert and co-workers[179,387] to explain the products of the photolysis of azomethane in the presence of oxygen, and by many others as a step in assumed mechanisms. All evidence indicates that reaction (VIII-60) is very much faster than (VIII-59), but how it compares with the reactions of alkoxyl with other radicals, (VIII-61) to (VIII-63), is not known.

With nitric oxide and nitrogen dioxide the most likely reactions of alkoxyl radicals are the associations

$$\dot{R}O + NO \rightarrow RONO \qquad (VIII\text{-}64a)$$

$$\dot{R}O + NO_2 \rightarrow RONO_2 \qquad (VIII\text{-}64b)$$

These reactions explain the formation of alkyl nitrites and nitrates, both in polluted air and in laboratory irradiations which produce alkoxyl radicals in the presence of NO or NO_2. They apparently also play an important part in the pyrolysis of nitrites and nitrates. Thus, Levy[259] concluded from his investigation of the ethyl nitrite decomposition that (VIII-64a) is much faster than the hydrogen abstraction reaction of alkoxyl radicals with the nitrite. The importance of (VIII-64b) is shown by the facts that added NO_2 retards the thermal decomposition of alkyl nitrates, and leads to the formation of ethyl nitrate in the pyrolysis of ethyl nitrite.[167] The rate constants and even the relative collision yields of the two reactions are unknown.

A speculative reaction

$$RCH_2O + NO \rightarrow RCHO + HNO \qquad (VIII\text{-}65)$$

may be involved to explain the formation of nitroxyl, HNO, in the methyl nitrite photolysis (Chapter III) as well as the formation of acetaldehyde during the ethyl nitrite photolysis in air, but there is no direct evidence in its support.

Alkoxyl radicals are known to add to olefins with eventual polymer formation, the first step probably being[61,317,406,419]

$$R_1\dot{O} + \underset{R_3}{\overset{R_2}{>}}C=C\underset{R_5}{\overset{R_4}{<}} \rightarrow R_1-O-\underset{R_3}{\overset{R_2}{\underset{|}{C}}}-\underset{R_5}{\overset{R_4}{\underset{|}{C}}}\cdot \qquad \text{(VIII-66)}$$

Decompositions of alkoxyl radicals,

$$CH_3\dot{O} \rightarrow HCHO + H \qquad \text{(VIII-67)}$$

$$C_2H_5\dot{O} \rightarrow HCHO + \dot{C}H_3 \qquad \text{(VIII-68)}$$

$$C_2H_5\dot{O} \rightarrow CH_3CHO + H \qquad \text{(VIII-69)}$$

probably occur at elevated temperatures, and have been postulated as steps in a number of room temperature mechanisms.[165,213,356,360,388] Gray[163] has calculated activation energies of 21 kcal for reaction (VIII-68) and 23 kcal for (VIII-69), while more recently Wijnen[452] has estimated 13 ± 2 kcal for the activation energy of (VIII-68). With an activation energy in this range a decomposition rate competitive with that of the reactions of alkoxyl radicals with nitric oxide and nitrogen dioxide is quite possible.

In summary, while the possibility of a reaction between alkoxyl radicals and oxygen, especially (VIII-55), cannot be excluded, on the basis of the available evidence it appears that the major avenues of disappearance of these radicals in polluted air are probably through their reactions with nitric oxide or nitrogen dioxide, with olefins, with other radicals, or through their decomposition.

As noted in Chapter III, to the extent that reaction (VIII-64a) is reversed by the photolysis of the resulting nitrite, this reaction will serve no promotional function unless the alkoxyl radicals re-formed by the photolysis contain excess energy which leads them to react in a different way. An increased decomposition rate or increased rate of reaction with oxygen are possibilities in this regard.

Applying equation (VIII-34) and the subsequent reasoning leads to conclusions similar to those reached for the peroxyl radicals; either one or more of the reactions removing alkoxyl radicals must be very fast, or their concentration during photochemical smog forming periods in polluted air must be surprisingly high.

7. Reactions of Hydroxyl and Hydroperoxyl Radicals

Hydroxyl, or hydroxy, radicals are produced by the photodissociation of hydrogen peroxide and possibly also by the photodissociations of nitrous and nitric acids (Chapter III). Their production in the decomposition of peroxyalkyl (VIII-32) and peroxyformyl (VIII-45) radicals, and in the reaction of alkoxyl radicals with oxygen (VIII-56) has been postulated, and it is possible that they may be formed to some extent by any of several other reactions, for example,

$$H + O_3 \rightarrow \dot{O}H + O_2 \qquad\qquad (VIII\text{-}70)$$

$$H + NO_2 \rightarrow \dot{O}H + NO \qquad\qquad (VIII\text{-}71)$$

$$H\dot{O}_2 + NO \rightarrow \dot{O}H + NO_2 \qquad\qquad (VIII\text{-}72)$$

$$HNO + O_2 \rightarrow \dot{O}H + NO_2 \qquad\qquad (VIII\text{-}73)$$

Unfortunately, little may be said as to the rate at which hydroxyl radicals are produced in polluted air. The available evidence indicates that none of the photodissociations is an important source of hydroxyl radicals, but their formation at a significant rate by one or more secondary reactions, or by the over-all sum of all contributing reactions, is a distinct possibility.

Hydroxyl radicals apparently do not react with oxygen, at least at ordinary temperatures. They do, however, abstract hydrogen, probably more rapidly than do alkyl or alkoxyl radicals. Thus, they appear to react rapidly at room temperature with hydrogen,[67,389]

$$\dot{O}H + H_2 \rightarrow H_2O + H + 15.4 \text{ kcal} \qquad\qquad (VIII\text{-}74)$$

with hydrocarbons, [16,74,75,164,290,305,453]

$$\dot{O}H + RH \rightarrow H_2O + \dot{R} + 15 \text{ to } 30 \text{ kcal} \qquad\qquad (VIII\text{-}75)$$

and with aldehydes, [16,305,336,430]

$$\dot{O}H + RCHO \rightarrow H_2O + R\dot{C}O + \sim 35 \text{ kcal} \qquad\qquad (VIII\text{-}76)$$

Callear and Robb[67] have estimated a room temperature collision yield for reaction (VIII-74) of $y_{74} \sim 10^{-3}$ to 10^{-4}, and estimates of doubtful accuracy by Avramenko and Lorentso[16] give 25°C collision yields of $y_{75} \sim 2 \times 10^{-5}$ and $y_{76} \sim 10^{-4}$; these are much higher than the corresponding values for hydrogen abstraction by alkyl radicals (Table 58).

In the case of the olefins an alternate possibility to the hydrogen abstraction is, as with alkoxyl and other radicals, an addition,

$$\dot{O}H + \begin{matrix} R_1 \\ \diagdown \\ \diagup \\ R_2 \end{matrix} C = C \begin{matrix} R_3 \\ \diagup \\ \diagdown \\ R_4 \end{matrix} \rightarrow HO - \begin{matrix} R_1 \\ | \\ C \\ | \\ R_2 \end{matrix} - \begin{matrix} R_3 \\ | \\ C \cdot \\ | \\ R_4 \end{matrix} \qquad (VIII-77)$$

Hydroxyl radicals might be expected to add to nitric oxide and nitrogen dioxide to form, respectively, nitrous and nitric acids, or nitrous and pernitrous acids,[167]

$$\dot{O}H + NO + M \rightarrow HNO_2 + M + \sim 60 \text{ kcal} \qquad (VIII-78)$$

$$\dot{O}H + NO_2 + M \begin{cases} \nearrow HNO_3 + M + \sim 53 \text{ kcal} \qquad (VIII-79a) \\ \searrow HOONO + M \qquad\qquad\qquad (VIII-79b) \end{cases}$$

In order for these reactions to compete with the hydrogen abstraction reactions of hydroxyl radicals in polluted air, they must actually be faster than the latter since the usual concentrations of nitric oxide and nitrogen dioxide are smaller than those of hydrogen, hydrocarbons, and aldehydes. If they require a third body, which appears to be the case, a competitive rate scarcely seems likely, and certainly there is no evidence that the reactions of hydroxyl radicals with nitric oxide or nitrogen dioxide are of any importance in air. Various reactions of hydroxyl with other radicals present still other possibilities.

Hydrogen atoms are produced by the photolysis of formaldehyde (III-53) and by the reaction of hydroxyl radicals with hydrogen (VIII-74). They may also be produced to some extent by any of several speculative reactions; the photolysis of nitrous acid (III-36), of formyl nitrite (III-90C) or pernitrite (III-91C), and the decompositions of formate (VIII-53) and alkoxyl (VIII-67), (VIII-69) radicals are examples. Taken together, these reactions may well add up to a significant rate of hydrogen atom formation in polluted air.

Hydrogen atoms react rapidly with oxygen to form hydroperoxyl radicals[18,22,48,67,348,389,433,444]

$$H + O_2 + M \rightarrow H\dot{O}O + M + 60 \text{ kcal} \qquad (VIII-80)$$

From the effect of oxygen on the photochemical hydrogen–chlorine reaction, Bodenstein and Schenk[48] in 1933 estimated an activation energy of ~ 1.5 kcal for this reaction. In air at atmospheric pressure and ordinary temperatures this would correspond to a collision yield of $y_{80} \sim 10^{-4}$ with respect to bimolecular $H + O_2$ collisions. More recently Volman,[433] from a study of the mercury photosensitized reaction of hydrogen with oxygen, concluded that at 40°C and atmospheric pressure the ratio of the rate constant for $H + O_2 \rightarrow HO_2$ to that for the adsorption of hydrogen atoms on the walls, $H + \text{wall} \rightarrow \text{removal}$, was 1.2×10^{-3}. This would set an upper limit of $y_{80} \sim 10^{-3}$ for bimolecular $H + O_2$ collisions in air. On the other hand, Callear and Robb[67] assume a collision yield of ~ 0.1 for the initial step $H + O_2 \rightarrow HO_2^*$, a life of 3×10^{-2} sec for the excited state, and a yield of unity for stabilizing collisions in H_2–O_2 mixtures. These assumptions would mean that in air at 1 atm nearly all of the HO_2^* formed would be stabilized and hence that the bimolecular yield for (VIII-80) would be $y_{80} \sim 10^{-1}$.

Hydrogen atoms also react with carbon monoxide, with ozone, with organic molecules, and probably with nitric oxide, but none of these reactions appear to be able to compete significantly with reaction (VIII-80) in air. Thus, for the reaction with carbon monoxide,

$$H + CO + M \rightarrow H\dot{C}O + M \tag{VIII-81}$$

the collision yield for bimolecular $H + CO$ collisions in air at atmospheric pressure and room temperature[128] is $y_{81} \sim 10^{-6}$ to 10^{-7}. At a carbon monoxide concentration of 20 ppm in air, if $y_{80} \sim 10^{-3}$ and $y_{81} \sim 10^{-6}$, the fraction of the hydrogen atoms reacting by (V-81) would be only $y_{81}(CO)/y_{80}(O_2) \approx 10^{-7}$.

For the reaction with ozone, (VIII-70), at the ozone concentrations achieved in polluted air, a similar estimate shows that only $\sim 0.1\%$ of the hydrogen atoms would react even if this process had a collision yield of unity.

In the case of hydrogen abstraction reactions with organic molecules

$$H + RH \rightarrow H_2 + \dot{R} \tag{VIII-82}$$

the room temperature collision yields are from $y_{82} \sim 10^{-10}$ to 10^{-11} when RH is methane, and from $\sim 10^{-6}$ to 10^{-8} when RH is ethane, ethylene, or propane.[398] For the direct addition of hydrogen atoms to olefins,

$$\tag{VIII-83}$$

the collision yields are higher; for ethylene, propylene, and the butenes they range from $y_{83} \sim 10^{-3}$ to 10^{-4}. Even in this case the fraction of the hydrogen atoms which will react in air is negligible. If the olefin concentration is 20 pphm and both y_{80} and y_{83} range from $\sim 10^{-3}$ to 10^{-4}, this fraction will be only $\sim 10^{-6}$, the ratio of olefin-to-oxygen concentrations.

Since the ratio of nitric oxide-to-oxygen concentrations during photochemical smog forming periods in air is only $\sim 10^{-7}$, if $y_{80} \sim 10^{-3}$, not more than $\sim 10^{-4}$ of the hydrogen atoms could react with nitric oxide, even if that reaction occurred at every collision. In similar manner it may be shown that the combination of hydrogen atoms

$$H + H + M \rightarrow H_2 + M + 103.2 \text{ kcal} \qquad \text{(VIII-84)}$$

is entirely negligible in air.

There thus appears to be no question but that any hydrogen atoms formed in polluted air will react almost exclusively with oxygen to yield hydroperoxyl radicals, by reaction (VIII-80). Hydroperoxyl radicals may also be formed by other reactions in air, such as that of formyl radicals (VIII-18), peroxyacyl radicals (VIII-35), or alkoxyl radicals (VIII-55) with oxygen.

The reactions of hydroperoxyl radicals are not well understood. There is no evidence that they react with oxygen, but there is evidence that they react with other radicals and with organic molecules. Thus, the photolysis of hydrogen peroxide and both the photochemical and mercury photosensitized hydrogen–oxygen reactions may be explained by mechanisms including the step[22,433]

$$H\dot{O}O + H\dot{O}O \rightarrow H_2O_2 + O_2 + 19 \text{ kcal} \qquad \text{(VIII-85)}$$

Although the rate constant of this reaction has not been determined, if the postulated mechanisms involving it are correct, the over-all quantum yields obtained indicate that it must be fast. Callear and Robb[67] estimate that it has a room temperature collision yield of $y_{85} \sim 10^{-1}$ to 10^{-2}.

In their experiments with hydrogen atoms produced in the hydrogen discharge tube, Geib and Harteck[150] found that when the H atoms were introduced into methane at room temperature there was no perceptible reaction, but when they were introduced into a mixture of methane and oxygen the methane was rapidly oxidized even at $-183°C$. This indicates a rapid reaction between hydroperoxyl radicals and methane, but the nature of the reaction is not known. On the basis of Walsh's estimate[444] of 78 kcal for the dissociation energy of $H_2O_2 \rightarrow HO_2 + H$, the abstraction of hydrogen from CH_4 by HO_2 is endothermic.

$$H\dot{O}O + CH_4 \rightarrow HOOH + \dot{C}H_3 - 19 \text{ kcal} \qquad \text{(VIII-86)}$$

If this is so, the collision yield at ordinary temperatures must be less than 10^{-14}, which would rule this reaction out of consideration. By the same token the reactions

$$H\dot{O}O + CH_4 \rightarrow 2 \dot{O}H + \dot{C}H_3 - 73 \text{ kcal} \qquad \text{(VIII-87)}$$

and

$$H\dot{O}O + CH_4 \rightarrow H_2 + O_2 + \dot{C}H_3 - 58 \text{ kcal} \qquad \text{(VIII-88)}$$

are so endothermic as to be out of the question. The reaction

$$HO\dot{O} + CH_4 \rightarrow H_2O + CH_3\dot{O} \qquad \text{(VIII-89)}$$

may be exothermic, but it involves so much rearrangement that one would expect it to be slow.

Among a number of reactions of hydroperoxyl radicals with formaldehyde which have been postulated,[398] the most likely seems to be the hydrogen abstraction

$$HO\dot{O} + HCHO \rightarrow HOOH + \dot{C}HO \pm \sim 0 \text{ kcal} \qquad \text{(VIII-90)}$$

On the basis of the bond energy estimates of Walsh[444] and Klein and Schoen[248] this would be very nearly thermoneutral. With acetaldehyde, the hydrogen abstraction reaction

$$HO\dot{O} + CH_3CHO \rightarrow HOOH + CH_3\dot{C}O + \sim 7 \text{ kcal} \qquad \text{(VIII-91)}$$

has also been postulated.[301,302]

With the olefins, not only hydrogen abstraction by hydroperoxyl radicals, but also other reactions have been postulated,[261,302] for example:

$$HO\dot{O} + C_2H_4 \rightarrow HOOH + \dot{C}_2H_3 \qquad \text{(VIII-92)}$$

$$HO\dot{O} + C_2H_4 \rightarrow 2HCHO + H \qquad \text{(VIII-93)}$$

$$HO\dot{O} + C_2H_4 \rightarrow C_2H_4O + \dot{O}H \qquad \text{(VIII-94)}$$

A high collision yield is not to be expected for any of these reactions.

Other reactions of hydroperoxyl radicals, which may be of importance in air pollution, may be postulated. Thus

$$HO\dot{O} + NO \rightarrow HOONO \rightarrow \dot{O}H + NO_2 \qquad \text{(VIII-95)}$$

$$HO\dot{O} + RO\dot{O} \nearrow \begin{array}{l} ROOH + O_2 \qquad \text{(VIII-96a)} \\ \\ \searrow R\dot{O} + \dot{O}H + O_2 \qquad \text{(VIII-96b)} \end{array}$$

$$HO\dot{O} + R\overset{\overset{\displaystyle O}{\|}}{C}O\dot{O} \rightarrow R\overset{\overset{\displaystyle O}{\|}}{C}OOH + O_2 \qquad \text{(VIII-97)}$$

$$HO\dot{O} + R\overset{\overset{\displaystyle O}{\|}}{\dot{C}}O \rightarrow R\overset{\overset{\displaystyle O}{\|}}{C}OH + O_2 \qquad \text{(VIII-98)}$$

$$HO\dot{O} + R\dot{O} \rightarrow ROH + O_2 \qquad \text{(VIII-99)}$$

$$HO\dot{O} + \begin{array}{c} R \\ \diagdown \\ R \diagup \end{array} C = C \begin{array}{c} R \\ \diagup \\ \diagdown R \end{array} \rightarrow HOO - \overset{R}{\underset{R}{C}} - \overset{R}{\underset{R}{C}} \cdot, \text{ etc.} \qquad \text{(VIII-100)}$$

It is not possible on the basis of present evidence to judge the relative importance of these reactions, and until more information is available none can be excluded from consideration. However, by analogy with peroxyalkyl and peroxyacyl radicals it may be said that the reactions of hydroperoxyl radicals most likely to be of importance in polluted air are their reaction with themselves (VIII-85), with other radicals, especially (VIII-99), with nitric oxide (VIII-95), and possibly their addition to olefins (VIII-100). The concentration of hydroperoxyl radicals in the air during smog forming periods should be far higher than that of hydrogen atoms, and may even be comparable with that of peroxyalkyl, peroxyacyl, or alkoxyl radicals.

8. SUMMARY OF FREE RADICAL REACTIONS

This study has indicated that at least eleven radicals or classes of radicals are probably formed by the action of sunlight on polluted urban air. These radicals, not all of equal importance, are:

alkyl	Ṙ	peroxyformyl	$\text{HCOO}\cdot$ (with =O)
alkoxyl	RȮ	peroxyacyl	$\text{RCOO}\cdot$ (with =O)
peroxyalkyl	ROȮ	formate	$\text{HCO}\cdot$ (with =O)
hydroxyl	ȮH	acylate	$\text{RCO}\cdot$ (with =O)
hydroperoxyl	HOȮ		
formyl	HĊO		
acyl	RĊO		

Some of these radicals are produced by the photolysis of original pollutants, some are produced by secondary reactions, and some may be produced by the photolysis of products of secondary reactions. The most, and possibly the only, important reaction in the first of these three categories is the photolysis of aldehydes to yield alkyl and formyl radicals. A special case which may be of some importance is the photolysis of formaldehyde to yield formyl radicals and hydrogen atoms. Other photolyses in this category, all apparently of minor importance, include that of ketones to yield alkyl and acyl radicals, and of peroxides to yield hydroxyl and alkoxyl radicals. Still other radical producing reactions which must be taken into account involve some of the products of the action of sunlight on, or of nonphotochemical reactions of, the original pollutants. Among these are the photolyses of nitrous and nitric acids, which may produce either hydroxyl radicals or hydrogen atoms in small amounts, the photolysis of alkyl nitrites to yield alkoxyl radicals or nitroxyl which may in turn react with oxygen to yield hydroxyl radicals, the photolysis of acyl nitrites and pernitrites which may yield alkyl or acyl radicals, and the thermal reactions between oxygen atoms or ozone and the olefins which may be a source of several classes of radicals, including alkyl, alkoxyl, and acyl.

The available evidence indicates that the alkyl, formyl, and acyl radicals, as well as the hydrogen atoms, formed in air will react almost exclusively with oxygen to form the corresponding peroxyl radicals, peroxyalkyl, peroxyformyl, peroxyacyl, and hydroperoxyl.

As a consequence of their rapid reactions with oxygen, the stationary concentrations of alkyl, formyl, and acyl radicals, as well as those of hydrogen atoms, will all be quite low in urban air, while the concentrations of some of the peroxyl radicals and of alkoxyl radicals may be surprisingly high.

The situation regarding the secondary reactions of peroxyl radicals is much less clear. For each type of peroxyl radical there are a number of reactions among which, on the basis of present information, it is impossible to decide. These consist of reactions with oxygen, with nitric oxide and nitrogen dioxide, with olefins, with other radicals, and decompositions. All of the peroxyl radicals except hydroperoxyl may possibly react with oxygen to yield ozone and alkoxyl, formate, or acylate radicals. The reactions with nitrogen dioxide probably consist of additions to give the corresponding nitrates, while those with nitric oxide may result either in an addition or in an oxygen transfer yielding alkoxyl, acylate, or hydroxyl radicals and nitrogen dioxide. With olefins, addition to yield other radicals appears to be more likely than hydrogen abstraction. With other radicals various products may result, including acids, alcohols, ethers, peroxides, peroxy acids, peroxy esters, and, from the reaction between peroxyalkyl radicals, alkoxyl radicals and oxygen. Finally, peroxyacyl and especially peroxyformyl radicals may directly decompose to yield carbon dioxide and alkoxyl or hydroxyl radicals.

With alkoxyl, hydroxyl, formate, and acylate radicals a similar situation exists, in that existing information is not sufficient to permit an assessment of the relative importance of several possible reactions. Alkoxyl radicals may react with oxygen to yield aldehyde and hydroperoxyl or other products, with nitric oxide and nitrogen dioxide to yield alkyl nitrites and nitrates; they may add to olefins, they may decompose, or they may react with other radicals to give various molecular products. An example of the latter, for which there is some experimental support, is the disproportionation between two alkoxyl radicals to yield alcohol and aldehyde (VIII-60). Hydroxyl radicals may abstract hydrogen atoms from hydrogen molecules or from hydrocarbons or aldehydes, they may add to olefins, to nitric oxide, or to nitrogen dioxide, or they may react with other radicals. Formate and acylate radicals may add to nitric oxide or nitrogen dioxide to give formyl or acyl nitrites or nitrates, with nitric oxide they might lose an oxygen atom to yield formyl or acyl radicals and nitrogen dioxide, they may react with other radicals, or they may decompose directly into carbon dioxide and hydrogen atoms or alkyl radicals.

Some of the molecular products of these reactions are in turn photolyzed in air, and as the product concentrations build up during the day some of these secondary photolyses probably become important. In this category are the photolyses of alkyl, acyl, and peroxyacyl nitrites. The products of these nitrite photolyses are not definitely known, but they probably result in the regeneration of free radicals which will again take part in secondary reactions.

Chapter IX

Reactions of Sulfur Dioxide

1. The Photooxidation of Sulfur Dioxide in Air

Sulfur dioxide, alone or in the presence of oxygen, is slowly photolyzed when exposed to solar radiation. The photolysis of sulfur dioxide alone yields sulfur and sulfur trioxide, but in the presence of oxygen or air no sulfur is formed. The only observed product in this case is sulfur trioxide, or if water is present, sulfuric acid.

The rate of the photooxidation reaction has been studied by Hall,[177] Gerhard and Johnstone,[152] and Renzetti and Doyle.[353] Hall, on exposing quartz tubes filled with 56 to 230 mm of SO_2 and with 50 to 200 mm of O_2 to sunlight, found the rate of sulfur trioxide formation to be directly proportional to the sulfur dioxide concentration and roughly independent of the oxygen concentration. Gerhard and Johnstone, using 5 to 30 ppm of sulfur dioxide in moist air, at 24 to 32°C and 32 to 91% R.H., enclosed in a Lucite cell and exposed to a mercury sunlamp, found the rate of sulfuric acid formation also to be directly proportional to the sulfur dioxide concentration. They did not vary the oxygen concentration.

In both of these investigations the absorption was weak, and it may be concluded that the observed proportionality between photolysis rate and sulfur dioxide concentration was due merely to the variation in absorption rate. If k is the observed photolysis rate constant relative to sulfur dioxide concentration, k_a the absorption rate constant, and Φ the over-all quantum yield, for weak absorption, if the reaction is indeed independent of oxygen concentration it follows that

$$\frac{-d(SO_2)}{dt} \cong k(SO_2) \cong \Phi k_a(SO_2) \qquad \text{(IX-1)}$$

from which $\Phi = k/k_a$.

The estimates of Φ which may be obtained from the three investigations show a wide variation. Beginning with the experiments in sunlight, Hall obtained an average value of $k = 5 \times 10^{-4}$ hr^{-1} for exposure to sunlight during the hours of 10 A.M. to 3 P.M., under the experimental conditions described in the preceding paragraph. Gerhard and Johnstone made a few runs with low concentrations of sulfur dioxide in air, contained in a 64-cu ft reaction chamber which was lined with Saran film and covered with Plexiglas windows. Exposed to sunlight, the conversion rate in this chamber correspond to a value of $k \sim 10^{-3}$ hr^{-1}. Both of these figures are much smaller than the estimated open air values of k_a for sulfur dioxide in Table 19, and even though no quantitative comparison is warranted they suggest a quantum yield of the order of 10^{-2} to 10^{-3}.

Several estimates of the quantum yield of the sulfur dioxide photooxidation may also be obtained from studies with artificial illumination. Gerhard and Johnstone, in their experiments with Lucite cell and mercury sunlamp, obtained a photolysis rate constant of $k = 6.8 \times 10^{-3}$ hr^{-1}. They estimate that the radiation intensity in the sulfur dioxide absorption region was approximately three times that of noon sunlight. From the data of Table 19, this would correspond to $k_a \approx 2$ hr^{-1}, from which the estimated quantum yield is $\Phi \approx 3 \times 10^{-3}$, in rough agreement with the experiments in sunlight. Hall reports one measurement of the quantum yield, using 12.7 mm of SO_2 and 10.6 mm of O_2 at 25°C in a 3×20-cm quartz reaction cell exposed to the 3130-A line from a mercury arc. The value obtained was $\Phi = 0.036$, which is an order of magnitude larger than the estimates based on the photolyses in sunlight, as well as those based on Gerhard and Johnstone's sunlamp experiments. Finally, Renzetti and Doyle have measured the rate of photolysis of sulfur dioxide at concentrations of 0.2 to 0.6 ppm in air of 50% R.H. at 30°C, using a 50-liter Pyrex flask, illuminated by four medium pressure mercury arcs, as a stirred flow reactor of variable residence time. The absorption rate, based on manufacturer's data for the intensity distribution of the mercury arc radiation and the absorption coefficients in Table 18, was estimated to be $k_a = 0.013$ min^{-1} and the observed photolysis rate constant averaged 0.0045 min^{-1}. From these the estimated quantum yield is $\Phi \approx 0.3$. The estimated quantum yields for the photooxidation of sulfur dioxide at small concentrations in air, as well as at larger concentrations with oxygen, thus cover a range of about two orders of magnitude. While some of these estimates are quite rough, the reasons for such a large variation are not apparent.

The mechanism of the photooxidation is likewise obscure. As noted in Chapter III, the bond dissociation energy of sulfur dioxide, either by the process

$$SO_2 \rightarrow SO + O - 135 \text{ kcal} \qquad \text{(IX-2)}$$

or by other reactions is much too high to be produced by absorption in the solar radiation region, and the primary photochemical processes following absorption in this region must therefore involve activated SO_2 molecules.

A primary mechanism involving activated molecules, based in part on that postulated by Hall [177] and Blacet,[34] and in part on that of Dainton and Ivin,[90] is

$$SO_2 + h\nu \rightarrow SO_2' \qquad\qquad\qquad\qquad\qquad (IX\text{-}3)$$
$$SO_2' \rightarrow SO_2'' \ (+M \rightarrow SO_2) \qquad\qquad\qquad (IX\text{-}4)$$
$$SO_2' + SO_2 \rightarrow SO_2 + SO_2 \qquad\qquad\qquad (IX\text{-}5a)$$
$$SO_2' + N_2 \rightarrow SO_2 + N_2 \qquad\qquad\qquad (IX\text{-}5b)$$
$$SO_2' + O_2 \rightarrow SO_2 + O_2 \qquad\qquad\qquad (IX\text{-}5c)$$
$$SO_2' + O_2 \rightarrow SO_4 \qquad\qquad\qquad\qquad (IX\text{-}6)$$

The excited state SO_2' might be a triplet, as postulated by Dainton and Ivin, which may degrade by internal transfer to a vibrationally excited ground state, SO_2'', which is subsequently deactivated by collision. As fluorescence of sulfur dioxide has not been observed at wavelengths above 2100 A, it must be assumed that the initial excited state SO_2' is deactivated only by this internal rearrangement, or by collision.

The collisonal deactivation $SO_2' + M \rightarrow SO_2 + M$ is broken down in the foregoing mechanism into separate reactions for the different molecules which might serve as M, for reasons which will appear shortly. The SO_4 molecule formed by (IX-6) would presumably have a peroxy structure, and if SO_2' is a triplet it might be a biradical,

$$\cdot \overset{\displaystyle O}{\underset{\displaystyle O}{\diagdown \diagup}} S - O - O \cdot$$

Even though this molecule must possess a considerable internal energy when formed, there is no evidence that a third body is required in (IX-6).

Secondary reactions of SO_4 which might lead to sulfur trioxide or sulfuric acid formation are

$$SO_4 + SO_2 \rightarrow 2SO_3 \qquad\qquad\qquad\qquad (IX\text{-}7)$$
$$SO_4 + O_2 \rightarrow SO_3 + O_3 \qquad\qquad\qquad (IX\text{-}8)$$
$$SO_3 + H_2O \rightarrow H_2SO_4 \qquad\qquad\qquad (IX\text{-}9)$$

Other reactions of this molecule, such as internal rearrangement, collisional stabilization, or decomposition into $SO_2 + O_2$, might be postulated but are not required by present experimental information. A search for ozone among the reaction products is obviously indicated by the postulation of (IX-8).

For weak absorption, such that $I_a \cong k_a(SO_2)$, the rate law approached by this mechanism is

$$-\frac{d(SO_2)}{dt} = \frac{k_a k_6(SO_2)(O_2)(f + 1)}{k_4 + k_{5a}(SO_2) + k_{5b}(N_2) + (k_{5c} + k_6)(O_2)} \qquad (IX\text{-}10)$$

where $f = k_7(SO_2)/[k_7(SO_2) + k_8(O_2)]$, the fraction of the SO_4 molecules which react by (IX-7).

Dainton and Ivin have obtained evidence (Section 2) that the efficiency of sulfur dioxide and nitrogen as the deactivating species in steps (IX-5a) and (IX-5b) is small relative to that of iodine. If it be assumed that they are also small relative to that of oxygen, at large oxygen concentrations the terms $k_{5a}(SO_2)$ and $k_{5b}(N_2)$ may be neglected, and the rate law simplifies to

$$-\frac{d(SO_2)}{dt} = \frac{k_a k_6 (SO_2)(O_2)(f + 1)}{k_4 + (k_{5c} + k_6)(O_2)} \tag{IX-11}$$

Expanding the term $(f + 1)$, the mechanism leads to the expression

$$\frac{1}{\Phi} = \left[1 + \frac{k_{5c}}{k_6} + \frac{k_4}{k_6(O_2)}\right] \cdot \left[\frac{k_7 + k_8 \dfrac{(O_2)}{(SO_2)}}{2k_7 + k_8 \dfrac{(O_2)}{(SO_2)}}\right] \tag{IX-12}$$

It may be seen from equation (IX-11) that the postulated mechanism will lead to a photooxidation rate which is essentially proportional to sulfur dioxide and independent of oxygen concentrations only at sulfur dioxide concentrations low enough to make the weak absorption approximation valid, only at oxygen concentrations high enough to make $(k_{5c} + k_6)(O_2)$ large relative to k_4, and only for conditions such that $(f + 1)$ is essentially constant, i.e., $k_8(O_2)$ is large relative to $k_7(SO_2)$ or vice versa. Equation (IX-12) predicts (1) at constant oxygen concentration there should be a range of sulfur dioxide concentrations over which the quantum yield increases by a factor of two, and (2) at constant $(O_2)/(SO_2)$ ratios $1/\Phi$ should be linear with respect to $1/(O_2)$.

These predictions, as well as the assumptions on which they are based, are susceptible to experimental test. In particular, the dependence on oxygen concentration in the presence of excess nitrogen has not been studied, and further work of this nature, as well as a solution of the quantum yield question, will be necessary before the kinetics, mechanism, and rate of the photooxidation of sulfur dioxide in air becomes established.

In a few experiments in which 3 ppm of 1,3-butadiene or 1-pentene was added to photooxidizing sulfur dioxide at a concentration of 0.3 ppm in air at 50% R.H., Renzetti and Doyle found that the addition of these olefins had a strong suppressive effect on the production of light scattering aerosol. They also obtained some evidence that addition of 1 ppm of nitric oxide hindered the formation of aerosol. It has not been established whether these effects are due to a retardation of the photooxidation reaction itself, or to a suppression of the formation of sulfuric acid droplets in the light scattering size range. If the former, the retardation might be accomplished through removal of excited sulfur dioxide molecules by the additives (Section 2), although at such low concentrations a serious competition with their removal by reaction (IX-5c) would be surprising. Another possibility, in the case of the olefins at least, would be offered by a reaction between SO_4 molecules and the olefin, perhaps analogous to the ozone–olefin reaction (Chapter VI). With nitric oxide, the reaction

$$SO_4 + NO \rightarrow SO_3 + NO_2 \tag{IX-13}$$

would have a retarding effect only in the event that in air more of the SO_4 reacts by (IX-7) than by (IX-8).

What effect adding nitrogen dioxide may have on the rate of photo-oxidation of sulfur dioxide in air has not been observed. In this case the reaction of oxygen atoms, from the photodissociation of NO_2, with the sulfur dioxide might lead to some enhancement, but various retarding reactions may be postulated as well, and the question can only be settled by experiment.

2. THE PHOTOCHEMICAL REACTION OF SULFUR DIOXIDE WITH HYDROCARBONS

In two important papers published in 1950, Dainton and Ivin[90] reported a photochemical reaction between sulfur dioxide and hydrocarbons, both paraffins and olefins. The reaction was studied in a cylindrical 2×7-cm quartz cell, thermostatted at temperatures of 15–100°C, and illuminated with the full radiation of a hot mercury arc. The reaction was followed by pressure decrease and chemical analysis for both reactants and products.

In all cases the reaction was accompanied by the formation of a mist which on settling gave a colorless or pale yellow involatile oil with a disagreeable odor, and which appeared to be capable of secondary polymerization. These oils, from both paraffins and olefins, showed the characteristics of sulfinic acids. They were slightly soluble in water, giving an acid solution with reducing properties. The product from the reaction with n-butane gave an ebullioscopic molecular weight in acetone of 139 ± 4 and an equivalent weight of the order of 129–160 on titration with alkali, as compared with a molecular weight of 122 for butyl sulfinic acid, $C_4H_9SO_2H$. Composition analyses of this product were in reasonable agreement with that of $C_4H_9SO_2H$, although a somewhat low C/S ratio, 3.6 to 3.8 vs. the theoretical 4.0, suggested a certain amount of disulfinic acid. The observed molecular weight also suggests this.

Analysis of the residual gases showed equimolar amounts of sulfur dioxide and hydrocarbon consumed, except for the short-chain hydrocarbons or when a large excess of sulfur dioxide was present. In no case was any noncondensable product observed, and the pressure decreases were in good agreement with the weight yield of condensable product.

Dainton and Ivin concluded from this evidence that the over-all reaction is

$$RH + SO_2 \rightarrow RSO_2H \tag{IX-14}$$

The approximate quantum yield of this reaction was determined by uranyl oxalate actinometry for starting mixtures of sulfur dioxide and n-butane, and extended to other hydrocarbons in a series of experiments with equal light intensities and starting concentrations. The results, for starting mixtures of 150 mm each of sulfur dioxide and hydrocarbon at 25°C, are given in Table 59.

TABLE 59

ESTIMATED QUANTUM YIELDS FOR THE SULFUR
DIOXIDE–HYDROCARBON REACTION

Hydrocarbon	Φ	Hydrocarbon	Φ
Methane	0.006		
Ethane	0.025	Ethylene	0.018
Propane	0.125	Propylene	0.020
n-Butane	0.23	1-Butene	0.044
Isobutane	0.18	2-Butene	0.033
Pentane	0.26		

The higher quantum yields for the paraffins, relative to those for the olefins, are noteworthy. The quantum yield for the disappearance of sulfur dioxide alone, at a starting pressure of 150 mm was found to be <0.01.

With both n-butane and 1-butene the quantum yield was found to be independent of the light intensity, but to increase slightly with decreasing wavelength. It was nearly independent of the sulfur dioxide concentration, but increased with hydrocarbon pressure in the manner shown in Fig. 40. Addition of up to 200 mm of nitrogen had no appreciable effect on the quantum yield, but iodine, butadiene, and in the case of n-butane, 1-butene exerted a marked retardation. For example, with sulfur dioxide and n-butane at a reactant pressure of 125 mm, addition of 0.2 mm of iodine reduced the quantum yield to about one-tenth of its previous value, and with 150 mm each of sulfur dioxide and n-butane addition of 9 mm of butadiene reduced the yield to about 25%

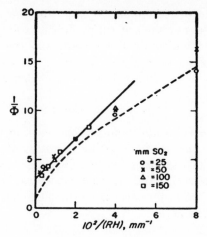

Fɪɢ. 40. Variation in quantum yield of the sulfur dioxide–1-butane reaction with butane pressure. The straight line is for $1/\Phi = 2.9 + 207/(\mathrm{RH})$, the dashed line for $1/\Phi = 1 + 23/(\mathrm{RH})^{0.5} + 87/(\mathrm{RH})$, with (RH) in mm. From F. S. Dainton and K. J. Ivin (Ref. 90).

of its value in the absence of butadiene. The effect of oxygen was not investigated.

With increasing temperature the rate, and hence the quantum yield, decreased. Plots of log rate against $1/T$ gave straight lines with slopes corresponding to a negative activation energy of ~1 to 2 kcal, depending on the hydrocarbon and starting pressure.

The mechanism proposed by Dainton and Ivin is

$$\mathrm{SO_2} + h\nu \rightarrow \mathrm{SO_2}' \qquad\qquad\qquad (\text{IX-3})$$
$$\mathrm{SO_2}' \rightarrow \mathrm{SO_2} \qquad\qquad\qquad (\text{IX-4})$$
$$\mathrm{SO_2}' + \mathrm{SO_2} \rightarrow \mathrm{SO_2} + \mathrm{SO_2} \qquad\qquad (\text{IX-5a})$$
$$\mathrm{SO_2}' + \mathrm{RH} \rightarrow \mathrm{SO_2} + \mathrm{RH} \qquad\qquad (\text{IX-5d})$$
$$\mathrm{SO_2}' + \mathrm{RH} \rightarrow \mathrm{RSO_3H} \qquad\qquad (\text{IX-15})$$

This mechanism leads to the expression for the quantum yield of sulfinic acid formation

$$\Phi = \frac{k_{15}(\mathrm{RH})}{k_4 + k_{5a}(\mathrm{SO_2}) + (k_{5d} + k_{15})(\mathrm{RH})} \qquad (\text{IX-16})$$

Since it was found experimentally that the quantum yield is independent of the sulfur dioxide pressure, $k_{5a}(\mathrm{SO_2})$ may be neglected and the equation rewritten in the form

$$\frac{1}{\Phi} = 1 + \frac{k_{5d}}{k_{15}} + \frac{k_4}{k_{15}(\mathrm{RH})} \qquad\qquad (\text{IX-17})$$

This equation predicts a quantum yield independent of light intensity and a linear relation between $1/\Phi$ and $1/(RH)$. From the intercept and slope of the straight line plotted in Fig. 40, Dainton and Ivin estimate that

$$\frac{k_{5d}}{k_{15}} = 1.9 \pm 0.2 \quad \text{and} \quad \frac{k_4}{k_{15}} = 207 \pm 17 \text{ mm} \qquad \text{(IX-18)}$$

Neglecting the term $k_{5a}(SO_2)$ involves the assumption that sulfur dioxide is ineffective in quenching the excited SO_2' molecules; the same assumption was made in deriving equation (IX-11) in connection with the sulfur dioxide photooxidation. The negative activation energy of the over-all reaction was tentatively suggested by Dainton and Ivin to be due to a positive temperature dependence of reaction (IX-4) in excess of that of the other reactions. If the retarding effects of butadiene and 1-butene on the reaction with n-butane are attributed to the effectiveness of these molecules in deactivating SO_2',

$$SO_2' + B \rightarrow SO_2 + B \qquad \text{(IX-5e)}$$

from the observed inhibitions at low pressures the quenching efficiencies of n-butane, 1-butene, and butadiene in reaction (IX-5) are in the ratio 1:110:220. On the same scale the efficiency of nitrogen would be close to zero while that of iodine would be in the neighborhood of 5000. This wide range suggests that the observed retardations involve something more than simple collisional deactivation, a suggestion which is supported by the observation that, with increasing pressure of 1-butene and butadiene, the apparent quenching efficiency markedly decreases, with the quenching rate approaching proportionality to $(B)^{0.5}$.

Assuming that the same situation also holds for n-butane, from the observed rates at constant sulfur dioxide and varying n-butane pressures Dainton and Ivin deduced, without reference to actinometric measurements, the equation

$$\frac{1}{\Phi} = 1 + 23/(RH)^{0.5} + 87/(RH) \qquad \text{(IX-19)}$$

Referring to Fig. 40, it is seen that with some adjustment in the numerical coefficients this equation would fit the observed points at least as well as the straight line required by (IX-17). A more complex mechanism than that assumed in deriving equations (IX-16) and (IX-17) is indicated by these variations, and accordingly the rate constant ratios given in (IX-18) must be accepted with reserve.

If the dependence of the quantum yield on the hydrocarbon concentration, observed by Dainton and Ivin, is maintained at very low concentrations, the quantum yield at the hydrocarbon concentrations attained in polluted air will be very small indeed. Thus either by equation (IX-17) or (IX-19) at an n-butane concentration of 50 pphm, the value of Φ would be $\sim 2 \times 10^{-6}$. In air, an additional reduction might be brought about by reaction (IX-5c) and to some extent by (IX-6). On the other hand, new reactions involving hydrocarbons, such as

$$SO_4 + \underset{R_2}{\overset{R_1}{\diagdown}} C = C \underset{R_4}{\overset{R_3}{\diagup}} \rightarrow \underset{\underset{SO_3}{\overset{\mid}{R_2}}}{\overset{R_1}{\diagdown}} C - C \underset{\underset{O}{\overset{\mid}{R_4}}}{\overset{R_3}{\diagup}} \rightarrow \text{unknown} \atop \text{products} \qquad \text{(IX-20)}$$

which is analogous to the ozone–olefin reaction, might become of some importance in air. The only observation so far reported on sulfur dioxide–hydrocarbon mixtures in air is that of Schuck and Doyle[377] that olefins suppress the formation of light scattering aerosol from the photo-oxidation reaction, an effect which might be accomplished by any of several reactions (Section 1), including (IX-20). This question, and in fact the entire field of photochemical sulfur dioxide–hydrocarbon reactions in air, undoubtedly merits further investigation.

3. The Photolysis of Mixtures of Sulfur Dioxide, Nitric Oxide–Nitrogen Dioxide, and Hydrocarbons in Air

In 1958 Schuck, Ford, and Stephens[379] reported that the addition of sulfur dioxide to automobile exhaust–air mixtures led to dramatic increases in the rate of aerosol formation or irradiation. The following year Doyle, with Schuck[377] and Renzetti,[353] reported the same effect on irradiation of nitric oxide–nitrogen dioxide–olefin mixtures in air, and observed that in such mixtures the rate of disappearance of sulfur dioxide was much greater than its photooxidation rate when present alone in air.

These experiments were conducted at $\sim 30°C$ in the 50-liter stirred flow reactor described in Section 1. The air used was first passed through a platinized alumina catalyst at 600°C, then through a carbon filter followed by a bed of activated alumina. After adjusting to the desired humidity by a split stream method, the air was again passed through hot platinized alumina, cooled, led into a mixer in which the reactants were added, then through an aerosol filter, and finally into the reactor. Sulfur dioxide was determined in the effluent stream by a continuous colorimetric recorder.

The results obtained, using nitric oxide and 2-methyl-2-butene, are summarized in Table 60. It is seen that the rate of sulfur dioxide disappearance in the presence of the nitrogen oxide–olefin mixture was from 3 to 13 times that which it would have been in their absence, and

TABLE 60

CONSUMPTION OF SULFUR DIOXIDE DURING THE PHOTOLYSIS OF MIXTURES OF NITRIC OXIDE AND 2-METHYL-2-BUTENE IN AIR

Entering concentrations (pphm)			Effluent SO₂ conc. (pphm)	Residence time (min)	Rate of SO₂ consumption (pphm min⁻¹)		Estimated absorption rate $k_a(SO_2)$ (pphm min⁻¹)	Ratios of	
NO (+NO₂)	Olefin	SO₂			In mixture	At entering conc. in air alone		$\dfrac{\text{Mixture rate}}{\text{Rate alone}}$	$\dfrac{\text{Mixture rate}}{\text{Absn. rate}}$
98	49	11	1	17	0.59	0.046	0.013	13	45
96	290	52	40	17	0.70	0.22	0.52	3.2	1.3
100	100	10	~0.5	44	0.22	0.038	~0.007	5.8	31
100	300	10	~0.5	44	0.22	0.038	~0.007	5.8	31
100	300	100	40–50	44	~1.2	0.38	~0.6	3.2	~2

in all cases it exceeded the estimated absorption rate of the sulfur dioxide in the reactor. The latter is open to doubt, as it was based on Doyle's estimate of $k_a = 0.013$ min^{-1} for sulfur dioxide in the reactor, which was not an actual measurement, and on the effluent sulfur dioxide concentrations, which when low could not be accurately determined. Nevertheless, the results in Table 60, taken together with the observation that either nitric oxide or olefin when added individually appear to retard rather than enhance the rate of aerosol formation from the sulfur dioxide photooxidation (Section 1), strongly suggest that the sulfur dioxide becomes involved in the nitrogen oxide–olefin photolysis, rather than vice versa.

The photochemical behavior of mixtures of nitric oxide with 2-methyl-2-butene in air is quite similar to that of nitric oxide with isobutene (Fig. 50) and other olefins.[377] The major immediate change is the conversion of nitric oxide to nitrogen dioxide. The major identified products, in static experiments with nitric oxide and 2-methyl-2-butene, were acetaldehyde, acetone, formaldehyde, carbon monoxide, ozone, and compound X. The estimated absorption rate constant of nitrogen dioxide in the reactor was $k_a \sim 1.2$ min^{-1}, or about 100 times that of sulfur dioxide, and during the residence time the reaction must have been rather far advanced.

In separate experiments Schuck and Doyle have obtained preliminary evidence of some effect of sulfur dioxide on the nitrogen dioxide–olefin reaction. These experiments were conducted statically in a 520-cu ft chamber with an irradiation intensity about one-third of that in the reactor. Using starting mixtures of 1 ppm of nitrogen dioxide and ~3 ppm of isobutene, the addition of up to 12 ppm of sulfur dioxide was found to have little if any significant effect on the rate of isobutene consumption, but to decrease markedly the yields of the products formed in its absence. For example, Fig. 41 shows the yields of formaldehyde and acetone, per mole of olefin consumed, in the presence and absence of sulfur dioxide. The other major products of the reaction in the absence of sulfur dioxide were similarly reduced by its presence. Thus in the same experiments after 50 min of irradiation, the yield of PAN per mole of olefin consumed was reduced from 0.20 to 0.15, that of carbon monoxide was reduced from 0.30 to 0.08, and the percentage of the carbon atoms in the olefin consumed which appeared among the observed products was decreased from 88 to 56. The sulfur dioxide and ozone concentrations were not followed in these experiments, and no new products were observed.

Not only the chemical nature of the products, but also the mechanism

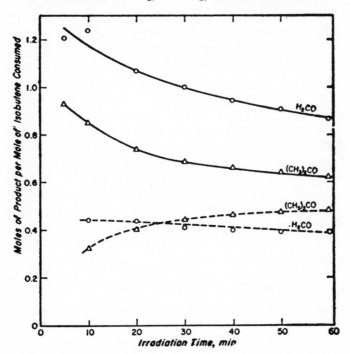

FIG. 41. Effect of sulfur dioxide on yields of formaldehyde and acetone from the nitrogen dioxide–isobutene photolysis in air. Starting mixtures: solid lines, 1 ppm $NO_2 + 3$ ppm isobutene; dashed lines, 1 ppm $NO_2 + 3$ ppm isobutene $+ 3$ ppm SO_2.

of involvement of sulfur dioxide in the nitrogen oxide–olefin photolysis are unknown. The reaction of oxygen atoms with sulfur dioxide is one possibility, but from the rate constants for the $O + SO_2 + M \rightarrow SO_3 + M$ and $O + O_2 + M \rightarrow O_3 + M$ reactions (Chapter V) in air only $2 \times 10^{-5}(SO_2)$, with (SO_2) in pphm, of the oxygen atoms produced would react with sulfur dioxide. Even with the most favorable assumptions regarding the rate of oxygen atom production in the reactor, this reaction could not account for more than a few per cent of the rate of sulfur dioxide consumption in any of the experiments in Table 60. Free radical reactions with sulfur dioxide offer another possibility, for example

$$\text{RO}\overset{\cdot}{\text{O}} + SO_2 \rightarrow \text{R}\overset{\cdot}{\text{O}} + SO_3 \tag{IX-21}$$

In order for any such reaction to account for the observed rates of sulfur dioxide consumption, the product of the collision yield and radical concentration, assuming the sulfur dioxide concentrations are given by the effluent concentrations in Table 60, would have to be $y(R) = 2.5 \times$

10^{-6} to 10^{-4} pphm, which is not impossible, nor is it impossible that in the reactor experiments free radicals were produced at rates equalling or exceeding those of sulfur dioxide consumption.

Other speculative possibilities might be offered, such as reactions or condensations of free radicals or zwitterions from the nitrogen oxide–olefin photolysis with sulfuric acid nuclei from the sulfur dioxide photo-oxidation, but further experimental work is obviously the major requirement for a satisfactory explanation of the photolysis of mixtures of sulfur dioxide, nitrogen oxides, and hydrocarbons in air. Profitable experiments would include identification of the products, use of monochromatic radiation at 3660 A to determine the extent to which absorption by sulfur dioxide is responsible, use of paraffin hydrocarbons instead of olefins, determination of whether or not sulfur dioxide becomes involved in the thermal ozone–olefin and oxygen atom–olefin reactions in air, and examination of free radical reactions with sulfur dioxide by producing known radicals in its presence.

4. SULFUR DIOXIDE AND PARTICULATE FORMATION

All three of the photochemical reactions of sulfur dioxide which have been discussed lead to the formation of particulates. In the photooxidation, in air of normal humidity the particulate consists of droplets of moderately dilute sulfuric acid ($\sim43\%$ H_2SO_4 at 50% R.H.). In the sulfur dioxide–hydrocarbon reaction in the absence of oxygen the particulate appears to consist chiefly of sulfinic acids; its nature in the presence of oxygen or air has not been determined.

Likewise not determined is the chemical nature of the particulate from the photolysis of mixtures of sulfur dioxide, nitric oxide or nitrogen dioxide, and hydrocarbons in air. It has been shown that the amount of particulate matter formed by the irradiation of dilute automobile exhaust in air is a function of the sulfur content of the fuel,[379] and analyses of this particulate have been conducted,[353] with the results shown in Table 61. The high organic content of the particulate, both from irradiated dilute exhaust and from photochemical smog, is noteworthy. Analysis of the benzene soluble fraction in the former case for carbon, hydrogen, and oxygen yielded the atomic ratios $C_{1.0}H_{1.85}O_{1.3}$.

Another noteworthy point which follows from Table 61 is the small amount of sulfur dioxide required to furnish the observed sulfate content of the particulate. Thus, to supply the sulfate in a particulate loading of 1000 $\mu g/m^3$, a value which is observed in the atmosphere only on days of severely limited visibility,[351] would have required the conversion of only 2.1 pphm of sulfur dioxide in the case of Fuel A, 1.5 pphm in the

TABLE 61

COMPOSITION OF PARTICULATE MATTER FROM IRRADIATED
AUTOMOBILE EXHAUST IN AIR

	Source of particulate		
	Irradiated auto exhaust at 4000 ppm in air		Photochemical smog, Los Angeles
Component	Fuel A[a]	Fuel B[b]	
Nitrate as NO_3^-	10.3%	9.4%	15.3%
Sulfate as SO_4^-	8.4	5.9	19.7
Water soluble, organic	24.3	14.1	—
Ether soluble, organic	42.2	54.3	32.9[c]
Other	14.8	16.3	32.1

[a] Fuel A, 0.22% sulfur.
[b] Fuel B, 0.08% sulfur.
[c] Benzene soluble.

case of Fuel B, and 5 pphm in the case of the particulate from photochemical smog.

The amount of light scattering by the aerosol from the sulfur dioxide photooxidation has been determined by Doyle and collaborators,[353,377] using the flow reactor previously described together with an O'Konski-Doyle aerosol counter photometer.[107] The results are shown in Fig. 42.

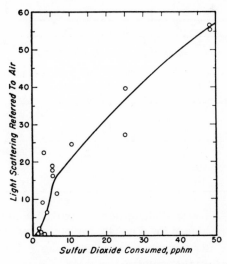

FIG. 42. Light scattering from the photooxidation of sulfur dioxide in air at 50% R.H.

The shape of the curve was probably determined by the variation in response of the counter photometer with average particle size. It appears that for sulfur dioxide consumptions greater than about 5 pphm, the majority of the particles were large enough to give a response approximately proportional to the square of the diameter, but when the consumption was less than this the diameters lie in the transition region where scattering is going from a square law to a sixth power response. In addition, the particle concentration may be varying rapidly in this region.

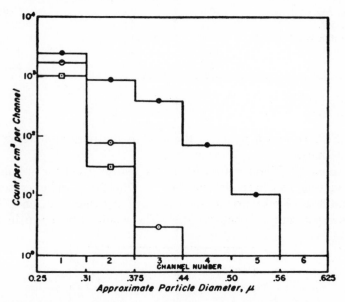

FIG. 43. Particle size distribution of aerosols produced by sulfur dioxide photooxidation. Air at 50% R.H. Residence time 27.5 min.

	SO₂ conc., ppm	
	Entering	Reacted
•	4.5	～0.49
⊙	2.3	～ .25
⊡	0.51	～ .06

The number and size distribution of particles above the threshold of the counter are shown in Fig. 43 for three influent concentrations of sulfur dioxide. It is obvious there must have been many particles with diameters below the counter threshold.

In one experiment both the light scattering and the number of condensation nuclei (for water) produced by the sulfur dioxide photo-oxidation in air at 50% R.H. were determined, using an Aitken nuclei counter. The results, as a function of time of irradiation, are shown in Fig. 44. It is evident that a great number of nuclei appeared almost immediately and then decayed to an intermediate value while the light scattering increased. The steady-state sulfur dioxide consumption during the 18 min residence time in the reactor in this experiment was estimated to be 2 pphm, which lies in the transition region of Fig. 42.

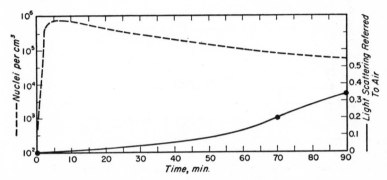

Fig. 44. Condensation nuclei and light scattering from sulfur dioxide photo-oxidation as a function of time of irradiation. Influent SO_2 conc. 24 pphm; residence time 18 min; air at 50% R.H.

Assuming an exponential relation for small irradiation times, the amount consumed at the time of peak nuclei concentration, about 6 min, would have been only ~0.6 pphm.

The results of similar experiments by Doyle on particulate formation during the photolysis of mixtures of sulfur dioxide, nitric oxide, and an olefin in air[353,377] are summarized in Figs. 45, 46, and 47.

Figure 45 shows that the amount of scattering approaches a maximum with increasing olefin concentration, probably due to complete consumption of the sulfur dioxide. With a longer residence time, 44 min, this maximum, together with virtually complete sulfur dioxide consumption, had already been reached at the lowest olefin concentration used, ~0.5 ppm. The average values of the maxima, referred to air, were not greatly different in the two cases.

The particle counts in Fig. 46 show that the water content of the air affects the particle size distribution, and at 50% R.H. the distribution in the observed range is much the same as that obtained from sulfur dioxide alone (Fig. 43). The immediate appearance and early maximum in condensation nuclei, and the gradual increase in light scattering with

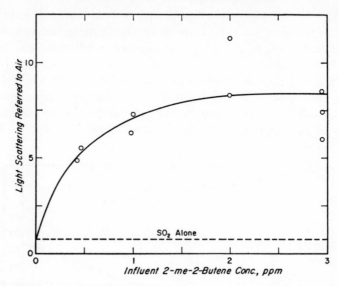

Fig. 45. Light scattering from the photolysis of mixtures of sulfur dioxide, nitric oxide, and 2-methyl-2-butene in air. Air at 50% R.H.; residence time 17 min; influent concentrations, 0.1 ppm SO_2, 1 ppm NO, 2-methyl-2-butene as shown.

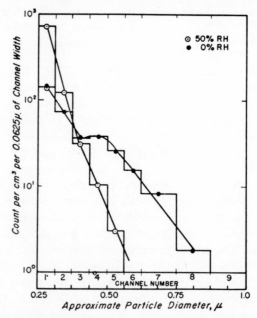

Fig. 46. Particle size distribution of aerosols produced from the photolysis of mixtures of sulfur dioxide, nitric oxide, and 2-methyl-2-butene in dry and humid air. Influent concentrations, 0.5 ppm SO_2, 1 ppm NO, 3 ppm 2-methyl-2-butene.

irradiation time (Fig. 47) are also quite similar to those obtained with sulfur dioxide alone (Fig. 44). Again, from the observed rate of sulfur dioxide consumption (Table 60), the amount consumed at the time of peak nuclei concentration, ~3 min, would have been only about 0.6 pphm.

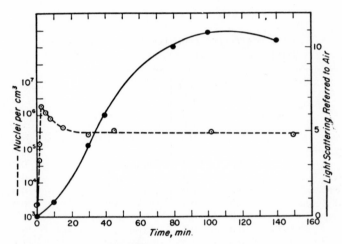

Fig. 47. Condensation nuclei and light scattering from the photolysis of a mixture of sulfur dioxide, nitric oxide, and tetramethylethylene as a function of time of irradiation. Air at 50% R.H.; residence time, 27.5 min; influent concentrations, SO₂ 0.1 ppm, NO 1.0 ppm, tetramethylethylene 3.0 ppm.

The enhancement of the rate of photochemical consumption of sulfur dioxide on addition of nitric oxide and an olefin (Table 60) is accompanied by enhancement of the rate of light scattering aerosol formation. This is shown by comparison of the solid and dashed lines in Fig. 45, and also by Table 62.

TABLE 62

LIGHT SCATTERING FROM IRRADIATION OF SULFUR DIOXIDE AND
NITRIC OXIDE–2-METHYL-2-BUTENE MIXTURES IN AIR[a]

Composition of influent mixture (ppm)			SO₂ Consumed (ppm)	Light scattering referred to air
NO	2-Me-2-butene	SO₂		
1	3	0	—	0.4
0	0	0.1	0.008	0.75
1	3	0.1	~0.1	8.5

[a] Reactor residence time, 17 min; air at 50% RH.

The amounts of light scattering obtained by Doyle from irradiation of mixtures of nitric oxide and a number of hydrocarbons in air, both alone and with added sulfur dioxide, are listed in Table 63. With the paraffins no light scattering was observed, either with or without added

TABLE 63

LIGHT SCATTERING FROM IRRADIATION OF VARIOUS
HYDROCARBON–NITRIC OXIDE MIXTURES IN AIR[a]

Hydrocarbon	Light scattering referred to air		Hydrocarbon	Light scattering referred to air	
	Without SO$_2$	With SO$_2$		Without SO$_2$	With SO$_2$
Methane	0.0	0.0	Ethylene	0.0	1.4
n-Pentane	0.0	0.0	1-Pentene	0.1	10.7
2-Methylbutane	0.0	0.0	Isobutene	0.0	4.5
2,2-Dimethylpropane	0.0	0.0	trans-2-Butene	0.0	16.0
Cyclopentane	0.0	0.0	2-Methyl-2-butene	0.4	10.7
Benzene	0.0	0.5	Tetramethylethylene	0.3	11.1
Toluene	0.0	1.0	Cyclohexene	11.1	11.7
Ethyl benzene	0.0	1.4	1,3-Butadiene	0.4	16.7
p-Xylene	0.0	0.0	1-Butyne	0.0	0.1

[a] Reactor residence time, 17 min; air at 50% RH. Influent conc. 3 ppm hydrocarbon, 1 ppm NO, 0.1–0.6 ppm SO$_2$.

sulfur dioxide. Since irradiation of sulfur dioxide alone at the concentrations used would have produced observable scattering, it must be presumed that this was suppressed by the nitric oxide–paraffin mixture. In some of these experiments the rate of sulfur dioxide consumption appeared to be greater in the presence of nitric oxide and a paraffin than in their absence, suggesting some process which consumes sulfur dioxide without producing aerosol. With the unsaturated hydrocarbons in only one case, cyclohexene, was any large amount of light scattering produced in the absence of sulfur dioxide, and in this case the addition of sulfur dioxide led to little increase in scattering.

An interesting comparison may be made, for the olefins, between the relative amounts of scattering produced by the photolysis of their mixtures with nitric oxide and sulfur dioxide, and the relative rates of their reactions with oxygen atoms, ozone, and photochemically with nitrogen dioxide. As shown in Table 64, the order for increasing amounts of scattering appears to correlate best with that for the rates of reaction with ozone.

TABLE 64

COMPARISON OF RELATIVE AMOUNTS OF LIGHT SCATTERING FROM THE SULFUR DIOXIDE–
NITRIC OXIDE–OLEFIN PHOTOLYSIS WITH THE RELATIVE RATES OF REACTION OF THE
OLEFINS WITH OXYGEN ATOMS, OZONE, AND PHOTOCHEMICALLY WITH NITRIC OXIDE-
NITROGEN DIOXIDE[a]

Olefin	Light scattering	Oxygen atoms	Ozone	Nitric oxide-nitrogen dioxide, photochemical
Ethylene	0.3	0.04	0.5	0.04
Isobutene	1.0	1.0	1.0	1.0
1-Pentene	2.4	2.5	1.1	0.5
2-Methyl-2-butene	2.4	—	3.2	2.6
Tetramethylethylene	2.5	4.2	3.8	6.4
Cyclohexene	2.6	—	3.7	0.9
trans-2-Butene	3.6	1.1	4.5	3.6
1-3-Butadiene	3.7	—	1.3	0.7

[a] Relative rates for scattering from Table 63, for oxygen atoms from Table 40, for ozone from Table 48, and for nitrogen dioxide from Table 66.

The work of Doyle, Schuck, and Renzetti clearly demonstrates that sulfur dioxide may play a large part in the photochemical formation of aerosols in polluted air. The sulfur dioxide–nitrogen oxide–olefin reaction is fast enough to account for the high sulfate and organic contents of the particulate and in some part at least for the low sulfur dioxide content of the air in the Los Angeles basin. In addition, the high rate of nuclei formation shows that the photooxidation of very small amounts of sulfur dioxide can supply ample acidic nuclei for either physical or chemical condensation of other materials present in the atmosphere.

Chapter X

General Discussion

1. The Photochemistry of Mixtures of Nitric Oxide or Nitrogen Dioxide with Hydrocarbons in Air

The photochemistry of low concentrations of nitrogen oxides and hydrocarbons in air, already referred to on several occasions in earlier chapters, has been studied by Stephens and collaborators[183,379,383,405] and by Schuck and Doyle.[377] The most extensive investigation, that of Schuck and Doyle, was conducted in a 520-cu ft glass lined chamber illuminated by an array of 24–400-watt H-1 mercury arcs and 78–30-watt Blacklight fluorescent bulbs. The ultraviolet irradiation intensity in the chamber, measured by a photocell calibrated with uranyl oxalate, led to an estimated absorption rate constant for nitrogen dioxide of $k_a = 0.40$ min^{-1}, and the observed photolysis rate constant for nitrogen dioxide in nitrogen was close to this figure. The observed photolysis rate constant for acetaldehyde in air was 1.2×10^{-3} min^{-1}, which, assuming a primary yield [69] of $\phi = 0.2$ corresponds to an absorption rate of $k_a = 6 \times 10^{-3}$ min^{-1}. Compared to these figures, the estimated absorption rates in sunlight at $z = 40°$, from Chapter III, are $k_a = 0.37$ min^{-1} for nitrogen dioxide and 3.6×10^{-3} min^{-1} for acetaldehyde. It may be concluded from this that the ultraviolet intensity in the chamber approximated that of full sunlight in the nitrogen dioxide absorption region, and possibly somewhat exceeded that of sunlight in the acetaldehyde absorption region.

The air used in the chamber was first passed through a platinized alumina catalyst at 600°C, and after cooling, through a charcoal filter. Prior to each experiment the chamber, and the cells of a long-path infrared spectrometer through which air from the chamber was circulated, were flushed for 5 hr at a flow rate of 10 cu ft per min, under full irradiation without cooling. The air temperature during this phase was 60°C, during the experiment proper it was reduced to ~30°C by a cooler and mixing fans. The desired quantities of reactants were introduced into the circulating air stream by hypodermic syringe, and became completely mixed in less than one minute. The concentrations of reactants and products were followed during each irradiation by infrared absorption and, for nitric oxide and nitrogen dioxide, by a continuous colorimetric recorder. In addition, spot samples were periodically removed for gas chromatographic analysis.

The rates and products observed by Schuck and Doyle are summarized in Tables 65 and 66, and the products reported by Stephens, Darley, Taylor, and Scott[401] from irradiations at somewhat higher concentrations are listed in Table 67.

TABLE 65

RATES AND PRODUCTS OF PHOTOCHEMICAL NITROGEN
OXIDE–SATURATED HYDROCARBON REACTIONS IN AIR[a]

Hydrocarbon		Oxide of nitrogen			Identified products (ppm)			
Name	Initial conc. (ppm)	Formula	Initial conc. (ppm)	Max. rate coeff. (min^{-1}) $\times 10^2$	Aldehydes	O$_3$	CO	PAN
Methane	6	NO$_2$	2	0.00	0	0	0	0
n-Pentane	6	NO$_2$	2	0.02	0	0.2	0	0
Isopentane	9	NO$_2$	3	0.02	0	0.15	0	0
3-Methyl pentane	6	NO$_2$	2	0.15	0	0.2	0	0
2-Methyl heptane	3	NO$_2$	1	—	0	0.45	0.40	0.15
Cyclohexane	6	NO	1	0.05	0	0.2	0.10	0

[a] Product concentrations are after 100 min of irradiation except for 2-methyl heptane which are after 180 min. Rate coefficients are the maximum observed values of $-d \log (\text{Hyd})/dt$.

Probably the first points to be noted are the generally low rates of photochemical consumption of the saturated, relative to those of the comparable unsaturated, hydrocarbons and the absence of aldehydes from the former relative to the high yields from the latter. This conforms with the relatively low rates of reaction of the saturated hydrocarbons with oxygen atoms and their inertness with respect to ozone, as reported in earlier chapters.

With the olefins, as in the case of their reactions with ozone, in the majority of cases the aldehydes or ketones corresponding to addition of an oxygen atom to one end of the olefin, with a split at the double bond, are among the major products. The results of Stephens, Darley, Taylor, and Scott show nearly a stoichiometric yield of these products, again reminiscent of the ozone–olefin reaction, but the results of Schuck and Doyle do not. In fact, Schuck and Doyle found a substantial change in product yields with time of irradiation. This effect is illustrated, for a starting mixture of isobutene and nitrogen dioxide in Fig. 48. Quite different behavior, particularly with respect to the yield of formaldehyde, is found on starting with nitric oxide (Fig. 49).

Minor products which have been observed from the olefins, mostly by

TABLE 66

RATES AND PRODUCTS OF PHOTOCHEMICAL NITROGEN OXIDE–OLEFIN REACTIONS IN AIR[a,b]

| Olefin | Oxide of nitrogen | Max. rate coeff. (min^{-1}) × 10^2 | Moles of product per mole of olefin consumed | | | | | | | % Recov.[c] |
| | | | Aldehydes | | Other | Acetone | O$_3$ | CO | PAN | |
			Formaldehyde	Acetaldehyde						
Ethylene	NO	0.15	0.63	—	—	—	0.30	0.56	—	60
Propylene	NO	1.9	0.68	0.68	—	—	0.39	NI	0.20	82
1-Butene	NO$_2$	1.46	0.47	—	1.00[d]	—	0.21	0.03	0.02	88
Isobutene	NO	3.45	0.56	—	—	0.66	0.25	0.26	0.11	75
Isobutene	NO$_2$	3.75	0.78	—	—	0.57	0.37	0.40	0.14	79
cis-2-Butene	NO	8.1	NI	0.84	—	—	0.17	0.31	0.17	58
trans-2-Butene	NO$_2$	13.6	NI	1.34	—	—	0.23	0.70	0.17	93
1-2-Butadiene	NO$_2$	0.74	0.14	—	—	—	0.28	0.28	0.07	14
1-3-Butadiene	NO$_2$	2.7	0.88	—	0.83[e]	—	0.32	0.39	0.02	95
1-Pentene	NO$_2$	1.7	1.04	—	0.78[f]	—	0.40	0.53	0.08	100
2-Methyl-2-butene	NO	9.0	0.47	0.72	—	0.42	0.12	0.19	0.27	78
1-3-Pentadiene	NO	3.5	0.65	1.33	0.33[e]	—	0.24	0.45	0.10	100
2-Methyl-1-3-butadiene	NO	5.0	0.50	0.80	0.35[e]	—	0.24	0.26	0.06	87
3-Heptene	NO$_2$	2.2	0.88	—	1.35[d,f]	—	—	0.31	0.06	~90
Tetramethylethylene	NO	22.	0.29	—	—	1.38	0.23	0.26	0.37	90
2-Ethyl-1-butene	NO	2.9	0.55	—	—	0.58[g]	0.25	0.21	0.06	63
Cyclohexene	NO	3.2	0.44	—	—	—	0.16	0.22	0.09	14
2,3-Dimethyl-1-3-butadiene	NO	3.8	0.48	0.93	—	—	0.15	0.29	0.13	64

[a] Initial olefin concentrations were ~3 ppm in all cases except ethylene, which was 6 ppm. Initial nitrogen oxide concentrations were ~1 ppm. Product recoveries given are after 100 min of irradiation, except for ethylene, which are after 4 hr. Rate coefficients are the maximum observed values of $-d \log (\mathrm{Hyd})/dt$. NI = no information.

[b] From Schuck and Doyle.

[c] Percentage of carbon atoms recovered in products listed.

[d] Propionaldehyde.

[e] Acrolein or homolog.

[f] Butyraldehyde.

[g] Diethylketone.

TABLE 67

PRODUCTS OF PHOTOCHEMICAL NITROGEN OXIDE–OLEFIN REACTIONS IN AIR[a]

| Olefin | Initial conc. (ppm) | | | Moles of product per mole of olefin consumed | | | | | % Re- cov.[c] |
| | Ole- fin[b] | NO | NO₂ | Aldehydes | | | Ace- tone | PAN | |
				Formal- dehyde	Acetal- dehyde	Propion- aldehyde			
Ethylene	11.2	—	10	0.79	—	—	—	—	40
Isobutene	10.2	11	—	0.48	—	—	0.61	—	58
	9.9	—	10	0.33	—	—	0.53	—	49
cis-2-Butene	11	9.3	—	—	1.01	—	—	0.27	64
	10.6	—	10	—	0.81	—	—	0.22	52
cis-3-Hexene	1.9	10	—	—	—	0.90	—	—	45
	10	10	—	—	—	0.97	—	—	48
	2.1	—	10	—	—	0.90	—	—	45
	5.0	—	10	—	—	0.96	—	—	43
	11.4	—	10.4	—	—	1.00	—	—	50

[a] From Stephens, Darley, Taylor, and Scott.
[b] Percentages of original olefin consumed during irradiation were ethylene 55%, isobutene 93%, cis-2-butene and cis-3-hexene 100%.
[c] Percentage of carbon atoms recovered in products listed.

gas-liquid chromatography, include epoxides, alkyl nitrates and nitrites, methyl alcohol, and ketene. In some cases small amounts of an aldehyde with the same number of carbon atoms as the original olefin, e.g., isobutyraldehyde from isobutene, have also been observed. The yields and the variations with irradiation time of these products have not been established.

Concentration vs. time curves obtained by Schuck and Doyle during irradiation of mixtures of isobutene with nitric oxide and nitrogen dioxide in air are shown in Figs. 50 and 51. These are representative of the behavior of a number of olefins, and disclose several interesting as well as puzzling features.

The first of these features is shown by the behavior during the first twenty minutes or so of irradiation in Fig. 50. Here the major change which occurs is the conversion of nitric oxide to nitrogen dioxide. During the process of introducing the nitric oxide into the chamber, a small amount (estimated at ~5%) becomes converted to nitrogen dioxide by thermal reaction with oxygen. This nitrogen dioxide is the only known photochemical absorber initially present, and if the conversion is indeed initiated by nitrogen dioxide absorption the unusual situation is presented that the photolysis of the absorbing substance results in an increase in its concentration. In other words, during this period the quantum yield of the nitrogen dioxide photolysis is negative.

This means, of course, that nitrogen dioxide is being formed by secondary reactions more rapidly than it is being photodissociated. The olefin must be present for this to occur, and the only known intermedi-

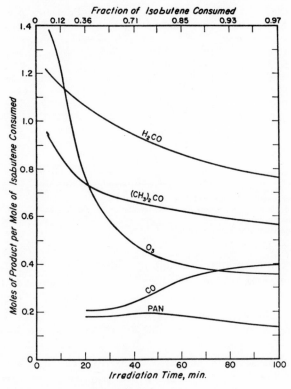

FIG. 48. Variation in product yields with time of irradiation for isobutene–nitrogen dioxide mixtures in air. An average of five experiments with starting concentrations of 2.3 to 3.2 ppm of isobutene and $\sim$1 ppm of nitrogen dioxide.

ate capable of reacting with the olefin at an appreciable rate at this stage is atomic oxygen.

Consider, for illustration, the situation at $t = 10$ min in Fig. 50. At this time the nitrogen dioxide concentration was about 0.3 ppm and was increasing at a rate of $\sim$0.035 ppm min^{-1}. The most important immediate reactions occurring are

$$NO_2 + h\nu \rightarrow NO + O \qquad \phi k_a(NO_2) \qquad\qquad (X\text{-}1)$$
$$O + O_2 + M \rightarrow O_3 + M \qquad k_2(O_2)(M) = 1.45 \times 10^6 \text{ min}^{-1} \qquad (X\text{-}2)$$
$$NO + O_3 \rightarrow NO_2 + O_2 \qquad k_3 \approx 30 \text{ ppm}^{-1} \text{ min}^{-1} \qquad (X\text{-}3)$$
$$O + \text{isobutene} \rightarrow \text{products} \qquad k_4 \approx (1 \text{ to } 3) \times 10^4 \text{ ppm}^{-1} \text{ min}^{-1} \qquad (X\text{-}4)$$

The rate constants shown are derived from Tables 35, 40, and 44. From these constants and the observed value of $k_a = 0.4$ min^{-1}, the estimated rate of the photodissociation (X-1) at $t = 10$ min in Fig. 50 was ~ 0.12 ppm min^{-1}, the rates of reactions (X-2) and (X-3) were each from

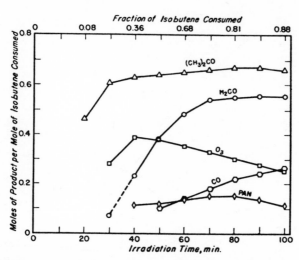

FIG. 49. Variation in product yields with time of irradiation for an isobutene–nitric oxide mixture in air. Starting concentrations were 3 ppm of isobutene, 1 ppm of nitric oxide, and ~ 0.05 ppm of nitrogen dioxide.

~ 0.113 to 0.118 ppm min^{-1}, and the rate of (X-4) was from ~ 0.0023 to 0.007 ppm min^{-1}. The latter is most simply estimated from the equation

$$S_1 = \frac{\phi k_a k_4 (NO_2)(HC)}{k_2(O_2)(M)} \qquad (X\text{-}5)$$

If no further processes occurred, reactions (X-1) to (X-4) would lead to a decrease in nitrogen dioxide concentration at a rate equal to that of (X-4), since the oxygen atoms reacting with the olefin must be subtracted from those reacting with oxygen to form ozone. The reactions of oxygen atoms with nitric oxide and nitrogen dioxide, and of ozone with nitrogen dioxide and isobutene, are all relatively unimportant at the time in question; they would produce a small additional decrease in the nitrogen dioxide concentration.

The observed conversion of nitric oxide to nitrogen dioxide shows that further reactions do occur, and the rate of conversion by these reactions at the time in question must equal the difference between the observed rate of nitrogen dioxide increase and the estimated decrease on the basis of reactions (X-1) to (X-4), or from $0.035 + (0.0023$ to $0.007) \approx 0.037$ to 0.042 ppm min^{-1}.

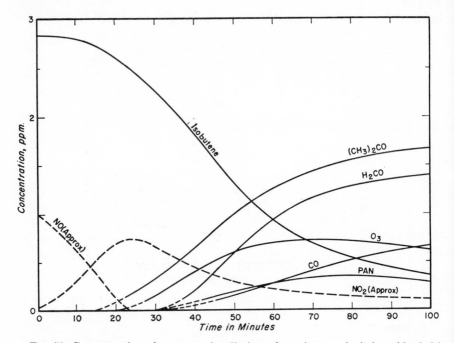

Fig. 50. Concentration changes on irradiation of a mixture of nitric oxide (with some nitrogen dioxide) and isobutene in air. The times of first appearance of products are approximate.

This is from 6 to 16 times the estimated rate of the oxygen atom–isobutene reaction at this time. It follows that if this reaction initiates the process responsible for the conversion, and its rate constant lies within the range indicated in (X-4), the process so initiated must involve a chain. Such a chain might produce the conversion in two ways; by direct reaction with nitric oxide or by forming ozone from molecular oxygen. The work of Cvetanović reported in Chapter V indicates some free radical formation from the oxygen atom–olefin reaction, and a free radical chain is an obvious possibility.

The buildup in ozone concentration shown in Figs. 50 and 51, which is a characteristic feature of the nitrogen oxide–olefin photolyses in air, is probably due to the same process. As in polluted air (Chapter VI), the relation between the nitric oxide and ozone concentrations is determined chiefly by reactions (X-1), (X-2), and (X-3), which yield the limiting expression,

$$\frac{(NO)(O_3)}{(NO_2)} = \frac{\phi k_a}{k_3} \tag{X-6}$$

As the nitric oxide concentration decreases, the ozone concentration will increase, or vice versa. Again this result may be accomplished either by

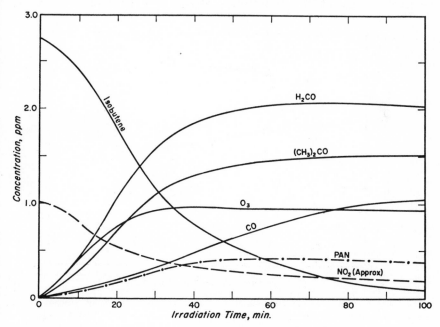

FIG. 51. Concentration changes on irradiation of mixtures of nitrogen dioxide and isobutene in air. The curves are averages of five experiments with starting concentrations of 2.3 to 3.2 ppm of isobutene and ∼ 1 ppm of nitrogen dioxide.

the oxidation of nitric oxide or by production of ozone from molecular oxygen, again the rate which must be accounted for is a number of times greater than that of the oxygen atom–olefin reaction, and again it must be concluded that if this reaction initiates the process, it involves a chain.

   As the irradiation proceeds the ozone concentration reaches a peak, beyond which it either falls off slowly or levels off at a more or less stable value. In the case of isobutene and nitrogen dioxide (Fig. 51), this stable terminal concentration of ozone is particularly well marked. Schuck and Doyle[377] found that, with starting mixtures of 1 ppm of nitrogen dioxide and 1, 3, and 6.6 ppm of isobutene the terminal ozone concentration was proportional to the square root of the light intensity. This again suggests a free radical chain, with radical recombination as the chain stopping step. On the other hand, at a higher initial isobutene concentration, 10.6 ppm, the terminal ozone concentration showed almost no dependence on light intensity.

The terminal ozone concentrations obtained after 2 hr of irradiation of various isobutene and nitrogen dioxide starting mixtures are summarized on Fig. 52. It is interesting to note that as long as the initial

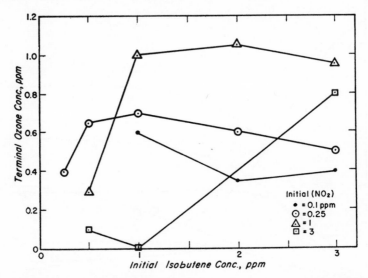

FIG. 52. Terminal ozone concentrations from the irradiation of isobutene and nitrogen dioxide in air. Initial nitrogen dioxide concentrations: · = 0.1 ppm; ⊙ = 0.25 ppm; △ = 1 ppm; ☐ = 3 ppm.

isobutene concentration equalled or exceeded that of the nitrogen dioxide. substantial ozone yields were obtained even at the lowest concentrations used. The lowest yields were obtained from mixtures in which the initial nitrogen dioxide concentration exceeded that of the olefin.

The buildup of ozone on irradiation with nitrogen dioxide in air is not limited to olefins. Many paraffin hydrocarbons, as well as aldehydes and other classes of organic compounds have been shown to produce ozone under these circumstances,[176] although with large differences in rate and in final concentration attained (Table 68). Moreover, ozone formation is not limited to irradiations with nitrogen dioxide. Alkyl nitrite–olefin mixtures in air, for example, closely resemble nitrogen dioxide–olefin mixtures in this regard, and even the irradiation of alkyl

TABLE 68

TERMINAL OZONE CONCENTRATIONS

Hydrocarbon	Initial conc. (ppm)		Terminal ozone conc. (ppm)	Irradiation time to reach terminal conc. (min)
	Hydrocarbon	NO₂		
Methane	6	2	0	—
n-Pentane	6	2	0.2	100
Isopentane	9	3	0.2	120
3-Methyl pentane	6	2	0.2	100
2-Methyl heptane	3	1	0.45	180
Cyclohexane	6	1 (NO)	0.2	80
Ethylene	6	2	1.1	140
Propylene	3	1	0.7	75
1-Butene	3	1	0.6	45
Isobutene	3	1	1.0	40
cis-2-Butene	3	1	0.6	35
trans-2-Butene	3	1	0.7	35
1-Pentene	3	1	0.6	45
2-Methyl-2-butene	3	1	0.4	40
Cyclohexene	3	1	0.45	35
1-3-Butadiene	3	1	0.65	45

nitrites alone in air results in ozone formation. Biacetyl and azomethane also produce some ozone on irradiation in air or oxygen, and aldehydes cause the conversion of nitric oxide to nitrogen dioxide in air, although more slowly than do the olefins. The processes of ozone buildup in all of these cases are photochemical, but the extent to which they are mechanistically related is not known.

Another puzzling feature of the nitrogen oxide–olefin photolysis in air concerns the rate of olefin consumption. This may best be seen by inspecting the rate vs. time curves in Figs. 53 and 54. After irradiation is started, some time is required for the rate of olefin disappearance, $-d(HC)/dt$, to reach a peak, and the length of this induction period is greater when starting with nitric oxide than it is with nitrogen dioxide. The rate of the oxygen atom–olefin reaction throughout the irradiation period may be estimated from equation (X-5), and that of the ozone–olefin reaction from the observed rate constant and reactant concentrations. The sum of these rates, shown on Figs. 53 and 54, reaches a peak at approximately the same time as that of the peak rate of olefin consumption, but even using the highest estimates of their rate constants these two reactions, except possibly during the first few minutes of irradiation, cannot account for all of the olefin consumed.

This excess in the rate of olefin consumption, over that which may be accounted for by the oxygen atom–olefin and ozone–olefin reactions, has been observed by both Schuck and Doyle and by Stephens and his collaborators for a number of olefins. While it appears to differ in extent and characteristics, in a manner which has not yet been defined, from olefin to olefin, it is apparently quite general, and indicates that in the nitrogen oxide–olefin photolyses in air there is at least one additional reaction which consumes olefin.

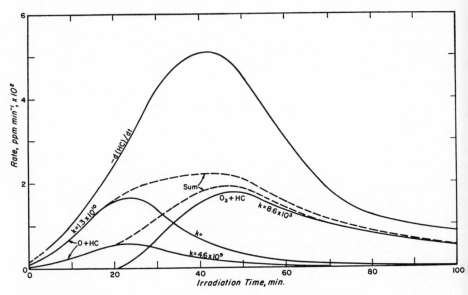

FIG. 53. Rate of olefin consumption compared to estimated rates of its reactions with oxygen atoms and ozone; isobutene and nitric oxide. Here and in Fig. 54 the rates of the oxygen atom–isobutene reaction are estimated for two values of the rate constant. Rate constants are in liter mole^{-1} sec^{-1}.

An exponential plot of the isobutene concentration against time, Fig. 55, shows that when starting with nitrogen dioxide, after the initial induction period the rate of olefin disappearance becomes directly proportional to its concentration and remains so through the balance of the irradiation. On starting with nitric oxide the induction period is much longer, the period over which the rate is proportional to the olefin concentration is shorter, and there is a break at between 60 and 80 min to a slower reaction.

A break of this type was observed by Schuck and Doyle in a number of experiments with different olefins, and was assigned by them to the termination of the reaction or reactions responsible for the excess rate of olefin removal. While it is true that after the break the rate of olefin consumption is nearly proportional to the sum of the estimated rates of the oxygen atom and ozone reactions, in most cases it is still in excess of that sum (Fig. 53). The difference can scarcely be due to an underestimate of the rate of the oxygen atom–olefin reaction, as the contribution of this reaction during the latter part of the irradiation period is quite small. An underestimate of the rate of the ozone–olefin reaction might be suspected, particularly in view of the nonstoichiometric nature observed

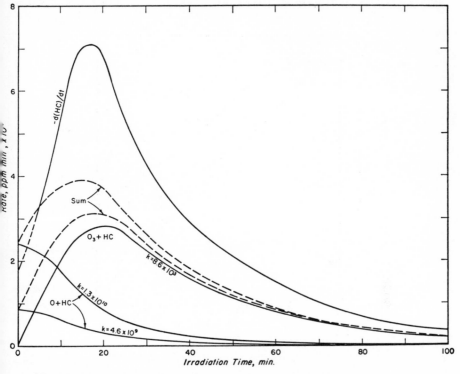

FIG. 54. Rate of olefin consumption compared to estimated rates of its reactions with oxygen atoms and ozone; isobutene and nitrogen dioxide.

by Schuck and Doyle in the case of isobutene (Chapter VI). Arguing against this are the facts that the rate constant used in Figs. 53 and 54 was determined at comparable concentrations in the same chamber, and on interrupting the illumination during a photolysis the rate at once dropped to a value in agreement with that estimated from this constant. It appears, therefore, that some olefin was still being removed by an additional process, even after the break.

The effect of varying the light intensity, over a fourfold range, on the rate of isobutene consumption was investigated by Schuck and Doyle. Although the variance of the data was too great to permit firm conclusions, the results suggest that with starting concentrations of 1, 3, and 6.6 ppm of isobutene, all with 1 ppm of nitrogen dioxide, the rate has two components, one directly proportional to the light intensity and the other proportional to the square root of the intensity. The correlation of the excess rate with light intensity was slightly in favor of the square root as compared with the first power. As in the case of the ozone buildup, this suggests that the excess removal of olefin is accomplished at least in

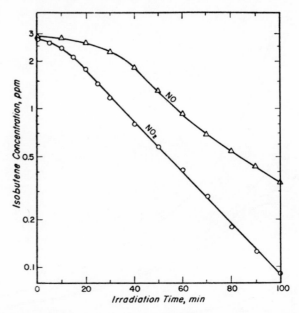

FIG. 55. Exponential plot of isobutene concentration against irradiation time.

part by a free radical chain. At a higher isobutene concentration, 10.6 ppm, there was no excess rate, and again as in the case of ozone buildup, the rate was nearly independent of light intensity.

The effects of varying nitrogen dioxide concentration on the rate of isobutene consumption resemble those of light intensity. The over-all rate varies with something between the square root and the first power of nitrogen dioxide concentration, and again the results suggest that the square root component is associated with the excess rate of olefin removal.

A number of special experiments conducted by Schuck and Doyle have yielded information which must be taken into account in any explanation of the photochemistry of nitrogen oxide–olefin mixtures in air. These experiments have indicated the following:

1. The photochemical nitrogen dioxide–olefin reaction is not initiated by visible radiation.

2. On irradiation of a nitrogen dioxide–olefin mixture (using *trans*-2-butene) in an atmosphere of nitrogen, the rate of olefin consumption can be accounted for solely by the oxygen atom–olefin reaction. Without oxygen there is no excess rate of olefin removal.

3. On interrupting the illumination, the excess rate of olefin consumption at once disappears and the rate drops to that of the ozone–olefin reaction. On resuming irradiation the excess rate builds up again.

4. In one experiment addition of a large excess (3000 ppm) of hydrogen wiped out most, if not all, of the excess rate of olefin consumption and substantially reduced the peak concentrations of formaldehyde, acetone, and ozone, but not that of PAN (Table 69). However, this result is questionable, as a later experiment showed no such effect.

TABLE 69

EFFECT OF ADDED HYDROGEN ON THE NITROGEN DIOXIDE–ISOBUTENE PHOTOLYSIS

	3 ppm Isobutene, 1 ppm NO$_2$ in air	3 ppm Isobutene 1 ppm NO$_2$ 3000 ppm H$_2$ in air
Maximum rate coeff. for isobutene consumption (min^{-1}):	3.75×10^{-2}	1.33×10^{-2}
Peak product concentrations:		
O$_3$	1.0	0.4
HCHO	2.1	1.3
(CH$_3$)$_2$CO	1.5	1.1
PAN	0.4	0.4
CO (after 100 min irrad.)	1.0	0.3

5. Irradiation of formaldehyde (6 ppm) and acetaldehyde (3 ppm) in the presence of isobutene (3 ppm) in air, with no NO or NO$_2$ present, produces no measurable photochemical consumption of the olefin.

6. Irradiation with the light used to produce the nitrogen dioxide–olefin reaction has no effect on the rate of the ozone–olefin reaction in air.

7. The addition of nitrogen dioxide, in the dark, has no effect on the rate of the ozone–olefin reaction in air. The products of this reaction, however, are affected by the presence of nitrogen dioxide. In particular, PAN is formed, even in the dark.

The determination of the mechanisms of the nitric oxide–nitrogen dioxide conversion, of ozone buildup, and of the consumption of olefin by processes other than the oxygen atom and ozone reactions constitute the major remaining problems in the photochemistry of nitrogen oxide–olefin mixtures in air. As we have seen, there are indications that all of these processes involve free radical chains, but no clear evidence has been obtained of this, of the radicals involved, or of the steps in the chains.

The effect of hydrogen on the excess rate of olefin consumption (experiment 4); if real, suggests a chain in which hydroxyl radicals are carriers. If hydroxyl radicals serve as carriers, some effect might have been expected on irradiating ozone–olefin mixtures alone in air, as there is evidence that ozone is photodissociated by ultraviolet radiation to yield ^1D oxygen atoms, which react rapidly with water to yield hydroxyl (Chapter III). The fact that no such effect was observed (experiment 6) might be explained in a number of ways, e.g., the radiation used does not dissociate ozone to yield ^1D oxygen atoms, hydroxyl radicals are not the carriers, or the presence of nitric oxide or nitrogen dioxide are necessary to the chain.

The induction period with respect to olefin consumption (Figs. 51, 55) suggests that the buildup of some intermediate is involved, and the immediate disappearance of the excess rate when the illumination is cut off (experiment 3) suggests, although not exclusively, an intermediate which is photolyzed. The shapes of the rate vs. time curves (Figs. 53, 54) indicate that the ozone–olefin reaction contributes to the initiation of the process responsible for the excess rate, but the fact that it cannot do so in the dark, even in the presence of NO_2 (experiment 7), again suggests an additional photochemical step, such as photolysis of an intermediate.

Possible intermediates which would appear to fulfill the requirements here are the alkyl and acyl nitrites and pernitrites, which have been discussed in some detail in earlier chapters. Alkyl nitrites, for example, are known to be formed in small concentrations during the nitrogen oxide–olefin photolyses in air, they are so rapidly photolyzed that no more than small concentrations would be expected, and their photolysis in the presence of isobutene in air leads to nearly the same rate of olefin consumption and to the same principal products as are obtained with nitrogen dioxide–isobutene mixtures. The absence of any effect from added formaldehyde or acetaldehyde when NO or NO_2 are not present (experiment 5) conforms with the hypothesis of a nitrite or pernitrite intermediate.

During the early stages of the photolysis at least, the most likely initial source of radicals is the oxygen atom–olefin reaction. However, both the extent to which this reaction produces radicals and the nature of the radicals produced are uncertain. The work of Cvetanović, reported in Chapter V, indicates that the reaction includes at least two fragmentation processes, one pressure dependent and the other not. One of the fragments may consist of a methyl radical or a hydrogen atom, and the other may be an acyl or some other oxygen containing radical. In addition, the initial oxygen atom–olefin addition product may react with oxygen with some eventual radical formation.

This opens a number of mechanistic possibilities, mostly speculative, which might account for the excess rate of olefin removal. For example, beginning with the production of methyl radicals from the oxygen atom–olefin reaction, with isobutene as the olefin, and assuming the intermediate formation and photolysis of methyl nitrite, the following reactions may be postulated:

$$O + C_4H_8 \rightarrow \dot{C}H_3 + C_3H_5\dot{O} \tag{X-7}$$

$$\dot{C}H_3 + O_2 \rightarrow CH_3O\dot{O} \tag{X-8}$$

$$CH_3O\dot{O} + O_2 \rightarrow CH_3\dot{O} + O_3 \tag{X-9}$$

$$CH_3\dot{O} + NO \rightarrow CH_3ONO \tag{X-10}$$

$$CH_3ONO + h\nu \rightarrow CH_3\dot{O}^* + NO \tag{X-11}$$

$$CH_3\dot{O}^* + O_2 \rightarrow H_2CO + HO\dot{O} \tag{X-12}$$

$$\left.\begin{array}{l} HO\dot{O} + C_4H_8 \rightarrow H_2CO + (CH_3)_2CO + H \qquad\qquad (\text{X-13})\\[4pt] H + O_2 \rightarrow HO\dot{O} \qquad\qquad (\text{X-14}) \end{array}\right\} \text{chain I}$$

$$\left.\begin{array}{l} HO\dot{O} + NO \rightarrow \dot{O}H + NO_2 \qquad\qquad (\text{X-15})\\[4pt] \dot{O}H + C_4H_8 \rightarrow (CH_3)_2CO + \dot{C}H_3 \qquad\qquad (\text{X-16})\\[4pt] \dot{C}H_3 + O_2 \rightarrow CH_3O\dot{O}, \text{etc, as above} \qquad (\text{X-8})\text{--}(\text{X-12}) \end{array}\right\} \text{chain II}$$

$$\left.\begin{array}{l} 2HO\dot{O} \rightarrow H_2O_2 + O_2 \qquad\qquad (\text{X-17})\\[4pt] 2\,\dot{O}H \rightarrow H_2 + O_2 \qquad\qquad (\text{X-18}) \end{array}\right\} \text{chain breaking}$$

$$\left.\begin{array}{l} \dot{O}H + H_2 \rightarrow H_2O + H \qquad\qquad\qquad (\text{X-19})\\[6pt] HO\dot{O} + H_2 \begin{array}{l} \nearrow H_2O + \dot{O}H \\[6pt] \searrow H_2O_2 + H \qquad (\text{X-20}) \end{array} \end{array}\right\} \text{effect of added H}_2$$

Most of these reactions have been discussed in earlier chapters, and all of them appear in the literature.[398] Either chain in the series might account for the excess rate of olefin removal, and chain II would also contribute to the conversion of nitric oxide to nitrogen dioxide and to ozone buildup. Both chains would account for the possible retarding effect of hydrogen, both yield rates proportional to the square root of light intensity, and both lead to formation of the principal observed carbonyl products, formaldehyde and acetone. The rapid consumption of olefin on photolysis of alkyl nitrite–olefin mixtures in air may be explained by reactions (X-11) and (X-12), followed by either chain I or II.

With other olefins the appropriate reactions may be substituted in the series. For example in the case of ethylene the reactions to be substituted would be

$$O + C_2H_4 \rightarrow \dot{C}H_3 + H\dot{C}O \qquad\qquad \text{(X-7a)}$$

$$H\dot{O}\dot{O} + C_2H_4 \rightarrow 2H_2CO + H \qquad\qquad \text{(X-13a)}$$

$$\dot{O}H + C_2H_4 \rightarrow H_2CO + \dot{C}H_3 \qquad\qquad \text{(X-16a)}$$

Again, these reactions account for the principal carbonyl product, in this case formaldehyde.

The series does not account for the formation of PAN or of carbon monoxide. Indeed, the fact that hydrogen does not retard the rate of PAN formation (Table 69) and the slow buildup of carbon monoxide (Fig. 51) suggest other processes for their formation. The reaction of acyl radicals with oxygen, and of the resulting peroxyacyl radicals with nitrogen diox-

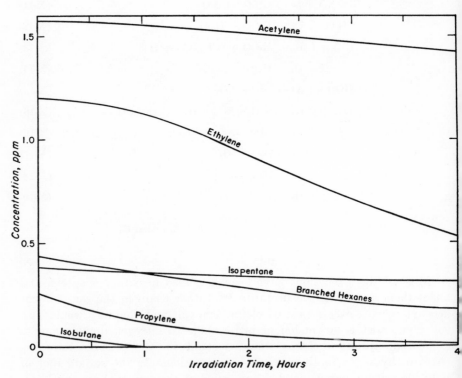

FIG. 56. Disappearance of certain hydrocarbons on irradiation of dilute automobile exhaust in air.

ide, has often been suggested for PAN formation, and this process appears to conform with all known data. Carbon monoxide may be formed by several processes, including the ozone–olefin reaction and the aldehyde photolysis.

Other series of reactions, equally competent to explain the data, may be postulated beginning with acyl or other radicals, and involving the intermediate photolyses of acyl nitrites or pernitrites rather than alkyl nitrites, and it is quite possible that several such series contribute to the over-all processes of ozone buildup and olefin consumption. It must be recognized, however, that these comments are speculative and that only by further experimental work will the mechanisms of these processes become established.

On irradiation of a mixture of hydrocarbons, such as in automobile exhaust, with nitric oxide or nitrogen dioxide in air, the different hydrocarbons are consumed at rates commensurate with their reactivity as measured singly, and the same general features are observed with regard to the nitric oxide–nitrogen dioxide conversion and the buildup of products. This is illustrated by Figs. 56 and 57, from Schuck et al.,[379] showing typical results obtained on irradiation of dilute automobile exhaust in air. A comparison of the two figures, and of the ozone producing capacity of the different hydrocarbons in Table 68 suggests that ethylene is responsible for a major part of the ozone buildup. On the other hand, ethylene

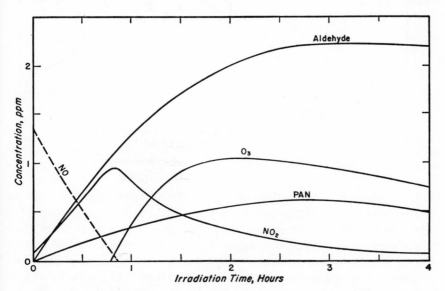

FIG. 57. Concentration changes in oxides of nitrogen and certain products on irradiation of dilute automobile exhaust in air.

produces little or no PAN, and the continued buildup in this product after the reactive olefins have disappeared, if true, is hard to explain.

2. Concentration Changes Produced by Irradiation of Polluted Air

It is well known that pollutant concentrations, measured at any specific point on any specific day, show quite erratic short-term fluctuations, and the same is true of solar radiation (Fig. 14). By taking averages over a number of days and if possible at a number of stations, these short-term fluctuations cancel out and the true diurnal variations become apparent. This is illustrated for oxidant concentrations at a specific station in Fig. 58. A complete evaluation of the reactions which occur would require

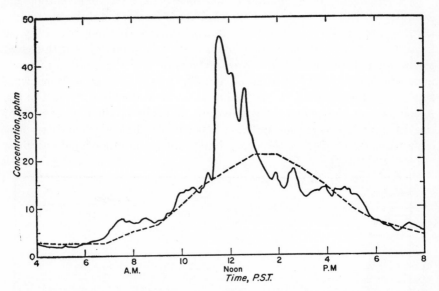

Fig. 58. Oxidant concentration on a single day, and averaged over a three month period at a specific station in Pasadena, California. Solid line is for Sept. 13, 1955; dashed line for Sept.–Nov., 1955.

that the short-term variations in concentration and light intensity be taken into account. In particular, they are important in determining the extent to which the concentrations of intermediates depart from their "stationary" concentrations (Chapter IV). For our present purposes, however, it is sufficient to consider concentrations only in terms of averages.

The averaged diurnal variations in concentration of a number of pollutants on days of eye irritation in Los Angeles are reproduced in Fig. 59. It will be noted that the data for nitric oxide and nitrogen dioxide were obtained during a different year, and hence are only qualitatively comparable with that for hydrocarbons, aldehydes, and ozone.

It is difficult, even with averages such as these, to distinguish between the effects due to photohcemical reactions and those due to such factors as the varying rate of contribution of pollutants to the atmosphere, air motion across the station, and changing ventilation rate. For these reasons, in order to evaluate the photochemical effects, it is necessary to rely on laboratory experiments, such as those described in the preceding

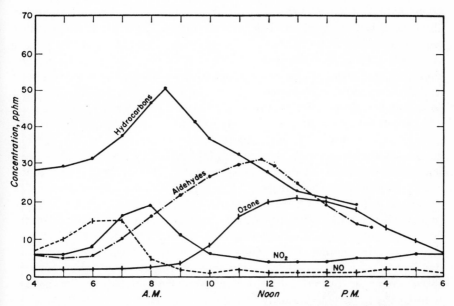

FIG. 59. Average concentrations during days of eye irritation in downtown Los Angeles. Hydrocarbons, aldehydes, and ozone for 1953–54. Nitric oxide and nitrogen dioxide for 1958. From data of the Los Angeles County Air Pollution Control District.

section, in which the variables of meteorology and human activity do not enter. Comparison of the concentration changes in such experiments with those in polluted air brings out some significant similarities as well as differences, but in making such a comparison the differences in conditions must be kept in mind. Thus, in the laboratory the reactants are generally introduced *in toto* before irradiation is commenced, and the irradiation starts at full intensity and remains at this intensity throughout the experiment; in outside air the reactants continue to be introduced at varying rates throughout the day, while the irradiation intensity increases throughout the morning and decreases throughout the afternoon.

In the air over urban areas subject to photochemical smog, generally the first change which occurs in the early morning is an increase in nitric oxide and hydrocarbon concentrations, due no doubt to the morning increase in automobile traffic. Shortly after sunrise a striking change sets in; the decrease of nitric oxide and increase in nitrogen dioxide. This process continues over a period of several hours, at the end of which the nitric oxide concentration has been reduced to a very low value and the ozone concentration starts to increase. This conversion of nitric oxide to nitrogen dioxide and the ensuing ozone buildup are undoubtedly brought about by the nitrogen oxide–hydrocarbon photolysis with olefins as the chief participants; a comparison of Figs. 50 and 59 is interesting in this regard.

These figures also disclose a marked difference, as irradiation continues, in the shape of the ozone concentration vs. time curves. Whereas in laboratory experiments such as shown in Figs. 50, 51, and 57, the ozone concentration drops off but slowly after passing its peak, in polluted air and sunlight it drops off almost as rapidly in the afternoon as it increases during the morning. This shape of the ozone curve, with a peak around noon or shortly after, is quite general and with minor variations has been reproduced whenever records have been taken. The difference is no doubt largely due to differences in conditions; fixed initial reactant concentrations and constant light intensity in the laboratory experiments; continued emission of pollutants which react with ozone accompanied by decreasing solar irradiance and improved ventilation during the afternoon in outside air. In fact, it has been shown[256,257] that for stations within the area in which the pollution originates or for averages taken over an entire area the diurnal variations in ozone concentration may be accounted for quite satisfactorily on this basis.

The midmorning peak in concentration of hydrocarbons may be assigned to the decrease in the rate of their contribution to the atmosphere after the morning traffic rush, combined with the increase in rate of their photochemical consumption with increasing solar irradiance. The gradual increase in concentration of aldehyde throughout the morning is probably due primarily to their production by the photochemical nitrogen oxide–olefin reaction. The rapid decrease in aldehyde concentration during the afternoon, shown on Fig. 59, like the rapid decrease in ozone concentration is not observed in the laboratory experiments of Figs. 50, 51, or 57. It is definitely too large to be accounted for by the aldehyde photolysis alone, and it appears likely that it is due to a combination of removal processes; direct photolysis, reactions with oxygen atoms, free radicals, ozone, and ventilation.

3. EYE IRRITANTS AND PHYTOTOXICANTS

A satisfactory understanding of the photochemistry of air pollution must include an understanding of the processes of formation of the substances responsible for its two major physiological effects, eye irritation and plant damage. With the exception of ozone the identification of these substances long eluded experimental attack, but now, due largely to the work of Stephens, Darley and their collaborators[94,401] and of Schuck and Doyle,[377] substantial progress has been made.

Through this work three specific eye irritants have been identified in photochemical smog, as well as in irradiated dilute automobile exhaust and in irradiated nitrogen oxide–olefin mixtures in air. These are formaldehyde, acrolein, and PAN.

The contribution of formaldehyde and acrolein to the observed eye irritation from irradiated dilute exhaust and nitrogen oxide–olefin mixtures has been evaluated by Schuck and Doyle, using an arbitrary index based on judgments of severity by a subjective panel. The irritation index from known concentrations of formaldehyde and acrolein was combined with the observed concentrations of these substances in each experiment to obtain a calculated index which could be compared with the observed value for that experiment. For nineteen olefins and exhausts from two fuels which gave significant irritation, the average ratio of calculated to observed indices was 0.83. At the time these experiments were conducted it was not known that PAN is also an eye irritant, and inclusion of its contribution would undoubtedly have raised the ratio to a value near unity; in any event the difference between the observed average and unity is not statistically significant.

It appears to be established, therefore, that formaldehyde, acrolein, and PAN account for most if not all of the eye irritation obtained from laboratory irradiation of nitrogen oxide–olefin mixtures and of automobile exhaust in air, with formaldehyde and acrolein as the major contributors.

In outside air, on the other hand, this has not been established. With the panel method used by Schuck and Doyle, the subjects were seated in booths outside the irradiation chamber. Each subject wore a loosely fitting Plexiglas helmet or shield to which the irradiated mixture was piped in such a manner that it flowed slowly downward across the eyes, but could not be breathed. Under these conditions the threshold concentrations required for significant irritation were about 1 ppm for formaldehyde and 0.4 ppm for acrolein. In experiments using a comparable subjective panel, Stephens, Darley, Taylor, and Scott[401] have obtained threshold values, for significant irritation in 5-min exposures, of 1 ppm for formaldehyde, less than 0.5 ppm for acrolein, and 2 ppm for PAN. The concentrations attained by these substances in photochemical smog are not well known, but are almost certainly below these thresholds, even during periods of severe eye irritation. Moreover, with this method of evaluation the concentrations of nitrogen oxides and olefins required to yield severe irritation were around an order of magnitude larger than those attained in outside air.

Renzetti and Schuck[354] have found that moving the subjects from separate booths to eyeports attached directly to the irradiation chamber, but shielded from the radiation, resulted in a doubling of the reported indices from irradiated nitrogen dioxide–olefin mixtures as well as a doubling of the index and halving of the threshold for known concentrations of formaldehyde, even in the dark. Even with this improvement in response, however, 1 ppm of formaldehyde still yielded only light to medium eye irritation and reactant concentrations several times those in outside air were still required to obtain comparable irritation. Another apparent discrepancy between the laboratory and outside air is in the response time. In the laboratory panel methods the thresholds decrease with time of exposure of the eyes to the air being tested and exposures of 5 min or more are often required to detect irritation, whereas in outside air it is common experience that irritation appears to occur almost immediately.

The next task, obviously, is to account for these discrepancies. They may be subjective, they may be due to differences in conditions such as the continued introduction of reactants in outside air as compared to their fixed initial introduction in the chamber experiments, they may be due to as yet unknown irritants in outside air, or they may be the resultant of some combination of these factors. The human eye is at best a capricious instrument and its use in the evaluation of irritation is subject to complex physiological and psychological variables which are little understood; the improvement in response in moving the subjects from booths to eyeports is an illustration of this. Until these matters are settled it cannot be assumed that formaldehyde, acrolein, and PAN are the only photochemically produced eye irritants in polluted air. Other possibilities which have been suggested include free radicals,[227] nitroolefins (Chapter VII), and the transmission of irritants to the eye by particulate matter.

The work of Darley, Stephens, Middleton, and Hanst,[94] and of Stephens, Darley, Taylor, and Scott[401] has disclosed three phytotoxicants, or classes of phytotoxicants, which are formed both in photochemical smog and in irradiated nitrogen dioxide–olefin mixtures in air. The first is ozone itself, which produces a mottling or bleaching of the upper surfaces of plant leaves. The other two produce a glazing or bronzing of the under surfaces of leaves, and are distinguished by the age or types of leaves affected and by the methods or reactions through which they are produced.

Based on their effects on the leaves of young Pinto bean plants, the sources of these two classes of phytotoxicants observed by Stephens, Darley, Taylor, and Scott are:

Class A. Damage to 7 to 8-day old Pinto bean leaves but not to 14-day old leaves. Produced by:

1. Irradiation of mixtures of nitrogen dioxide and olefins in air. Long lived.

2. Irradiation of automobile exhaust in air.

3. Irradiation of mixtures of ozone with 1-pentene, 1-hexene, and 3-heptene, but not with *cis*-2-butene, in air.

4. Irradiation of butyraldehyde and propionaldehyde, but little with acetaldehyde, and none with formaldehyde, in air.

5. Irradiation of nitrogen dioxide–*n*-hexane–air mixtures with light of short wavelengths (λ 2537 and 1849 A).

Class B. Damage to 14-day old Pinto bean leaves, but not to 7 to 8-day old leaves. Produced by the dark reaction of ozone with olefins containing a chain of 3 or more carbon atoms on one side of the double bond. Short lived; the half-life of the toxicant from ozone + 2-pentene was 3 min, that from ozone + 3-heptene was 15 min.[14]

Darley, Stephens, and their co-workers[94,401] have investigated a number of individual compounds which might be responsible for these effects, with the result that PAN has been demonstrated to be a class A phytotoxicant. Exposure for 5 hr to concentrations of 0.1 ppm of the purified acetyl member of the PAN series (Chapter III) caused moderate damage on 8-day old Pinto bean leaves and severe damage on petunia leaves; it was indistinguishable from the damage caused by the photolyses of nitrogen dioxide–olefin mixtures and dilute automobile exhaust, as well as from much of the damage caused by polluted ambient air. However, the fact that damage in the class A category was observed from irradiated aldehyde–air and ozone–olefin–air mixtures, in which no oxides of nitrogen were present, indicates that PAN is not the only photochemically produced phytotoxicant in this class.

Hydrogen peroxide at high concentrations, and acrolein at concentrations of ~2 ppm have been found to produce class B injury. Ozonides, organic acids, including formic acid, aldehydes, and peroxyacetic acid were found either to be nontoxic or to produce atypical injury. A zwitterion or an ozone–olefin complex have been suggested as the class B phytotoxicant produced by ozone–olefin reactions; this possibility has already been discussed (Chapter VI).

The production of a class A phytotoxicant by the irradiation of ozone–olefin mixtures and of aldehydes in air deserves some comment. The olefins which produced this effect yield aldehydes with chains of three or more carbon atoms on reaction with ozone, and it was precisely these aldehydes, propionaldehyde and butyraldehyde (valeraldehyde, a product of the ozone–1-hexene reaction, was not investigated) which gave the greatest class A damage on irradiation. It may be concluded that the effect in both cases was the result of the aldehyde photolysis in air. The products of the photooxidation of propionaldehyde and butyraldehyde have not been determined, but by analogy with acetaldehyde[69] they would be expected to include three or four carbon atom peroxy acids, the toxic effects of which have not yet been determined.

The major products of the photooxidation of acetaldehyde, which produced little class A effect, include methanol, formic acid, and peroxyacetic acid. Darley, Stephens, and co-workers have found formic acid to be nontoxic, while peroxyacetic acid produced atypical damage. This explains the absence of class A damage from irradiated mixtures of ozone with cis-2-butene, as the only aldehyde produced from their dark reaction is acetaldehyde. The absence of class B damage from the thermal ozone–olefin reaction using ethylene, propylene, or cis-2-butene suggests that whatever the class B toxicant is, here also a chain of three or more carbon atoms is necessary for it to be effective.

4. SUMMARY

It has been established that all of the major photochemical products, all of the photochemically produced eye irritants and phytotoxicants which have thus far been identified, and probably a major share of the photochemically originated organic particulates (Chapter IX) in photochemical smog are due to the nitrogen dioxide–olefin photolysis and the reactions which follow. Although much remains to be disclosed concerning the details of this immensely complicated process, there is no longer any doubt but that removal of the oxides of nitrogen and the olefins from polluted air, by proper control of their sources, will eliminate this unwelcome by-product of present day civilization.

References

1. Abbot, C. G.; *Smithsonian Ser.,* **2,** 116 (1949).
2. Abbot, C. G., and Aldrich, L. B.; *Ann. Astrophys. Observatory Smithsonian Inst.,* **3,** 21, 73 (1913); **4,** 99 (1922).
3. Abbott, C. G., Aldrich, L. B., and Fowle, F. E.; *Ann. Astrophys. Observatory Smithsonian Inst.,* **5,** 103, 133 (1932).
4. Abbot, C. G., Aldrich, L. B., and Hoover, W. H.; *Ann. Astrophys. Observatory Smithsonian Inst.,* **6,** 83 (1942).
5. Abbot, C. G., and Fowle, F. E.; *Ann. Astrophys. Observatory Smithsonian Inst.,* **2,** 21, 83 (1908).
6. Akeroyd, E. I., and Norrish, R. G. W.; *J. Chem. Soc.,* p. 890 (1939).
7. Almasy, F.; *J. chim. phys.,* **30,** 528 (1932).
8. Almy, G. M., and Anderson, S.; *J. Chem. Phys.,* **8,** 205 (1940).
9. Almy, G. M., Fuller, H. Q., and Kinzer, G. D.; *J. Chem. Phys.,* **8,** 37 (1940).
10. Almy, G. M., and Gillette, P. R.; *J. Chem. Phys.,* **11,** 188 (1943).
11. Anderson, H. W., and Rollefson, G. K.; *J. Am. Chem. Soc.,* **63,** 816 (1941).
12. Angström, A.; "Actinometric Measurements," Compendium of Meteorology; Am. Meteorol. Soc., Boston, Massachusetts, 1951, p. 50.
13. Arnell, A. R., and Daniels, F.; *J. Am. Chem. Soc.,* **74,** 629 (1952).
14. Arnold, N. N.; *Intern. J. Air Pollution,* **2,** 167 (1959).
15. Avramenko, L. E., Joffee, E. E., and Lorentso, P. V.; *Doklady Akad. Nauk S.S.S.R.,* **66,** 1111 (1949).
16. Avramenko, L. E., and Lorentso, P. V.; *Doklady Akad. Nauk S.S.S.R.,* **67,** 867 (1949).
17. Bäckström, H. L. J.; *Z. physik. Chem.,* **B25,** 99 (1934).
18. Badin, E. J.; *J. Am. Chem. Soc.,* **70,** 3651 (1948).
19. Bailey, P. S.; *Chem. Revs.,* **58,** 925 (1958).
20. Bateman, L., and Gee, G.; *Proc. Roy. Soc.,* **A195,** 376 (1949).
21. Bates, D. R.; "The Earth as a Planet" (G. P. Kuiper, ed.) University of Chicago Press, Chicago, Illinois, 1954, p. 586.
22. Bates, J. R.; *J. Chem. Phys.,* **1,** 457 (1933).
23. Baur, E.; *Helv. Chim. Acta* **1,** 186 (1918).
24. Baur, E., and Neuweiler, G., *Helv. Chim. Acta* **10,** 901 (1927).
25. Baur, E., and Perret, A.; *J. chim. phys.,* **23,** 97 (1927); *Helv. Chim. Acta* **7,** 910 (1924).
26. Baxter, W. P.; *J. Am. Chem. Soc.,* **52,** 3920 (1930).
27. Beeck, O., and Rust, F. F.; *J. Chem. Phys.,* **9,** 480 (1941).
28. Bell, E. R., Raley, J. H., Rust, F. F., Seubold, F. H., and Vaughan, W. E.; *Discussions Faraday Soc.,* **10,** 242 (1951).
29. Bell, W. E., and Blacet, F. E.; *J. Am. Chem. Soc.,* **76,** 5332 (1954).
30. Benson, S. W., and Axworthy, A. E., Jr.; *J. Chem. Phys.,* **26,** 1718 (1957).
31. Benson, S. W., and Forbes, G. S.; *J. Am. Chem. Soc.,* **65,** 1399 (1943).
32. Beretta, V., and Schumacher, H. J.; *Z. physik. Chem.,* **B17,** 417 (1932).
33. Bickel, A. F., and Koogman, E. C.; *J. Chem. Soc.,* p. 2215 (1956).
34. Blacet, F. E.; *J. Phys. & Colloid Chem.,* **52,** 534 (1948); *Ind. Eng. Chem.,* **44,** 1339 (1952).
35. Blacet, F. E., and Bell, W. E.; *Discussions Faraday Soc.,* **14,** 70 (1953).

36. Blacet, F. E., and Blaedel, W. J.; *J. Am. Chem. Soc.*, **62**, 3374 (1940).
37. Blacet, F. E., and Calvert, J. G.; *J. Am. Chem. Soc.*, **73**, 661, 667 (1951).
38. Blacet, F. E., Fielding, G. H., and Roof, J. G.; *J. Am. Chem. Soc.*, **59**, 2375 (1937).
39. Blacet, F. E., and Heldman, J. D.; *J. Am. Chem. Soc.*, **64**, 889 (1942).
40. Blacet, F. E., and LuValle, J. E.; *J. Am. Chem. Soc.*, **61**, 273 (1939).
41. Blacet, F. E., and Moulton, R. W.; *J. Am. Chem. Soc.*, **63**, 868 (1941).
42. Blacet, F. E., and Pitts, J. N., Jr.; *J. Am. Chem. Soc.*, **74**, 3382 (1952).
43. Blacet, F. E., and Roof, J. G.; *J. Am. Chem. Soc.*, **58**, 73 (1936).
44. Blacet, F. E., and Volman, D. H.; *J. Am. Chem. Soc.*, **61**, 582 (1939).
45. Blaedel, W. J., Ogg, R. A., Jr., and Leighton, P. A.; *J. Am. Chem. Soc.*, **64**, 2499, 2500 (1942).
46. Blake, A. R., and Kutschke, K. O.; *Can. J. Chem.*, **37**, 1462 (1959).
47. Bodenstein, M.; *Z. angew. Chem.*, **31**, 145 (1918); *Z. Elektrochem.*, **24**, 183 (1918); *Z. physik. Chem.*, **100**, 68 (1922).
48. Bodenstein, M., and Schenk, P. W.; *Z. physik. Chem.*, **B20**, 420 (1933).
49. Bowen, E. M., and Tietz, E. L.; *J. Chem. Soc.*, p. 234 (1940).
50. Briner, E., and Meier, R.; *Helv. Chim. Acta*, **12**, 529 (1929).
51. Briner, E., Pfeiffer, W., and Malet, G.; *J. chim. phys.*, **21**, 25 (1924).
52. Briner, E., and Schnorf, P.; *Helv. Chim. Acta*, **12**, 154, 181 (1929).
53. Briner, E., Susz, B., and Dallwigk, E.; *Compt. rend. acad. sci.*, **234**, 1932 (1952); *Helv. Chim. Acta*, **35**, 353 (1952).
54. Briner, E., and Wunenburger, R.; *Helv. Chim. Acta*, **12**, 786 (1929).
55. Brinton, R. K., and Volman, D. H.; *J. Chem. Phys.*, **20**, 1053 (1952).
56. Broadwell, S. J.; private communication, Los Angeles County Air Pollution Control District (1960).
57. Brown, F. B., and Crist, R. H.; *J. Chem. Phys.*, **9**, 840 (1941).
58. Brown, H. W., and Pimentel, G. C.; *J. Chem. Phys.*, **29**, 883 (1958).
59. Brown, J. F., Jr.; *J. Am. Chem. Soc.*, **79**, 2480 (1947).
60. Buckley, R. P., Leavitt, F., and Szwarc, M.; *J. Am. Chem. Soc.*, **78**, 5557 (1956).
61. Burnett, G. M., and Melville, H. W.; *Chem. Revs.*, **54**, 225 (1954).
62. Cadle, R. D.; "Conference on Chemical Reactions in Urban Atmospheres," Rept. No. 15, Air Pollution Foundation, Los Angeles, California, 1956, p. 27.
63. Cadle, R. D., Eastman, R. H., Littman, F. E., and Benedict, H. M.; *Interim Tech. Rept. Jan. 1, 1952 to July 1, 1952*, Project C-466, Stanford Research Institute, Stanford, California (1952).
64. Cadle, R. D., and Johnston, H. S.; *Proc. Natl. Air Pollution Symposium, 2nd Symposium, Pasadena Calif., 1952*, p. 28.
65. Cadle, R. D., Littman, F. E., Eastman, R. H., and Silverstein, R. M.; *Interim Tech. Rept. July 1, 1951 to Jan. 1, 1952*, Project C-466, Stanford Research Institute, Stanford, California (1952).
66. Cadle, R. D., and Schadt, C.; *J. Am. Chem. Soc.*, **74**, 6002 (1952); *J. Chem. Phys.*, **21**, 163 (1953).
67. Callear, A. B., and Robb, J. C.; *Trans. Faraday Soc.*, **51**, 649 (1955).
68. Calvert, J. C.; "Conference on Chemical Reactions in Urban Atmospheres," Rept. No. 15, Air Pollution Foundation, Los Angeles, California, 1956, p. 91.
69. Calvert, J. G., and Hanst, P. L.; *Can. J. Chem.*, **37**, 1671 (1959).
70. Calvert, J. G., and Layne, G. S.; *J. Am. Chem. Soc.*, **75**, 856 (1953).
71. Calvert, J. G., Pitts, J. N., Jr., and Thompson, D. D.; *J. Am. Chem. Soc.*, **78**, 4239 (1956).

72. Calvert, J. G., and Steacie, E. W. R.; *J. Chem. Phys.,* **19,** 176 (1951).
73. Calvert, J. G., Theurer, K., Rankin, G. T., and MacNevin, W. M.; *J. Am. Chem. Soc.,* **76,** 2575 (1954).
74. Chamberlain, G. H. N., Hoare, D. E., and Walsh, A. D.; *Discussions Faraday Soc.,* **14,** 89 (1953).
75. Childs, W. H. J., and Mecke, R.; *Z. Physik,* **68,** 344 (1931).
76. Childs, W. H. J., and Mecke, R.; *Z. Physik,* **68,** 344 (1931).
77. Chilton, H. T. J., and Gowenlock, B. J.; *Nature,* **172,** 73 (1953).
78. Christie, M. I.; *Proc. Roy. Soc.,* **A244,** 411 (1958).
79. Christie, M. I., Harrison, A. J., Norrish, R. G. W., and Porter, G.; *Proc. Roy. Soc.,* **A231,** 446 (1955).
80. Coblentz, W. W., and Stair, R.; *J. Research Natl. Bur. Standards,* **15,** 123 (1935); **16,** 315 (1936); **30,** 435 (1943); **33,** 21 (1944).
81. Coe, C. W., and Doumani, T. F.; *J. Am. Chem. Soc.,* **70,** 1516 (1948).
82. Colange, G.; *J. phys. radium,* **8,** 256 (1927).
83. Coward, N. A., and Noyes, W. A., Jr.; *J. Chem. Phys.,* **22,** 1207 (1954).
84. Cretien, P. D., and Boh, G.; *Compt. rend. acad. sci.,* **220,** 822 (1945).
85. Criegee, R., Blust, G., and Zinke, H.; *Chem. Ber.,* **87,** 766 (1954).
86. Cullis, C. F., and Hinshelwood, C. N.; *Discussions Faraday Soc.,* **2,** 117 (1947).
87. Cvetanović, R. J.; *J. Chem. Phys.,* **23,** 1375 (1955); **25,** 376 (1956).
88. Cvetanović, R. J.; *Can. J. Chem.,* **33,** 1684 (1955); **36,** 623 (1958).
89. Cvetanović, R. J.; *J. Chem. Phys.,* **30,** 19 (1959).
90. Dainton, F. S., and Ivin, K. J.; *Trans. Faraday Soc.,* **46,** 374, 382 (1950).
91. Dalby, F. W.; *Can. J. Phys.,* **36,** 1336 (1958).
92. Dalmon, R.; *Mém. serv. chim. état,* **30,** 141 (1943).
93. Danby, C. J., and Hinshelwood, C. N.; *Proc. Roy. Soc.,* **A179,** 139 (1931).
94. Darley, E. F., Stephens, E. R., Middleton, J. T., and Hanst, P. L.; *Intern. J. Air Pollution,* **1,** 155 (1959).
95. Davidson, N., and Schott, G. L.; *J. Chem. Phys.,* **27,** 317 (1957).
96. Davis, W., Jr.; *Chem. Revs.,* **40,** 201 (1947).
97. Davis, W., Jr.; *J. Am. Chem. Soc.,* **70,** 1867, 1868 (1948).
98. Davis, W., Jr., and Noyes, W. A., Jr.; *J. Am. Chem. Soc.,* **69,** 2513 (1947).
99. Deichmann, W. B., Keplinger, M. L., and Lanier, G. E.; *A.M.A. Arch. Ind. Health,* **18** (4), 312 (1958).
100. Deirmendjian, D., and Sekera, Z.; *Tellus,* **6,** 382 (1954).
101. Dickinson, R. G., and Baxter, W. P.; *J. Am. Chem. Soc.,* **50,** 774 (1928).
102. Dieke, G. H., and Babcock, H. D.; *Proc. Natl. Acad. Sci. U.S.,* **13,** 670 (1927).
103. Dixon, J. K.; *J. Chem. Phys.,* **8,** 157 (1940).
104. Dobson, G. M. B.; *Proc. Roy. Soc.,* **A129,** 411 (1930).
105. Dorfman, L. M., and Noyes, W. A., Jr.; *J. Chem. Phys.,* **16,** 557 (1948).
106. Dorfman, L. M., and Salsburg, Z. W.; *J. Am. Chem. Soc.,* **73,** 255 (1951).
107. Doyle, G. J., and Renzetti, N. A.; *J. Air Pollution Control Assoc.,* **8,** 23 (1958).
108. Duncan, A. B. F., Ells, V. R., and Noyes, W. A., Jr.; *J. Am. Chem. Soc.,* **58,** 1454 (1936).
109. Dunkelman, L, and Scolnik, R.; *J. Opt. Soc. Am.,* **49,** 356 (1959).
110. Durham, R. W., and Steacie, E. W. R.; *J. Chem. Phys.,* **20,** 582 (1952).
111. Durham, R. W., and Steacie, E. W. R.; *Can. J. Chem,* **31,** 377 (1953).
112. Eastman, R. H., and Silverstein, R. M.; *J. Am. Chem. Soc.,* **75,** 1493 (1953).
113. Eibner, A.; *Chem. Zeitung,* **35,** 786 (1911).
114. Elias, L., Ogryzlo, E. A., and Schiff, H. I.; *Can. J. Chem.,* **37,** 1680 (1959).

115. Ells, V. R., and Noyes, W. A., Jr.; *J. Am. Chem. Soc.*, **61**, 2492 (1939).
116. Erlenmeyer, H., and Schoenaur, W.; *Helv. Chim. Acta*, **19**, 338 (1936).
117. Eucken, A.; *Z. physik. Chem.*, **107**, 436 (1923).
118. Evans, M. G., and Uri, N.; *Trans. Faraday Soc.*, **45**, 224 (1949).
119. Everett, A. J., and Minkoff, G. J.; *Symposium on Combustion, 3rd Symposium, Madison, Wisconsin, 1948*, p. 390 (1949).
120. Fabry, C.; *Proc. Phys. Soc. (London)*, **39**, 1 (1926).
121. Fabry, C., and Buisson, H.; *J. phys., Paris*, **3**, 196 (1913).
122. Fabry, C., and Buisson, H.; *Compt. rend. acad. sci.*, **192**, 457 (1931).
123. Faith, W. L.; "Combustion and Smog," Rept. No. 2, Air Pollution Foundation, Los Angeles, California (1954).
124. Faith, W. L., Hitchcock, L. B., Neiburger, M., Renzetti, N. A., and Rogers, L. H.; Second Technical Progress Report, Rept. No. 12, Air Pollution Foundation, Los Angeles, California (1955).
125. Faith, W. L., Renzetti, N. A., and Rogers, L. H.; Third Technical Progress Report, Rept. No. 17, Air Pollution Foundation, Los Angeles, California (1957).
126. Faith, W. L., Renzetti, N. A., and Rogers, L. H.; Fourth Technical Progress Report, Rept. No. 22, Air Pollution Foundation, San Marino, California (1958).
127. Falk, R., and Pease, R. N.; *J. Am. Chem. Soc.*, **76**, 4746 (1954).
128. Farkas, L., and Sachsse, H.; *Z. physik. Chem.*, **B27**, 111 (1935).
129. Fischer, F. G., Dill, H., and Volz, J. L.; *Ann. Chem. Liebigs*, **486**, 80 (1931).
130. Foizik, L., and Reichamt, O. R.; *Wetterdienst, Wiss. Abb., Berlin*, **4** No. 5 (1938).
131. Fok, N. V., and Nalbandyan, A. B.; *Doklady Akad. Nauk S.S.S.R.*, **86**, 589 (1952); **89**, 125 (1953); *Voprosy Khim. Kinetiki, Kataliza, i Reaktsionnoi Sposobnosti; Akad. Nauk S.S.S.R., Otedel. Khim. Nauk*, p. 219 (1955).
132. Ford, Hadley W.; Tech. Rept. No. X, Project C-1388, Stanford Research Institute, Stanford, California (1955).
133. Ford, H. W.; "An Experimental Study of Oxidants and Organics in Urban Atmospheres," Tech. Repts. Nos. XI, XII, XIII, Project S-1388, Stanford Research Institute, Stanford, California (1956).
134. Ford, H. W., Progress Rept. 20-393, Jet Propulsion Laboratory, Inst. of Technology, Pasadena, California (1960); *Can. J. Chem.*, **38**, 1780 (1960).
135. Ford, H. W., Doyle, G. J., and Endow, N.; *J. Chem. Phys.*, **26**, 1336, 1337 (1957).
136. Ford, H. W., and Endow, H.; *J. Chem. Phys.*, **27**, 1156, 1277 (1957).
137. Forsyth, J. S. A.; *Trans. Faraday Soc.*, **37**, 312 (1941).
138. Forsythe, W. E.; "Smithsonian Physical Tables," 9th ed., rev., Smithsonian Institution, Washington, 1954, p. 720.
139. Fowle, F. E.; *Monthly Weather Rev.*, **42**, 2 (1914); *Astrophys. J.*, **40**, 435 (1914); *Smithsonian Misc. Collections*, **69**, No. 3 (1918).
140. Fowle, F. E.; *Trans. Illum. Eng. Soc., N.Y.*, **30**, 273 (1935).
141. Fritz, S.; "Solar Radiant Energy and its Modification by the Earth and its Atmosphere," Compendium of Meteorology, Am. Meteorol. Soc., Boston, Massachusetts, 1951, p. 13.
142. Fritz, S.; *J. Opt. Soc. Am.*, **45**, 820 (1955).
143. Fritz, S.; *Sci. Monthly*, **84**, 55 (1957).
144. Fulweiler, W. H.; *Am. Gas. Assoc. Proc.*, **15**, 829 (1933).
145. Fulweiler, W. H.; *Am. Gas J.*, p. 27 (June 1935).

146. Gachkovskii, V., and Terenin, A.; *Bull. acad. sci., U.R.S.S., Classe sci. math. nat., Sér. chim.,* p. 805 (1936).

147. Garvin, D.; *J. Am. Chem. Soc.,* **76,** 1523 (1954).

148. Gaydon, A. G.; *Proc. Roy. Soc.,* **A183,** 111 (1944); *Trans. Faraday Soc.,* **42,** 292 (1946).

149. Geib, K. H., and Harteck, P.; *Ber.,* **66B,** 1815 (1933).

150. Geib, K. H., and Harteck, P.; *Z. physik. Chem.,* **A170,** 1 (1934).

151. Geiger, R.; "The Climate Near the Ground," Harvard University Press, Cambridge, Massachusetts, 1950, p. 219.

152. Gerhard, E. R., and Johnstone, H. F.; *Ind. Eng. Chem.,* **47,** 972 (1955).

153. Giauque, W. F., and Johnston, H. L.; *J. Am. Chem. Soc.,* **51,** 1436, 3528 (1929).

154. Giauque, W. F., and Kemp, J. D.; *J. Chem. Phys.,* **6,** 40 (1939).

155. Glissman, A., and Schumacher, H. J.; *Z. physik. Chem.,* **21B,** 323 (1933).

156. Glueckauf, E.; "The Composition of Atmospheric Air, Compendium of Meteorology, Am. Meteorol. Soc., Boston, Massachusetts, 1951, p. 3.

157. Goetz, F. W. P., Meehan, A. R., and Dobson, G. M. B.; *Proc. Roy. Soc.,* **A145,** 416 (1934).

158. Gomer, R., and Kistiakowsky, G. B.; *J. Chem. Phys.,* **19,** 85 (1951).

159. Gomer, R., and Noyes, W. A., Jr.; *J. Am. Chem. Soc.,* **72,** 101 (1950).

160. Goodeve, C. F.; *Trans. Faraday Soc.,* **33,** 340 (1937).

161. Goodeve, J. W.; *Trans. Faraday Soc.,* **30,** 504 (1934).

162. Gorin, E.; *Acta Physicochim. U.R.S.S.,* **8,** 513 (1938); **9,** 681 (1938); *J. Chem. Phys.,* **7,** 256 (1939).

163. Gray, J. A.; *J. Chem. Soc.,* p. 3150 (1952).

164. Gray, J. A.; *J. Chem. Soc.,* p. 741 (1953).

165. Gray, J. A., and Style, D. W. G.; *Trans. Faraday Soc.,* **48,** 1137 (1952); **49,** 52 (1953).

166. Gray, P.; *Trans. Faraday Soc.,* **51,** 1367 (1955).

167. Gray, P., and Yoffee, A. D.; *Chem. Revs.,* **55,** 1069 (1955).

168. Greaves, J. C., and Garvin, D.; *J. Chem. Phys.,* **30,** 348 (1959).

169. Groh, H. J., Jr.; *J. Chem. Phys.,* **21,** 674 (1953).

170. Groh, H. J., Jr., Luckey, G. W., and Noyes, W. A., Jr.; *J. Chem. Phys.,* **21,** 115 (1953).

171. Groth, W. E., and Schierholz, H.; *J. Chem. Phys.,* **26,** 973 (1957).

172. Haagen-Smit, A. J.; *Ind. Eng. Chem.,* **44,** 1342 (1952).

173. Haagen-Smit, A. J.; *Ind. Eng. Chem.,* **48,** 65A (Dec. 1956).

174. Haagen-Smit, A. J., Bradley, C. E., and Fox, M. M.; *Ind. Eng. Chem.,* **45,** 2086 (1953).

175. Haagen-Smit, A. J., and Fox, M. M.; *Air Repair,* **4,** 105 (1954); *S. A. E. Trans.,* **63,** 575 (1955).

176. Haagen-Smit, A. J., and Fox, M. M.; *Ind. Eng. Chem.,* **48,** 1484 (1956).

177. Hall, T. C., Jr.; "Photochemical Studies of Nitrogen Dioxide and Sulfur Dioxide," Doctoral Thesis, University of California, Los Angeles (1953).

178. Hall, T. C., Jr., and Blacet, F. E.; *J. Chem. Phys.,* **20,** 1745 (1952).

179. Hanst, P. L., and Calvert, J. G.; paper presented at the *133rd Meeting of Am. Chem. Soc., San Francisco,* April 14, 1958; *J. Phys. Chem.,* **63,** 71, 2071 (1959).

180. Hanst, P. L., and Stephens, E. R.; *Interim Repts. I-2372-1, 2, 3, 5,* Project SF-7, The Franklin Institute, Philadelphia, Pennsylvania (1954–55).

181. Hanst, P. L., and Stephens, E. R.; *Interim Repts. I-2373-4, 5,* Project SF-6, The Franklin Institute, Philadelphia, Pennsylvania (1954–55).

182. Hanst, P. L., and Stephens, E. R.; Interim Rept. I-2495-1, Project SF-8, The Franklin Institute, Philadelphia, Pennsylvania (1955).

183. Hanst, P. L., Stephens, E. R., and Scott, W. E.; *Proc. Am. Petrol. Inst.*, 35, III, 175 (1955).

184. Hanst, P. L., Stephens, E. R., Scott, W. E., and Doerr, R. C.; "Atmospheric Ozone-Olefin Reactions," The Franklin Institute, Philadelphia, Pennsylvania (1958).

185. Harteck, P.; *Trans. Faraday Soc.*, 30, 134 (1934).

186. Harteck, P., and Kopsch, V.; *Z. Elektrochem.*, 36, 714 (1930); *Z. physik. Chem.*, B12, 327 (1931).

187. Harteck, P., Reeves, R. R., and Mannella, G.; *J. Chem. Phys.*, 29, 1333 (1958).

188. Haurwitz, B.; *J. Meteorol.*, 5, 110 (1948).

189. Hautefeuille, P., and Chappuis, J.; *Compt. rend. acad. sci.*, 92, 80 (1881); 94, 1111, 1302 (1882).

190. Heidt, L. J.; *J. Am. Chem. Soc.*, 57, 1710 (1935).

191. Henri, V.; "Etudes de photochemie," Gautier-Villars, Paris, 1919.

192. Henri, V., and Schou, S. A.; *Z. Physik*, 49, 774 (1928).

193. Herr, D. S., and Noyes, W. A., Jr.; *J. Am. Chem. Soc.*, 62, 1052 (1940).

194. Herron, J. T., and Schiff, H. I.; *Can. J. Chem.*, 36, 1159 (1958).

195. Herzberg, G.; *Trans. Faraday Soc.*, 27, 378 (1931).

196. Herzberg, G.; "Molecular Spectra and Molecular Structure," Van Nostrand, New York, 1950.

197. Herzberg, G., and Franz, K.; *Z. Physik*, 76, 720 (1932).

198. Herzberg, G., and Ramsay, D. A.; *Proc. Roy. Soc.*, A233, 34 (1955).

199. Hisatsune, I. C., Crawford, Bryce, Jr., and Ogg, R. A., Jr.; *J. Am. Chem. Soc.*, 79, 4648 (1957).

200. Hoare, D. E.; *Trans. Faraday Soc.*, 53, 791 (1957).

201. Hoare, D. E., and Walsh, A. D.; *Trans. Faraday Soc.*, 53, 1102 (1957).

202. Hoey, G. R., and Kutschke, K. O.; *Can. J. Chem.*, 33, 496 (1955).

203. Holmes, H. H., and Daniels, F.; *J. Am. Chem. Soc.*, 56, 630 (1934).

204. Holt, R. B., McLane, C. K., and Oldenberg, O.; *J. Chem. Phys.*, 16, 225 (1948).

205. Horner, E. C. A., Style, D. W. G., and Summers, D.; *Trans. Faraday Soc.*, 50, 1201 (1954).

206. Houghton, H. G., and Chalker, W. R.; *J. Opt. Soc. Am.*, 39, 955 (1949).

207. Hulburt, E. O.; *J. Opt. Soc. Am.*, 31, 467 (1941).

208. Hulburt, E. O.; *J. Opt. Soc. Am.*, 37, 405 (1947).

209. Hull, J. N., *Trans. Illum. Eng. Soc.*, N.Y., 19, 21 (1954).

210. Hunt, R. E., and Noyes, W. A., Jr.; *J. Am. Chem. Soc.*, 70, 467 (1948).

211. Hurn, R. W.; Progr. Rept., Bur. Mines Air Pollution Control Projects (1958).

212. Ingold, C. K.; "Structure and Mechanism in Organic Chemistry," Cornell University Press, Ithaca, New York, 1953, p. 649.

213. Ingold, K. U., and Bryce, W. A.; *J. Chem. Phys.*, 24, 360 (1956).

214. Ingold, K. U., and Lossing, F. P.; *J. Chem. Phys.*, 21, 1135 (1953).

215. Inn, E. C. Y., and Tanaka, Y.; *J. Opt. Soc. Am.*, 43, 870 (1953).

216. Ives, J. E.; *Public Health Bull.*, *Washington, D.C.*, No. 224 (1936).

217. Ivin, K. J., and Steacie, E. W. R.; *Proc. Roy. Soc.*, A208, 25 (1951).

218. Jackson, W. F.; *J. Am. Chem. Soc.*, 56, 2631 (1934).

219. Jaquiss, M. T., Roberts, J. S., and M. Szwarc; *J. Am. Chem. Soc.*, 74, 6005 (1952).

220. Jarvie, J. M. S., and Cvetanović, R. J.; *Can. J. Chem.*, 37, 529 (1959).

221. Johnson, F. S.; *J. Meteorol.*, **11**, 431 (1954).
222. Johnson, F. S.; *Proc. Toronto Meteorol. Conf.*, **1953**, 17 (1954).
223. Johnson, F. S., Purcell, J. D., and R. Tousey; *J. Geophys. Research*, **56**, 583 (1951).
224. Johnson, F. S., Purcell, J. D., Tousey, R., and Watanabe, K.; *J. Geophys. Research*, **57**, 157 (1952).
225. Johnson, F. S., Purcell, J. D., Tousey, R., and Wilson, N.; "Rocket Exploration of the Upper Atmosphere," Pergamon, New York, 1954, p. 279.
226. Johnston, H. S.; *J. Am. Chem. Soc.*, **73**, 4542 (1951).
227. Johnston, H. S.; *Ind. Eng. Chem.*, **48**, 1488 (1956).
228. Johnston, H. S., and Crosby, H. J.; *J. Chem. Phys.*, **22**, 689 (1954).
229. Johnston, H. S., Foering, L., and Thompson, R. J., *J. Phys. Chem.*, **57**, 390 (1953).
230. Johnston, H. S., and Yost, D. M.; *J. Chem. Phys.*, **17**, 386 (1949).
231. Johnstone, H. F., and Coughanowr, D. R.; *Ind. Eng. Chem.*, **50**, 1169 (1958).
232. Jones, H. J., and Wulf, O. R.; *J. Chem. Phys.*, **5**, 873 (1937).
233. Jones, M. H., and Steacie, E. W. R.; *Can. J. Chem.*, **31**, 505 (1953).
234. Jordan, C. W., Smoker, E. H., and Fulweiler, W. H.; Paper Presented at Spring Meeting, *Am. Chem. Soc.*, New York, 1935; abstracted in *Brennstoff-Chem.*, **16**, 212 (1935).
235. Jordan, C. W., Ward, A. L., and Fulweiler, W. H.; *Ind. Eng. Chem.*, **26**, 947 (1934).
236. Karasch, M. S., Rowe, J. L., and Urry, W. H.; *J. Org. Chem.*, **16**, 905 (1951).
237. Kaskan, W. E., and Duncan, A. B. F.; *J. Chem. Phys.*, **16**, 407 (1948).
238. Kaskan, W. E., and Duncan, A. B. F.; *J. Chem. Phys.*, **18**, 427 (1950).
239. Kassel, L. S.; "The Kinetics of Homogeneous Gas Reactions," Am. Chem. Soc., Monograph No. 57, The Chemical Catalog Co., New York, 1932.
240. Kaufman, F.; *Proc. Roy. Soc.* **A247**, 123 (1958).
241. Kaufman, F., Gerri, N. J., and Bowman, R. E.; *J. Chem Phys.*, **25**, 106 (1956).
242. Keidel, E.; *Farben-Ztg.*, **34**, 1242 (1929).
243. Kimball, H. H.; "Solar Radiation and Its Role," Physics of the Earth, III— Meteorology. Natl. Research Council, Natl. Acad. Sci., Washington, D.C. 1931.
244. Kimball, H. H.; *Monthly Weather Rev.*, **63**, 1 (1935).
245. Kistiakowsky, G. B., and Kydd, P. H.; *J. Am. Chem. Soc.*, **79**, 4825 (1957).
246. Kistiakowsky, G. B., and Roberts, E. K.; *J. Chem. Phys.*, **21**, 1637 (1953).
247. Kistiakowsky, G. B., and Volpi, G. G.; *J. Chem. Phys.*, **27**, 1141 (1957).
248. Klein, R., and Schoen, L. J.; *J. Chem. Phys.*, **24**, 1094 (1956).
249. Klein, W. H.; *J. Meteorol*, **5**, 119 (1948).
250. Koller, L. R.; "Ultraviolet Radiation," Wiley, New York, 1952.
251. Kutschke, K. O., Wijnen, M. H. J., and Steacie, E. W. R.; *J. Am. Chem. Soc.*, **74**, 714 (1952)
252. Läuchli, A.; *Helv. Phys. Acta*, 1, 208 (1928); *Z. Physik*, **53**, 92 (1929).
253. Leighton, P. A., and Blacet, F. E.; *J. Am. Chem. Soc.*, **55**, 1766 (1933).
254. Leighton, P. A., Levanas, L. D., Blacet, F. E., and Rowe, R. D.; *J. Am. Chem. Soc.*, **59**, 1843 (1937).
255. Leighton, P. A., and Perkins, W. A.; "Solar Radiation, Absorption Rates, and Photochemical Primary Processes in Urban Air," Rept. No. 14, Air Pollution Foundation, Los Angeles, California, 1956.
256. Leighton, P. A., and Perkins, W. A.; "Conference on Chemical Reactions in

Urban Atmospheres," Rept. No. 15, Air Pollution Foundation, Los Angeles, California, 1956.

257. Leighton, P. A., and Perkins, W. A.; "Photochemical Secondary Reactions in Urban Air," Rept. No. 24, Air Pollution Foundation, Los Angeles, California, 1958.

258. Lemon, J. T., and Lowry, T. M.; *J. Chem. Soc.,* p. 1409 (1936).

259. Levy, J. B.; *J. Am. Chem. Soc.,* **75**, 1801 (1953); **78**, 1780 (1956).

260. Levy, N., and Scaife, C. W.; *J. Chem. Soc.,* p. 1093 (1946).

261. Lewis, B., and von Elbe, G.; "Combustion, Flames, and Explosions of Gases," Macmillan, New York, 1951.

262. Light, L.; *Z. physik. Chem.* **122**, 414 (1926).

263. Linke, F., and v. dem Borne, H.; *Gen. Bereits, Zin. Geophys.,* **37**, 49 (1932).

264. List, R. J.; "Smithsonian Meteorological Tables," 6th ed., Washington, D.C. (1951).

265. Littman, F. E.; Tech. Rep. No. IX, Project C-844, Stanford Research Institute, Stanford, California (1955).

266. Littman, F. E., Ford, H. W., and Endow, N.; *Ind. Eng. Chem.,* **48**, 1492 (1956).

267. Lossing, F. P., Ingold, K. U., and Tickner, A. W.; *Discussions Faraday Soc.,* **14**, 34 (1953).

268. Lowry, T. M., and Seddon, R. V.; *J. Chem. Soc.,* p. 1461 (1947); p. 626 (1938).

269. Luckey, G. W., and Noyes, W. A., Jr.; *J. Chem. Phys.,* **19**, 227, (1951).

270. Luckiesh, M.; "Germicidal, Erythemal, and Infrared Energy," Van Nostrand, New York, 1946, p. 52.

271. Lunge, G., and Berl, E.; *Z. angew. Chem.,* **19**, 861 (1906).

272. McDowell, C. A.; *Discussions Faraday Soc.,* **14**, 132 (1953).

273. McDowell, C. A., and Sharples, L. K.; *Can. J. Chem.,* **36**, 251, 258, 268 (1958).

274. McDowell, C. A., and Thomas, J. H.; *J. Chem. Soc.,* pp. 2208, 2217 (1949); p. 1462 (1950).

275. McGrath, W. D., and Norrish, R. G. W.; *Proc. Roy. Soc.,* **A242**, 265 (1957); *Nature,* **182**, 235 (1958); *Z. physik. Chem., Frankfurt,* **15**, 245 (1958).

276. Mader, P. P., MacPhee, R. D., Lofberg, R. T., and Larson, G. P.; *Ind. Eng. Chem.,* **44**, 1352 (1952).

277. Magill, P. L., Hutchison, D. H., and Stormes, J. M.; *Proc. Natl. Air Pollution Symposium, 2nd Symposium, Pasadena, California,* 1952, p. 71.

278. Mandelcorn, L., and Steacie, E. W. R.; *Can. J. Chem.,* **32**, 79 (1954).

279. Marcotte, F. B., and Noyes, W. A., Jr.; *Discussions Faraday Soc.,* **10**, 236 (1951); *J. Am. Chem. Soc.,* **74**, 783 (1952).

280. Markham, M. C., and Laidler, K. J.; *J. Phys. Chem.,* **57**, 363 (1953).

281. Martin, E. V., and Jenkins, F. A.; *Phys. Rev.,* **39**, 549 (1932).

282. Martin, R. B., and Noyes, W. A., Jr.; *J. Am. Chem. Soc.,* **75**, 4183 (1953).

283. Martin, T. W., and Pitts, J. N., Jr.; *J. Am. Chem. Soc.,* **77**, 5465 (1955).

284. Masson, C. R.; *J. Am. Chem. Soc.,* **74**, 4731 (1952).

285. Matheson, M. S., and Zabor, J. W.; *J. Chem. Phys.,* **7**, 536 (1939).

286. Melvin, E. H., and Wulf, O. R.; *J. Chem. Phys.,* **3**, 755 (1935).

287. Middleton, J. T., Kendrick, J. B., Jr., and Darley, E. F.; *Proc. Natl. Air Pollution Symposium, 3rd Symposium, Los Angeles, California, 1955,* p. 191.

288. Middleton, W. E. K.; "Visibility in Meteorology," Univ. of Toronto Press, Ontario, 1935.

289. Middleton, W. E. K.; *J. Opt. Soc. Am.,* **44**, 793 (1954).

290. Milas, N. A., Stahl, L. E., and Dayton, B. B.; *J. Am. Chem. Soc.*, **71**, 1448 (1949).

291. Miller, D. M., and Steacie, E. W. R.; *J. Chem. Phys.*, **19**, 73 (1951).

292. Mills, R. L., and Johnston, H. S.; *J. Am. Chem. Soc.*, **73**, 938 (1951).

293. Moon, P.; *J. Franklin Inst.*, **230**, 583 (1940).

294. Moore, W. J., Jr., and Taylor, H. S.; *J. Chem. Phys.*, **8**, 466, 504 (1940).

295. Morriss, F. V., and Bolze, C.; "Reactions of Auto Exhaust in Sunlight," Rept. No. 19, Air Pollution Foundation, Los Angeles, California, 1957.

296. Mulliken, R. A.; *Revs. Modern Phys.*, **14**, 204 (1942).

297. *Natl. Bur. Standards (M.S.), Circ.* **500**. Washington, D.C. (1952).

298. Neiburger, M.; *J. Meteorol.*, **6**, 98 (1949).

299. Neuberger, D., and Duncan, A. B. F.; *J. Chem. Phys.*, **22**, 1693 (1954).

300. Nicholson, A. J. C.; *Rev. Pure and Applied Chem. (Australia)*, **2**, 174 (1952).

301. Niclause, M.; *J. chim. phys.*, **49**, 157 (1952).

302. Niclause, M., Combe, A., and Letort, M.; *J. chim. phys.*, **49**, 604 (1952).

303. Norman, I., and Pitts, J. N., Jr.; *J. Am. Chem. Soc.*, **77**, 6104 (1955).

304. Norrish, R. G. W.; *J. Chem. Soc.*, pp. 1158, 1611 (1929).

305. Norrish, R. G. W.; *Discussions Faraday Soc.*, **10**, 269 (1951).

306. Norrish, R. G. W.; *Proc. Chem. Soc.*, p. 247 (1958).

307. Norrish, R. G. W., Crone, A. G., and Saltmarsh, O. D.; *J. Chem. Soc.*, p. 1456 (1934).

308. Norrish, R. G. W., and Griffiths, J. G. A.; *J. Chem. Soc.*, p. 2829 (1928).

309. Norrish, R. G. W., and Thrush, B. A.; *Quart. Revs.*, *(London)*, **10**, 149 (1956).

310. Noyes, W. A., Jr., and Dorfman, L. M.; *J. Chem. Phys.*, **16**, 788 (1946).

311. Noyes, W. A., Jr., Duncan, A. B. F., and Manning, W. M.; *J. Chem. Phys.*, **2**, 717 (1934).

312. Noyes, W. A., Jr., and Finkelstein, A.; *Discussions Faraday Soc.*, **10**, 308 (1951).

313. Noyes, W. A., Jr., and Henriques, F. C., Jr.; *J. Chem. Phys.*, **7**, 767 (1929).

314. Noyes, W. A., Jr., and Leighton, P. A.; "The Photochemistry of Gases," Reinhold, New York (1941).

315. Noyes, W. A., Jr., Porter, G. B., and Jolley, J. E.; *Chem. Revs.*, **56**, 49 (1956).

316. Ny Tsi-Ze and Choong Shin-Piaw; *Compt. rend. acad. sci.*, **195**, 309 (1932); **196**, 916 (1933); *Chinese J. Phys.*, **1**, 38 (1933).

317. Offenbach, J., and Tobolsky, A. V.; *J. Am. Chem. Soc.*, **79**, 278 (1957).

318. Ogg, R. A., Jr.; *J. Chem. Phys.* **15**, 337, 613 (1947); **18**, 572 (1950).

319. Ogg, R. A., Jr., Richardson, W. S., and Wilson, M. K.; *J. Chem. Phys.*, **18**, 573 (1950).

320. Ogg, R. A., Jr., and Sutphen, W. T.; *Discussions Faraday Soc.*, **17**, 47 (1954).

321. Orgyzlo, E. A., and Schiff, H. I.; *Can. J. Chem.*, **37**, 1690 (1959).

322. Oster, G. K., and Marcus, R. A.; *J. Chem. Phys.*, **27**, 189, 472 (1957).

323. "Oxidation"; *Discussions Faraday Soc.*, pp. 184, 190, 204, 215, 222, 233, 239, 249, 267, 272 (1945).

324. Paneth, F.; *Quart. J. Roy. Meteorol. Soc.*, **63**, 433 (1937); **65**, 304 (1939).

325. Penndorf, R.; *J. Opt. Soc. Am.*, **47**, 176 (1957).

326. Pettit, E.; *Astrophys. J.*, **75**, 185 (1932).

327. Pettit, E.; *Astrophys. J.*, **91**, 159 (1940).

328. Pfund, A. H.; *J. Opt. Soc. Am.*, **24**, 143 (1943).

329. Pimentel, G. C.; *J. Am. Chem. Soc.*, **80**, 62 (1958).

330. Pimentel, G. C.; *Chem. & Eng. News*, p. 47 (Apr. 20, 1959).

331. Pitts, J. N., Jr., and Blacet, F. E.; *J. Am. Chem. Soc.*, **72**, 2810 (1950).

332. Pitts, J. N., Jr., and Blacet, F. E.; *J. Am. Chem. Soc.,* **74,** 455 (1952).
333. Pitts, J. N., Jr., and Norman, I.; *J. Am. Chem. Soc.,* **76,** 4815 (1954).
334. Pitts, J. N., Jr., Thompson, D. D., and Woolfolk, R. W.; *J. Am. Chem. Soc.,* **80,** 66 (1958).
335. Pitts, J. N., Jr., Tolberg, R. S., and Martin, T. W.; *J. Am. Chem. Soc.,* **79,** 6370 (1957).
336. Pollard, F. H., and Wyatt, R. M. H.; *Trans. Faraday Soc.,* **46,** 281 (1950).
337. Porter, C. W., and Iddings, C.; *J. Am. Chem. Soc.,* **48,** 40 (1926).
338. Pressman, J., Aschenbrand, L. M., Marmo, F. F., Jursa, A., and Zelikoff, M.; *J. Chem. Phys.,* **25,** 187 (1956).
339. Pretorius, V., Henderson, I. H., and Danby, C. J.; *J. Chem. Soc.,* 1076 (1955).
340. Raal, F. A., and Danby, C. J.; *J. Chem. Soc.* p. 2222 (1949).
341. Rabinowitch, E., and Wood, W. C.; *J. Chem. Phys.,* **4,** 497 (1936); *Trans. Faraday Soc.,* **32,** 907 (1936).
342. Raley, J. H., Porter, L. M., Rust, F. F., and Vaughan, W. E.; *J. Am. Chem. Soc.,* **73,** 15 (1951).
343. Raley, J. H., Rust, F. F., and Vaughan, W. E.; *J. Am. Chem. Soc.,* **70,** 88 (1948).
344. Ramsay, D. A.; *J. Chem. Phys.,* **21,** 960 (1953).
345. Ramsay, D. D.; *Ann. N. Y. Acad. Sci.,* **67,** 485 (1957).
346. Ranz, W. E., and Johnstone, H. F.; *Proc. Natl. Air Pollution Symposium, 2nd Symposium, Pasadena, California, 1952,* p. 35.
347. Rayleigh, Lord; *Phil. Mag.,* **47,** 375 (1899).
348. Rebbert, R. E., and Laidler, K. J.; *J. Chem. Phys.,* **20,** 274 (1952).
349. Regener, E., and Regener, V. H.; *Physik. Z.,* **35,** 388 (1934).
350. Remkaum, A., and Szwarc, M.; *J. Am. Chem. Soc.,* **77,** 3486 (1955).
351. Renzetti, N. A. (ed.); "An Aerometric Survey of the Los Angeles Basin" August–November, 1954, Rept. No. 9, Air Pollution Foundation, Los Angeles, California, 1955.
352. Renzetti, N. A., *Advances in Chem. Ser.,* **21,** 230 (1959).
353. Renzetti, N. A., and Doyle, G. J.; *J. Air Pollution Control Assoc.,* **8,** 293 (1959); *Intern. J. Air Pollution,* **2,** 327 (1960).
354. Renzetti, N. A., and Schuck, E. A.; *J. Air Pollution Control Assoc.,* **11,** 121 (1961).
355. Reynolds, W. C., and Taylor, W. H.; *J. Chem. Soc.,* p. 131 (1912).
356. Rice, F. O., and Herzfeld, K. F.; *J. Am. Chem. Soc.,* **56,** 284 (1934).
357. Richards, L. M.; *J. Air Pollution Control Assoc.,* **5,** 216 (1956).
358. Rieche, A.; "Alkylhydroperoxides and Ozonides," Theodor Steinkopff, Dresden, 1931.
359. Ritchie, M.; *Proc. Roy. Soc.,* **A146,** 848 (1939).
360. Robinson, P. L., and Smith, E. J.; *J. Chem. Soc.,* p. 3895 (1952).
361. Roebber, J. L., Rollefson, G. K., and Pimentel, G. C.; *J. Am. Chem. Soc.,* **80,** 255 (1958).
362. Rogers, L. H.; "Second Technical Progress Report," Rept. No. 12, Air Pollution Foundation, Los Angeles, California, 1955.
363. Rogers, L. H.; *J. Air Pollution Control Assoc.,* **8,** 124 (1958).
364. Rogers, L. H.; *J. Chem. Educ.,* **35,** 310 (1958).
365. Roof, J. G., and Blacet, F. E.; *J. Am. Chem. Soc.,* **63,** 1126 (1941).
366. Rosser, W. A., Jr., and Wise, H.; *J. Chem Phys.,* **25,** 1078 (1956).

367. Rubin, T. R., Calvert, J. G., Rankin, G. T., and MacNevin, W. M.; *J. Am. Chem. Soc.*, **75**, 2850 (1953).
368. Ruehrwein, R. A., and Hashman, J. S.; *J. Chem. Phys.*, **30**, 823 (1959).
369. Saltzman, B. E.; *Ind. Eng. Chem.*, **50**, 677 (1958).
370. Saltzman, B. E., and Gilbert, N.; *Ind. Eng. Chem.*, **51**, 1415 (1959).
371. Sato, S., and Cvetanović, R. J.; *Can. J. Chem.*, **36**, 279, 970, 1668 (1958).
372. Sato, S., and Cvetanović, R. J.; *Can. J. Chem.*, **37**, 953 (1959).
373. Scheer, M. D., and Taylor, H. A.; *J. Chem. Phys.*, **20**, 653 (1952).
374. Schott, G., and Davidson, N.; *J. Am. Chem. Soc.*, **80**, 1841 (1958).
375. Schou, S. A.; *J. chim. phys.*, **26**, 665 ((1929).
376. Schuck, E. A.; "Eye Irritation from Irradiated Automobile Exhaust," Rept. No. 18, Air Pollution Foundation, Los Angeles, California, 1957.
377. Schuck, E. A., and Doyle, G. J.; "Photooxidation of Hydrocarbons in Mixtures Containing Oxides of Nitrogen and Sulfur Dioxide," Rept. No. 29, Air Pollution, San Marino, California, 1959.
378. Schuck, E. A., Doyle, G. J., and Endow, N.; "A Progress Report on the Photochemistry of Polluted Atmospheres," Rept. No. 31, Air Pollution Foundation, San Marino, California, 1960.
379. Schuck, E. A., Ford, H. W., and Stephens, E. R.; "Air Pollution Effects of Irradiated Automobile Exhaust as Related to Fuel Composition," Rept. No. 26, Air Pollution Foundation, San Marino, California, 1958.
380. Schumacher, H. J.; *J. Am. Chem. Soc.*, **52**, 2377, 2584 (1930).
381. Schumacher, H. J.; *Z. physik. Chem.*, **B17**, 405 (1932).
382. Schumacher, H. J., and Sprenger, G.; *Z. physik. Chem.*, **136**, 77 (1928); **140**, 281 (1929); **B2**, 267 (1929); *Z. angew. Chem.*, **42**, 697 (1929).
383. Scott, W. E., Stephens, E. R., Hanst, P. L., and Doerr, R. C.; "Further Developments in the Chemistry of the Atmosphere," *Proc. Am. Petrol. Inst.*, **37**, III, 171 (1957).
384. Shepp, A.; *J. Chem. Phys.*, **24**, 939 (1956).
385. Shepp, A., and Kutschke, K. O.; *J. Chem. Phys.*, **26**, 1020 (1957).
386. Sickman, D. V., and Rice, O. K., *J. Chem. Phys.*, **4**, 608 (1936).
387. Sleppy, W. C., and Calvert, J. G.; *J. Am. Chem. Soc.*, **81**, 769 (1959).
388. Smith, E. J.; *J. Chem. Soc.*, p. 1271 (1933).
389. Smith, H. A., and Napravnik, A.; *J. Am. Chem. Soc.*, **62**, 385 (1940).
390. Smith, H. E.; "The Vapor Phase Reaction of 2,3-Dimethyl-2-Butene and Ozone," M.S. Thesis, Stanford University, Stanford, California, (1954).
391. Smith, J. H.; *J. Am. Chem. Soc.*, **65**, 74 (1943).
392. Smith, J. H., and Daniels, F.; *J. Am. Chem. Soc.*, **69**, 1735 (1947).
393. Smith, J. H. C.; *Carnegie Inst. Wash. Yearbook*, No. 27, 178 (1928).
394. Sprenger, G.; *Z. Elektrochem.*, **37**, 674 (1931).
395. Stair, R.; *Proc. Natl. Air Pollution Symposium, 3rd Symposium, Pasadena, California, 1955*, p. 48.
396. Stair, R., and Johnston, R. G.; *J. Research Natl. Bur. Standards*, **57**, 205 (1956).
397. Stanford Research Institute; "The Smog Problem in Los Angeles County," Western Oil and Gas Association, Los Angeles, California, 1954.
398. Steacie, E. W. R.; "Atomic and Free Radical Reactions," Reinhold, New York, 1954.
399. Steiner, W.; *Trans. Faraday Soc.*, **31**, 623 (1935).

400. Stephens, E. R., Darley, E. F., and Taylor, O. C.; "Air Pollution Research at the University of California, Riverside," Interim Rept. (April 1959).
401. Stephens, E. R., Darley, E. F., Taylor, O. C., and Scott, W. E.; *Proc. Am. Petrol. Inst.* **40, III** (1960), also *Intern. J. Air Pollution,* in press.
402. Stephens, E. R., Hanst, P. L., Doerr, R. C., and Scott, W. E.; *Franklin Inst. Tech. Rept. I-A1845-1* (1956).
403. Stephens, E. R., Hanst, P. L., Doerr, R. C., and Scott, W. E.; *Ind. Eng. Chem.,* **48,** 1498 (1956).
404. Stephens, E. R., Prager, M. J., Doerr, R. C., and Labes, M. M.; *Progr. Rept.,* API S and F, Project 678, the Franklin Institute, Philadelphia, Pennsylvania (Dec. 1957).
405. Stephens, E. R., Scott, W. E., Hanst, P. L., and Doerr, R. C.; *J. Air Pollution Control Assoc.,* **6,** 159 (1956); *Proc. Am. Petrol. Inst.* **36, III,** 288 (1956).
406. Stockmayer, W. H., Billinger, F. W., Jr., and Beasley, J. K.; *Ann. Rev. Phys. Chem.,* **6,** 359 (1955).
407. Stratton, J. A., and Houghton, H. G.; *Phys. Rev.,* **38,** 159 (1936).
408. Strong, R. L., and Kutschke, K. O.; *Can. J. Chem.,* **37,** 1456 (1959).
409. Style, D. W. G., and Summers, D.; *Trans. Faraday Soc.,* **35,** 899 (1939).
410. Style, D. W. G., and Ward, J. C.; *Trans. Faraday Soc.,* **49,** 999 (1953).
411. Sutphen, W. T.; "Kinetic Study of the Thermal Decomposition of Ozone," Doctoral Thesis, Stanford University, Stanford, California (1955).
412. Tanaka, Y., and Shimazu, M.; *J. Sci. Research Inst. Tokyo,* **43,** 241 (1949).
413. Taylor, H. A., and Bender, H.; *J. Chem. Phys.,* **9,** 761 (1941).
414. Taylor, H. S., and Jungers, J. C.; *Trans. Faraday Soc.,* **33,** 1353 (1937).
415. Taylor, R. P., and Blacet, F. E.; *Ind. Eng. Chem.,* **48,** 1505 (1956).
416. Taylor, R. P., and Blacet, F. E.; *J. Am. Chem. Soc.,* **78,** 706 (1956).
417. Thompson, H. W., and Purkis, C. H.; *Trans. Faraday Soc.,* **32,** 674 (1936).
418. Thompson, H. W., and Purkis, C. H.; *Trans. Faraday Soc.,* **32,** 1466 (1936).
419. Tobolsky, A. V.; *Ann. Rev. Phys. Chem.,* **7,** 167 (1956).
420. Tolberg, R. S.; Doctoral Thesis, Northwestern Univ., Evanston, Illinois (1954).
421. Trautz., M.; *Z. Elektrochem.,* **22,** 104 (1916).
422. Treacy, J. C., and Daniels, F.; *J. Am. Chem. Soc.,* **77,** 2033 (1955).
423. Trotman-Dickenson, A. F.; *Quart. Revs. (London),* **7,** 198 (1953).
424. Trotman-Dickenson, A. F., and Steacie, E. W. R.; *J. Phys. & Colloid Chem.,* **55,** 908 (1951).
425. Tunitzki, N. N.; *J. Phys. Chem. (U.S.S.R.),* **20,** 1137 (1946).
426. Ubbelohde, A. R.; *Proc. Roy. Soc.,* **A152,** 372 (1935).
427. Urey, H. C., Dawsey, L. H., and Rice, F. O.; *J. Am. Chem. Soc.,* **51,** 1371 (1929).
428. Vail, C. B., Holmquist, J. P., and White, L., Jr.; *J. Am. Chem. Soc.,* **76,** 624 (1954).
429. Van de Hulst, H. C.; "Light Scattering by Small Particles," Wiley, New York (1957).
430. Van Tiggelen, A.; *Bull. soc. chim. Belges.,* **55,** 202 (1946).
431. Verhoek, F. H., and Daniels, F.; *J. Am. Chem. Soc.,* **53,** 1250 (1931).
432. Vesselovskii, I., and Shub, D. M.; *Zhur. Fiz. Khim.,* **26,** 509 (1952).
433. Volman, D. H.; *J. Chem. Phys.,* **14,** 707 (1946); **17,** 947 (1949).
434. Volman, D. H.; *J. Am. Chem. Soc.,* **73,** 1018 (1951).
435. Volman, D. H.; *J. Am. Chem. Soc.,* **76,** 6034 (1954).
436. Volman, D. H., and Craven, W. M.; *J. Chem. Phys.,* **20,** 919 (1952); *J. Am. Chem. Soc.,* **75,** 3111 (1953).

437. Volman, D. H., Leighton, P, A., Blacet, F. E., and Brinton, R. K.; *J. Chem. Phys.,* **18**, 203 (1950).
438. von Elbe, G., and Lewis, B.; *J. Am. Chem. Soc.,* **59**, 976 (1937).
439. Vrbaški, T., and Cvetanović, R. J.; *Can. J. Chem.,* **38**, 1053, 1063 (1960).
440. Wagner, H.; *Farben-Ztg.,* **34**, 1243 (1929).
441. Wagner, H., and Zipfel, M.; *Faben-Ztg.,* **37**, 1480 (1932).
442. Walling, Cheves; "Free Radicals in Solution," Wiley, New York, 1957, pp. 475, 491–493.
443. Walsh, A. D.; *Trans. Faraday Soc.,* **43**, 297 (1947).
444. Walsh, A. D.; *J. Chem. Soc.,* p. 331 (1948).
445. Warburg, E., and Leithauser, G.; *Ann. Physik,* **20**, 743 (1906); **23**, 209 (1907).
446. Wayne, L. G., and Yost, D. M.; *J. Chem. Phys.,* **19**, 41 (1951).
447. Wenger, F., and Kutschke, K. O.; *Can. J. Chem.,* **37**, 1546 (1959).
448. Whiteway, S. G., and Masson, C. R.; *J. Chem. Phys.,* **25**, 233 (1956).
449. Whittingham, G.; *Nature,* **159**, 232 (1947).
450. Wigner, E., and Witmer, E. E.; *Z. Physik,* **51**, 859 (1928).
451. Wijnen, M. H. J.; *J. Chem. Phys.,* **27**, 710 (1957); **28**, 271 (1958).
452. Wijnen, M. H. J.; Informal Conference on Photochemistry, National Bureau of Standards, 1959.
453. Wijnen, M. H. J., and Van Tiggelen, A.; *Bull. soc. chim. Belges,* **57**, 446 (1948).
454. Wulf, O. R.; *Proc. Natl. Acad. Sci. U.S.,* 16, 507 (1930), *Smithsonian Misc. Collections,* **85**, No. 9 (1931).
455. Wulf, O. R., and Melvin, E. H.; *Phys. Rev.,* **38**, 330 (1931).
456. Zatsiorskii, M., Kondrateev, V., and Solnishkora, S.; *J. Phys. Chem. (U.S.S.R.),* **14**, 1521 (1940).

SUBJECT INDEX

A

Absorbing species in polluted air, 43
Absorption coefficients, *see also* specific
    compounds
  averaging, 134
  discrete spectra, 133
Absorption rates, estimation of, 26–30
Acetaldehyde, *see also* Aldehydes
  absorption coefficients, 74
  absorption rates, 75
  formation by nitrogen dioxide-olefin
    photolysis, 256, 257
  by ozone-olefin reactions, 168, 172,
    173, 176
  photooxidation, 278
  primary processes, 77-79
  primary yields, 78
Acetone, *see also* Ketones
  absorption coefficients, 74
  absorption rates, 75
  formation by nitrogen dioxide-olefin
    photolysis, 245, 256–261
  by ozone-olefin reactions, 171, 172,
    176
  primary processes, 79-81
  primary yields, 80
Acetylene
  in automobile exhaust, 179, 270
  reaction with oxygen atoms, 141, 145
  with ozone, 179
Acetyl nitrate, 90
Acetyl radicals, *see* Acyl radicals
Acrolein
  absorption coefficients, 74
  absorption rates, 75
  eye irritation from, 275–276
  photochemical stability, 81
  phytotoxicant, as, 277
Actinic irradiance, 26–33
  diurnal variations in, 31
  rate of change, 33
  variation with latitude, 31–32
  with solar altitude, 30
  table, 29
Acyl nitrate, 89–90

Acyl nitrite, 89, 94
Acyl pernitrite, *see* Peroxyacyl nitrite
Acyl radicals, 211–215
  decomposition, 214
  formation by acyl nitrite photolysis, 94
  by ketone photolysis, 80–86, 103
  by oxygen atom-olefin reaction, 269
  by ozone-olefin reaction, 170–177
  reactions, 211–213
Acylate radicals, 222–223
Air, *see also* Transmissivity
  mass, 9
  purification, 242, 254
  refractive index, 13
Albedo, 39
Aldehydes, 71–86
  as radical source, 84
  formation by alkyl nitrite photolysis,
    66–68, 103
  by nitrogen dioxide-olefin photolysis,
    256–258, 269
  by oxygen atom-olefin reaction, 136–
    140
  by ozone-olefin reaction, 168–177
  in air, 84, 273–274
  light absorption, 71–73
  photolysis, 73–80
  primary processes, 74–79
  primary yields, 78
  reaction with oxygen atoms, 146
  with ozone, 180–183
  structural effects on absorption, 71–73
Alkoxyl radicals, 223–225
  fluorescence, 63
  formation by alkyl nitrite photolysis,
    66–71, 013
  by ozone-olefin reaction, 170, 177
  by peroxyalkyl radical reactions, 215,
    217, 218
  reactions, 223–225
Alkyl nitrates, 62–64
  primary process, 63
Alkyl nitrites, 64–71
  absorption rates, 65–66, 70
  formation, 70, 224, 257

Physical Chemistry

A Series of Monographs

Ernest M. Loebl, Editor

Department of Chemistry, Polytechnic Institute of

Brooklyn, Brooklyn, New York

Physical Chemistry

A Series of Monographs